T0215486

The Business of Cyber

This book examines the cybersecurity phenomenon, looking at the folklore, the hype, and the behaviour of its practitioners. A central theme is that the management of cybersecurity needs to be owned by the people running the organisation, rather than by the cybersecurity team, who frequently don't have management as a core skill. In order to effect that change, managers need to have the background and detail to challenge what they are being told, enabling them to engage in a way that will result in more appropriate outcomes for the business. This book provides that background and detail. It debunks a number of cyber-myths, and calls out basic errors in the accepted thinking on cyber. The content is strongly rooted in available research and presented in an accessible manner, with a number of business-related case studies. Each chapter in the book takes a theme such as end-user behaviours and compares the available evidence with what the industry would like to have its customers believe. The conclusion is that there is definitely a problem, and we certainly need cyber defences. Just not the ones the industry is currently selling.

The Business of Cyber

Why You Should Question What Your Security Team Are Telling You

Peter Fagan

CRC Press
Taylor & Francis Group
Boca Raton London New York

CRC Press is an imprint of the
Taylor & Francis Group, an **informa** business

Designed cover image: Shutterstock

First edition published 2024
by CRC Press
2385 NW Executive Center Drive, Suite 320, Boca Raton, FL 33431

and by CRC Press
4 Park Square, Milton Park, Abingdon, Oxon, OX14 4RN

CRC Press is an imprint of Taylor & Francis Group, LLC

ISBN: 9781032462868 (hbk)
ISBN: 9781032462905 (pbk)
ISBN: 9781003380962 (ebk)

DOI: 10.1201/9781003380962

Typeset in Times
by Newgen Publishing UK

Contents

Preface

The field of information security thrives on the use of jargon and an air of magic. The security problem ("cyber" for those in the know) is presented as an arcane practice, a field for specialists only. An area with an established and sophisticated body of knowledge.

But at its heart, the cybersecurity industry exists to shift products and make a profit. So really, are there any grounds for seeing cyber as a formal discipline in its own right? Or is the argument that cyber is a recognised profession simply there to sell more product?

This book takes a look at five principles underpinning the practice of cybersecurity. To one degree or another, each is treated as a "given" by the security community, and it's generally accepted that, in combination, they show that information security is a worthy standalone discipline. However, if you accept what's in this book, then none of the five should be given credence. Those claims are:

- That users are "the weakest link" – that they just don't "get it". An alternative view put forward by Cormac Herley [1] is that users are right to reject security advice, because it loads them up with additional work for no additional benefit. Albrechtsen and Hovden [2] suggest the existence of a divide between security practitioners and users – that the two groups have different world views. The argument in this book is that security people, not users, are the ones that need to change their thinking.
- That the security community treats security as a business issue. In fact, there are no business principles built into existing security models and there is no recognition of established business paradigms. There is, however, evidence that the security community would like to claim that cyber is a business issue, in order to establish a basis for "educating" managers in the importance of following their guidance.
- That security is a unique and specialised discipline and therefore needs its own versions of more generally accepted concepts. The idea of "security culture", for example, is proposed as something quite special, and separate from the idea of company culture. An examination of the available evidence shows an absence of any accepted definition, and at best, only shaky foundations in supporting theory.
- That security is a technical problem – that it can be broken down into a number of smaller problems which can then be solved independently. When you've solved the smaller ones, you've automatically solved the bigger ones. The CIA model (Confidentiality, Integrity, Availability) is perhaps the most egregious example here. A large body of evidence suggests that, instead, security is shaped by the context of its use.
- That security can be done by numbers. The security community uses algorithms to "calculate" risk and underpins the results with claims of near-accuracy. However, to quote John Adams [3]: *"[r]isk management isn't rocket*

science – it's much more complicated". In practice, risk calculations as currently conducted are based on guesswork. It's more appropriate to see security as a negotiation, rather than a calculation.

For each of the alleged principles, this book presents a workable alternative that doesn't require cybersecurity to be a specialism. Each alternative is based on evidence and first-hand experience. The failings underlying the original principles are clearly set out. Broadly (and you'll have to read the book to see the detail), those failings relate to the use of an engineering approach to problems involving human behaviour, and the assumption that it's the users and/or management that are at fault.

The argument presented here takes a strongly evidence-based approach and looks at the viewpoint of pretty much everyone except that of the security practitioner. It suggests that to be effective, security needs to be based on the world as it is, and not on the way security practitioners would like it to be [4]. The central intention of this book is to provide managers with the tools they need to own cyber for themselves.

There's no magic to managing security. In fact, it's best done by those who have domain expertise. But at the minute, we have people who don't have management as a core skill, saying that cyber is so special, only the security team can manage it. As a consequence, after 25 years of record expenditure, we're still seeing the same problems. But then, to quote Mark Neocleous [5], once you've built an industry based on selling security, the last thing you want to do is actually deliver any.

If you're a practitioner, you might find some of these ideas challenging. If you're in the small percentage that makes it past that stage, welcome. If you're a manager about to engage a security practitioner, you might find this a useful source of questions to ask at the interview. Whatever your reason for proceeding, this is a fairly condensed book. There's no gentle introduction. Honestly, this is a difficult book to read.

We start with a review of where cybersecurity stands at the minute (and how it got there), followed by an examination of where the industry might be heading.

REFERENCES

1. Herley, C., So long, and no thanks for the externalities: the rational rejection of security advice by users. In *Proceedings of the 2009 Workshop on New Security Paradigms*. 2009. ACM.
2. Albrechtsen, E. and J. Hovden, The information security digital divide between information security managers and users. *Computers & Security*, 2009. 28(6): p. 476–490.
3. Adams, J., Risk management: It's not rocket science...... It's much more complicated. *Risk Management*, 2007. 54(5): p. 36.
4. Machiavelli, N., *The prince*. 2011: Penguin.
5. Neocleous, M., *Critique of security*. 2008: Edinburgh University Press.

About the Author

Peter Fagan has been working in the information security industry for well over 20 years, in a variety of roles and environments. About eight years ago, he asked himself the question, "Why isn't this working?". After all, if we're selling security, surely after a while there ought to be less of a need for it? Asking that question kicked off a journey of personal research, academic research, and the hands-on practical implementation of contemporary approaches, based on the way people actually behave rather than the way security teams would like them to behave. That journey ultimately led to this book, which presents the argument that an industry focused on profit is more concerned with selling compliance than it is with selling protection. Along the way, the author draws upon formal business knowledge gained through an MBA and an MSc in organisational psychology.

1 The Current and Future State of Cyber

THE CURRENT STATE OF CYBER

SOME STATISTICS

As a number of people have pointed out, it's difficult to get an accurate figure on the cost of cybercrime [1–3], partly because it depends on how you define it. A 2016 White House report [4] suggested that the impact on the US economy alone lay somewhere between a lower estimate of US$57Bn and an upper figure of US$109Bn. For reference, that upper figure is roughly equal to the gross domestic product (GDP) of Ecuador (population 17 million) in the same year [5].

Other estimates quote US$600Bn per year for 2017 [6], US$1Tn per year for 2020 [7], and a projected US$10Tn per year by 2025 [8]. That suggested figure of US$1Tn is equivalent to about one-third of the GDP of India; the predicted figure of US$10Tn is equivalent to about 50% of the GDP of the United States in 2020, and about two-thirds of the GDP of the People's Republic of China [9]. Others in the industry [10] have suggested that the cost of identity fraud alone will amount to US$20Tn by 2025. That's about the same as completely removing the United States from the global economy.[1]

Really? I'm not sure those numbers look credible. The message from the cyber industry, however, seems to be "it's a big problem, keep spending".

In 2019, a European advisory body (LSEC) presented their analysis of the market for cyber security, at a European Union conference on cross-border collaboration [11]. Interesting point made by the authors [12] – their estimate of spending on cybersecurity (€600Bn, equivalent to about US$650Bn at the time of writing) was greater than their estimate of the global cost of cybercrime (around US$450Bn). The authors of the report acknowledged that their figure for industry size came out higher than some other estimates, because they included e.g. companies that supplied cyber services as well as other services, in order to obtain a wider picture of economic activity.

The broad principles of the report, however, are supported by a similarly painstaking investigation by Anderson et al. [13], summarised by Bruce Schneier [14]: "*[w]e spend more money on cyber defense than we do on the actual losses*". Which, on the face of it, is an odd situation. A generous interpretation might be that the current level

DOI: 10.1201/9781003380962-1

of expenditure is at least driving down the total cost of cybercrime, and that potentially the costs would be much greater without those defences. However, it raises the question of diminishing returns – how much more should we spend on security in order to reduce the global costs of cybercrime by e.g. another US$1Bn? In fact, do we even know how much benefit we're getting from the current spend?

There's no real incentive to find out, because spending on cyber security is predicted to keep growing anyway. It depends who you ask, but compound annual growth rate (CAGR) is estimated by a number of sources (e.g. [15, 16]) to be around 10% on average, although the distribution of growth across the industry isn't completely even [11]:

The global Cybersecurity market has grown rapidly across all sub-sectors over the last 3 years, varying from 5% for Training and Education to 25% for Identity and Access and for Outsourced/ Managed Services in 2015/16, with the number of global companies and employment growing at similar rates. Each Cybersecurity sub-sector is forecast to continue growing rapidly at a similar rate (above 10% per annum out to 2021) apart from Training and Education which is forecast to grow at a rate of just above 5%.

These numbers are obviously good from the industry's viewpoint. Figures for cyber start-ups in Israel [17], for example, indicate an average runtime of about five years before being bought out, at an average valuation of around US$130M. Nasdaq figures for 2017 on quoted cyber suppliers [18] showed that "... *the ISE Cyber Security UCITS Index has outperformed the benchmark over the last 5 years*", i.e. over that time, the value of the cybersecurity sector outstripped the market average.

For privately held organisations, company valuation is more of an art than a science, but it's commonly based on a multiple of pre-tax profit. A multiple of ten or so is quite generous. When FireEye acquired the forensic security specialists Mandiant [19] in 2014, they were reported to have paid US$1Bn, equivalent to a multiple of ten (10) on gross revenue (that's a multiple of *income*, not profit [20]). At the time, the deal added an estimated US$1.7Bn to FireEye's own market capitalisation [21]. Nice work. However, two years later their acquisition of iSight was for a maximum of US$275M, despite an earlier informal valuation of around US$1Bn i.e. the same amount as had been paid for Mandiant [22]. The difference was blamed on a general fall in the valuations of cyber companies over the period.

Market capitalisation and company valuation aren't the same, obviously. But as noted in the Reuters report on the iSight deal [22], the fall in valuations affected both privately held and publicly listed companies. The point is that the overall level of performance of cyber companies, as quoted in the Nasdaq report, is higher than the benchmark, *despite* a market correction occurring in the same period.

In the immediate aftermath of the 2017 Wannacry virus, the combined market capitalisation of five leading cybersecurity companies increased by a total of around US$5.9Bn, with no apparent effort on their part [23]. Wannacry was a ransomware package that exploited a vulnerability in Microsoft operating systems. The National Health Service (NHS) in the United Kingdom was quite badly hit, partly because at the time it was using an operating system that was about 20 years old [24]. However, some months earlier, Microsoft had issued a patch that would have plugged much of the vulnerability [25, 26]. To quote a contemporary BBC report [27]: *"[i]f all IT departments everywhere had implemented this patch immediately, the WannaCry ransomware worm wouldn't have been able to run riot across the globe"*. A retrospective review of the impact on the NHS [28], quoting a report from the National Audit Office (NAO), noted that *"... none of the organisations affected by WannaCry had followed advice by NHS Digital (the national information and technology partner to the health and social care system) to apply a Microsoft update patch"*. A 2019 report into preventable health incidents noted that *"[i]n the example of the WannaCry incident, a failure to install a simple operating system patch because of the inadequate funding of support services led to the entirely preventable disruption of care for many thousands of patients"* [29, p133]. That is, the underlying issue seems to have been to do with ineffective local procedures [30–33], rather than the absence of advanced technical security products.

Nonetheless, when news of the attack broke, the share price for Symantec, who claimed that their product would have stopped the infection [34], went up by about 4%. The share price of antivirus vendor Sophos, whose web site up until that point had said *"[t]he NHS is totally protected with Sophos"* [35, 36], rose by nearly 8%, i.e. they saw twice the rise seen by Symantec [37]. Microsoft's share price *dropped* by about 1% [38] despite the fact that they had issued a fix [39]. The Financial Times [40] noted that cyber insurance companies could also expect their stock to rise, even though the amount demanded from victims (about US$500) would have been below the policy excess set by most insurers.

When FireEye were themselves hacked, leading to the loss of a number of advanced security scanning tools [41], their share price dropped by about 12% over the next couple of days.[2] About ten days later, when the scale of the SolarWinds attack [42] became known, their share price rose by about 45%.[3] Now, correlation is not causation, as anyone will tell you, but on the basis of these figures, the price rise seen when demand was expected to increase, was about four times higher than the drop occasioned by a breach affecting the company itself.

Overall, not a bad position for cyber providers.

It's Complicated

What about customers – what happens if the protection offered by the cyber industry fails to live up to the promises?

It can be difficult to assess the long-term internal costs of a breach, so the impact on stock price is often taken as a proxy for the level of damage [43–52]. To take one example from Cavusoglu et al. [53], the average next-day drop in share price for a breached company was about 2%. And a day or so after the announcement, cybersecurity suppliers could expect to see a corresponding 1.36% *rise*. As pointed out by Harkins [54], there are very few industries where you can expect to be rewarded for failure. That figure of about 2% for victims contrasts with a drop of just 0.6% for vendors announcing a security vulnerability in their own product. That is, when things go wrong, security product suppliers seem to be hit much less badly than their customers [55]. Further, as stated by Modi et al. [56], "... *service failures due to the front-end service provider lead to greater shareholder losses than such failures due to the buyer firm*", i.e. if you outsource a corporate security function and your managed security service provider has an incident, then you can expect to get hit harder than you would have been if you'd kept the function inhouse.

The reverse situation (the stock market benefit of investing in security) also seems to be less than straightforward. Malliouris and Simpson [57] found that when a company gained certification against the Cyber Essentials scheme (a UK scheme providing a demonstration of a baseline measure of cybersecurity [58]), there was usually a positive market response, whereas certification against ISO 27001 (an international standard for security [59]) was seen in some cases to lead to a drop in share price. The paper suggests that stock markets prefer to see investments that have clear commercial benefits. Cyber Essentials, for example, has been mandated for organisations wishing to bid for some UK Government contracts [60]. Successful certification could therefore be seen as facilitating access into an otherwise inaccessible market, whereas gaining security certification for its own sake doesn't come across as a sensible use of capital.

In fact, investments to gain security certification that haven't been preceded by a publicised cybersecurity failure can lead to a negative response [61]. Unpacking that: if you pre-emptively get your security systems certified, the markets reserve the right to punish you for it. On the other hand, if you delay investing, you can expect to be rewarded as you subsequently shut and firmly bolt the stable door. It also seems to be the case [62] that a publicised cyber security incident affects not only the short-term share price of the breached firm, but also potentially, the share prices of its competitors. So if perhaps sensibly, you invest in protection, but your competitors don't, then the market reserves the right to cane you when one of your competitors has an incident.

Long story short, cyber stocks tend to go up, especially after a breach. That seems to be the case even for suppliers that weren't relevant to the breach, and (it could be argued) those that failed to contain the breach. Whereas the benefits for listed companies investing in cybersecurity aren't quite so straightforward, largely because the outcomes of both investment and security incidents seem to be complex [13, 63–65].

So to the evangelists and salespeople who say it's a matter of (a) implementing cybersecurity and (b) reaping corporate benefits, the message is: "I think you'll find it's a bit more complicated than that". Unless of course you're a cybersecurity company, in which case it seems to be money all the way. It's interesting to consider how the industry got itself into such a unique position.

INDUSTRY GROWTH AND POSITIONING

THE GROWTH OF CYBER

Brito and Watkins [66] point to the decision by the United States to maintain a substantial standing army after WWII as a driver for defence companies to over-inflate the threat in order to bolster demand for materiel, and to over-inflate the benefits of their own solution in order to move up the queue for funding. Much the same process was seen when the US Government announced their decision to establish a cyber unit, with new buildings, new staff, new infrastructure, etc. States that felt they had a chance of hosting the shiny thing started offering incentives, pressing their case, and doing whatever they felt would be effective in attracting the spending to their constituency. Cyber was clearly the coming thing, and there was no reason why anyone should hold back on stressing its importance. An idea which surprisingly also caught on amongst the companies selling it.

There are now clear parallels between the cybersecurity industry and what's known as the "military industrial complex"; the hype, pressure groups, and lobbying that go with the traditional arms industry. Jellenc [67] noted a huge increase in global Government expenditure on cyber (from about US$10Bn in 2007 to about US$100Bn in 2012) and that consequently *"[a]lmost every defense contractor in the developed world has, since 2007, created cyber security or 'cyber solutions' units, whereas only a handful previously provided such capability"*. Over the same period there was also a four-fold increase in the number of US Government lobbyists declaring interests relating to the cyber industry [68].

The subsequent development of the economics of cyber has been set out in some detail by Professor Ross Anderson [69, 70], and it's generally recognised that we now have some sort of "cyber industrial complex" [71]. Essentially, both the cyber threat and the cyber promises had to be inflated in order to justify the initial spending, and at the time nobody had any facts to contradict the claims [72]. But once you start it's hard to stop. So although there is a threat, and in some aspects it's serious, now that we have the hype it's difficult to step away from it [73–75]. The increase in state-sponsored offensive cyber capability [67] as demonstrated in a number of high-profile events [68] has simply fanned the flames.

But at the same time, we have stocks rising, Governments spending, and individuals getting rich. That all sounds good. Although those circumstances haven't come for free. A 2014 paper published by the Royal United Services Institute (RUSI) proposed 13 reasons why threat inflation leads to problems [76]. Taking the top three: hype leads to confusion over what security is meant to encompass; it makes it difficult to assess whether or not an investment in cyber will return a result; and third, hype inevitably clouds planning objectives.

Part of the problem is that hype relies on simplification, which comes with its own price tag. Lawson and Middleton [77], for example, suggest that an excessive focus on the idea of a single, disastrous "cyber Pearl Harbor" led the US Government to overlook a number of more likely, but nonetheless significant real-world threats.

Measuring Success

In the United Kingdom, a Public Accounts Committee (PAC) report in 2019, commenting on the Cabinet Office implementation of the UK's cybersecurity strategy [78], noted that although the UK is particularly vulnerable to the risk of cyber-attacks, *"[t]he Department cannot justify how its approach to cyber security is delivering value for money"* and *"[t]he Department lacks the robust evidence base it needs to make informed decisions about cyber security"* [79, 80]. The Cabinet Office seemed to be criticised in the report, but the detail of the text contains a slightly more nuanced message – that it's difficult to measure success when what you want is societal change, but you're measuring progress in terms of technology. The report noted, for example, that out of 12 strategic objectives, only 1 was predicted with any confidence to be achievable in the timescales, not because the work hadn't been done, but because it was difficult to measure success.

There's a lot of stuff buried in that last point: the "difficulty of measuring success". A report from the Swedish National Board of Trade on cyber standards [81] catches the underlying issue:

> *When policy makers and regulators address IT security in ICT products, they should take note of a large number of interdependencies, including acknowledging that modern life is dependent on a multitude of interconnected and interdependent infrastructures so that separating cyberspace (as its own domain) from sectors such as food, health and transportation has become impossible. Cyberspace can be best understood as a thin layer running through all sectors, enabling them to communicate and function.*

Their point is that cyberspace, and by implication cybersecurity, can't be considered as a separate, bounded topic. It's so closely tangled up with so many other issues that it's difficult to take high-level objectives and extract standalone metrics for success. The report also suggests that it's not sensible to assume a linear model (every time you pull this lever, this light comes on), because applying either view leads to unexpected outcomes. As an example, they suggest that addressing security through lower level bilateral deals, rather than addressing it as a wider issue, would inevitably impact other areas:

> *The handling of security concerns could in the future be dependent on bilateral gentlemen's agreements between economic powers. Such a result would deviate from our existing trade patterns and risk further undermining multilateral trade policy processes... [i]t is important to understand that IT security is to a high degree a policy challenge.*

Essentially, doing what might seem sensible at the level of the organisation can lead to an anomalous result overall. And yet, working back the other way, starting out with strategic objectives at the national level, and breaking them down into lower-level targets, doesn't always work either. The environment for cyber is complex, with many interlinked factors, and the simplification inherent in the industry's approach is at odds with those circumstances.

SYSTEMS THINKING

This kind of situation was described by Peter Checkland [82], who built on the principles of "systems thinking" set out by von Bertalanffy [83]. Checkland argued that some problems are so complex that when you break them down into smaller ones, you lose information on the relationships between the constituent parts, which means that the essence of the problem disappears. So when you try to build a solution to the bigger problem from the set of solutions to the smaller ones, it doesn't work.

They don't add up, because you're trying to create a solution in the original problem space, but with no information on the original relationships.

This is the difference between analysis (breaking a problem down) and synthesis (seeing the whole picture) [84]. Problems requiring a systems thinking approach, i.e. ones based on synthesis, tend to be characterised by the importance of relationships between components rather than by the components themselves. Examples would be the relationship between a company and its investors, the relationship between an employee and their working environment, and relationships between trading nations. You can't take any of those components (markets, people, nations) out of the context in which you want to examine them and look at them in isolation. At least, not sensibly. You need to view them in the round.

There's no reason why systems thinking can't be applied to cyber (e.g. [85]), but it does require a shift in approach. The problem is, from an economic viewpoint, the best option for the industry is to ignore all this real-world complexity and continue to market cyber on the basis of a causal link between investment and benefits. It's a simple message, and as we'll see later, by using compliance as a proxy for protection, the cyber industry can claim to have delivered, without necessarily having improved things for the customer. Against a background of complexity and nuance, the industry therefore remains committed to a one-point operating model originally formulated nearly a quarter of a century ago, largely because it's the most profitable option.

OUTCOMES FOR THE CUSTOMER

ACHIEVING PROTECTION

But surely, investment in cyber *must* lead to protection?

A 2019 cyber readiness survey conducted by UK insurance firm Hiscox [86] reported that amongst 5,400 companies across seven countries: "*... only one in ten (10%) achieved 'expert' status this year, slightly down from 11% in 2018. Nearly three-quarters (74%) ranked as unprepared 'novices'*".

It's difficult to compare the findings in the 2019 report with those from 2020 [87] and 2021 [88], largely because of changes in approach. The 2020 report, for example, included Ireland for the first time, and Ireland seemingly had a large proportion of companies in the "expert" bracket [87, p10]. That said, the 2020 report noted a jump in the number of "expert" companies – from 10% to 18%, i.e. there seemed to have been a significant improvement in cyber preparedness [87, p10]. Partly that may have been due to a rise in reported spending on cybersecurity, up 39% on the year, at an average of US$2.1M per organisation [87, p14]. Yet the median cost of a cyber incident (the midpoint of the range of costs) had reportedly also risen, by a factor of six [87, p7]. That is, despite better reported levels of preparedness and increased levels of expenditure, the median impact of a breach had gone up.

The 2020 report was based on 5,569 survey respondents [87, p17] and stated that 39% of those respondents had been "*... affected by a security event*" [87, p3]. Amongst the 2,172 companies affected (i.e. 0.39 × 5,569) the total estimated costs of cyber breaches was US$1.8Bn [87, p7]. Assuming I've interpreted the figures correctly, that's an average impact of about US$0.8M per *affected* company (well below half of the population), against reported average spending (across *all* companies) of US$2.1M.

The 2021 report made another adjustment to the terms of the survey, in the way "expert" was defined. There are no numbers for overall losses in the 2021 report (at least none that I could find), but it's noted that amongst the companies taking part in the survey, expenditure on cybersecurity had increased yet again, to about 20% of the average IT budget.

Examined in sequence, the reported figures for average company expenditure on cyber were: £1.2M (2018); £1.45M (2019); £2.03M (2020); and £3.25M (2021). That's a fairly clear trend.[4] The numbers of firms reporting an attack in the same years were: 45% (2018); 61% (2019); 39% (2020); and 43% (2021). That's obviously not such a clear pattern and may not be providing the right information anyway, since in 2020 the survey was amended to distinguish between incidents (events not leading to a compromise) and breaches (events leading to a material loss). Previously, respondents simply reported "events". However, the report goes on to set out "... *impacts of incidents or breaches*" [87, p8] so it's not clear whether the terms are being used consistently. The 2021 report [88, p9] suggests that respondents are more able to "... *measure the business impact of security incidents that disrupt their business*", so again, I'm not sure it's possible to compare like-for-like across these reports, at least in terms of a potential link between expenditure and protection.

I was hoping that the annual Department for Digital, Culture, Media and Sport (DCMS) security breach survey could be taken instead, to demonstrate a simple pattern of increasing investment and declining breach numbers. As far as I can see, that's not the case, partly because in 2020 the questions on cyber investment were dropped to make room for others, on the basis that "*[t]he overall estimates of spending on cyber security had been relatively consistent across the years and we did not expect to see any measurable changes this year*" [89, p19]. That statement alone, however, seems to contradict the findings from the Hiscox reports.

For the record, in previous DCMS reports, the average investment was given as £4,590 (2017); £3,580 (2018); and £5,100 (2019). The proportions of businesses reporting a cyberattack were 46% (2017); 43% (2018); 32% (2019); 46% (2020); and 39% (2021). So again, there seems to be no clear pattern linking expenditure to outcome, although arguably in the period 2017–20, it was the breach count leading expenditure, not the other way around. That is, it may have been the failure of existing investments in security that led to an increase in expenditure in the following year.

In the United States, the Ponemon Institute [90] found that despite spending a reported average of US$18M annually on cyber security, over half the companies they surveyed (53%) agreed with the statement "*[o]ur IT security leadership is not certain if the technologies deployed are working as promised and protecting the network*". Some 69% of respondents agreed with the statement "*[o]ur organization's security approach is reactive and incident driven*". Yet more than half of the respondents in the survey (58%) indicated that they were planning to increase their IT security budget in the coming year, and by average of 14%. Which begs the question – why keep spending? The answer might be found in a 2013 UK Government report on cyber standards [91], which noted that *"34% of organisations who purchased certified products or services did so purely to achieve compliance as an outcome"*. That is, one in three organisations who bought those products were aiming to get a ticket rather than expecting improved levels of protection.

So overall, depending on which survey you believe, there seems to be quite a lot of money going into cybersecurity, but no clear indication of any associated outcome for the customer, in terms of reduced numbers of incidents and/or reduced impacts.

It must be worth asking where that money's going.

WHERE THE MONEY GOES

THE IMPORTANCE OF DECISION-MAKING

Amazon's Simple Storage Service (S3) is part of the Amazon Web Services (AWS) portfolio. AWS provide a means for organisations to create their own virtual IT infrastructure with no capital expenditure. S3 is one of the component offerings, and it comes in the form of "buckets", although "balloons" might perhaps be more appropriate. For your money you get an Internet-accessible URL that you can use to put data into a notional bucket, take it out again, replace it, delete it, etc., and all the hard work is done behind the scenes. However, it's up to the owner to manage access permissions. It's entirely possible to make the contents of the bucket, however sensitive, open to anyone with an Internet connection. And that's exactly what many people have done [92–94], in most cases with large amounts of data, and in some cases with sensitive personal data.

AWS have since moved to make it more difficult to leave an S3 bucket too open [95, 96], but the general consensus is that people will continue to make optimistic assumptions on access configurations. The underlying lesson seems to be that effective security is about making good decisions, rather than simply employing more technology. The 2019 Imperva leak, for example, which was caused by a loss of control over AWS keys [97] was concisely summed up by their CTO Kunal Anand:

> *We take ownership of the fact that the incident was a result of our choices, actions we took and failed to take before, during, and after our database migration. We recommend all organizations take the time to fully understand the shared responsibility of deploying and managing applications and data in Infrastructure as a Service (IaaS) solutions.*

AWS provide two methods for accessing their services: one is a console-type interface, the other is a web-based Command Line Interface (CLI). Access via this second route is controlled through privately managed keys, and of course it's up to the owner to make sure that those keys are protected. Any other individual gaining access to the keys can pretend to be the owner. They can then delete virtual networks and virtual machines, etc., although the most common action is to create new ones – specifically, very large virtual machines and lots of them – and set them to the task of mining cryptocurrency. Charges for virtual machines depend on how big they are, how many you have, and how long you've had them running. The largest machines can be eye-wateringly expensive. Consequently, if you lose your keys and someone gains access to your account, you can end up holding the bill while they walk away with the profit. Typically you might end up with a bill for thousands of dollars after just a few hours [98].

The usual route for losing the keys is to absent-mindedly publish them to public source code repositories [99]. Therefore, in addition to offering ways of checking S3 configurations, AWS and third parties now also offer tools to scan source code files for keys before they're uploaded to public areas [100]. But in an odd way, maybe that's the wrong response.

The "Peltzman Effect" [101] remains a somewhat contentious proposal, but the premise is that when technology is introduced as a means of reducing risk, people increase their risk-taking to compensate, because they feel as though the system "has their back". Under those circumstances, adding in further technical controls may do little more than persuade users that they can afford to take more risks. Greg Ip, for example [102, pp94, 99, 101], argues that the introduction of Antilock Braking Systems (ABS) as a safety measure was correlated closely with recorded increases in speeding fines, but with virtually no reduction in the numbers of crashes. McMahon [103] goes further and suggests that when users are shielded with technology in this way, they're less well prepared to deal with a threat when they're eventually faced with it [104–109]. Describing the situation as an "irony of automation" [110], McMahon notes that this has come about because "... *the stupid human has been largely designed out of how the system handles risk*" [103, p1390].

Possibly a better approach would have been to engineer a higher level of perceived risk, in order to trigger a more cautious set of behaviours. This converse effect is summarised as "if you want to drive more safely, take your seat belt off". You may have seen this referred to elsewhere as a "risk thermostat". To be fair the argument over whether or not there is an effect is still going on, with evidence both for (on the basis of experimental results [111–113]) and against (mostly on the basis of an argument relating to statistical methods [114, 115]). And to be scrupulously fair – one study went as far as stating that it might not be possible to design an experiment that would bring the debate to a conclusion [116]. For the purposes of this chapter, it's enough to note that there is doubt over whether or not the apparently rational act of putting in more technical security measures is having the right effect on risk-taking behaviour [117].

All of which brings us to a salutary episode in cloud computing. Code Spaces was a company that rented out pre-built software development environments based on the AWS offering. It was noted earlier that AWS provide two means of managing your virtual environment, one being a web-based console. It's possible to add two-factor authentication (2FA) to your password for the console, and indeed it's strongly recommended. It means that someone has to steal not only your password but also your phone, or a hardware token, if they want to get access. Not implementing two-factor authentication means that you're relying on just a password protecting your "do-anything-you-want" account. Although it's not 100% clear how it happened, one way or another Code Spaces lost control of that root password. An attacker got into their account and started deleting things. Virtual machines, backups, anything they wanted. Subsequent investigations indicated that this was possible because the live environments and the backups were both accessible from a single AWS management account, rather than being held separately [118]. In short, while controls existed at the time to support a more resilient approach, they weren't engaged. As you may have guessed, the company simply ceased to exist. Not because of technical weaknesses, but because of the decisions that had been made.

In case it looks as though I have a problem with AWS (I don't, I think it's a really amazing creation), let's turn to the case of a US security technology company, HBGary. The company had two parts, one dealing with slightly spooky US Government work [119]. The CEO of that group picked an argument with the hacktivist group Anonymous, who responded by taking a close look at HBGary's corporate IT. The events thereafter were summarised by Ars Technica [120]:

- An unpatched web site content management system allowed Anonymous to establish a foothold.
- A weak password used by the CEO was easily cracked, giving access to the associated email account.
- Because the CEO had used the same passwords across multiple platforms, Anonymous were able to gain administrator privileges, and then gain access to social media accounts belonging to the CEO, and after that gain access to other email accounts, specifically the account belonging to the CTO.
- A forged email from the CTO was then sent to the system administrator, asking them to drop the firewall for a while. That was 100% successful. The rest is history [121, 122].

The "pivot points", the areas which gave Anonymous a further step into the system [123], weren't technical weaknesses. They were flawed decisions: a failure to maintain patching; the use of weak passwords; the reuse of passwords; and a susceptibility to social engineering [124]. People problems.

There's an interesting diagram in the 2017 UK Security Breaches survey [125, Figure 5.2] showing the proportion of respondents reporting specific types of attack, and also the proportion saying that the attack was the worst they had seen. If you draw a line about halfway up, the attacks can be divided into two groups (see Figure 1.1). The ones below the line are direct electronic attacks – denial of service, hacking, etc. The proportions of respondents experiencing those attacks range from 5% (deliberate misuse) to 10% (unauthorised use by external parties). The ones above the line (anywhere from 17% to nearly three quarters of respondents, 72%) represent attacks vectored through people's decision-making (phishing, malware, misdirection, impersonation).

That is, the worst and most often reported incidents arise through the exploitation of people's decision-making. Against that background, if you look back at the quote from the LSEC report, you will see that the slowest growing sector is training and awareness. The aspect of IT security that is already pretty much the smallest item of expenditure (at around 4% of total spend) is also growing at the slowest rate, further increasing the spending gap between it and technical measures (where the incidence

Q: Which of the following have happened to your business in the last 12 months

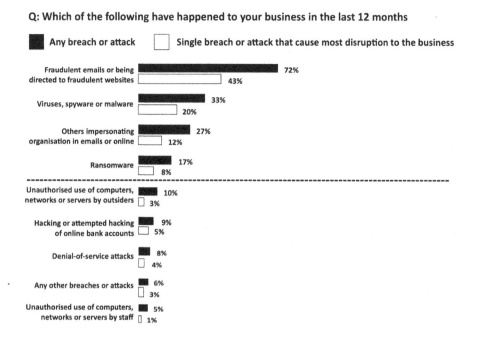

FIGURE 1.1   Distribution of incident types. (Leapfrog Creative Ltd, reproduced with permission. From DCMS Security Breaches Survey 2017, accessed under the Open Government Licence v3.0.)

and severity of reported attacks are already much lower, and where paradoxically the spend on technology may be aggravating the problem of behaviour).

Despite the fact that other approaches could be more effective in solving the underlying problems, the industry remains focused on pushing "build one, sell many" technical products.

All of which could explain the observed non-outcomes. A report from "Debate Security" [126] draws on interviews conducted with over 100 individuals in businesses and in the cybersecurity industry. The key finding is that security technology simply isn't performing as claimed: "... *90% of interviewees in our research say there is an efficacy problem with cybersecurity technology which compromises defences and is partially responsible for the continued success of attackers*" [126, p7]. The report goes on to say that without improvements in technology efficacy, cybersecurity will "*continue to fail*" [126, p5].

Biancotti [127] references a Financial Times interview with a former GCHQ deputy director for intelligence and cyber operations [128]:

The reason breaches are growing is because companies aren't protecting themselves properly, because they are being made confused by the cyber security vendors. A "cyber mythology" has been created by the industry, to sell unnecessarily expensive solutions through fear. All recent high profile cyber-attack incidents could and should have been prevented with relatively low cost solutions.

Whenever I give advice to clients on this subject to business or at a national level to formulate national security policies, the client emphasis is always around finding expensive technical solutions. The unfortunately more boring but more realistic (however considerably more effective and cheaper) solutions reflect a blend of technology, human education and procedural measures.

It isn't either expensive or complicated to understand and manage these risks. But while it is still made so – the figures in these reports will continue to grow and we will be no safer.

If true, it may not be stretching the point to suggest that the industry focus on profits is acting to *reduce* the level of protection provided to the customer.

The question posed earlier was: "where's the money going, and what are we getting for it?". The answer to the first bit seems to be "on tech, mostly". The answer to the second seems to be "more problems".

THE ROLE OF THE CUSTOMER IN THE CYBER MARKET

Ironically, the numbers being what they are, a slight drop in spending on pure technology would equate to a very large percentage rise in spending on human-centric security, which again, given the numbers, could result in easy wins in some of the areas of most concern. However, as pointed out by Malcolm Harkins in his keynote presentation at PreventCon 2018 [54], the cyber security industry isn't motivated to solve problems – it's motivated to sell products. A Security Week article by Bowers [129] goes so far as to state that: "*[t]he primary goal is not to solve the security problems, but sell you a product that you think can solve your security problems*". Harkins argues persuasively that the cyber industry has let down its customers, and he isn't alone in suggesting that – the concept of "expense in depth" [71] has been raised by others [130].

Questions have also been asked regarding the underlying rationale for investment in cyber – the claimed huge cost of breaches [131–133]. As pointed out by Dunn Cavelty [134], a number of people [e.g. 2, 135] are now asking if the cost of a cyber breach is actually as high as it's claimed to be, or if this is all just a marketing exercise [136].

Although perhaps "sponsored marketing" might be more appropriate. The emergence of cyber insurance has created a secondary market in warranties for security products, and on the face of it, this is a good thing – customers let down by ineffective security products can make a claim for compensation to offset the impacts arising from a breach. However, it's worth looking at the detail, as shown in the paper by Woods and Moore [137]:

1. Insurance companies are now selling "product insurance" to cybersecurity product manufacturers, in the same way as they have historically offered the same type of cover to other industries. The insurance company underwrites a guarantee which the manufacturer then bundles into their product. Should a

claim be made by a customer against the manufacturer, then the manufacturer in turn makes a claim on their policy with the insurer.

2. The sales pitch from the insurance company to the manufacturer seems to be along the lines of "not all people will qualify for cover, so adopting our insurance will make your product stand out from its competitors". The benefit offered by the insurer is therefore market differentiation, which can be important. The firewall sector, for example, could be seen as a commodity market in which differentiation from your competitors is crucial.

3. In commercial situations where there is information asymmetry i.e. the seller knows more about a product's quality than the buyer does, the argument from Akerlof [138] is that the situation becomes a "market for lemons". Akerlof's example related to the market for used cars. He suggested that buyers' concerns that a car might turn out to be a "lemon" would become the dominant factor determining maximum possible pricing [139].

One of the mechanisms suggested to offset the risk of buying a lemon is branding (as in, it's not second hand, it's "pre-loved"). Another is the use of guarantees, which are intended to act as a signal of quality [140]. The guarantee ostensibly reduces the buyer's risk, and that apparent reduction in risk acts to maintain the asking price. As in "we're so sure of our product, we can afford to take the risk of giving you a guarantee". Through the use of warranties, prices can be maintained, and the market doesn't collapse.

Woods and Moore examined the use of such warranties when applied to cyber security products. Their conclusion was that the use of guarantees is *probably* more than just marketing, but also that the exclusions and qualifications attached to the guarantees they examined meant that in most cases there was no appreciable risk transfer. That is, in most cases the customer was running pretty much the same risk as they would have been running in the absence of a guarantee. As the authors did, you can engage a popular Internet search engine to look for "cyber product warranties" or something similar, and then scroll through the list of exclusions, restrictions, and conditions applying to a typical guarantee. One example might be the requirement for a claimant to supply evidence that the attack they suffered was state-sponsored. Good luck with that.

As suggested by Woods and Moore, it's likely that in the end, the costs incurred by the manufacturer in taking out the policy will be passed onto the customer, in one form or another. In the short term, the manufacturer might absorb it as an investment to increase sales, but longer term, the cost of the insurance will be reflected in the price – after all, we're selling a top-notch product that stands out from the competition, so we can afford to charge a premium.

Putting all this together – customers for "guaranteed" products seem to be covering the cost of the policy taken out by the manufacturer to underwrite the warranty. The warranty, in turn, is intended to make the product stand out, so that the manufacturer can justify the asking price. And in the meantime, there seems to be no appreciable reduction in risk for the buyer. One interpretation might be that the customer is paying to help the manufacturer differentiate their product, so that the customer can be asked to pay more.

CONCLUSION

So, back to the question that's been running through this section. Setting aside the obvious financial benefits accruing to suppliers, does the industry deliver for its customers? A reasonable answer might be that it delivers technology (at a price), but there's no hard evidence that it delivers on the claimed benefits, in part because it ignores the human setting for that technology.

The industry's position is perhaps best reflected in a quote from an unnamed individual in the banking sector, expressing their view just before the global financial meltdown [141]: *"I didn't really understand what was going on, but we were making lots of money"*.

THE FUTURE OF CYBER

ONE POSSIBLE FUTURE

Instead of treating cyber as a unique discipline, it might be better to see it as a specialist activity within a number of domains, tailored to meet the needs of each of those domains. Achieving alignment between the nature of the solution and the nature of the problem is generally recognised as being sensible [142].

That would place the management of risk where it is best understood i.e. in the hands of people with domain expertise, rather than in the hands of security practitioners. Also the management of risk would be alongside the management of reward. The two tend to go together. Cyber would cease to be a separate discipline, if indeed it ever was, and would become a tool used by managers to deliver specific outcomes in a range of fields, which, as we'll see later, is how businesses would like to see it anyway. In effect, cyber would become a distributed concept, rather than a centralised one.

Clearly, it would be optimistic to think that such a change could happen in the normal course of events. With the current levels of profit and current levels of growth, cyber security product manufacturers and security service providers aren't going to welcome changes in direction. More importantly perhaps, change requires an accepted baseline – a common understanding of what cybersecurity means at present. Whereas it's actually quite difficult to find an accepted definition.

THE DEFINITION OF CYBERSECURITY

The European Union Agency for Cybersecurity (ENISA) concluded that there were indeed multiple definitions [143]. Their solution, probably underpinned with the best of intentions, was to suggest another one. Their definition runs to just over 90 words and comes with a rider: *"[e]xisting use of the terms under the CIA paradigm when applied to single interfaces and single classes of object shall explicitly not use the term Cybersecurity"*. Their paper seems well-considered, and well researched. I'm just not sure it's all that helpful.

Others (e.g. von Solms and van Niekerk [144] and Bay [145]) have attempted to define cybersecurity by distinguishing it from related terms such as "information security". As subsequently reported [146], that line of thinking leads to anomalies, indicating that perhaps the original distinctions were somewhat artificial. In fact, these (and other) attempts to draw some kind of distinction means that this book will continue to follow the lead of Bishop [e.g. 147] and use the terms "cybersecurity" and "IT/computer/information security" interchangeably. It seems to me that fine-grained distinctions in terminology amount to not much more than sophistry – purposely adding a level of complication in order to make the subject seem more relevant.

Schatz et al. [148] applied semantic and lexical analysis to the largest set of definitions they could assemble (nearly 30 in total) and concluded that "*[o]ur review of primary sources unveiled a clear lack of congruence across the sources as to the meaning and scope of the term*". Other people have found the same, e.g. Craigen et al. [149]:

> *Based on the literature review described in this article, we found that the term is used broadly and its definitions are highly variable, context-bound, often subjective, and, at times, uninformative. There is a paucity of literature on what the term actually means and how it is situated within various contexts. The absence of a concise, broadly acceptable definition that captures the multi-dimensionality of cybersecurity potentially impedes technological and scientific advances by reinforcing the predominantly technical view of cybersecurity while separating disciplines that should be acting in concert to resolve complex cybersecurity challenges.*

Not surprisingly, a common theme running through the definitions examined by Schatz et al. is that cyber is about the protection of assets. But as we saw earlier, and as hinted at by Craigen, it's not that simple – cyber has effects in areas well beyond the concept of protecting assets, and the outcome of security investments and/or breaches is highly dependent on context. So, is cyber just about the protection of assets, and we don't care about those wider outcomes? Dunn Cavelty [150] looked into the ways in which cybersecurity has been presented [150, p28]:

> *Two dominant perspectives were identified. The first sees cybersecurity as the practice of fixing broken objects and the second sees cybertechnologies as tools to further political goals. With relatively little overlap between them, the first view neglects social construction and meaning-making processes whereas the second focuses too much on preconceived notions of politics and security, with too little knowledge of how the materiality of the artefacts constrains their use. What we therefore need for innovative cybersecurity research is to combine both perspectives at the intersection between the technical and the social to the greater benefit of both communities.*

My reading is that you can either see cyber as an end in itself, or you can see it as a means to an end [151]. However, those two approaches are mutually exclusive. You won't meet wider expectations if you insist that cyber is just about protecting assets. You have to lift your gaze up a little bit and stop viewing cyber as a matter of controlling which user can access which file.

An End in Itself vs a Means to an End

Choi et al. [152] looked at two groups of hospitals in the United States. One group had never suffered a publicised security breach, whereas the other group had been involved in a breach and, as a result, had implemented additional security measures. The study looked at how long it took to see a patient with a suspected heart attack, starting with their time of arrival at the hospital, and also at the 30-day mortality rates for those patients. For hospitals with additional security measures, waiting times were longer, by nearly 3 minutes. The 30-day mortality rates were up by 0.23 percentage points one year after the implementation, 0.36 percentage points two years later, and 0.35 percentage points three years later. As noted in the report, that's not just a bad clinical outcome, it's a bad security outcome, since *"[f]rustrated clinicians bypassing new systems and processes with ad hoc workarounds avoid system safeguards and create new opportunities for errors"*. Koppel et al. [153] summarise the ways in which healthcare workers circumvent security controls (and feel as though they have to), when security is seen as an end in itself.

Miller and Tucker [154] found that in the absence of any other drivers, when one hospital chose to implement an Electronic Medical Records system, it caused a ripple effect amongst its peers, encouraging them to do the same. The outcome of this cooperation was an improved level of patient care. Amongst hospitals located in states with privacy laws however, there was no such effect. Those hospitals seemed to view security compliance as the overriding requirement and ignored any potential for wider improvements. They missed out on achieving business benefits, because security in and of itself had been presented to them as the desired outcome.

In contrast, in 2015, exports from Israel's cyber industry [155] amounted to more than 7% of the global cybersecurity product market [156, p119]. According to one report [157], in 2018, inward investment for Israel's cyber start-ups came to 20% of the global total [158]. And despite having a population only about the same as that of London, Israel claims to be one of the top five countries in terms of cybersecurity capabilities [159].

Israel didn't explicitly set out a fixed national strategy, but chose instead to develop a cyber ecosystem [160], reflecting a shift towards the concept of resilience [134]. As a consequence, Israel views cyber as a technology to be used in a variety of ways [156, 161]. The relaxation of rules applying to the export of cyber technologies [162] provides an example [163].

This isn't just a soundbite – it's a major factor shaping Israel's approach [159], reflected in the creation of a multi-disciplinary research unit at Tel Aviv University looking into the social implications of cyber [164].

Conclusions

Papakonstantinou's paper examining the impact of EU cyber regulations [165] argues that networks and information systems *"... cannot be the subject matter of cybersecurity. The protection of a computer system cannot be an end in itself"* [165, p5]. The argument in the paper is that what's being protected is the rights of EU citizens, not the data held on the system.

The absence of a widely accepted definition of cybersecurity is also explained, using the observation from Papakonstantinou [165, p2]: *"[d]ifferent actors understand cybersecurity differently under different circumstances"* i.e. multiple definitions exist precisely because the meaning of cyber depends upon the context of its use.

But, from the viewpoint of the cyber industry, selling protection as an end state is so much easier, and what's more, it enables the industry to package up a standard offering, which of course maximises profits. Such an approach is heavily weighted towards what the industry wants to achieve, rather than what the customer might want. To draw a transport analogy, at the minute it seems to be all about where the bus driver wants to go, rather than the wishes of the fare-paying passengers.

DRIVERS FOR CHANGE

INTERNAL DRIVERS FOR CHANGE

If cyber is to become more outcome-based, then pressure will be needed to bring that about. At the simplest level, that pressure can either come from within the industry, or from outside. Are there any indications, for example, that the industry might naturally change direction, or is it more likely that change, if it comes, will be imposed?

Shires [166] examined the processes of ritualisation in cybersecurity, concluding that the industry implicitly recognises a division between the commercial activity of selling services and products, and the promotion of cyber as a specialism. At security conferences for example, there's a formalised division between people going up on stage, usually in a separate room, to deliver speeches on *"pure"* cyber [166, p32], and the same people going back to their exhibition stands in the main hall, to engage in the tawdry business of selling security products. Shires argues that this ritual of separation is intended to promote a sense of value in practitioners' claims of expertise. The logical extension of this is perhaps seen in invitation-only cyber conferences – events where what might be viewed as the "purest of the pure" cyber discussions are held between practitioners, usually *in camera*. Generally, no proceedings are issued, so it's difficult to tell what goes on, although human behaviour seems to be a hot topic.

For me, partitioning off "pure cyber" doesn't fit in with the idea of getting to know what your customers might want, and without that understanding, it's unlikely that any pressures will arise from within the industry to move to a more customer-focused model. In fact if anything, the view from the industry seems to be just the opposite. Over about the same period, the cyber industry has been actively debating whether or not *"the user is the enemy"* of cybersecurity [167–173]. As far as I can see, the central argument is that users (which I would read as "customers") ruin what would otherwise be a smoothly running approach to cyber, in much the same way as passengers getting on and off trains might be viewed as a source of inconvenient delays for train operators.

Ashenden [174] sums up the problem as a failure to adopt an appropriate viewpoint, rather than as a failing on the part of the user:

Unfortunately humans are not very predictable. They do not operate as machines where if the same information is input and processed in the same way then the result that is output will be the same time after time. They can appear erratic in behaviour because we often fail to take account of the individual belief systems that humans bring into the organisation.

However, that probably doesn't represent the majority opinion within the practitioner community.

Klimburg-Witjes and Wentland [175] offer a really interesting analysis of the security practitioners' view of users, highlighting two key points. The first is that users are seen as a problem that needs to be fixed, usually by trying even harder to convince them of the correctness of the security practitioners' approach [176]. The second is that a lack of compliance amongst users is increasingly being framed as a moral failing on the part of the user. That's perhaps exemplified in a questionnaire-based approach identifying "high risk" individuals on the basis of their assessed personality characteristics, and/or their scores on security tests. The suggestion [177] being that those individuals (/customers) can then be debarred from accessing sensitive corporate assets, on the basis that their assessed personality traits don't meet the criteria laid down by the security team.

Nothing in that approach, of course, looks at the contribution that those individuals might bring to the company. Consequently, it would seem to be the security tail wagging the corporate dog. The implication is that security concerns are completely separate to business concerns. Security is there to control access, not to evaluate costs and benefits.

It will be interesting to see the first test case under UK or EU employment law, involving an employee being "let go" on the basis that they couldn't do their job, because their employer prevented them from doing it, on the basis of a security personality assessment. Although in practice that might be preceded by the first case brought by an ex-employee who was taken on by a company with a declared policy on neuro-diversity.

As noted by MacEwan [178, p9], quoting Sparks [179], *"every system of risk management creates a blaming system as its counterpart"*. You can see that in comments from practitioners, stating that a large percentage of security incidents are caused "... *either through ignorance or stupidity"* [180, p8], that the job of the security practitioner is to "... *rectify the damage caused by the incurably stupid"* [180, p9], and that the best thing to do with users is to "*[l]et them know what they are to do, and let them know what's expected of them"* [180, p15]. This viewpoint of users as something to be corralled and controlled in the name of cyber is evident elsewhere e.g. [181, Ch9]:

We need to accept that there will always be mavericks who cannot, whatever is done, make the transition from "infosec denier" to "security convert"... [and] what do you do when you encounter someone who won't or can't comply? It's a business decision as to whether they remain or have no place in the organisation, even if they are your best salespeople.

On that precise topic, Google [182] sponsored an interesting piece of work in 2021 – they asked over 200 security practitioners "if you had to provide just three bits of security advice to users in order to help them stay safe online, what would they be?". After sorting through and removing duplicates, etc., they found 152 different suggestions across 15 distinct categories, leading the authors to conclude that "... *the expert community as a whole lacks consensus*". Quite.

Some of the views were interesting, given that the survey related to advice intended for non-tech-savvy users:

- Check for a green HTTPS to the left of the domain name.
- Check SSL certificates.
- Don't enter sites whose reputation isn't clearly (and positively) assessed in a public database.
- Disable Java browser plug-ins or uninstall Java.
- Disable root certificates for entities that you would be alarmed to see certifying your bank's login page.
- Let Gmail render your mail attachments instead of opening them locally.

Some of it seemed to be completely divorced from reality:

- Be aware of why your computer asks you for permission or passwords.
- Never click on a link in an email.
- Don't blindly trust every message even if it came from someone you know and trust.
- Always be suspicious; don't trust everybody.
- Never give out personal information.
- Don't look for porn.
- If you didn't ask for the attachment, don't open it.
- Don't trust email.
- Don't give out your email [address].

The report draws a number of general conclusions, amongst them:

> *Our finding that there are 152 pieces of advice spread across 15 categories suggests a wide breadth of security advice that experts consider important to follow. Just considering these numbers, it's perhaps unsurprising that users don't follow all the advice on offer – there's a lot of it, it spans diverse areas, and it's not clear where to start. Users are probably not receiving a consistent message on what's most important and exactly what to do in each area.*

A study conducted by Frey et al. [183] created a game in which teams of three to four people had to decide how to allocate cybersecurity spending for a fictional local utility company. The game ran as a series of "rounds", with security issues being introduced by a game organiser at the start of each new round. The teams were made up of either managers, computer experts, or cybersecurity practitioners. Success was judged in terms of the proportion of cybersecurity incidents that were prevented or contained in each round. It will come as no surprise to hear that the cybersecurity teams performed worst overall, mostly because they saw "stupid users" as a problem and instead, put their faith in technology. There are a number of illuminating quotes from the worst-performing team (made up of security people), which the study puts forward as evidence of over-confidence, e.g. *"[we're] security experts – we don't need a threat assessment"*, and after being briefed on the details for the next round, *"[y]ou told us what we already knew"* [183, p529].

Observations on the performance of security teams highlighted tunnel vision, and a tendency to blame circumstances and/or a lack of budget for poor outcomes. Other teams performed much better, largely because they adopted an approach that balanced technology against "people issues", and because they showed a willingness to question their decisions. The paper concludes that in real life, security teams should perhaps be drawn not just from a pool of cyber people but should include other sources of expertise such as technicians and managers. That is, perhaps it might be an idea to ask people what they want from cyber before you give it to them, and perhaps it might be an idea to see cyber as a negotiation, rather than something handed down from Mount Olympus.

So on this basis, is there any evidence that the wider cybersecurity community understands the user, or wants to understand the user, or even understands the context of their customers' use of cybersecurity? I would say no, not really. A paper by Menges et al. [184] goes further and suggests that the relationship between security people and users has now become "dysfunctional".

Rather than engaging with the user [185], cyber practitioners tend to fall back on a simpler, standard solution: add in more technology [186]:

Many secure systems rely on a "human in the loop" to perform security-critical functions. However, humans often fail in their security roles. Whenever possible, secure system designers should find ways of keeping humans out of the loop. However, there are some tasks for which feasible or cost effective alternatives to humans are not available. In these cases secure system designers should engineer their systems to support the humans in the loop and maximize their chances of performing their security-critical functions successfully.

Klimburg-Witjes and Wentland [175] broaden this out, referencing an idea proposed by Morozov [187] – that the cyber industry takes a "solutionist" approach, even when it comes to human behaviour. The underlying proposal that technology should be used to constrain the wayward user has been noted by others, e.g. Zimmermann and Renaud [188], who suggest that such a view is rooted in an out of date, technically oriented approach aimed at achieving *"security by resistance"* [188, p9]. Zimmermann and Renaud go further and suggest that users should be treated as adults, rather than as "the problem" [188, p6] and/or as a convenient scapegoat [189]. It's also interesting to compare the industry's perceived need to manage users, with the relatively small degree of investment allocated to understanding them [12].

Whatever the future holds for cyber as a business, it seems that any movement towards a more customer-based approach is unlikely to be driven by internal pressures. The mindset that sees users/customers as a problem, and the view that assets are items to be shielded from being accessed by those users, seems too deeply entrenched.

External Drivers for Change

Michael Porter [190] identified five factors that drive competitive strategy and, in so doing, set out the key characteristics shaping any industry:

- **Threat of new entrants.** How easy is it for new companies to get into the industry? This is sometimes described as "barriers to entry".
- **Power of suppliers.** If you're reliant on a single supplier to provide a key element of your product, then you're not really in control of your costs.
- **Industry rivalry.** How intense is the competition between companies that are already in the market?
- **Power of buyers.** If there are many companies offering the product and/or your customers aren't locked in, then the bargaining power of customers becomes a factor.
- **Threat of substitutes.** This isn't so much the threat of new competitors selling similar products, but other ways in which the underlying need can be met.

Porter's model isn't so much a description of what all markets have to look like, it's more a framework for analysing market characteristics. Any successful corporate strategy will be shaped by some balance of these five main factors.

If we turn that around, any change in direction for the one or more elements of the cyber industry would have to be driven by a change in one of or more of those external factors. So, picking the cyber consultancy sector as an example...

There isn't really a key supplier for this sector – it's not as though it depends on e.g. specialist chips, and it's difficult to see any way in which that might change, mostly because the "raw material" for this sector is people. For penetration testing companies in some markets, there are requirements for skills to be formally assessed before the company can offer its services, i.e. there are barriers to entry, but that doesn't apply across the security industry as a whole. And there don't seem to be any obvious routes that would change current levels of industry rivalry, short of a significant influx of new companies, or a dramatic decline in demand. The threat of substitutes is a possible factor, but we've already seen cyber insurance emerge as a potential substitute, and the market has just absorbed it.

So if there is going to be an evolution of the cybersecurity industry, it's going to have to come at least in part through the bargaining power of customers – people who buy cyber products and services demanding something different to what they're currently getting.

Derek Abell [191] proposed a slightly different model: as markets evolve, strategic windows open and close, and the "fit" between a business and their customers only works within that temporary window. He suggested four types of change that could lead to a current window closing and a new one opening:

- **New primary demand.** After the fall of the Berlin Wall, a new tranche of customers became available to Western electronics companies. That previously untapped demand created opportunities for fast-moving companies to increase their market share.

- **New technology.** A classic if perhaps now slightly dated example used in the original paper concerned the introduction of electronic calculators, which displaced sales of slide rules (millennials, ask your grandparents).
- **New channels.** Although it might seem odd now, petrol stations didn't always sell food. They used to sell things for cars. When supermarkets started franchising food outlets in petrol stations, they opened up a new channel to reach their customers, which in turn led to an increase in sales.
- **Market redefinition.** This means that customers buy essentially the same product, but they look for different benefits. Levitt [192] said that whatever you're selling, there's a tangible component (e.g. a security policy document) and an intangible component (the customer feeling that they know what risks they're running). Market redefinition, it's always seemed to me, occurs when the intangible benefit sought by a customer changes, even if the tangible product doesn't. Companies that are able to meet that emerging need can therefore gain an advantage.

A sudden surge in primary demand isn't going to happen in the cyber industry, or at least, it seems unlikely. Similarly, new technology doesn't seem like a way in which the industry would evolve. The industry is built around constantly changing technology and has been since its inception. New channels? Perhaps, but it's hard to see how. The development of security as a service is a potential example, although that's more to do with suppliers moving to a subscription arrangement, thereby increasing "visibility" (clarity of future revenue), which in turn allows them to achieve a higher valuation for their company.

Which leaves market redefinition – people still buying cyber, but for new reasons, and that's similar to the result we saw from applying Porter's model.

CONCLUSION

The future of cyber can be about more of the same, or it can be about change. If the analysis presented here stands up, then industry change will only come about through customers demanding more than just the protection of assets. That pressure has to come from outside – there are no intrinsic pressures that would force the industry to deviate from its existing position. You can either view that as customers saying "I'm not getting a sensible return on my investment in cyber – I want something more", or as the industry being presented with an unmet need, and adapting to meet it. Those two options correspond to the outcome of applying Porter's market-based model, and the outcome of applying Abell's industry-based model. However, unless the cyber industry sees that there is an unmet need and/or customers point it out, then we're stuck with the current situation.

CASE STUDY: MARKET REDEFINITION

BACKGROUND

KnowBe4 is a US-based cybersecurity training company. Their key market (phishing awareness training) has a large number of small players, as you can see if you carry out an online search for security training providers. That alone indicates that the market has low barriers to entry, and limited scope for differentiation. Security training is seen as a commodity. Anyone can do it.

KnowBe4 claimed revenues of over US$100M in 2019, whereas (depending on who you ask, and depending on you think are their competitors) their nearest eight direct competitors had combined revenues of around US$75M.

KnowBe4 has devastatingly good UK-oriented marketing (assuming it's still available on YouTube, I recommend it – it's engaging, disruptive, and very funny). Year-on-year revenue was initially reported to be growing at 40% (Q1 2019 vs Q1 2018, and a claimed 55% in Q3). You can see the Q4 2022 figures here [193] (broadly, 33% growth in revenue, and about the same in annual recurring revenue). In 2019 they attracted US$300M of venture capital investment, valuing the company at around US$1Bn, although the company has since gone through an IPO, and at the time of writing, their market capitalisation is a little over US$5.5Bn. Also, they seem to have been voted "cyber company of the decade". Other companies now seem to regard Knowbe4 as the industry benchmark [e.g. 194].

CAUSES

In what appears to be a commodity market with low barriers to entry, how can one company do this?

Well, possibly through market redefinition – selling broadly the same product as their competitors, but in a way that packages up different benefits to the customer.

The CEO and founder Stu Sjouwerman suggests that what differentiates KnowBe4 from other suppliers is that [195]:

> *The main difference is that both [competitor 1] and [competitor 2]'s plat-form were developed for InfoSec pros that do this full-time. Powerful but not user-friendly and the learning curve is much longer than KnowBe4, which was developed from day one for an IT Admin who has 16 other fires to put out.*

To be clear, there are other differences, in price and in overall target market, to name but two. However, KnowBe4 is aimed at overworked IT admins, not cyber professionals, and the benefit is a reduction in workload, and more specifically, a reduction in workload for key resources. This is exactly as predicted by Levitt – the linking of a different intangible benefit to the same tangible product.

According to research conducted by Cavusoglu et al. [196], businesses find it relatively easy to spend money on security if it means they achieve certified compliance against published standards, whereas a more robust business case is needed where an investment is being made simply to meet best practice. Security training in particular is seen as being only weakly linked to any organisational benefits – companies only invest in training because they feel as though they ought to. My reading of KnowBe4's success is that they have created that missing link between security training and business benefits, and therefore sidestepped the need for a formal business case. Companies buying these services aren't investing in security – they're investing in outcomes. The benefit of adopting the product isn't just 'more security'.

KNOWBE4: CONCLUSION

Against that background, I would argue, the success of KnowBe4 reflects the benefits of market redefinition. You can see it as people buying more of the same, but for different reasons, or as security being reframed as something more relevant to customer needs. But either way, the perceived and desired outcome isn't just "more security".

CASE STUDY: MEETING UNMET NEEDS

COMPETITIVE ADVANTAGE

Porter [197] set out three generic routes by which companies can achieve competitive advantage: through cost leadership; through product differentiation; and through the use of niche marketing.

Cost leadership involves reducing your operating expenses so that you can offer a lower price to your customers, assuming a lower price will matter to them. Product differentiation involves making your product look different to the customer, making it stand out, so that they buy it in preference to other offerings in the same market.

The niche aspect is about offering your product solely to a corner of the market that your competitors aren't addressing, or which they can't address. This is often misinterpreted as offering services to specific markets e.g. high-net-worth individuals. An example might be offering free cyber insurance as part of a package on the customer's credit card. The trouble is, any of your competitor banks can do the same, whereas ideally you want to work to a niche that only you have access to.

USE OF NICHE MARKETING

In early 2022, the Belgian Data Protection Agency (DPA), acting on complaints from privacy activists, concluded that an implementation of Real Time Bidding (RTB – advertisers bidding in real time for ad space on your browser window [198]) was contrary to the principles of the GDPR. They issued a €250,000 fine to the named broker (the Interactive Advertising Bureau, IAB) and demanded a remediation plan, with a six-month implementation timescale [199]. The IAB has appealed against the judgement [200], and as of October 2022 there has been a referral to the European Court of Justice [201], which has been asked to rule on several aspects of law, including (according to the IAB) on whether or not the original ruling by the Belgian DPA was itself lawful. In the United Kingdom, the Open Rights Group initiated action against the Information Commissioners Office for (allegedly) failing to proceed with a similar case [202]. Both complainants cite widespread societal damage arising from advertising companies exploiting consumer data for commercial purposes and claim that the use of RTB constitutes an abuse of human rights.

The same activists point to the Brave browser [203] as an example of an alternative (and "privacy-aware") approach, in which consumers can decide for themselves whether or not to see ads. The technical approach for Brave [204] uses the local device's bandwidth and processing power to load up country-specific advert catalogues into the browser, with machine learning then matching the user's search terms and browsing history against the contents of the catalogue. In this way, sensitive information can be kept on the local machine.

The business model for the company behind Brave [205] rests on consumers willingly engaging with Brave-endorsed ads, and being incentivised to do so, via payments made to them in a special-to-purpose cryptocurrency. Advertising companies, in turn, are required to register with Brave (the company) in order to have their ads hosted on Brave servers [206]. One of the major issues with online advertising is that it's difficult to be sure about the actual level of effectiveness [207]. The investment pitch for Brave [208] claims that they can provide a unique level of insight into an otherwise unreachable target population – people who routinely use ad blockers and VPN's, and who aren't on TikTok [209]. A basic Internet search shows that the company's funding comes from a number of Venture Capitalists (VCs) [209], who presumably see a return in being able to present advertising to a group of consumers who can't be reached in any other way.

A criticism voiced by some is that this business model, while it might be novel, is not so far removed from the approach that the same privacy activists are seeking to dismantle [210, 211]. It's also been alleged that the company has blocked the "forking" of their software to provide a completely ad-free version [212], and that the company has had at least one privacy breach themselves [213]. It's also fair to point out that the channels to both consumers and advertisers involve significant degrees of lock-in. However, the approach has been undeniably successful. At the launch of their in-house cryptocurrency, Brave reportedly raised US$35M worth of investment within 30 seconds [214].

CONCLUSIONS

Brave's positioning is oriented to appeal to individuals who see online privacy as an issue, and the overall implementation is designed to ensure that only Brave (the company) has access to that sector of the market.

Notwithstanding any reservations that may have been expressed, the Brave model shows that cybersecurity can be used to gain competitive advantage, through searching out and meeting unmet market needs.

NOTES

1   Although this may itself provide an illustration of how figures are treated when it comes to cyber, since the source quoted in the article seems to refer to "billions" rather than "trillions".
2   Dec 8, 2020: US$15.31; Dec 10, 2020: US$13.50.
3   Dec 18, 2020: US$14.68; Dec 22, 2020: US$21.29.

4 If you do go and look at the source documents, you should note that the summary annual figures provided in the 2021 report differ slightly from those in the individual yearly reports.

REFERENCES

1. HOSAC, Understanding the costs of cyber crime. 2018 [Accessed 10 April 2021]; Available from: https://assets.publishing.service.gov.uk/government/uploads/system/uploads/attachment_data/file/674046/understanding-costs-of-cyber-crime-hor r96.pdf
2. Florêncio, D. and C. Herley, Sex, lies and cyber-crime surveys. In *Economics of information security and privacy III*, B. Schneier, Editor. 2013: Springer, p. 35–53.
3. McGuire, M., It ain't what it is, it's the way that they do it? Why we still don't understand cybercrime. In *The human factor of cybercrime*, R. Leukfeldt and T.J. Holt, Editors. 2019: Routledge, p. 3–28.
4. CEA, CEA report: The cost of malicious cyber activity to the U.S. economy 2018 [Accessed 9 April 2021]; Available from: www.hsdl.org/?view&did=808776
5. WorldBank, Ecuador GDP. 2023 [Accessed 9 April 2021]; Available from: https://data.worldbank.org/indicator/NY.GDP.MKTP.CD?locations=EC
6. McAfee, Economic impact of cybercrime – No slowing down. 2018 [Accessed 14 January 2023]; Available from: www.mcafee.com/enterprise/en-us/assets/reports/restricted/rp-economic-impact-cybercrime.pdf
7. McAfee, New McAfee report estimates global cybercrime losses to exceed $1 trillion. 2021 [Accessed 19 June 2021]; Available from: www.businesswire.com/news/home/20201206005011/en/New-McAfee-Report-Estimates-Global-Cybercrime-Losses-to-Exceed-1-Trillion
8. INTRUSION, Cybercrime to cost the world $10.5 trillion annually by 2025. 2020 [Accessed 19 June 2021]; Available from: www.globenewswire.com/news-release/2020/11/18/2129432/0/en/Cybercrime-To-Cost-The-World-10-5-Trillion-Annually-By-2025.html
9. Silver, C., The top 25 economies in the world. 2020 [Accessed 19 June 2021]; Available from: www.investopedia.com/insights/worlds-top-economies/#5-india
10. Quinn, K., The world has changed: So must cybersecurity. 2022 [Accessed 3 January 2023]; Available from: www.forbes.com/sites/forbesbusinessdevelopment council/2022/11/22/the-world-has-changed-so-must-cybersecurity
11. EU, European Commission, Directorate-General for Communications Networks, Content and Technology, cybersecurity industry market analysis: CIMA. 2019 [Accessed 28 April 2021]; Available from: https://data.europa.eu/doi/10.2759/018751
12. Seldeslachts, U., ECSO EUNITY workshop: Cybersecurity industry market analysis. 2019 [Accessed 9 April 2021]; Available from: www.eunity-project.eu/m/filer_public/4b/62/4b6262dc-3bca-4145-a84b-b514049156ce/1_lsec_japan_eunity_ecso_wg2_cima_seldeslachts_ulrich_20190124881.pdf
13. Anderson, R., et al., *Measuring the changing cost of cybercrime*. Workshop on the Economics of Information Security (WEIS) 2019.
14. Schneier, B., Schneier on security: The cost of cybercrime. *Schneier on security*. 2019 [Accessed 10 April 2021]; Available from: www.schneier.com/blog/archives/2019/06/the_cost_of_cyb_1.html
15. Mordor, Europe cyber security market. 2021 [Accessed 10 April 2021]; Available from: www.mordorintelligence.com/industry-reports/europe-cyber-security-market

16. Gartner, Gartner *forecasts worldwide information security spending to exceed* $124 *billion in 2019*. 2018 [Accessed 10 April 2021]; Available from: www.gartner.com/en/ newsroom/press-releases/2018-08-15-gartner-forecasts-worldwide-information-secur ity-spending-to-exceed-124-billion-in-2019

17. Schreiber, O. and I. Reznikov, The state of Israel's cybersecurity market. 2018 [Accessed 10 April 2021]; Available from: https://techcrunch.com/2018/01/14/the-state-of-israels-cybersecurity-market

18. Nasdaq, Cybersecurity: Proliferation of cybercrimes & reaction by governments/ corporations. 2017 [Accessed 10 April 2021]; Available from: https://indexes.nasdaq. com/docs/Cybersecurity_Research_NQCYBR.pdf

19. Reuters, FireEye buys cyber forensics firm Mandiant for about $1 billion. 2014 [Accessed 10 April 2021]; Available from: www.reuters.com/article/us-mandiant-fire eye/fireeye-buys-cyber-forensics-firm-mandiant-for-about-1-billion-idUSBREA01 0W220140102

20. Aronson, Key *observations from FireEye's ~$1.0B acquisition* of Mandiant. 2014 [Accessed 23 December 2022]; Available from: https://aronsonllc.com/key-observati ons-from-fireeyes-1-0b-acquisition-of-mandiant

21. Reuters, FireEye market value surges by a third after Mandiant deal. 2014 [Accessed 14 January 2023]; Available from: www.reuters.com/article/us-mandiant-fireeye-idUSBREA010W220140103

22. Reuters, FireEye buys cyber intelligence firm iSight Partners for $200 million. 2016 [Accessed 14 January 2023]; Available from: www.reuters.com/article/us-isight-fire eye-m-a-idUSKCN0UY2OU

23. Forbes, These *cybersecurity stocks are beating the WannaCry Ransomware hackers*. 2017 [Accessed 10 April 2021]; Available from: https://fortune.com/2017/05/15/ran somware-wanna-cry-stock-market

24. Field, M., WannaCry cyber attack cost the NHS £92m as 19,000 appointments can-celled. 2018 [Accessed 10 April 2021]; Available from: www.telegraph.co.uk/technol ogy/2018/10/11/wannacry-cyber-attack-cost-nhs-92m-19000-appointments-cancelled

25. Schneier, B., Schneier on *security: WannaCry Ransomware*. 2017 [Accessed 10 April 2021]; Available from: www.schneier.com/blog/archives/2017/05/wannacry_ ransom.html

26. Microsoft, Customer guidance for WannaCrypt attacks. 2017 [Accessed 30 July 2021]; Available from: https://msrc-blog.microsoft.com/2017/05/12/customer-guidance-for-wannacrypt-attacks

27. Wall, M. and M. Ward, WannaCry: What can you do to protect your business? 2017 [Accessed 10 April 2021]; Available from: www.bbc.co.uk/news/business-39947944

28. Ghafur, S., et al., A retrospective impact analysis of the WannaCry cyberattack on the NHS. NPJ Digital Medicine, 2019. 2(1): p. 1–7.

29. Martin, G., et al., The effects and preventability of 2627 patient safety incidents related to health information technology failures: a retrospective analysis of 10 years of incident reporting in England and Wales. The Lancet Digital Health, 2019. 1(3): p. e127–e135.

30. NHE, WannaCry cyber-attack cost the NHS £92m after 19,000 appointments were cancelled. 2018 [Accessed 30 July 2021]; Available from: www.nationalhealthexecut ive.com/News/wannacry-cyber-attack-cost-the-nhs-92m-after-19000-appointments-were-cancelled

31. NHE, DH warned about risk of cyber-attack a year before WannaCry incident. 2017 [Accessed 30 July 2021]; Available from: www.nationalhealthexecutive.com/News/ dh-warned-about-risk-of-cyber-attack-a-year-before-wannacry-incident/186316

32. NHE. NHS cyber-attack fears return as all tested trusts fail assessments. 2018 [Accessed 30 July 2021]; Available from: www.nationalhealthexecutive.com/Health-Care-News/nhs-cyber-attack-fears-return-as-all-tested-trusts-fail-assessments

33. Boiten, E. and D.S. Wall, WannaCry report shows NHS Chiefs knew of security danger, but management took no action. 2017 [Accessed 21 January 2023]; Available from: www.scientificamerican.com/article/wannacry-report-shows-nhs-chiefs-knew-of-security-danger-but-management-took-no-action

34. Symantec, What you need to know about the WannaCry Ransomware. 2017 [Accessed 10 April 2021]; Available from: www.symantec.com/blogs/threat-intelligence/wanna cry-ransomware-attack

35. Fletcher, N. and H. Siddique, Cybersecurity stocks boom after ransomware attack. 2017 [Accessed 10 April 2021]; Available from: www.theguardian.com/technology/2017/may/16/cybersecurity-stocks-boom-ransomware-attack

36. Leyden, J., Sophos waters down 'NHS is totally protected' by us boast. 2017 [Accessed 10 April 2021]; Available from: www.theregister.com/2017/05/15/sophos_nhs

37. Monaghan, A., WannaCry attack lifts shares in cybersecurity firm Sophos to record high. 2017 [Accessed 10 April 2021]; Available from: www.theguardian.com/technol ogy/2017/may/17/shares-in-cybersecurity-firm-sophos-record-high-wannacry-attack

38. MarketWatch, Anti-virus stocks rally with 'WannaCry' cyber attack expected to hit again. 2017 [Accessed 10 April 2021]; Available from: www.marketwatch.com/story/anti-virus-stocks-rally-with-wannacry-cyber-attack-expected-to-go-on-the-ramp age-again-2017-05-15

39. Wikipedia, Eternal Blue. 2021 [Accessed 10 April 2021]; Available from: https://en.wikipedia.org/wiki/EternalBlue

40. FT, Cyber insurance market expected to grow after WannaCry attack. 2017 [Accessed 10 April 2021]; Available from: www.ft.com/content/25bf97e8-3a27-11e7-821a-6027b8a20f23

41. Sanger, D.E. and N. Perlroth, FireEye, a top cybersecurity firm, says it was hacked by a nation-state. 2020 [Accessed 10 August 2021]; Available from: www.nytimes.com/2020/12/08/technology/fireeye-hacked-russians.html

42. NCSC, NCSC annual review 2021: SolarWinds. 2021 [Accessed 14 January 2023]; Available from: www.ncsc.gov.uk/collection/ncsc-annual-review-2021/the-threat/sol arwinds

43. Acquisti, A., A. Friedman, and R. Telang, Is there a cost to privacy breaches? An event study. In *ICIS 2006 Proceedings*, 2006: p. 94.

44. Kammoun, N., et al., Financial market reaction to cyberattacks. *Cogent Economics & Finance*, 2019. 7(1): p. 1645584.

45. Hilary, G., B. Segal, and M.H. Zhang, Cyber-risk disclosure: Who cares? Georgetown McDonough School of Business Research Paper, 2016(2852519).

46. Spanos, G. and L. Angelis, The impact of information security events to the stock market: A systematic literature review. *Computers & Security*, 2016. 58: p. 216–229.

47. Rosati, P., et al., Social media and stock price reaction to data breach announcements: Evidence from US listed companies. *Research in International Business and Finance*, 2019. 47: p. 458–469.

48. Ishiguro, M., et al., *The effect of information security incidents on corporate values in the Japanese stock market.* In International Workshop on the Economics of Securing the Information Infrastructure (WESII). 2006.

49. Campbell, K., et al., The economic cost of publicly announced information security breaches: Empirical evidence from the stock market. *Journal of Computer Security*, 2003. 11(3): p. 431–448.

50. Morse, E.A., V. Raval, and J.R. Wingender Jr, *Market price effects of data security breaches. Information Security Journal: A Global Perspective*, 2011. 20(6): p. 263–273.

51. Bianchi, D. and O.K. Tosun, Cyber attacks and stock market activity. Available at SSRN 3190454, 2019.

52. Ko, M. and C. Dorantes, The impact of information security breaches on financial performance of the breached firms: an empirical investigation. *Journal of Information Technology Management*, 2006. 17(2): p. 13–22.

53. Cavusoglu, H., B. Mishra, and S. Raghunathan, The effect of internet security breach announcements on market value: Capital market reactions for breached firms and internet security developers. *International Journal of Electronic Commerce*, 2004. 9(1): p. 70–104.

54. Harkins, M., Trust and the economics of insecurity. 2017 [Accessed 9 April 2021]; Available from: https://icitech.org/author/malcolm-harkins

55. Telang, R. and S. Wattal, An empirical analysis of the impact of software vulnerability announcements on firm stock price. *IEEE Transactions on Software Engineering*, 2007. 33(8): p. 544–557.

56. Modi, S.B., M.A. Wiles, and S. Mishra, Shareholder value implications of service failures in triads: The case of customer information security breaches. *Journal of Operations Management*, 2015. 35: p. 21–39.

57. Malliouris, D.D. and A. Simpson, The stock market impact of information security investments: The case of security standards. In *Workshop on the Economics of Information Security (WEIS)*. 2019.

58. HMG, Cyber essentials scheme: Overview. 2018 [Accessed 10 April 2021]; Available from: www.gov.uk/government/publications/cyber-essentials-scheme-overview

59. ISO, ISO/IEC 27000 family – Information security management systems. 2013 [Accessed 10 April 2021]; Available from: www.iso.org/isoiec-27001-information-security.html

60. HMG, Government mandates new cyber security standard for suppliers. 2014 [Accessed 21 January 2023]; Available from: www.gov.uk/government/news/governm ent-mandates-new-cyber-security-standard-for-suppliers

61. Szubartowicz, E. and G. Schryen, Timing in information security: An event study on the impact of information security investment announcements. 2018; *Journal of Information Systems Security*, 2020. 16(1): p. 3–31

62. Parameswaran, S., S. Venkatesan, and M. Gupta, Cloud computing security announcements: Assessment of investors' reaction. *Journal of Information Privacy and Security*, 2013. 9(1): p. 17–46.

63. Anderson, R., et al., Measuring the cost of cybercrime (presentation). 2012 [Accessed 10 April 2021]; Available from: www.econinfosec.org/archive/weis2012/presentation/ Moore_presentation_WEIS2012.pdf

64. Anderson, R., et al., Measuring the cost of cybercrime. In *The economics of information security and privacy*, R. Böhme, Editor. 2013: Springer, p. 265–300.

65. Fielder, A., et al., Decision support approaches for cyber security investment. *Decision Support Systems*, 2016. 86: p. 13–23.

66. Brito, J. and T. Watkins, Loving the cyber bomb-the dangers of threat inflation in cybersecurity Policy. *Harvard National Security Journal*, 2011. 3: p. 39.

67. Jellenc, E., The emerging cyber arms race and international security: Theoretic explanation and empirical foundation. Proceedings of the 9th European Conference on Information Warfare and Security. 2012.

68. Grenier-Chalifoux, W., The new virtual battlefield: Washington's institutionalized cyber strategy and the militarization of cyberspace. In 55th ISA Annual Conference. 2014: Toronto.
69. Anderson, R., *Security engineering*. 2008: John Wiley & Sons.
70. Anderson, R., Why information security is hard-an economic perspective. In Seventeenth Annual Computer Security Applications Conference. 2001. IEEE.
71. Harkins, M., The rise of the cyber industrial complex. 2019 [Accessed 11 January 2023]; Available from: https://blogs.blackberry.com/en/2019/02/the-rise-of-the-cyber-industrial-complex
72. Lewis, J.A., *Cybersecurity and critical infrastructure protection*. 2006: Center for Strategic and International Studies.
73. Chrapavy, P., Cybersecurity risks: Are they inflated? *Salus Journal*, 2016. 4(2): p. 19.
74. Guinchard, A., Between hype and understatement: Reassessing cyber risks as a security strategy. *Journal of Strategic Security*, 2011. 4(2): p. 75–96.
75. Guitton, C., Cyber insecurity as a national threat: Overreaction from Germany, France and the UK? *European Security*, 2013. 22(1): p. 21–35.
76. Lee, R.M. and T. Rid, OMG Cyber! Thirteen reasons why hype makes for bad policy. *The RUSI Journal*, 2014. 159(5): p. 4–12.
77. Lawson, S. and M.K. Middleton, *Cyber Pearl Harbor: Analogy, fear, and the framing of cyber security threats in the United States, 1991–2016*. 2019: First Monday.
78. HMG, National Cyber Security Strategy 2016 to 2021. 2017 [Accessed 10 April 2021]; Available from: www.gov.uk/government/publications/national-cyber-security-strategy-2016-to-2021
79. HMG, National *Cyber Security Str*ategy needs long-term plan. 2019 [Accessed 10 April 2021]; Available from: https://old.parliament.uk/business/committees/committees-a-z/commons-select/public-accounts-committee/news-parliament-2017/cyber-security-in-the-uk-report-published-17-19
80. NAO, Progress of the 2016–2021 National Cyber Security Programme. 2019 [Accessed 10 April 2021]; Available from: www.nao.org.uk/wp-content/uploads/2019/03/Progress-of-the-2016-2021-National-Cyber-Security-Programme-Summary.pdf
81. Lund, H., The cyber effect: The implications of IT security regulation on international trade. 2018 [Accessed 10 April 2021]; Available from: www.kommers.se/Documents/dokumentarkiv/publikationer/2018/The-Cyber-Effect.pdf
82. Checkland, P., *Systems thinking, systems practice: Includes a 30-year retrospective*. 1999: John Wiley and Sons Ltd.
83. Von Bertalanffy, L. and A. Rapoport, *General systems*. 1956: Yearbook of the Society for the Advancement of General System Theory, 1: p. 1–10.
84. Colchester, J., Systems *thinking. 2016* [Accessed 2 March 2022]; Available from: www.scribd.com/document/385251035/Systems-Thinking-Book
85. Yan, D., A *systems thinking for cybersecurity mod*eling. arXiv preprint arXiv: 2001.05734, 2020.
86. Hiscox, Hiscox Cyber Readiness Report 2019. 2019 [Accessed 4 May 2021]; Available from: www.hiscoxlondonmarket.com/hiscox-cyber-readiness-report-2019.
87. Hiscox, Hiscox Cyber Readiness Report 2020. 2020 [Accessed 4 May 2021]; Available from: www.hiscox.co.uk/sites/uk/files/documents/2020-06/Hiscox_Cyber_Readiness_Report_2020_UK.PDF
88. Hiscox, Hiscox Cyber Readiness Report 2021. 2021 [Accessed 4 May 2021]; Available from: www.hiscoxgroup.com/cyber-readiness

89. DCMS, Cyber *Security Breaches Sur*vey 2020. 2020 [Accessed 11 January 2023]; Available from: www.gov.uk/government/statistics/cyber-security-breaches-sur vey-2020

90. Ponemon, The *cybersecurity illusion: The emperor has no clothes.* 2019 [Accessed 9 April 2021]; Available from: www.businesswire.com/news/home/20190730005215/ en/Ponemon-Study-53-Percent-of-IT-Security-Leaders-Don't-Know-if-Cybersecur ity-Tools-are-Working-Despite-an-Average-of-18.4-Million-Annual-Spend

91. BIS, UK *Cyber Security Sta*ndards: Research *R*eport. 2013 [Accessed 9 April 2021]; Available from: https://assets.publishing.service.gov.uk/government/uploads/system/ uploads/attachment_data/file/261681/bis-13-1294-uk-cyber-security-standards-resea rch-report.pdf

92. BBC, Data on 540 million Facebook users exposed. 2019 [Accessed 10 April 2021]; Available from: www.bbc.co.uk/news/technology-47812470

93. BBC, Exposed Amazon cloud storage clients get tip-off alerts. 2018 [Accessed 10 April 2021]; Available from: www.bbc.co.uk/news/technology-42839462

94. Williams, C., Someone's in hot water: Tea party super PAC group 'spilled 500,000+ voters' info' all over web. 2018 [Accessed 10 April 2021]; Available from: www.ther egister.co.uk/2018/10/17/republican_tea_party_fund_security_blunder

95. Thomson, I., Amazon's answer to all those leaky AWS S3 buckets: A dashboard warning light. 2017 [Accessed 10 April 2021]; Available from: www.theregister.co.uk/ 2017/11/07/amazon_aws_s3_alert

96. AWS, How can I secure the files in my Amazon S3 bucket? 2021 [Accessed 10 April 2021]; Available from: https://aws.amazon.com/premiumsupport/knowledge-center/secure-s3-resources

97. Imperva, Imperva *security u*pdate. 2019 [Accessed 10 April 2021]; Available from: www.imperva.com/blog/ceoblog

98. Guru, Exposing your AWS access keys on Git*H*ub can be extremely costly. A personal experience. 2017 [Accessed 10 April 2021]; Available from: https://medium.com/@ nagguru/exposing-your-aws-access-keys-on-github-can-be-extremely-costly-a-perso nal-experience-960be7aad039

99. Guo, D., I *p*ublished *m*y AWS *s*ecret key to GitHub. 2018 [Accessed 10 April 2021]; Available from: www.dannyguo.com/blog/i-published-my-aws-secret-key-to-github

100. Rzepa, P., AWS *a*ccess *k*eys *l*eak in GitHub *r*epository and *s*ome *i*mprovements in Amazon *r*eaction. 2020 [Accessed 21 January 2023]; Available from: https://medium. com/swlh/aws-access-keys-leak-in-github-repository-and-some-improvements-in-amazon-reaction-cc2e20e89003

101. Peltzman, S., The effects of automobile safety regulation. *Journal of Political Economy*, 1975. 83(4): p. 677–725.

102. Ip, G., *Foolproof: Why safety can be dangerous and how danger makes us safe.* 2015: Hachette UK.

103. Mc Mahon, C., In defence of the human factor. *Frontiers in Psychology*, 2020. 11: p. 1390.

104. Alsharnouby, M., F. Alaca, and S. Chiasson, Why phishing still works: User strategies for combating phishing attacks. *International Journal of Human-Computer Studies*, 2015. 82: p. 69–82.

105. Junger, M., L. Montoya, and F.-J. Overink, Priming and warnings are not effective to prevent social engineering attacks. *Computers in Human Behavior*, 2017. 66: p. 75–87.

106. Kearney, W.D. and H.A. Kruger, Considering the influence of human trust in practical social engineering exercises. In *2014 Information Security for South Africa*. 2014. IEEE.

107. Caputo, D.D., et al., Going spear phishing: Exploring embedded training and awareness. *IEEE Security & Privacy*, 2013. 12(1): p. 28–38.

108. Burns, A., M.E. Johnson, and D.D. Caputo, Spear phishing in a barrel: Insights from a targeted phishing campaign. *Journal of Organizational Computing and Electronic Commerce*, 2019. 29(1): p. 24–39.

109. Herley, C., More is not the answer. *IEEE Security & Privacy*, 2013. 12(1): p. 14–19.

110. Bainbridge, L., Ironies of automation. In *Analysis, design and evaluation of man–machine systems*, G. Johannsen and J. E. Rijnsdorp, Editors. 1983: Elsevier, p. 129–135.

111. Conybeare, J.A., Evaluation of automobile safety regulations: The case of compulsory seat belt legislation in Australia. *Policy Sciences*, 1980. 12(1): p. 27–39.

112. Traynor, T.L., The Peltzman hypothesis revisited: An isolated evaluation of offsetting driver behavior. *Journal of Risk and Uncertainty*, 1993. 7(2): p. 237–247.

113. Singh, H. and M. Thayer, Impact of seat belt use on driving behavior. *Economic Inquiry*, 1992. 30(4): p. 649–658.

114. Robertson, L.S., Rejoinder to Peltzman. *Journal of Economic Issues*, 1977. 11(3): p. 679–683.

115. Robertson, L.S., A critical analysis of Peltzman's "The Effects of Automobile Safety Regulation". *Journal of Economic Issues*, 1977. 11(3): p. 587–600.

116. Renaud, K. and M. Warkentin, Risk homeostasis in information security: Challenges in confirming existence and verifying impact. In Proceedings of the 2017 New Security Paradigms Workshop. 2017.

117. Kearney, W.D., *Risk homeostasis as a factor in information security*. 2016: North-West University (South Africa), Potchefstroom Campus.

118. Goodin, D., Code spaces closes shop after attackers destroy Amazon-hosted customer data. 2014 [Accessed 10 April 2021]; Available from: https://arstechnica.com/informat ion-technology/2014/06/aws-console-breach-leads-to-demise-of-service-with-pro ven-backup-plan

119. Schneier, B., HBGary and the *future* of the IT Security Industry. *Schneier on Security*. 2011 [Accessed 10 April 2021]; Available from: www.schneier.com/blog/archives/ 2011/02/hbgary_and_the.html

120. ArsTechnica, The HBGary *saga*. 2011 [Accessed 10 April 2021]; Available from: https://arstechnica.com/series/the-hbgary-saga

121. Anderson, N., Anonymous vs. HBGary: *The* aftermath. 2011 [Accessed 10 April 2021]; Available from: https://arstechnica.com/tech-policy/2011/02/anonymous-vs-hbgary-the-aftermath

122. Bright, P., With arrests, HBGary hack saga finally ends. 2012 [Accessed 10 April 2021]; Available from: https://arstechnica.com/tech-policy/2012/03/the-hbgary-saga-nears-its-end

123. Bright, P., Anonymous speaks: *The* inside story of the HBGary hack. 2011 [Accessed 10 April 2021]; Available from: https://arstechnica.com/tech-policy/2011/02/anonym ous-speaks-the-inside-story-of-the-hbgary-hack

124. Conheady, S. and E. Leverett, *Social engineering in IT security: Tools, tactics, and techniques*. 2014: McGraw-Hill Education.

125. DCMS, Cyber Security Breaches Survey 2017. 2017 [Accessed 9 April 2021]; Available from: https://assets.publishing.service.gov.uk/government/uploads/system/ uploads/attachment_data/file/609186/Cyber_Security_Breaches_Survey_2017_mai n_report_PUBLIC.pdf

126. Debate, Cyber *security technology effi*cacy: Is cybersecurity the new "market for lemons"? 2020 [Accessed *16 September 2021*]; Available from: www.debatesecurity. com/downloads/Cybersecurity-Technology-Efficacy-Research-Report-V1.0.pdf

127. Biancotti, C., The price of cyber (in) security: Evidence from the Italian private sector. *Bank of Italy Occasional Paper*, 2017(407).

128. Kaminska, I., Introducing the rise of cyber mythology. 2017 [Accessed 30 July 2021]; Available from: www.ft.com/content/6470595a-a17f-3740-8c47-a4464 6174681

129. Bowers, K., Fighting cyber security FUD and hype. 2017 [Accessed 16 September 2021]; Available from: www.securityweek.com/fighting-cyber-security-fud-and-hype

130. Forrester, The *data security money pit*: Expense *in depth hinders maturity*. 2017 [Accessed 10 April 2021]; Available from: https://info.varonis.com/hubfs/docs/resea rch_reports/Varonis_TLP.pdf

131. Romanosky, S., Examining the costs and causes of cyber incidents. *Journal of Cybersecurity*, 2016. 2(2): p. 121–135.

132. Edwards, B., S. Hofmeyr, and S. Forrest, Hype and heavy tails: A closer look at data breaches. *Journal of Cybersecurity*, 2016. 2(1): p. 3–14.

133. Richardson, V., M.W. Watson, and R.E. Smith, Much ado about nothing: The (lack of) economic impact of data privacy breaches. *Journal of Information Systems*, 2019. 33(3): p. 227–265.

134. Dunn Cavelty, M., A resilient Europe for an open, safe and secure cyberspace. *UI Occasional Papers*, 2013. 23.

135. Maass, P. and M. Rajagopalan, Does cybercrime really cost $1 trillion. 2012 [Accessed 10 April 2021]; Available from: www.propublica.org/article/does-cybercrime-really-cost-1-trillion

136. Espiner, T., Cybercrime cost estimate is "Sales Exercise", say experts. *ZDNet* 2011 [Accessed 10 April 2021]; Available from: www.zdnet.com/article/cybercrime-cost-estimate-is-sales-exercise-say-experts

137. Woods, D.W. and T. Moore, Cyber warranties: Market fix or marketing trick? *Communications of the ACM*, 2020. 63(4): p. 104–107.

138. Akerlof, G.A., The market for "lemons": Quality uncertainty and the market mechanism. In *Essential readings in economics*, S. Estrin and A. Marin, editors. 1995: Palgrave, p. 175–188.

139. Emons, W. and G. Sheldon, The market for used cars: New evidence of the lemons phenomenon. *Applied Economics*, 2009. 41(22): p. 2867–2885.

140. Woods, D.W., *The economics of cyber risk transfer*. 2019: University of Oxford.

141. Lanchester, J., *Whoops! Why everybody owes everyone and no one can pay*. 2010: Allen Lane/Penguin. Kindle Edition.

142. Snowden, D.J. and M.E. Boone, A leader's framework for decision making. *Harvard Business Review*, 2007. 85(11): p. 69–76.

143. ENISA, Definition of Cybersecurity – Gaps and overlaps in standardisation. 2016 [Accessed 10h April 2021]; Available from: www.enisa.europa.eu/publications/definit ion-of-cybersecurity

144. Von Solms, R. and J. Van Niekerk, From information security to cyber security. *Computers & Security*, 2013. 38: p. 97–102.

145. Bay, M., What is cybersecurity? In search of an encompassing definition for the post-Snowden era. ...*French Journal for Media Research*, 2016. 6/2016: p. 1–28.

146. Reid, R. and J. van Niekerk, From information security to cyber security cultures. In 2014 Information Security for South Africa. 2014. IEEE.

147. Talbot, E.B., D. Frincke, and M. Bishop, Demythifying cybersecurity. *IEEE Security & Privacy*, 2010. 8(3): p. 56–59.

148. Schatz, D., R. Bashroush, and J. Wall, Towards a more representative definition of cyber security. *Journal of Digital Forensics, Security and Law*, 2017. 12(2): p. 8.

149. Craigen, D., N. Diakun-Thibault, and R. Purse, Defining cybersecurity. *Technology Innovation Management Review*, 2014. 4(10): p. 13–21.

150. Cavelty, M.D., Cybersecurity research meets science and technology studies. *Politics and Governance*, 2018. 6(2): p. 22–30.

151. Seddon, J., *Systems thinking in the public sector: The failure of the reform regime... and a manifesto for a better way.* 2008: Triarchy Press Limited.

152. Choi, S.J., M.E. Johnson, and C.U. Lehmann, Data breach remediation efforts and their implications for hospital quality. *Health Services Research*, 2019. 54(5): p. 971–980.

153. Koppel, R., et al., Workarounds to computer access in healthcare organizations: You want my password or a dead patient? *ITCH*, 2015. 15(4): p. 215–220.

154. Miller, A.R. and C. Tucker, Privacy protection and technology diffusion: The case of electronic medical records. *Management Science*, 2009. 55(7): p. 1077–1093.

155. BICOM, UK-Israel relations after Brexit: Cyber security. 2018 [Accessed 10 April 2021]; Available from: www.bicom.org.uk/wp-content/uploads/2018/04/cyber-security-UK-Israel-relations-after-Brexit.pdf

156. Adamsky, D., The Israeli Odyssey toward its National Cyber Security Strategy. *The Washington Quarterly*, 2017. 40(2): p. 113–127.

157. Halon, E., Israeli cyber investments exceed $1 billion for first time in 2018. 2019 [Accessed 2 March 2022]; Available from: www.jpost.com/israel-news/investment-in-israeli-cyber-exceeds-1-billion-for-first-time-in-2018-578906

158. Solomon, S., Israel cybersecurity firms raise record $3.4b, 41% of global sector investment. 2021 [Accessed 5 March 2022]; Available from: www.timesofisrael.com/israel-cybersecurity-firms-raise-record-3-4b-41-of-global-sector-investment

159. Press, G., 6 reasons Israel became a cybersecurity powerhouse leading the $82 billion industry. 2017 [Accessed 10 April 2021]; Available from: www.forbes.com/sites/gilpress/2017/07/18/6-reasons-israel-became-a-cybersecurity-powerhouse-leading-the-82-billion-industry/#4cbecc0c420a

160. Kfir, I., Israel's cyber ecosystem. 2018 [Accessed 10 April 2021]; Available from: www.policyforum.net/israels-cyber-ecosystem

161. Tabansky, L., Towards a theory of cyber power: The Israeli experience with innovation and strategy. In 2016 8th International Conference on Cyber Conflict (CyCon). 2016. IEEE.

162. Srivastava, M. and T. Bradshaw, Israeli group's spyware 'offers keys to Big Tech's cloud'. *Financial Times* 3 August 2019 [Accessed 10 April 2021]; Available from: www.ft.com/content/95b91412-a946-11e9-b6ee-3cdf3174eb89

163. Reuters, Israel eases rules on cyber weapons exports despite criticism. 2019 [Accessed 10 April 2021]; Available from: www.reuters.com/article/us-israel-hackers/israel-eases-rules-on-cyber-weapons-exports-despite-criticism-idUSKCN1VC0XQ

164. Gandal, N., Values and cyber security [Accessed 10 April 2021]; Available from: https://icrc.tau.ac.il/research/valuesandsybersecurity

165. Papakonstantinou, V., Cybersecurity as praxis and as a state: The EU law path towards acknowledgement of a new right to cybersecurity? *Computer Law & Security Review*, 2022. 44: p. 105653.

166. Shires, J., Enacting expertise: Ritual and risk in cybersecurity. *Politics and Governance*, 2018. 6(2): p. 31–40.

167. Adams, A. and M.A. Sasse, Users are not the enemy. *Communications of the ACM*, 1999. 42(12): p. 41–46.

168. Vidyaraman, S., M. Chandrasekaran, and S. Upadhyaya, Position: The user is the enemy. In Proceedings of the 2007 Workshop on New Security Paradigms. 2008. ACM.

169. Wurster, G. and P.C. van Oorschot. The developer is the enemy. In Proceedings of the 2008 New Security Paradigms Workshop. 2009. ACM.

170. Green, M. and M. Smith, *Developers are not the enemy!: The need for usable security APIs. IEEE Security & Privacy*, 2016. 14(5): p. 40–46.

171. Shirley, J. and D. Evans, The user is not the enemy: Fighting malware by tracking user intentions. In Proceedings of the 2008 New Security Paradigms Workshop. 2009. ACM.

172. Besnard, D. and B. Arief, Computer security impaired by legitimate users. *Computers & Security*, 2004. 23(3): p. 253–264.

173. Riley, S., Password security: What users know and what they actually do. *Usability News*, 2006. 8(1): p. 2833–2836.

174. Ashenden, D., Information security management: A human challenge*? Information Security Technical Report*, 2008. 13(4): p. 195–201.

175. Klimburg-Witjes, N. and A. Wentland, *Hacking humans? Social engineering and the construction of the "deficient user" in cybersecurity discourses.* Science, Technology, & Human Values, 2021. 46(6): p. 1316–1339.

176. Sasse, A., Scaring and bullying people into security won't work. *IEEE Security & Privacy*, 2015. 13(3): p. 80–83.

177. Shropshire, J., et al., Personality and IT security: An application of the five-factor model. In *AMCIS 2006 Proceedings*, 2006: p. 415.

178. MacEwan, N.F., *Responsibilisation, rules and rule-following concerning cyber security: Findings from small business case studies in the UK.* 2017: University of Southampton.

179. Sparks, R., Degrees of estrangement: The cultural theory of risk and comparative penology. *Theoretical Criminology*, 2001. 5(2): p. 159–176.

180. McIlwraith, A., *Information security and employee behaviour: How to reduce risk through employee education, training and awareness.* 2021: Routledge.

181. Hallas, B., *Re-thinking the human factor: A philosophical approach to information security awareness behaviour and culture.* 2018: Hallas Institute.

182. Reeder, R.W., I. Ion, and S. Consolvo, 152 simple steps to stay safe online: Security advice for non-tech-savvy users. *IEEE Security & Privacy*, 2017. 15(5): p. 55–64.

183. Frey, S., et al., The good, the bad and the ugly: A study of security decisions in a cyber-physical systems game. *IEEE Transactions on Software Engineering*, 2017. 45(5): p. 521–536.

184. Menges, U., et al., Why IT security needs therapy. In *European Symposium on Research in Computer Security.* 2021: Springer.

185. Haney, J., Users are not stupid: Six cyber security pitfalls overturned. *Cyber Security: A Peer-Reviewed Journal*, 2023. 6(3): p. 230–241.

186. Cranor, L.F., A framework for reasoning about the human in the loop. Proceedings of the Conference on Usability, Psychology, and Security. USENIX Association, 2008.

187. Morozov, E., *To save everything, click here: The folly of technological solutionism.* 2013: Public Affairs.

188. Zimmermann, V. and K. Renaud, Moving from a "human-as-problem" to a "human-as-solution" cybersecurity mindset. *International Journal of Human-Computer Studies*, 2019. 131: p. 169–187.

189. Renaud, K., A. Musarurwa, and V. Zimmermann. Contemplating blame in cyber security. In *ICCWS 2021 16th International Conference on Cyber Warfare and Security.* 2021: Academic Conferences Limited.

190. Porter, M.E., The five competitive forces that shape strategy. *Harvard Business Review*, 2008. 86(1): p. 25–40.

191. Abell, D.F., Strategic windows. *The Journal of Marketing*, 1978. 42(3): p. 21–26.

192. Levitt, T., Marketing intangible products and product intangibles. *Cornell Hotel and Restaurant Administration Quarterly*, 1981. 22(2): p. 37–44.

193. KnowBe4, KnowBe4 announces third quarter 2022 financial results. 2022 [Accessed 11 January 2023]; Available from: https://investors.knowbe4.com/news-releases/news-release-details/knowbe4-announces-third-quarter-2022-financial-results

194. TitanHQ, KnowBe4 alternatives and competitors. 2023 [Accessed 11 January 2023]; Available from: www.titanhq.com/knowbe4-alternative

195. SpiceWorks, KnowBe4 *vs* PhishMe *vs* Wombat. 2017 [Accessed 10 April 2021]; Available from: https://community.spiceworks.com/topic/2095280-knowbe4-vs-phishme-vs-wombat

196. Cavusoglu, H., et al., Institutional pressures in security management: Direct and indirect influences on organizational investment in information security control resources. *Information & Management*, 2015. 52(4): p. 385–400.

197. Porter, M., Competitive advantage: Creating and sustaining superior performance. *Chap*, 1985. 1: p. 3–52.

198. Jones, H., Real-time bidding: The Ad Industry has crossed a very dangerous line. 2021 [Accessed 9 November 2022]; Available from: www.forbes.com/sites/hessiejones/2021/10/18/real-time-bidding-the-ad-industry-has-crossed-a-very-dangerous-line/?sh=5006197848ca

199. Drucker, J. and P. Guidotti, IAB Europe's transparency & consent framework does not comply with the GDPR. 2022 [Accessed 9 November 2022]; Available from: www.bristows.com/news/iab-europes-transparency-consent-framework-does-not-comply-with-the-gdpr

200. IAB, FAQ: APD decision on IAB Europe and TCF – updated 7 October 2022. 2022 [Accessed 9 November 2022]; Available from: https://iabeurope.eu/wp-content/uploads/2022/10/IAB-Europe-IAB-Europe-APD-FAQ-October-2022.docx.pdf

201. DPA, IAB Europe case: The Market Court refers preliminary questions to the Court of Justice of the EU. 2022 [Accessed 9 November 2022]; Available from: www.dataprotectionauthority.be/citizen/iab-europe-case-the-market-court-refers-preliminary-questions-to-the-court-of-justice-of-the-eu

202. ORG, Our Adtech *challenge*: What we won, what we lost and what we do next. 2021 [Accessed 9 November 2022]; Available from: www.openrightsgroup.org/blog/our-adtech-challenge-what-we-won-what-we-lost-and-what-we-do-next

203. Brave, About Brave. 2022 [Accessed 9 November 2022]; Available from: https://brave.com/about

204. Brave, An *introduction* to Brave's *in-browser a*ds. 2020 [Accessed 9 November 2022]; Available from: https://brave.com/intro-to-brave-ads

205. Cuofano, G., How does Brave make money? The Brave business model in a nutshell. 2022 [Accessed 9 November 2022]; Available from: https://fourweekmba.com/how-does-brave-make-money

206. Brave, Expand your business with Brave ads. 2023 [Accessed 14 March 2023]; Available from: https://brave.com/brave-ads

207. Aral, S., What digital advertising gets wrong. 2021 [Accessed 9 November 2022]; Available from: https://hbr.org/2021/02/what-digital-advertising-gets-wrong

208. Brave, Major changes to the digital ads landscape. 2022 [Accessed 9 November 2022]; Available from: https://brave.com/web3/changes-digital-ad-landscape

209. crunchbase, Brave (financials). 2022 [Accessed 9 November 2022]; Available from: www.crunchbase.com/organization/brave-software/company_financials

210. Muldoon, K., Do *not use* Brave *browser.* 2020 [Accessed 9 November 2022]; Available from: www.kevinmuldoon.com/do-not-use-brave-browser

211. unknown, The *cowardice* of Brave. 2020 [Accessed 9November 2022]; Available from: https://practicaltypography.com/the-cowardice-of-brave.html

212. O'Neal, S., Brave *browser* Fork *makes a 'bold' move citing legal pressure.* 2020 [Accessed 9 November 2022]; Available from: https://cointelegraph.com/news/brave-browser-fork-makes-a-bold-move-citing-legal-pressure

213. Lyons, K., Brave browser CEO apologizes for automatically adding affiliate links to cryptocurrency URLs. 2020 [Accessed 9 November 2022]; Available from: www. theverge.com/2020/6/8/21283769/brave-browser-affiliate-links-crypto-privacy-ceo-apology

214. Russell, J., Former Mozilla CEO raises $35M in under 30 seconds for his browser startup Brave. 2017 [Accessed 9 November 2022]; Available from: https://techcrunch. com/2017/06/01/brave-ico-35-million-30-seconds-brendan-eich.w

2 Security Culture Will Fix Things

INTRODUCTION TO SECURITY CULTURE

CONTEXT

The cyber industry is relatively young, so you might expect to see a number of tried and subsequently discarded ideas littering the place, as the industry evolves and hopefully moves on. For example:

- At one time the thinking was "we can do all this with logic". Security was seen as a matrix with permissions granted to individuals along one axis, and sensitivity labels assigned to data on the other. Access to data could therefore be mediated through fixed rules applied to each cell [1].
- Later the thinking was "we can fix this if we write enough standards" [2–4]. A number of mostly technical documents were developed, initially in the United States and then in the United Kingdom and Europe, dealing with e.g. database security and computer security, usually defining combinations of countermeasures aimed at providing hierarchical levels of protection [5].
- Subsequently the thinking was "we can do all this using maths" (e.g. [6]). By setting out the requirements for a computer system in a formal mathematical notation, it was supposedly possible to refine a specification into a design and then into an implementation, at each stage producing evidence that the translation had been achieved without error or omission.

Few of these approaches have stood the test of time. The Bell and LaPadula model of security matrices conflicted with the parallel Biba model [7], also based on matrices. And as it turned out, having as many security standards as we could possibly write didn't help the situation. Those older, rigid standards which were strictly security-focused are now being replaced with more flexible standards such as Service Operational Controls (SOC) [8]. Formal mathematical methods such as Z and VDM did not become mainstream components of information systems specification and design, partly because of the effort required, and partly because of the complexity of the tools needed to generate the necessary levels of evidence.

DOI: 10.1201/9781003380962-2

A central characteristic in most of these ideas is that they tended to offer a single, point solution, boiling down a complex problem into just one issue. Recently, and in the same vein, the idea of a "security culture" has been proposed [e.g. 9, 10–12]. Instilling a security culture into an organisation will (it's claimed) remedy the problem of users not behaving in line with security guidance.

At this point I would like to provide you with a summary of what a security culture is. However, as we'll see later, nobody seems to know. Most people in the industry will give you the answer "it's the way we do security around here" [e.g. 13, p56], which is at best a description rather than a definition. The best I can suggest is that in a good security culture, people behave in line with the expectations of the security team, but naturally and without coercion [14]. That is, the views, values, and beliefs of the security team are reflected in the attitudes and behaviours of everyone else in the organisation, but with no effort required on the part of the security team. Sounds perfect.

REVIEWING THE EVIDENCE

THE BASIS FOR SECURITY CULTURE

A number of literature reviews have been conducted – exercises looking at what can be said about security culture, based on the available evidence. The review by Oost and Chew [15] makes a number of interesting points:

> A review of published research on the topic suggests that it is not the information security panacea that has been suggested. Instead it tends to refer to a range of existing techniques for addressing the human aspect of information security, oversimplifying the link between culture and behaviour, exaggerating the ease with which a culture can be adjusted, and treating culture as a monolith, set from the top. Evidence for some of the claims is also lacking. The paper finds that the term "information security culture" is ambiguous and vague enough to suggest the possibility of achieving an almost mystical state whereby behaviour consistent with information security is second nature to all employees, but when probed does not deliver.

Karlsson et al. [16] provide a summary of shortcomings, noting that "... *existing research has focused on a broad set of research topics, but with limited depth*". The review by Karyda [17] concluded that "... *the academic field of information security culture has been described as immature, lacks empirical validation, while the constituents of the concept as well as methods, tools, frameworks and metrics for fostering and evaluating it within organisations remain elusive*". The goal of creating a reliable tool for "measuring" security culture seems to be proving similarly elusive [18, 19].

There's not much better news when you look for evidence linking security culture with something potentially useful. A review in 2018 by Nasir et al. [20] found over 100 research and discussion papers on the subject of security culture, of which only 6 met their criteria for being based on an empirical study of the relationship between information security culture and behaviour. It's always dangerous to summarise research in a single line, but for me that says that only about 5% of the papers they examined used experimental results, leaving the rest as either theoretical, or based on conjecture. Uchendu et al. found a similar picture [21].

It's also dangerous to draw firm conclusions from just those six remaining papers; however, the authors note that:

Interestingly, despite strong recommendations from information security scholars that the cultivation of positive [Information Security Culture] will influence employees' security behavior in line with [Information Security Policy], there is actually lack of empirical findings to confirm this relationship.

That is, it's difficult to find any evidence linking security culture with secure behaviour. Others have found the same [22]. Nasir et al. reference a study by Dugo [23] that examined among other things, the relationship between the strength of a prevailing security culture and people's beliefs and attitudes towards deliberately contravening security policies. That study showed no significant link in either case. That is, even where there were factors supposedly driving a security culture, attitudes towards security were no different, let alone behaviour.

Dugo used the process described by Knapp [24] to measure the strength of an organisation's security culture, although I gather there are other, equally valid ways of doing it, such as the process described by Martins and Eloff [25]. The fact that there's more than one way to measure security culture looks like a warning sign here – it suggests that there's more than one set of factors that people claim to be drivers. In fact, as reported by Nasir et al. [26], if you gather together the factors that supposedly go into a good security culture, and then eliminate the duplicates and combine similar-sounding concepts, you get a list of nearly 50 papers drawing on 26 issues that various people use to define their particular view. Da Veiga et al. for example [27] proposed a total of 5 external factors and another 20 internal ones. So when security person "A" is talking to you about security culture, they're unlikely to be thinking about the same thing as security person "B" when they're talking to you about security culture. There's no common definition, no shared understanding.

But surely all this has been done in the safety field – there's such a thing as a "safety culture"? Well, it depends who you ask. Dekker [28] suggests that the implementation of a safety culture may have only a weak relationship with people behaving safely, i.e. the situation is much the same as with cyber. Dekker's book cites the example of a company with rules relating to carrying a hot drink without a lid (a sackable offence) and not holding onto a handrail when using a gangway (a reportable offence). Obviously very safety-conscious. Excellent safety culture. The company in question being BP [29]. One place in which the rules were applied being the Deepwater Horizon drilling rig [30], where "ineffective and bypassed" safety regulations [31–33] led to the world's worst recorded oil spill [34]. Dekker's argument is that the desire to implement a safety culture stems mostly from a requirement to offload responsibility rather than to improve safety, which sounds enormously familiar. A number of texts [35–37] suggest that the safety industry is quietly abandoning the idea of safety culture, an approach which necessarily involves responsibilising people as "stupid users" and as "a problem to control", and which sees non-compliance as a failing.

To sum up, there's very little supporting evidence for the idea of a security culture. I might be quoting Lacey a little bit out of context [38, p7], but the point is valid – "*[m]any security practitioners would like to introduce a better 'security culture' into their organizations, but few can define precisely what that actually means*".

REVIEWING THE THEORY

BACKGROUND

Two main approaches have been taken to underpin the idea of security culture. Both are based on models of organisational culture.

Detert et al. [39] suggested an eight-factor model of organisational culture. It hasn't been widely adapted for use in security, possibly because of its relative complexity. Instead, the more popular approach has been to adapt Schein's three-layer model [40]. The three layers being artefacts (what you see around the place – posters, tees, mugs) espoused values (formal statements of e.g. security's place in the organisation) and tacit assumptions (unstated but underlying beliefs).

Two key points from Schein's paper are that:

- As you go down through the layers, it becomes more difficult to "get at" the indicators of culture.
- Partly as a result, questionnaires are not an appropriate means of assessing organisational culture [41, 42].

A widely used adaptation of this model to information security was proposed by Van Niekerk and Von Solms [43], who added another component ("security knowledge") below the bottom layer of Schein's original model. If the structure of Schein's model has been preserved in the transition across to security, then security knowledge, being right at the bottom [44], should be more or less impossible to measure. That clearly isn't the case.

More importantly perhaps, most people [e.g. 45] use a questionnaire to assess security culture, despite Schein's warning. David Ogilvy, a legend in the field of consumer behaviour [46], provides an astute observation on the use of questionnaires: "*[t]he trouble with market research is that consumers don't think how they feel, they don't say what they think, and they don't do what they say*".

A DIGRESSION ON QUESTIONNAIRES

If you happen to read an article saying that some intervention or other affected people's security behaviour, it's worth looking at whether the study actually measured *intent*, rather than behaviour. If the work was based on an Internet survey, then almost certainly, it will have measured self-reported intentions. Intentions are easier to gather [47], but you have to make a couple of assumptions if you want to use them to predict actual behaviours [48]. First, that using self-report is itself a reliable process, and second, that security intentions drive security behaviour.

Neither of which may be true. Wash et al. [49] found that the link between declared security intentions and actual security behaviours was reliable in only a small number of situations, and that for most people, security wasn't sufficiently salient to allow them to self-report in a meaningful way.

The authors cite Sheeran's study into the intention-behaviour gap [50], which found that only about 28% of observed variances in behaviours could be explained by looking at self-declared intentions. D'Arcy and Cram [51] go further, and suggest that particularly in relation to security, there's very little point in asking people about their intention to comply with a security policy, because you're asking them about what they *think* the policy says, rather than what the authors of the policy might have meant to say.

Gratian et al. [52] looked for connections between personality traits and security intentions, and found a mixed picture, noting that in some aspects their results were completely new, and that their results agreed with previous findings in some areas but contradicted them in others. They concluded that "*... the influence of individual differences on security behavior intentions can vary between environments*" and that consequently, "*[i]nsights into user behavior intentions may not generalize across all settings and user populations*". That is, even setting aside the issue of a link or otherwise between intention and action, self-reported intentions themselves seem to be affected by context. Guo et al. [53] also found that attitudes weren't significant factors when users engaged in security violations, and that decisions to breach security rules seemed to be taken on the fly. More widely, Sommestad [54] conducted an extensive examination of the supposed driving factors and theories for security behaviours and found "*no clear winner*" [54, p13].

Alessandro Acquisti is a recognised expert in the field of privacy and decision-making. So, it's with a degree of trepidation that I cite some of his findings to support this argument. However, nothing ventured... Acquisti and colleagues [55] found that when people were asked to make a *hypothetical* decision on privacy, it was absolute scales that made a difference to the individual's choices, i.e. when asked "what would you do if...", it was the economist's view of humans as rational actors that was displayed, with people weighing up the pros and cons. But when *behaviour* was measured i.e. when people were asked to make an actual decision, it was relative values that drove their choices. The significance is that Kahneman and Tversky [56] found that when we make real-life decisions, we tend to be swayed more by relative differences between alternatives than we are by the absolute measures assumed by economists. That's been shown a number of times in the field of consumer decision-making [57, 58].

In other words – comparative behaviour is displayed when people are asked to make actual decisions, in contrast to the rational, absolute thinking displayed when people are asked to make hypothetical decisions. Consequently, when you use a questionnaire to ask people what they would do under a specific set of circumstances, you get rational answers. But in order to understand actual behaviours, you have to ask them to go through the whole process and make real decisions.

The bottom line is that the link between intention and action depends on context. It's not fixed. Real-world security decisions are shaped by a number of factors applying at the time of the decision, only some of which are to do with security. For example, Gerber [59] found that when employees were strongly motivated to achieve performance targets, even self-reported levels of adherence to security regulations were reduced. As pointed out in the report, this doesn't make security a special case – exactly the same behaviours were reported by Welsh and Ordonez [60], who found that repeated applications of reward-driven targets tended to erode people's resistance to engaging in unethical behaviour when trying to achieve those targets.

Concern over the implicit assumption that security intentions are linked to security behaviours is such that there have been calls for increased measurement of actual behaviour in security research, and for a corresponding reduction in the use of self-report (e.g. [59, 61, 62], also [63, p1062, 1063]). Renaud and Flowerday sum this up [64, p79]:

> *We could stop asking people about their security behaviour and rather observe what they do. We know people are not necessarily frank and open about their security behaviours, and this leads to responses informed by social desirability instead of reality. Moreover, surveys measure intention, and not actual behaviour, and the two are weakly correlated.*

Essentially, and contrary to the wishes and beliefs of security practitioners, people don't take information security as the most important factor in their decision-making, even when it comes to making a security decision. As Gerber et al. noted, *"[w]ith regard to actual security policy compliance, intention to comply is only of predictive value as long as no other predictors are considered"*. So unless you're measuring actual security behaviour (rather than measuring e.g. "culture"), then it's not clear that you're measuring anything relevant.

CULTURE AND NUDGING

CONTEXT

As a tentative summary of the evidence regarding security culture:

- There's no accepted definition.
- Literature reviews show an absence of supporting evidence.
- There's no clear link between culture and useful outcomes.
- There are doubts over the theoretical background.
- There doesn't seem to be a reliable way of assessing it.
- Similar questions have been asked of "safety culture".

The central claim seems to be that a single measure will somehow "fix" behaviours, however to quote Checkland [65, p191]: *"real life is more complex than that"*. In that light, and as pointed out by Oost and Chew [15], the idea of a security culture magically making unwanted behaviours go away seems to be more of a sales message than a strategy.

Nevertheless, the idea of security culture is still being promoted and has now become conflated with the idea of "nudging" [66].

BACKGROUND

It's almost inconceivable that the term "nudge" [67] will be unfamiliar to anyone reading this book. Certainly in the United Kingdom, nudging has been at the front and centre of public sector policy for some time [68], since the formation in 2010 of what was then the Behavioural Insights Team, as part of the Cabinet Office [69]. Readers may recall that during the pandemic, the members of that team developed a number of nation-wide interventions, gently encouraging compliance with Government recommendations. More recently, the team have been proposing the use of embedded messages within TV programmes, in order to *"... shift the behaviour of millions of people"* [70]. Nudging was originally intended as a means of encouraging individuals to adopt a course of action that they themselves would agree was in their interests, but its field of application seems to have broadened.

BIASES AND HEURISTICS

Nudging is based on the idea that we've evolved to make our decision-making more efficient, through the use of weightings towards particular behaviours (biases) and through the use of established rules of thumb (heuristics). I'm not going to go through the detail, because they've been pretty much covered in a number of other places (e.g. [71]). I'm also reluctant because they've been presented elsewhere as almost automatic rules ("we always behave in this way") whereas in practice it's unlikely to be so cut and dried.

If you do want to look at the history, the key articles are probably those by Kahneman and Tversky [72, 73] which present evidence that we don't make decisions in the way economists would like, i.e. we don't simply maximise the cost/benefit balance.

The commonly understood premise is that we have two means of making a decision – System 1 and System 2. System 1 is associative, and for that reason, it's fast. We like fast. A significant proportion of the glucose budget for your body is related to cognitive effort, so if you can cut down on thinking time, then you get an evolutionary advantage. You can go a bit longer without having to run out and catch something to eat. Consequently, System 1 is our default mechanism for making a decision.

Using biases and heuristics, System 1 gets a "good enough" answer most of the time, but because it takes short cuts, it's prone to occasionally making mistakes, and it's prone to being led astray, and that's where nudging comes in. Priming is an example – when you walk into a supermarket in the UK, the chances are you'll see a National Lottery terminal placed very close to the entrance. It could be you!™ You could already (or very soon) be a multimillionaire. So it's ok to spend a little bit more than you were planning to, especially if it's on luxuries. Loss aversion is a second, and currently less controversial example. If you were asked to gamble £5 on the toss of a coin, how much would you need to be offered to make it worth gambling? Kahneman showed that most people would ask for about £10 – we value losses to be about twice as important as gains. It's an inbuilt bias that over the years has worked to our evolutionary advantage. And despite claims to the contrary [74], key experiments in loss aversion (which more or less forms the basis for behavioural economics) do seem to have been successfully replicated [75, 76].

System 2 on the other hand is slower. It takes a logical approach, working through from first principles, on a rational basis, and is therefore less likely to be affected by the choice of font on the sign above the avocados. When System 1 can't find a sensible solution, it gives up and hands the problem to System 2. But since System 2 uses more glucose, we only invoke it when we absolutely have to.

That's the standard explanation anyway, although the detail may be more nuanced [77]. Transitions from System 1 to System 2 require a trigger, which leads to complications [78, 79], partly because the decision to hand over the problem must be a rational one, i.e. one which is itself based on System 2 thinking. So is System 2 running all the time and steps in when it sees that System 1 is struggling? In that case are we saving any glucose by having System 1? Or is there some third, executive function overseeing the process? Partly because of these kinds of questions, people are now exploring hybrid approaches [80, 81] and approaches involving a mixture of the two types of thinking ("quasi-rationality"), such as Cognitive Continuum Theory [82, 83]. More on this later.

EXAMPLES OF SECURITY NUDGING

In 2014, researchers at Northumbria University [84] were looking for ways in which they could encourage mobile phone users to join secure wireless networks, and to steer them away from using open ones. Ordering the display of available networks according to their security level helped a little, as did colour coding. The combination of ordering and colour coding was more effective than either. However, doing both of those and also removing the padlock symbol resulted in about 99% of the people in the trial choosing one of the secure networks. The suggestion put forward by the researchers was that the padlock was being interpreted as a sign saying "secure area – do not enter". Rather than being an indicator of safety, it seemed to be an unhelpful nudge, deterring users from selecting those networks.

The key points being that:

1. The work was oriented towards a specific behaviour – choosing a secure wireless network – rather than a vague aim of "improving security".
2. A combination of measures gave the best result (c.f. the approach to security culture as a point solution).
3. The outcome was achieved through repeated trials and refinement rather than the one-off application of a single principle.

You can see some of the same points in work conducted by Bullée et al. [85]. Staff at a university in the Netherlands were asked by an experimenter pretending to be from the IT department to hand over their access tokens ("dongles") so that they could be taken away, checked, and if necessary reprogrammed, on the basis that "a fault has developed in the issuing system". Prior to the experiment, posters and leaflets warning about social engineering attacks were distributed to one group, together with a lanyard saying "Don't give me to a stranger" (see Figure 2.1 below).

The key takeaway (sorry…) is that about 63% of people handed over their token when asked. That fell to 37% in the group that received the warning materials and

FIGURE 2.1 Experimental materials. (Bullée et al. [85]. Republished under STM guidelines.)

the lanyard. It's not possible to disentangle the effect of each component, but it's worth noting that a subsequent experiment [86] on consumer behaviour, using just a warning notice based on the one used in the dongle experiment, found that the notice alone had no effect. It seemed that the message on the lanyard, observed at the very moment of handing over the dongle, was the main factor.

APPLICATION OF NUDGING

Security decisions can be adjusted, if you present the security message in an appropriate way, and if you present it at an appropriate time. These are ways in which System 1 might therefore be harnessed to redirect inbuilt "short-cut" thinking. But you have to target the nudge towards a specific, identified behaviour, rather than just saying that you want "better security". What's more, nudges may need to be developed and refined through repeated trials [87], which is going to be expensive if there are a number of behaviours to address. And even though the application of nudging in cybersecurity is still in its infancy, there are already a couple of warning signs. An ENISA report [88] suggests that the idea of the "stupid user" is still a theme – that the use of nudging seems to be tied to a strong underlying desire within practitioners to find something wrong with users, so that they can be "fixed".

There may also be a couple of more practical issues. Szaszi et al. [89] reviewed a wide range of literature on nudging, and found that most studies looked at just a single intervention in a specific setting, and made little effort to understand why the nudge worked. Quoting a number of sources, the paper concludes that very few of the nudging studies they examined looked at the statistical power of their experiment (the ability to detect an effect, assuming one is present), that small sample sizes tended to predominate (small sample sizes can lead to less reliable results), and also that sample populations tended to be heterogenous (i.e. when comparing the results across two groups, there may have been other differences between the groups that led to the published result). It was also noted that 93% of the studies they examined claimed to have found at least one positive outcome, and that only 18% concluded that the intervention had not worked as intended. The implication being that the number of unsuccessful interventions might have been expected to be rather higher, all things being equal. The work has sparked a debate [90–92], with a suggestion that the wider context for a nudge is a significant factor in deciding whether or not it has any noticeable effect [93].

It's not for me to say – however, on the basis of the available evidence, it seems that the fundamentals of behavioural economics do seem to be turning out to be reliable. But given Szaszi's findings, it could be argued that the practical applications of nudge theory, particularly in cyber, tend to rely on a simplified approach in which the outcomes are occasionally oversold [94–98]. Speaking personally, I believe that behavioural science can offer a means of addressing some of the wider and more serious problems in security, but the long-standing idea of the "stupid user" and the constant search for a single-point solution seem to be tainting its use in cyber. In particular, and in relation to nudging as an adjunct to the idea of security culture, it's the ongoing belief that there are silver bullets that really seems to be causing the problems.

DEBIASING

BACKGROUND

There are alternatives to the use of nudging. Gamification is a popular option [99], one that has been used as the basis for a number of products, such as cyber "escape rooms" [100, 101], and immersive experiences in which teams of managers learn almost first-hand what it feels like to have your organisation hacked (e.g. [102, 103]). The effectiveness of gamification does seem to be strongly dependent on the method of implementation, however [104, 105]. The approaches that seem to work involve small teams of people working and learning as a group. Which is fine, but that might prove to be expensive when larger populations are involved. An interesting development is the use of chatbots to provide interactive advice at the point of the decision [106]. A further emerging option is to try and reduce the effects of biases, rather than exploiting them.

REDUCING THE EFFECTS OF BIASES

Confirmation bias and optimism bias are two elements of short-cut thinking directly relevant to security decision-making [e.g. 107, p15]. Confirmation bias is the tendency to ignore evidence that conflicts with an existing belief, and to selectively engage with evidence that supports it [108]. Optimism bias is the idea that "things will work out ok" [109] even when there is evidence saying that they probably won't.

You can see confirmation bias working in our tendency to over-trust. When we first meet someone, we tend to employ confirmation bias to find reasons why we should trust them, rather than look for reasons why we shouldn't [110, 111]. From an evolutionary point of view that makes perfect sense. If I had to come round to your cave for dinner on alternate Friday nights for a couple of months or so before I trusted you enough to go hunting together, we'd both have starved to death. It makes much more sense for me to trust you from the outset. However, in an online world, that process doesn't always work out so well – it might, for example, provide a clue as to why people are so willing to give their savings to a stranger they've just met on a webcam.

Optimism bias has been examined in an earlier chapter, at least indirectly, in the discussion on AWS online storage. The tendency to think "I'm sure it'll be ok" without checking privacy settings has led to a number of well-publicised breaches [112–114].

If we could reduce the levels of those biases, it's possible that we might get fewer breaches, through encouraging the use of more considered decision-making. It's by no means guaranteed, but it may be possible.

Shortly after 9/11, the US Government commissioned some research into improving the performance of its intelligence analysts. As part of that, Carey Morewedge [115, 116] developed an animated video taking participants through a fictional detective story. The volunteers in the experiment were invited to review the evidence, pick up clues, and solve the mystery of a disappearance. Their tendency to display confirmation bias was tested beforehand, then afterwards, and then again after a number of weeks. Obviously, confirmation bias isn't great for roles that are meant to objectively assess the available evidence and extract meaning from it.

As you may have guessed, Morewedge found that levels of confirmation bias fell after people were exposed to the video. It seemed that solving the puzzle had required them to think more analytically, and that the effect had "stuck".

There were two other findings. One was that the effect was relatively long-lasting. After a number of weeks, a re-test showed that although the level of confirmation bias had gone back up, it was still below pre-test levels. The second was that other biases had also been reduced, and with the same pattern. That is, the effect had spilled over into other areas. Dunbar et al. [117–119] reported similar findings – that the use of a game encouraging people to think more rationally seemed to reduce confirmation bias (although interestingly, the game had to be explicit about its purpose). The work by Morewedge has since been taken out of the laboratory and tried under more realistic conditions [120], with similar results.

At the time of writing, the wider evidence on debiasing remains somewhat mixed [121–124], although a general review in health settings [125] concluded that "...*most of the interventions reviewed here are found to be effective, pointing to the utility of debiasing in the health context*". The point in relation to cyber is that while debiasing might be no more effective than traditional nudging, it might be more generally applicable, and therefore cheaper.

THEORETICAL BACKGROUND

There are at least two competing ideas on how debiasing might work. The first is Cognitive Continuum Theory [83, 126–128], which says that our approach to decision-making lies somewhere on a spectrum from analytical to intuitive. Whereabouts on that continuum we sit when we solve a problem is determined partly by the nature of the problem that we're faced with, and partly by the way in which the problem has been presented to us. By default we start at the intuitive end; however, sometimes the nature and/or presentation of the problem can pull us up towards to the analytical end. That is, by adjusting the presentation of the problem, people can be moved away from their default intuitive position, and towards using a more analytical approach. The experiment known as the "Moses Illusion" [129] may or may not illustrate that, depending on which bit of evidence you prefer to believe. This fits in well with the idea of System 1 (intuitive) and System 2 (rational), but because it uses a continuum, there's no need for a switching mechanism.

A fundamental part of the theory is that when the nature of the approach is aligned with the nature of the problem, the outcome is more likely to be appropriate. But using an analytical approach on an intuitive problem, or vice versa, is likely to result in a lower quality decision. That sounds like a detail, but it's critical. Because as a result, while we might see a general improvement from using debiasing to encourage more deliberative security decision-making, there might also be a price to pay in terms of worse outcomes for those decisions that should have been made on the default, intuitive basis.

Research into clinical diagnosis [130], for example, indicates that when a patient's symptoms are relatively complex or relatively unusual, taking an analytical approach improves the proportion of correct diagnoses. The same study also concluded that taken overall, debiasing delivered a better result. However, when the patient's symptoms were relatively straightforward, an intuitive approach to diagnosis was no worse, and in some cases, slightly better than an analytical approach [130, Figure 1].

The key conclusion being that debiasing isn't a fix – it might improve the situation, but if our approach to a problem needs to be suited to the nature of the problem itself, then some decisions may turn out to be less appropriate, if you always nudge people up towards the analytical end of the scale.

The second model is Fuzzy Trace Theory [131, 132], which says that when we approach a problem, we form different models of it ranging from verbatim (percentages, numbers, facts) to "gist-based" models, which instead contain the essential nature of the problem. The core messages of the research being that our decision-making approach changes as we mature, but also that when we make a decision, we prefer to use the most gist-based model we can get away with [133]. Studies on patients making choices regarding elective joint replacement surgery, for example [134], found that when presented with information that formed a verbatim model (e.g. simple numerical representations of percentages of patients suffering complications, and average timescales for recovery), their decisions were frequently not optimal, given the patient's lifestyle. The quality of decision-making was improved (i.e. patients were happier with the outcomes) when the information was presented in a way that prompted a gist-based model e.g. through the use of diagrams to convey a feeling, rather than using numerical percentages.

Debiasing: Summary

The amount of evidence is limited, although what there is says that while debiasing may not deliver benefits under all conditions, it does seem to be beneficial in most cases. And while it isn't a "one-shot" solution (the effect wears off over time), it does seem to be relatively long lasting, and further, since it's not aimed at specific behaviours or choices, it might be cheaper to apply than bespoke nudges. However, a key conclusion is that there are no silver bullets – encouraging more considered security decision-making comes at a cost.

BOOSTS

BACKGROUND

Recently, "boosts" have been proposed as an alternative to nudges [135–140]. The difference between the two isn't completely clear, and it's been argued that a boost is simply another type of nudge (also that nudges can turn into boosts, and/or have boost-like side effects). When you look into it, the definitions do start to get a bit muddy [141, 142]. Also the evidence for boosts seems to rely on a small number of experiments [143] and arguments from a small number of proponents. The key difference, if there is one, is that nudges act directly on behaviour, whereas boosts make new decision tools available, i.e. they provide additional "rules of thumb". In effect, the individual hasn't been nudged; their set of heuristics has been extended [137, Table 1]. Boosts are therefore educative, in that they promote longer lasting changes. A critical claim is that in contrast to nudges, boosts leave people with "agency" – the ability to make their own choices [144]. The logical conclusion being that those individuals also then have the ability to learn from their mistakes.

THEORETICAL BACKGROUND

The underlying theory is based on the idea that heuristics aren't always applied automatically – some are explicitly chosen and then applied as part of the decision-making process [145, p249].

The way I've come to view it is that we may have a mechanism that comes up with a set of possible narratives to explain a problem – "perhaps this is what's going on?", and a second mechanism that validates each suggested narrative against a set of criteria chosen according to the prevailing context [146]. The acceptability of any one narrative depends on how much conflict there is between the narrative and the applicable criteria, and also on how much conflict we are prepared to accept, depending on context e.g. whether or not we're under pressure to make a decision [147].

If the first process comes up with an initial suggestion that's "good enough" (because we satisfice rather than maximise), then *to the outside observer*, that looks like a quick, intuitive decision. If, however, the narrative system needs a number of iterations to meet the selected criteria, perhaps because they're more stringent, then it will seem to have been a slower, more deliberative decision, again, *to the outside observer*. On this basis, it's likely that the distribution of processing times will tend towards the short end of the scale, i.e. the majority of decisions will look like fast, instinctive choices [148]. So you get a distribution in processing times, with a peak at the low end, and a long tail stretching out to the right [148].

In this context, boosts give the individual a rule that should always be chosen, i.e. "no matter what other criteria you apply depending on the context for the decision, you should always consider this one". So you get a more consistent, more deliberative outcome, even if it takes a little bit longer.

Boosts, it's said, empower individuals to better exert their own agency [139, 149]. It's also claimed that boosts require the individual's understanding, approval and active participation, and that to be effective, boosts need to be explicit, visible, and transparent. Essentially, individuals are advised, but still left to make their own decisions, rather than being unconsciously steered towards whatever outcome was desired by the choice architect, and that's an important difference. Theil et al. [150] found that when a sense of agency was taken away from individuals, there was a kind of moral disengagement. If I'm not being left to make the decision myself, then I don't own any of the outcomes, and indeed, under those conditions, I might even be tempted to engage in deliberate rule-breaking. The key findings from that study were that a sense of agency is associated with a sense of ownership, and that when people feel that they're being treated fairly, they're more likely to be tolerant of measures such as monitoring of their actions.

BOOSTS: SUMMARY

There are, undeniably, issues that need to be bottomed out. Nonetheless, the preceding argument suggests that perhaps our decisions sit somewhere on a spectrum [151, 152] rather than flipping between two modes, and that the approach taken to decision-making depends on the context for the decision [153]. All of which indicates the possibility that boosts (or whatever you want to call them) could be employed to leave people with the right to make their own security decisions, while at the same time providing them with the tools to make more deliberative decisions.

THE ETHICS OF SECURITY

BACKGROUND

It might seem odd to talk about the ethics of information security, but the behaviour of security teams can have a significant effect on people's view of cyber. During the pandemic for example, security teams busied themselves sending out fake phishing emails, to remind users not to click on links. That's fair enough, but what constitutes reasonable behaviour depends on context [154]. Sending out emails offering employees a "thank you" bonus for risking their health by working throughout the pandemic is one example [155]. As you can guess, in that case, instead of a reward, staff were admonished and directed towards a remedial training session if they clicked on the link. From a security point of view, that might seem to be perfectly legitimate. From the employee's point of view, and also in the view of HR and general management (not to mention the unions), it was perceived as crass and clumsy. That sort of action, it seems to me, exemplifies the need for managers, and not security people, to own the way in which security is implemented within an organisation. The security teams involved don't seem to have spent any time considering the potential consequences of their own behaviour. It's all about the reprehensible behaviour of the user. And yet as pointed out by NCSC, significant organisational issues are almost certain to arise when you phish your own users [156]. I've personally seen examples in which users were summarily disconnected from their email accounts because they failed to respond to a (genuine) request asking them to acknowledge updated procedures, and the same team castigating users for responding to a fake email threatening to remove access unless they open the attachment. The subsequent link to remedial training, of course, being sent as a clickable item in an email.

Example: Personalised Nudging

Hirsch [157] suggests that nudges can be made more effective by tailoring them according to an individual's personality traits (the "Big 5", or "OCEAN" model of personality characteristics). That is, an understanding of the personality of the individual can be used to shape nudges to fit that individual, so that you achieve a greater overall impact in terms of changes in behaviour.

Specifically in relation to cyber, Peer and colleagues [158] suggested that security nudges could be made more effective by tailoring them according to an individual's decision-making style. This has led to claims that "*[t]he future of nudging will be personal*" [159], and that "*... the next frontier in privacy and security research will be to tailor mitigations to users' individual differences*" [160].

In practice, tailoring nudges would, of course, involve gaining access to someone's potentially private information, in order to create a profile of that individual, so that the security team could then nudge them towards being more careful about who has access to their private information.

Peer notes that if that such information is being gathered already, then using it to improve privacy behaviours "*somewhat [mitigates] the harm to privacy caused by collecting and storing consumers' personal information*". Possibly I'm being overly sensitive, but that could be read as legitimising the collection of personal data, on the basis that the information has now become of value to the security team.

Peer also notes that there will need to be guards, because "*[l]ike any other persuasion method, personalized nudges might also be used in sinister motives by less-benevolent or less-democratic governments or organizations*". The implication being that the security team is justified in doing this, on the basis that they occupy the moral high ground. Interesting, because as described by Mills, the data-gathering process could involve methods that have, in the past, been decried as unacceptable by the cybersecurity industry itself [161].

Egelman et al. [160] note that "*[a]s a minimum, this data needs to be highly protected*". That is, additional controls would need to be enforced over the data being used to make people more compliant with privacy controls.

Setting aside any heavy-handed use of mandatory profiling, some less visible means would presumably be employed to segment the target groups. Techniques hinted at in the literature include the use of natural language processing of emails in order to infer personality type [162], and the analysis of personal posts on social media [163]. Others [164–167] have suggested analysing password choices, actions when using a keyboard and mouse, or mobile phone usage patterns, to assess decision-making style and/or personality characteristics. Whether or not those techniques would work is not the point – the point is that they're being suggested. To the untrained eye, that looks like a situation in which every action in, and potentially outside the workplace, is open to being monitored, so that the security team can build up a Facebook-style portfolio identifying individuals for "improvement". I'm sure that can't be right [168]. That would amount to not much more than 1900's style Taylorism [169].

Mills notes that such problems will need to be resolved, in order to "… *improve people's decisions and welfare*". The concept of "libertarian paternalism" is at the heart of the nudging movement. It's been some time since there was an open discussion on the subject [170, 171], but presumably the argument is still going on. In the context of cyber, the unstated premise is that the security team can be relied upon to have everyone's best interests at heart. Of course.

Lee et al. [172] looked into role of the psychological contract between an employee and their employing organisation and found that where the psychological contract was perceived as having been broken, employees reported reduced intentions to comply with information security rules. The psychological contract is the set of unstated beliefs relating what the employee owes the company, and what the company should be doing in return. It's quite separate from the formal, documented contract of employment. Breaches of the psychological contract come about when the employee feels that they aren't being treated as expected. For example, that they feel they aren't being treated fairly. Given that such breaches lead to reduced intentions to comply with security policy, it follows that if you want people to behave in a secure way, one issue you might address is the tendency for the security team to treat people as "work units".

IMPLICATIONS

This is a difficult area. Behavioural measures do seem to be an effective way of addressing some real-world security issues, especially those related to decision-making.

However, a number of characteristics emerge from the preceding review:

- A central belief that the target is simply to achieve the maximum degree of compliance.
- A lack of appreciation of the potential for damage arising from the practitioners' own actions.
- The ever-present view that users are malfunctioning work units that need to be "fixed".

The application of behavioural science isn't being seen by the cyber community as a new opportunity. It's being seen as a new way to achieve the old targets. There's very little consideration of the ethics of applying it, which leads to a deepening estrangement between users and the cyber team, and the generation of corporate costs which then have to be picked up by other parts of the organisation.

The practical application of behavioural science to cyber needs to take into account the fact that those "items" being nudged are individuals. What's more, these techniques need to be applied more critically – we can get benefits from them, not a solution. I'm personally not sure that simple compliance is what we want (see below). But if it is, then that goal needs to be balanced against the costs of achieving it – there needs to be a recognition of the context for compliance, and in particular, the ethical context. The only way I can see that happening is if the process is owned and supervised by the management team, and not by the security team.

A Modest Suggestion

Security rules can't be written to cover every situation. In fact, the range of possible circumstances could be viewed as an expanse of open ocean, with occasional islands of firm guidance dotted here and there. If you're in a situation that's precisely described in the guidance, then you're on solid ground. However, for most decisions, you're going to be a long way from land. As a result, it's not possible to achieve 100% compliance, because it's not possible to define what compliance looks like in 100% of all situations. You can't concrete over the ocean. Rather than aiming to provide perfect advice under every set of circumstances, it makes more sense to give users a set of additional tools to make more considered decisions on security, and then allow them the agency to make those decisions themselves.

It's been suggested that variability in our decision-making is a failing. On the face of it, the idea that we might give a slightly different judgement on two consecutive occasions, under what seem to be identical circumstances, does indeed look like inconsistency. In fact, by introducing "jitter" into our decisions, we're able to find out if our default decision is the best option. If we arrived at the same conclusion each and every time, then we'd never find out if there was a better choice. Greg Ip [173, p252] summarises this by quoting Amalberti: *"mistakes are cognitively useful"*. Decision-making involves a degree of variability. If it didn't, then our decision-making would never improve.

If that argument holds, then not only would it be more ethically acceptable to give people the right to make their own choices, it might also lead to security decision-making based on experience and knowledge, rather than on external enforcement, and in particular, external enforcement from a group of people who themselves may not have a full grasp of the circumstances for their actions.

The use of an ethical framework has already been suggested by Renaud in relation to the development of cyber-related nudging [174]. For example, should we be sending out COVID bonus emails – is that "us" as an organisation? Are we ok with using debiasing covertly, or should we be more open about it? Should we gamify it or perhaps make it optional? How much choice do we want to give to the people working for us? These aren't decisions that should be made by the security team – they're decisions that should be made by the people managing the organisation. Schmidt and Engelen [175, p2] note the difference between nudging for the benefit of the individual and nudging for the benefit of the company, and conclude that [176, p9]:

> *Overall, our view is that no "knockdown" objection has appeared to date that should make us reject the nudge approach overall. At the same time, serious ethical concerns have emerged that should guide and inform discussions around whether and which particular nudge policies should be pursued, and, if so, how.*

Just as with other aspects of employment, possibly what's needed is a per-company statement setting out how far the organisation is prepared to go, in order to improve its security posture. That might at least serve to constrain the occasionally wayward actions of the cyber team. It might also give fresh meaning to the term "security policy".

SECURITY CULTURE: CONCLUSIONS

SECURITY CULTURE

The concept of security culture is based on industry need to search out a single-point solution that will make people "work" when it comes to security. However, there seems to be very little evidence to support the concept, and its implementation seems to be based on a circular argument, in that compliance is seen as both a precursor to, and an outcome of, an effective security culture [176, 177].

ALTERNATIVES

If you don't want to go down the pixie dust route, there are alternatives. The available evidence suggests, for example, that you can affect decisions by nudging people to "do the right thing" [68]. However, first you have to define "the right thing", because the goal of "improved security" is too vague to be useful. More significantly perhaps, there are questions of ethics, particularly when you start singling people out for special treatment.

Reducing the level of irrationality ("debiasing") provides a less targeted option. The evidence shows that it does have an impact, and it seems to be a more generalised approach. However, pulling decisions up towards the more considered end of the spectrum may not work in all cases.

There's also an emerging new option: boosts. The evidence may be thin at the moment, but there's an argument that boosts could combine the effectiveness of nudging with an openness and transparency that leaves users with the right to make their own decisions.

Zimmermann and Renaud [178] make the point that "*[t]reating everyone as a problem does not seem to work, given the current cyber security landscape*". They propose a different model, one in which users are actively engaged as part of the solution. A key suggestion in their paper is that we could start with an assumption that users are basically well-intentioned. That, and the argument presented earlier, makes a strong case for taking cyber management away from the security team, where the view of users might perhaps be described as somewhat jaundiced, and putting it instead, into the hands of the management team. The clue is in the name.

REFERENCES

1. Bell, D.E. and L.J. LaPadula, *Secure computer systems: Mathematical foundations*. 1973: MITRE CORP BEDFORD MA.
2. BSI, *BS part 2: Code of practice for information security management*. 1999: British Standards Institute.
3. Fomin, V.V., H. Vries, and Y. Barlette, ISO/IEC 27001 information systems security management standard: Exploring the reasons for low adoption. In *EUROMOT 2008 Conference, Nice, France*, 2008.

4. Hearn, J., Does the common criteria paradigm have a future?[security and privacy]. *IEEE Security & Privacy*, 2004. 2(1): p. 64–65.

5. Murdoch, S.J., M. Bond, and R. Anderson, How certification systems fail: Lessons from the Ware report. *IEEE Security and Privacy*, 2012. 10(6): p. 40.

6. Wing, J.M., A symbiotic relationship between formal methods and security. In *Proceedings Computer Security, Dependability, and Assurance: From Needs to Solutions (Cat. No. 98EX358)*. 1998: IEEE.

7. Jin, J. and M. Shen, Analysis of security models based on multilevel security policy. In *2012 International Conference on Management of E-commerce and E-government*.

8. Ryoo, J., et al., Cloud security auditing: Challenges and emerging approaches. *IEEE Security & Privacy*, 2013. 12(6): p. 68–74.

9. AlHogail, A. and A. Mirza, Information security culture: A definition and a literature review. In *Computer Applications and Information Systems (WCCAIS), 2014 World Congress on*. 2014: IEEE.

10. Alnatheer, M., T. Chan, and K. Nelson, Understanding and measuring information security culture. In *PACIS*. 2012.

11. Chia, P., S. Maynard, and A. Ruighaver, Understanding organizational security culture. In *Proceedings of PACIS2002*. Japan, 2002.

12. Da Veiga, A., N. Martins, and J.H. Eloff, Information security culture-validation of an assessment instrument. *Southern African Business Review*, 2007. 11(1): p. 147–166.

13. McIlwraith, A., *Information security and employee behaviour: How to reduce risk through employee education, training and awareness*. 2021: Routledge.

14. ISACA, *Narrowing the culture gap for better business results*. 2018 [Accessed 21 January 2023]; Available from: https://library.cyentia.com/report/report_002 567.html

15. Oost, D. and E.K. Chew, Investigating the concept of information security culture. In *Strategic and practical approaches for information security governance: Technologies and applied solutions*, R. Sharman, M. Gupta, and J. Walp, Editors. 2012: IGI Global. p. 1–12.

16. Karlsson, F., J. Åström, and M. Karlsson, Information security culture–state-of-the-art review between 2000 and 2013. *Information & Computer Security*, 2015. 23(3): p. 246–285.

17. Karyda, M., *Fostering information security culture in organizations: A research agenda*. 2017.

18. Wiley, A., A. McCormac, and D. Calic, More than the individual: Examining the relationship between culture and information security awareness. *Computers & Security*, 2020. 88: p. 101640.

19. Sas, M., et al., Measuring the security culture in organizations: A systematic overview of existing tools. *Security Journal*, 2020. 34: p. 340–357.

20. Nasir, A., A.A. Ruzaini, and A.H. Rashid, Information security culture guidelines to improve employee's security behavior: A review of empirical studies. *Journal of Fundamental and Applied Sciences*, 2018. 10(2S): p. 258–283.

21. Uchendu, B., et al., Developing a cyber security culture: Current practices and future needs. *Computers & Security*, 2021. 109: p. 102387.

22. Nasir, A. and R.A. Arshah, Information security culture dimensions in information security policy compliance study: A review. *Advanced Science Letters*, 2018. 24(2): p. 943–946.

23. Dugo, T., *The insider threat to organizational information security: A structural model and empirical test*. 2007. PhD dissertation from Auburn University. https://etd.auburn.edu/handle/10415/1345

24. Knapp, K.J., *A model of managerial effectiveness in information security: From grounded theory to empirical test*. 2005: AUBURN UNIV AL.
25. Martins, A. and J. Eloff, Assessing information security culture. In *ISSA*. 2002.
26. Nasir, A., et al., An analysis on the dimensions of information security culture concept: A review. *Journal of Information Security and Applications*, 2019. 44: p. 12–22.
27. Da Veiga, A., et al., Defining organisational information security culture – Perspectives from academia and industry. *Computers & Security*, 2020. 92: p. 101713.
28. Dekker, S., *The safety anarchist: Relying on human expertise and innovation, reducing bureaucracy and compliance*. 2017: Routledge.
29. Elkind, P., D. Whitford, and D. Burke, *BP: 'An accident waiting to happen'*. 24 January 2011: Fortune.
30. Urbina, I., *Workers on doomed rig voiced concern about safety*. 2010 [Accessed 10 April 2021]; Available from: www.nytimes.com/2010/07/22/us/22transocean.html
31. Broder, J.M., *BP shortcuts led to Gulf oil spill, report says*. 2011 [Accessed 20 February 2022]; Available from: www.nytimes.com/2011/09/15/science/earth/15sp ill.html
32. Mullins, J., *The eight failures that caused the Gulf oil spill*. 2010 [Accessed 20 February 2022]; Available from: www.newscientist.com/article/dn19425-the-eight-failures-that-caused-the-gulf-oil-spill
33. Pilkington, E., *BP oil spill: Safety breaches revealed*. 2010 [Accessed 20 February 2022]; Available from: www.theguardian.com/environment/2010/jul/24/oil-spill-deepwater-horizon-safety-breaches
34. Guardian, *Investigation into 2010 BP oil spill finds failures, poor testing and ongoing risks*. 2014 [Accessed 10 April 2021]; Available from: www.theguardian.com/envi ronment/2014/jun/05/bp-deepwater-horizon-spill-report-failures-risks
35. Dekker, S., Safety differently: Human factors for a new era. *Collegiate Aviation Review*, 2016. 34(2): p. 107.
36. Conklin, T., *Pre-accident investigations: An introduction to organizational safety*. 2012: Ashgate Publishing, Ltd.
37. Dekker, S., *The field guide to understanding "human error"*. 2017: CRC Press.
38. Lacey, D., *Understanding and transforming organizational security culture*. 2010: Information Management & Computer Security.
39. Detert, J.R., R.G. Schroeder, and J.J. Mauriel, A framework for linking culture and improvement initiatives in organizations. *Academy of Management Review*, 2000. 25(4): p. 850–863.
40. Schein, E.H., *Organizational culture*. Vol. 45. 1990: American Psychological Association.
41. Schein, E.H., *Organizational culture and leadership*. Vol. 2. 2010: John Wiley & Sons.
42. Schein, E.H., *The corporate culture survival guide*. Vol. 158. 2009: John Wiley & Sons.
43. Van Niekerk, J. and R. Von Solms, Information security culture: A management perspective. *Computers & Security*, 2010. 29(4): p. 476–486.
44. Nasir, A., et al., How to cultivate cyber security culture? The evidences from literature. *International Journal of Synergy in Engineering and Technology*, 2023. 4(1): p. 13–19.
45. Da Veiga, A. and N. Martins, Information security culture: A comparative analysis of four assessments. In *Proceedings of the 8th European Conference on IS Management and Evaluation*. 2014.
46. Sutherland, R., *Alchemy: The surprising power of ideas that don't make sense*. 2019: WH Allen.

47. Pattinson, M., et al., Assessing information security attitudes: A comparison of two studies. *Information & Computer Security*, 2016. 24(2): p. 228–240.
48. Egelman, S., M. Harbach, and E. Peer, Behavior ever follows intention?: A validation of the security behavior intentions scale (SeBIS). In *Proceedings of the 2016 CHI Conference on Human Factors in Computing Systems*. 2016. ACM.
49. Wash, R., E. Rader, and C. Fennell, Can people self-report security accurately?: Agreement between self-report and behavioral measures. In *Proceedings of the 2017 CHI Conference on Human Factors in Computing Systems*. 2017: ACM.
50. Sheeran, P., Intention – Behavior relations: A conceptual and empirical review. *European Review of Social Psychology*, 2002. 12(1): p. 1–36.
51. Cram, W.A. and J. D'Arcy, *Barking up the wrong tree? Reconsidering policy compliance as a dependent variable within behavioral cybersecurity research*. Hawaii International Conference on System Sciences (HICSS), 2023: p. 4139–4148.
52. Gratian, M., et al., Correlating human traits and cyber security behavior intentions. *Computers & Security*, 2018. 73: p. 345–358.
53. Guo, K.H., et al., Understanding nonmalicious security violations in the workplace: A composite behavior model. *Journal of Management Information Systems*, 2011. 28(2): p. 203–236.
54. Sommestad, T., et al., Variables influencing information security policy compliance: A systematic review of quantitative studies. *Information Management & Computer Security,* 2014. 22(1): p. 42–75.
55. Adjerid, I., E. Peer, and A. Acquisti, *Beyond the privacy paradox: Objective versus relative risk in privacy decision making*. Available at SSRN 2765097, 2016.
56. Tversky, A. and D. Kahneman, The framing of decisions and the psychology of choice. *Science*, 1981. 211(4481): p. 453–458.
57. Azar, O.H., Relative thinking theory. *The Journal of Socio-Economics*, 2007. 36(1): p. 1–14.
58. Azar, O.H., Relative thinking in consumer choice between differentiated goods and services and its implications for business strategy. *Judgment and Decision Making*, 2011. 6(2): p. 176.
59. Gerber, N., et al., Understanding information security compliance – Why goal setting and rewards might be a bad idea. In *HAISA*. 2016.
60. Welsh, D.T. and L.D. Ordóñez, The dark side of consecutive high performance goals: Linking goal setting, depletion, and unethical behavior. *Organizational Behavior and Human Decision Processes*, 2014. 123(2): p. 79–89.
61. Crossler, R.E., et al., Future directions for behavioral information security research. *Computers & Security*, 2013. 32: p. 90–101.
62. Warkentin, M., D. Straub, and K. Malimage, Featured talk: Measuring secure behavior: A research commentary. In *Annual Symposium of Information Assurance & Secure Knowledge Management, Albany, NY*. 2012: Citeseer.
63. Lebek, B., et al., Information security awareness and behavior: A theory-based literature review. *Management Research Review*, 2014. 37(12): p. 1049–1092.
64. Renaud, K. and S. Flowerday, Contemplating human-centred security & privacy research: Suggesting future directions. *Journal of Information Security and Applications*, 2017. 34: p. 76–81.
65. Reynolds, M. and S. Holwell, *Systems approaches to managing change: A practical guide*. 2010: Springer.
66. Subramanian, S., *Nudging our way to successful information security awareness*. 2021 [Accessed 11 January 2023]; Available from: www.isaca.org/resources/isaca-journal/issues/2021/volume-1/nudging-our-way-to-successful-information-security-awareness

67. Leonard, T.C., Richard H. Thaler, Cass R. Sunstein, Nudge: Improving decisions about health, wealth, and happiness. *Constitutional Political Economy*, 2008. 19(4): p. 356–360.

68. Halpern, D., *Inside the nudge unit: How small changes can make a big difference.* 2016: Random House.

69. Wintour, P., *David Cameron's "nudge unit" aims to improve economic behaviour.* 2010 [Accessed 15 November 2022]; Available from: www.theguardian.com/society/2010/sep/09/cameron-nudge-unit-economic-behaviour

70. Sky, *Behaviour change on climate can be driven by TV, says Sky.* 2021 [Accessed 23 December 2022]; Available from: www.skygroup.sky/article/behaviour-change-on-climate-can-be-driven-by-tv-says-sky

71. Dennis, A.R. and R.K. Minas, Security on autopilot: Why current security theories hijack our thinking and lead us astray. *ACM SIGMIS Database: The DATABASE for Advances in Information Systems*, 2018. 49(SI): p. 15–38.

72. Kahneman, D., P. Slovic, and A. Tversky, *Judgment under uncertainty.* 1982: Cambridge University Press Cambridge.

73. Kahneman, D. and A. Tversky, Prospect theory: An analysis of decisions under risk. In *Econometrica*. 1979: Citeseer.

74. Gal, D. and D.D. Rucker, The loss of loss aversion: Will it loom larger than its gain? *Journal of Consumer Psychology*, 2018. 28(3): p. 497–516.

75. Ruggeri, K., et al., Replicating patterns of prospect theory for decision under risk. *Nature Human Behaviour*, 2020. 4(6): p. 622–633.

76. Mrkva, K., et al., Moderating loss aversion: Loss aversion has moderators, but reports of its death are greatly exaggerated. *Journal of Consumer Psychology*, 2020. 30(3): p. 407–428.

77. Hollingworth, C. and L. Barker, *Debunking myths and re-establishing truths – New frontiers in behavioural science series – article 5.* 2019 [Accessed 16 February 2022]; Available from: www.marketingsociety.com/think-piece/system-1-and-system-2-thinking

78. Evans, J.S.B., On the resolution of conflict in dual process theories of reasoning. *Thinking & Reasoning*, 2007. 13(4): p. 321–339.

79. Batool, N., M.N. Riaz, and M.A. Riaz, Integrated use of rational and intuitive decision making style: Modern trends in organizational decision making. *Pakistan Business Review*, 2015. 17(1): p. 147–161.

80. De Neys, W., Bias and conflict: A case for logical intuitions. *Perspectives on Psychological Science*, 2012. 7(1): p. 28–38.

81. Banerjee, S. and P. John, Nudge plus: Incorporating reflection into behavioral public policy. *Behavioural Public Policy*, 2021. 5717(332): p. 1–16.

82. Dhami, M.K. and J.L. Mumpower, Kenneth R. Hammond's contributions to the study of judgment and decision making. *Judgment and Decision Making*, 2018. 13(1): p. 1–22.

83. Dhami, M.K. and M.E. Thomson, On the relevance of cognitive continuum theory and quasirationality for understanding management judgment and decision making. *European Management Journal*, 2012. 30(4): p. 316–326.

84. Jeske, D., et al., Nudging whom how: IT proficiency, impulse control and secure behaviour. In *CHI Workshop on Personalizing Behavior Change Technologies, CHI.* 2014.

85. Bullée, J.-W.H., et al., The persuasion and security awareness experiment: Reducing the success of social engineering attacks. *Journal of Experimental Criminology*, 2015. 11(1): p. 97–115.

86. Junger, M., L. Montoya, and F.-J. Overink, Priming and warnings are not effective to prevent social engineering attacks. *Computers in Human Behavior*, 2017. 66: p. 75–87.
87. Coventry, L., et al. SCENE: A structured means for creating and evaluating behavioral nudges in a cyber security environment. In *International Conference of Design, User Experience, and Usability*. 2014. Springer.
88. ENISA, *Cybersecurity culture guidelines: "Technical annex: Evidence reviews"*. 2019 [Accessed 10 April 2021]; Available from: www.enisa.europa.eu/publications/cybers ecurity-culture-guidelines-technical-annex-evidence-reviews
89. Szaszi, B., et al., A systematic scoping review of the choice architecture movement: Toward understanding when and why nudges work. *Journal of Behavioral Decision Making*, 2018. 31(3): p. 355–366.
90. Szaszi, B., et al., No reason to expect large and consistent effects of nudge interventions. *Proceedings of the National Academy of Sciences*, 2022. 119(31): p. e2200732119.
91. de Ridder, D., et al., Simple nudges that are not so easy. *Behavioural Public Policy*, 2020: p. 1–19.
92. Mertens, S., et al., Reply to Maier et al., Szaszi et al., and Bakdash and Marusich: The present and future of choice architecture research. *Proceedings of the National Academy of Sciences*, 2022. 119(31): p. e2202928119.
93. Szaszi, B. and B. Aczel, *Extending the choice architecture toolbox: The choice context mapping*. PF: PsyArXiv, 24 September 2020.
94. House of Lords Science and Technology Select Committee, *Behaviour change (2nd report of session 2010–12, HL paper 179)*. 2011 [Accessed 28 November 2021]; Available from: www.publications.parliament.uk/pa/ld201012/ldselect/ldsctech/179/ 179.pdf
95. French, J., Why nudging is not enough. *Journal of Social Marketing*, 2011. 1: p. 154–162.
96. Mols, F., et al., Why a nudge is not enough: A social identity critique of governance by stealth. *European Journal of Political Research*, 2015. 54(1): p. 81–98.
97. Gross, T., *Why most results of socio-technical security user studies are false*. arXiv preprint arXiv:2109.10839, 2021.
98. Coopamootoo, K. and T. Gross, *A systematic evaluation of evidence-based methods in cyber security user studies*. School of Computing Technical Report Series, 2019. Newcastle University School of Computing Technical Report No. CS-TR-1528 July 2019.
99. Hart, S., et al., Riskio: A serious game for cyber security awareness and education. *Computers & Security*, 2020. 95: p. 101827.
100. Deloitte, *Serious gaming: The security awareness escaperoom*. 2022 [Accessed 16 February 2022]; Available from: www2.deloitte.com/content/dam/Deloitte/nl/Docume nts/risk/deloitte-nl-cyber-risk-the-security-awareness-escape-room.pdf
101. CGI, CGI cyber escape. 2023 [Accessed 19 October 2023]; Available from: www.cgi. com/uk/en-gb/cyberescape
102. Kaspersky, *KIPS*. 2021 [Accessed 10 April 2021]; Available from: https:// media.kaspersky.com/en/business-security/enterprise/KL_SA_KIPS_overview_ A4_Eng_web.pdf
103. PWC, *Game of threats*. 2022 [Accessed 14 January 2023]; Available from: www.pwc. com/lk/en/services/consulting/cybersecurity/game-of-threats.html
104. Gjertsen, E.G.B., et al., Gamification of information security awareness and training. In *ICISSP*. 2017.
105. Lindgren, N., *How can gamification enable behavior change related to information security: A literature review*. 2020. Masters Degree project, University of Skövde.

106. Gulenko, I., Chatbot for IT security training: Using motivational interviewing to improve security behaviour. In *AIST (supplement)*. 2014.

107. CertNZ, *Cyber change*. 2022 [Accessed 11 January 2023]; Available from: www.cert. govt.nz/assets/resources/cert-nz-cyber-change-behavioural-insights-2022-online-vers ion.pdf

108. Moravec, P., R. Minas, and A.R. Dennis, *Fake news on social media: People believe what they want to believe when it makes no sense at all*. Kelley School of Business Research Paper, 2018(18–87).

109. Meyer, W.G., The effect of optimism bias on the decision to terminate failing projects. *Project Management Journal*, 2014. 45(4): p. 7–20.

110. Hardin, R., The street-level epistemology of trust. *Politics & Society*, 1993. 21(4): p. 505–529.

111. McKnight, D.H., L.L. Cummings, and N.L. Chervany, Initial trust formation in new organizational relationships. *Academy of Management Review*, 1998. 23(3): p. 473–490.

112. Nichols, S., *Twilio: Someone waltzed into our unsecured AWS S3 silo, added dodgy code to our JavaScript SDK for customers*. 2020 [Accessed 10 April 2021]; Available from: www.theregister.com/2020/07/21/twilio_javascript_sdk_code_injection

113. Nichols, S., *Small business loans app blamed as 500,000 financial records leak out of … you guessed it, an open S3 bucket*. 2020 [Accessed 10 April 2021]; Available from: www.theregister.com/2020/03/18/smb_loan_app_leaks

114. Nichols, S., *When did you last check your AWS S3 security? Here's four scary words: 17k Magecart infections*. 2019 [Accessed 10 April 2021]; Available from: www. theregister.com/2019/07/12/riskiq_magecart_s3

115. Morewedge, C.K., *How a video game helped people make better decisions*. Harvard Business Review, October, 2015. 13. https://hbr.org/2015/10/how-a-video-game-hel ped-people-make-better-decisions

116. Morewedge, C.K., et al., Debiasing decisions: Improved decision making with a single training intervention. *Policy Insights from the Behavioral and Brain Sciences*, 2015. 2(1): p. 129–140.

117. Dunbar, N.E., et al., Implicit and explicit training in the mitigation of cognitive bias through the use of a serious game. *Computers in Human Behavior*, 2014. 37: p. 307–318.

118. Dunbar, N.E., et al., Mitigation of cognitive bias through the use of a serious game. In *Proceedings of the Games Learning Society Annual Conference*. 2013.

119. Dunbar, N.E., et al., MACBETH: Development of a training game for the mitigation of cognitive bias. *International Journal of Game-Based Learning (IJGBL)*, 2013. 3(4): p. 7–26.

120. Sellier, A.-L., I. Scopelliti, and C.K. Morewedge, Debiasing training improves decision making in the field. *Psychological Science*, 2019. 30(9): p. 1371–1379.

121. Hueber, L. and R. Schwaiger, Debiasing through experience sampling: The case of myopic loss aversion. Journal of Economic Behavior & Organization, 2021. 198, p. 87–138.

122. Sherbino, J., et al., Ineffectiveness of cognitive forcing strategies to reduce biases in diagnostic reasoning: A controlled trial. *Canadian Journal of Emergency Medicine*, 2014. 16(1): p. 34–40.

123. Hartigan, S., et al., Review of the basics of cognitive error in emergency medicine: Still no easy answers. *Western Journal of Emergency Medicine*, 2020. 21(6): p. 125.

124. Smith, B.W. and M.B. Slack, The effect of cognitive debiasing training among family medicine residents. *Diagnosis*, 2015. 2(2): p. 117–121.

125. Ludolph, R. and P.J. Schulz, Debiasing health-related judgments and decision making: A systematic review. *Medical Decision Making*, 2018. 38(1): p. 3–13.

126. Custers, E.J.F.M., Medical education and cognitive continuum theory: An alternative perspective on medical problem solving and clinical reasoning. *Academic Medicine*, 2013. 88(8): p. 1074–1080.

127. Hamm, R.M., Clinical intuition and clinical analysis: Expertise and the cognitive continuum. In *Professional judgment: A reader in clinical decision making*, J Dowie and A. Elstein, Editors. 1988: Cambridge University Press. p. 78–105.

128. Hammond, K.R., et al., Direct comparison of the efficacy of intuitive and analytical cognition in expert judgment. *IEEE Transactions on Systems, Man, and Cybernetics*, 1987. 17(5): p. 753–770.

129. Song, H. and N. Schwarz, Fluency and the detection of misleading questions: Low processing fluency attenuates the Moses illusion. *Social Cognition*, 2008. 26(6): p. 791–799.

130. Shimizu, T., K. Matsumoto, and Y. Tokuda, Effects of the use of differential diagnosis checklist and general de-biasing checklist on diagnostic performance in comparison to intuitive diagnosis. *Medical Teacher*, 2013. 35(6): p. e1218–e1229.

131. Reyna, V.F., A theory of medical decision making and health: Fuzzy trace theory. *Medical Decision Making*, 2008. 28(6): p. 850–865.

132. Reyna, V.F., A new intuitionism: Meaning, memory, and development in Fuzzy-Trace Theory. *Judgment and Decision Making*, 2012. 7(3): p. 332–359.

133. Blalock, S.J. and V.F. Reyna, Using fuzzy-trace theory to understand and improve health judgments, decisions, and behaviors: A literature review. *Health Psychology*, 2016. 35(8): p. 781.

134. de Achaval, S., et al., Impact of educational and patient decision aids on decisional conflict associated with total knee arthroplasty. *Arthritis Care & Research*, 2012. 64(2): p. 229–237.

135. Drexler, A., G. Fischer, and A. Schoar, Keeping it simple: Financial literacy and rules of thumb. *American Economic Journal: Applied Economics*, 2014. 6(2): p. 1–31.

136. Hertwig, R., When to consider boosting: Some rules for policy-makers. *Behavioural Public Policy*, 2017. 1(2): p. 143–161.

137. Hertwig, R. and T. Grüne-Yanoff, Nudging and boosting: Steering or empowering good decisions. *Perspectives on Psychological Science*, 2017. 12(6): p. 973–986.

138. Hertwig, R. and T. Grüne-Yanoff, Nudging and boosting financial decisions. *Bancaria: Journal of Italian Banking Association*, 2019. 73(3): p. 2–19.

139. Roekel, H.v., J. Reinhard, and S. Grimmelikhuijsen, *Building the behavior change toolkit: Designing and testing a nudge and a boost*. 2021 [Accessed 29 November 2021]; Available from: https://behavioralscientist.org/building-the-behavior-change-toolkit-designing-and-testing-a-nudge-and-a-boost

140. OFCOM, Boosting users' safety online: Microtutorials. 2023 [Accessed 19 October 2023]; Available from: www.ofcom.org.uk/research-and-data/behavioural-insights/boosting-users-safety-online-microtutorials

141. Sims, A. and T.M. Müller, Nudge versus boost: A distinction without a normative difference. *Economics & Philosophy*, 2019. 35(2): p. 195–222.

142. Grüne-Yanoff, T. and R. Hertwig, Nudge versus boost: How coherent are policy and theory? *Minds and Machines*, 2016. 26(1): p. 149–183.

143. van Roekel, H., J. Reinhard, and S. Grimmelikhuijsen, Improving hand hygiene in hospitals: Comparing the effect of a nudge and a boost on protocol compliance. *Behavioural Public Policy*, 2021. 6(1): p. 52–74.

144. Hertwig, R. and M.D. Ryall, Nudge versus boost: Agency dynamics under libertarian paternalism. *The Economic Journal*, 2020. 130(629): p. 1384–1415.

145. Grüne-Yanoff, T., C. Marchionni, and M.A. Feufel, Toward a framework for selecting behavioural policies: How to choose between boosts and nudges. *Economics & Philosophy*, 2018. 34(2): p. 243–266.

146. Kahneman, D. and S. Frederick, Representativeness revisited: Attribute substitution in intuitive judgment. *Heuristics and Biases: The Psychology of Intuitive Judgment*, 2002. 49: p. 81.

147. Franssens, S. and W. De Neys, The effortless nature of conflict detection during thinking. *Thinking & Reasoning*, 2009. 15(2): p. 105–128.

148. Hayes, A., *Poisson distribution formula and meaning in finance*. 2022 [Accessed 26 December 2022]; Available from: www.investopedia.com/terms/p/poisson-distribut ion.asp

149. Grüne-Yanoff, T., Boosts vs. nudges from a welfarist perspective. *Revue d'économie politique*, 2018. 128(2): p. 209–224.

150. Thiel, C.E., et al., Stripped of agency: The paradoxical effect of employee monitoring on deviance. *Journal of Management*, 2021. 49(2): p. 709–740.

151. Wittenbraker, J. and V. Venkatraman, *Ipsos dynamic decision making model*. Scientific Report. 2019: Global Science Organization.

152. Nicks, G. and Y. Carriou, Emotion, attention and memory in advertising. *IPSOS Connect*, 2016: p. 1–12.

153. Frank, M.J., M.X. Cohen, and A.G. Sanfey, Multiple systems in decision making: A neurocomputational perspective. *Current Directions in Psychological Science*, 2009. 18(2): p. 73–77.

154. Sunstein, C.R., The ethics of nudging. *Yale Journal on Regulation*, 2015. 32: p. 413.

155. Topham, G., *Train firm's "worker bonus" email is actually cybersecurity test*. 2021 [Accessed 17 February 2022]; Available from: www.theguardian.com/uk-news/2021/ may/10/train-firms-worker-bonus-email-is-actually-cyber-security-test

156. Kate_R., *The trouble with phishing*. 2018 [Accessed 11 January 2023]; Available from: www.ncsc.gov.uk/blog-post/trouble-phishing

157. Hirsh, J.B., S.K. Kang, and G.V. Bodenhausen, Personalized persuasion: Tailoring persuasive appeals to recipients' personality traits. *Psychological Science*, 2012. 23(6): p. 578–581.

158. Peer, E., et al., Nudge me right: Personalizing online security nudges to people's decision-making styles. *Computers in Human Behavior*, 2020. 109: p. 106347.

159. Mills, S., *The future of nudging will be personal*. [Accessed 10 April 2021]; Available from: https://behavioralscientist.org/the-future-of-nudging-will-be-personal

160. Egelman, S. and E. Peer., The myth of the average user: Improving privacy and security systems through individualization. In *Proceedings of the 2015 New Security Paradigms Workshop*. 2015.

161. TechCrunch., *5 Design Tricks Facebook Uses to Affect Your Privacy Decisions*. 2012 [Accessed 10 April 2021]; Available from: https://techcrunch.com/2012/08/25/5-des ign-tricks-facebook-uses-to-affect-your-privacy-decisions

162. Ahmad, F., et al., A deep learning architecture for psychometric natural language processing. *ACM Transactions on Information Systems (TOIS)*, 2020. 38(1): p. 1–29.

163. Azucar, D., D. Marengo, and M. Settanni, Predicting the Big 5 personality traits from digital footprints on social media: A meta-analysis. *Personality and Individual Differences*, 2018. 124: p. 150–159.

164. Qu, L., R. Xiao, and W. Shi, Towards practical personalized security nudge schemes: Investigating the moderation effects of behavioral features on nudge effects. In *International Conference on Science of Cyber Security*. 2022. Springer.

165. Khan, I.A., et al. Measuring personality from keyboard and mouse use. In *Proceedings of the 15th European Conference on Cognitive Ergonomics: The Ergonomics of Cool Interaction*. 2008.

166. Stachl, C., et al., Predicting personality from patterns of behavior collected with smartphones. *Proceedings of the National Academy of Sciences*, 2020. 117(30): p. 17680–17687.

167. Qu, L., et al., Design and evaluation of CFC-targeted security nudges. In *Extended abstracts of the 2021 CHI Conference on Human Factors in Computing Systems*. 2021.

168. Galič, M., T. Timan, and B.-J. Koops, Bentham, Deleuze and beyond: An overview of surveillance theories from the panopticon to participation. *Philosophy & Technology*, 2017. 30(1): p. 9–37.

169. DeWinter, J., C.A. Kocurek, and R. Nichols, Taylorism 2.0: Gamification, scientific management and the capitalist appropriation of play. *Journal of Gaming & Virtual Worlds*, 2014. 6(2): p. 109–127.

170. Mitchell, G., Libertarian paternalism is an oxymoron. *Northwestern University Law Review*, 2004. 99: p. 1245.

171 Sunstein, C.R. and R.H. Thaler, Libertarian paternalism is not an oxymoron. *University of Chicago Law Review*, 2003. 1 October: p. 1159–1202.

172. Lee, D., H.S. Lallie, and N. Michaelides, The impact of an employee's psychological contract breach on compliance with information security policies: Intrinsic and extrinsic motivation. *Cognition, Technology & Work*, 2023: p. 1–17.

173. Ip, G., *Foolproof: Why safety can be dangerous and how danger makes us safe*. 2015: Hachette UK.

174. Renaud, K. and V. Zimmermann, Ethical guidelines for nudging in information security & privacy. *International Journal of Human-Computer Studies*, 2018. 120: p. 22–35.

175. Schmidt, A.T. and B. Engelen, The ethics of nudging: An overview. *Philosophy Compass*, 2020. 15(4): p. e12658.

176. Tolah, A., S. Furnell, and M. Papadaki, A comprehensive framework for cultivating and assessing information security culture. In *HAISA*. 2017.

177. Alnatheer, M.A., Information security culture critical success factors. In *2015 12th International Conference on Information Technology – New Generations*. 2015. IEEE.

178. Zimmermann, V. and K. Renaud, Moving from a "human-as-problem" to a "human-as-solution" cybersecurity mindset. *International Journal of Human-Computer Studies*, 2019. 131: p. 169–187.

3 If Only Users Would "Get It"

WHY WON'T THEY LISTEN?

USERS...

Practitioners tend to be puzzled when users don't behave in line with expectations. Surely if people are given a logical argument and shown the importance of security, then that will shape their behaviour? The counter-argument from Herley [1] is that the behaviour of users is perfectly rational; they reject security advice because it burdens them with additional effort for no apparent benefit.

The usual reaction from the security community is to add in more restrictive technology (thereby increasing the burden on the user) and in parallel, to "educate" the user through mandatory training. Typically, the approach is based on a model of knowledge, attitudes and behaviours. If I give you some new knowledge, that will change your attitudes, which will in turn affect your behaviour [2]. Bearing in mind the preceding discussions, there are probably two key questions to ask of this approach: first, how are we doing in terms of getting knowledge across to people; and second, what effect is that having on their behaviour?

COMMUNICATION

Lacey and Stewart [3] describe traditional security awareness courses as a "*broadcast of facts*", usually from individuals selected for their technical skills rather than their expertise in communication.

You can see the outcome in the qualitative study by Reeves et al. [4], which provides a number of interview responses from users:

Get a red-hot poker and open up my eyes, it's so boring.
I think it could be a little bit of our IT is a bit... anal retentive? Obsessed? Sometimes you look at them like... calm down just a touch!.
I don't think the people who build most of this training really have a good understanding of how to build something that people would be happy to sit through, people just think it's a chore.

 DOI: 10.1201/9781003380962-3

Stanton et al. [5] use the term "security fatigue" to describe the disengagement caused when security training comes across as vague, inconsistent and contradictory:

This weariness often manifests as resignation or a loss of control in people's responses to online security. People are told they need to be constantly on alert, constantly "doing something", but they are not even sure what that something is or what might happen if they do or do not do it.

D'Arcy et al. [6] suggest that *"burdensome, complex, and ambiguous information security requirements"* lead to a kind of moral disengagement on the part of users.

Renaud et al. [7] looked into the emotions that people felt when asked about security, and perhaps not surprisingly, found the responses to be generally negative. Reeves et al. found the same picture [8] and suggested that when users don't act in the ways expected by practitioners, it might be more productive to look at the causes of the reaction, rather than to schedule more training [9], since it's perhaps the nature of the training itself that's driving the disengagement [10].

In the early 1960s, the US brewing company Anheuser-Busch conducted a number of experiments examining the effectiveness of their advertising budget [11]. Initial trials indicated that increased marketing effort didn't necessarily lead to increased sales. Based on this and prior findings, the researchers postulated that there might be two peaks of effectiveness – one at a relatively low level of advertising (about 50% of the then-current spend), and one slightly higher (about 50% more than the existing spend). So they gradually reduced the expenditure on communication, moving the sales outcome into the first (less expensive) peak of effectiveness. The company reached a position in which [11, p502]:

Advertising expenditure per barrel was $0.80 in contrast to $1.89 which it had been when the research was initiated... [d]uring this period (1962–68) sales of BUDWEISER increased from approximately 7.5 million to 14.5 million barrels, and its market share increased from 8.14 to 12.94 percent.

The first point to note is that the work wasn't aimed at improving awareness of the brand. It measured the only thing that mattered – the outcome.

Second, as a result of these findings, the advertising companies involved were weaned off a deal whereby they were paid according to the extent of their advertising and moved across onto a deal where they were paid according to the impact of their advertising on sales. That is, the people claiming to deliver on all this expenditure were judged by their results rather than by their actions.

The researchers went on to show that it was possible to pulse the advertising to get a similar result i.e. rather than having a continuous message selling the product, they found that switching the message off for a while seemed to improve sales. People were perhaps becoming habituated to the message when it was on continuously, whereas seeing it disappear and then re-appear seemed to get their attention.

There's a really useful source called the Advertising Concept Book [12] that picks out the factors and approaches that make advertising campaigns effective. The book presents and analyses a number of successful campaigns and provides hints and suggestions for achieving similar outcomes. There's ample evidence for example [13–17] that words are processed by the brain more slowly than images (we've been processing images for much longer) and that images are not only processed much more quickly, but also processed more extensively. So when posters have a single, simple message conveyed in a graphic, with a single congruent message in the supporting text, the message from the text arrives just after the processed message from the graphic, and supports it, so you get more effective communication.

These are established concepts, ones that have been shown to work. And yet having seen what's on offer for security awareness campaigns, it's clear that talking cartoon dogs are a "must have" item. Even the more earnest attempts crowd as much text as possible onto the page, as though the objective were simply to make information available, rather than to achieve communication.

IMPACT ON BEHAVIOURS

Field experiments indicate that raising people's awareness of social engineering seems to have only a short-term effect on susceptibility [18], and that under some circumstances, making people aware of the risks actually increases their willingness to part with information [19].

Worse, Sawaya et al. [20] found that, in their words, *"confidence trumps knowledge"* i.e. what people thought they know about security seemed to affect their behaviour to a greater degree than their actual level of knowledge.

Making people aware of possible sanctions may not work either. D'Arcy and Herath [21] found *"... an uneven and often contradictory picture regarding the influence of sanctions and deterrence theory in general in the IS security context"*. That is, they found no simple link between the severity of threatened punishment, and the level of compliance with security instructions.

In fact, in related research, Herath and Rao [22] found that:

Certainty of detection was found to be significant while surprisingly, severity of punishment was found to have a negative effect on security behavior intentions... further research may be needed to evaluate the role of penalty and reward systems in shaping information security behaviors.

Essentially, if the level of punishment is perceived as being disproportionate to the crime, then people's willingness to comply with the rules can actually be *reduced.*

A report in 2014 by Bada and Sasse [23], quoting an ISF survey [24] listed six high-level reasons why security awareness campaigns fail to change behaviour:

1. Solutions are not aligned to business risks.
2. Neither progress nor values are measured.
3. Incorrect assumptions are made about people and their motivations.
4. Unrealistic expectations are set.
5. The correct skills are not deployed.
6. Awareness is just background noise.

Others have seen similar results [25]. More worryingly, the report implied that the knowledge/attitude/behaviours chain might not actually hold up in practice:

People know the answer to awareness questions, but they do not act accordingly [in] real life... simple transfer of knowledge about good practices in security is far from enough.

Behaviours amongst the very people that expect awareness training to work on others indicate that it doesn't even work on them, according to a survey conducted by Symantec amongst information security professionals [26]. Their study found "*a huge disconnect between belief and action*". To quote the report:

The vast majority of users expressed concern over personal information disclosure. However, the actions taken (or more frequently) not taken show a massive disregard for these concerns... [it] is not possible to attribute this disconnect to technological naiveté.

Barth and de Jong investigated attitudes to mobile phone security amongst "privacy and cybersecurity experts" and found that: "*[o]ur results not only show that experts appear to behave online as unsafely as lay users; the arguments they provide to justify their risky online behaviors are comparable to those of lay users*" [27, p9] and that "*[d]espite their technical knowledge, results showed that the experts' perceptions and reported behaviors resembled those of lay users*" [27, p1].

In related work which looked at actual behaviours, the results suggested that "*... neither technical knowledge and privacy awareness nor financial considerations affect the paradoxical behavior observed in users in general. Technically-skilled and financially independent users risked potential privacy intrusions despite their awareness of potential risks*" [28, p1].

Security literate and technically aware individuals have also been shown to pick up and use USB sticks found in the street [29], despite the fact that widely publicised attacks such as Stuxnet [30] are known to have relied upon exactly that behaviour to propagate.

To be clear, the people displaying these behaviours are security practitioners. The same people actively promoting awareness as a means of improving cyber security.

CONCLUSIONS

In terms of reaching a point where users "get it", security awareness campaigns as currently formulated don't, and maybe can't work. There are a number of ways of presenting the reasons why not, but for me the key issues are (a) a lacklustre approach to delivery and (b) unchallenged assumptions concerning the role of awareness.

None of which will come as news, especially if you've experienced a typical security awareness course. But it does beg the question: if this is a known failing, why hasn't the industry done anything about it? Over the years, these issues ought to have been acknowledged and addressed. It's been long enough. But here we are, with the same approach and the same, widely recognised failings. In fact, in 2020, Van Steen et al. [31] reviewed a number of cyber awareness initiatives, all of which assumed by default that increased awareness would lead to changed behaviours – yet none of the schemes looked for post-hoc changes in behaviour, i.e. none of them checked to see if their assumption was correct.

The fact that very few people look to see whether or not awareness training has been effective is a clear sign that it doesn't matter if it's been effective. The only thing that matters is that the training has been conducted. Why?

Security awareness training isn't really about changing security behaviours. It's to do with legitimisation. Enforcing control. Putting the security team in a position where they can say "you were told". On that basis, it's working just fine. Well... except that it's masquerading as a means of changing security behaviours. And the fact that the organisation employing the security team might want to see some return on the money they're putting in.

There are approaches that might be more effective in changing behaviours, but the industry doesn't seem interested. We saw earlier that nudges could be used to exploit the gut feel decision stage, that debiasing could act to reduce the level of irrationality at the point of the decision, and that boosts, if they work, could add new rules of thumb into the decision. But as far as I can see [32, 33], none of those approaches have been integrated into mainstream security practice. My strong suspicion is that because they're not about enforcing control, they're not seen as relevant.

It's hard not to draw the conclusion that security awareness training as currently practised isn't seen by the cyber community as a failure. It's achieving the aims required of it. It doesn't need fixing.

EXAMPLE

In his book "Influence: The Psychology of Persuasion", Robert Cialdini identifies six techniques of persuasion [34]. To be fair, a seventh "Unity" has since been added [35], but the original six still provide a sound basis:

- **Scarcity.** If we think (or can be made to think) that a resource is in short supply, then we tend to value it more highly. Supermarkets putting up signs saying "no more than two per customer" is an example.
- **Social proof.** What are other people doing? You can see this in newspaper stories about crowds walking over collapsed shoppers to get to the bargains in sales. It's ok for me to do it, because other people have done it. Nobody likes to stand out. I'm sure he'll be fine.
- **Reciprocity.** If someone does something for you, especially if unasked, it's almost impossible to resist when they ask for the favour to be returned. In a social and evolutionary context that makes perfect sense. In the context of free taster samples given out in a supermarket, maybe not so much.
- **Authority.** People dressed as authority figures tend to have a significant influence on our decisions – we tend to obey even if reluctantly. Milgram's experiments and their more recent near-replications [36–38] provide the standard (and literally shocking) example.
- **Commitment and consistency.** We feel more comfortable when we think that we're being consistent with our previous behaviour.
- **Liking.** People whom we like are able to exert a significant degree of influence over our decisions, possibly because it's important for us to have the relationship intact even after the decision.

These principles have been used successfully to affect decisions in a variety of settings, most significantly in retail [39]. But are they relevant to security?

As it turns out they are – the content of phishing emails has been analysed using the same framework, by e.g. Parsons et al. [40]. Top of the list in most phishing emails is authority ("you have to do as I say"), but as Akbar shows, it's not necessarily used on its own [41, Table 14]. In much the same way as a supermarket wouldn't rely on just free samples to drive sales, phishing sources also use "mix and match". So you see other techniques being used e.g. social proof ("other people are doing this") and scarcity ("act immediately to prevent further losses"). The blend of techniques has been shown to vary by market sector, in that the balance of messages used in phishing emails (the "sales mix") is often adjusted according to the target audience [41, Table 31]. Phishing emails aimed at Government employees, for example, don't tend to use reciprocity ("I've done something nice for you, now do something nice for me"), and they don't tend to use social proof ("your peers are doing this"). Instead, they tend to rely primarily upon authority ("I'm in a position to tell you to do this").

Cialdini's principles are sometimes used in combination with other approaches when analysing phishing emails [42] but on balance, given the evidence that crops up in pretty much every security breach survey e.g. [43], they do seem to be relevant [44, p227]. They've also been shown to be central to other forms of social engineering [45–48]. Essentially, cybercriminals employ these techniques in a sophisticated way, and to great effect. They seem to work. But those same principles have yet to be adopted by the cyber industry as a means of changing security behaviours for the better. The attempts that have been made seem to have used social proof with a very simple message (as in "you're friends are doing security, you should too"), with perhaps predictably mixed results [33, 49]. Again, it's hard to avoid the conclusion that awareness training isn't really about improving security.

This need for control seems to come from an argument that non-compliance with security rules can be equated with non-compliance with society's rules. By taking on the role of security lawmakers, the cyber team can claim the right to define what non-compliance looks like, and hence claim the right to take whatever steps are necessary to make people more "honest".

APPLYING BEHAVIOURAL SCIENCE

ENCOURAGING HONESTY

Daniel Ariely's 2012 book "The (Honest) Truth About Dishonesty" [50] identified a set of drivers for dishonest behaviour, and a corresponding set of techniques for improving the level of honesty in people's decision-making [51]. The book was based on the results of field experiments and suggested that dishonesty is driven by a number of factors such as conflicts of interest, our physical state (if we're tired, then we find it harder to resist being dishonest), and whether or not we feel that someone will benefit from our actions.

However, some of the central findings in the research have since been re-examined using more powerful experimental procedures, and the effect sizes found in the replications are turning out to be much smaller than those that were originally reported. Specifically, the impact of moral reminders [52], the use of pledges [53], and the effect of ego depletion [54], each of which has been proposed as a way of increasing honest behaviour, have all since been challenged [55]. There has been a successful replication showing that people will return money given to them by mistake, providing the value is over a certain threshold [56]. There's also evidence [57, 58] that the emotional centre of the brain shows reducing levels of activity when individuals perform serial acts of dishonesty (i.e. one bit of dishonest behaviour does seem to facilitate another). Gneezy et al. [59] also found Ariely's idea of a "social self" to be relevant, in that participants seemed to be less willing to cheat when they thought that others might think less of them. That aligns with the findings from one replication, possibly two [60], although it contradicts the findings of at least one other.

In 2015, Ariely and colleagues suggested a reduced framework of just three principles. The framework was called REVISE [61]. It was based on the principles of moral **RE**minders, **VI**sibility, and **SE**lf-engagement. The framework has been subjected to a conceptual replication by Schild et al. [62] in which participants were asked to manually type in a promise to be honest, before then being given a chance to cheat and obtain more rewards than they should have been given. The replication also looked at combinations such as RE+VI, RE+SE, and all three principles combined. The results showed little evidence for the idea of moral reminders, but there was support for the effect of visibility (whether or not your dishonest actions are visible to others). There was also a small and separate effect seen from encouraging self-engagement (asking people to reflect on what they're doing). However, combining all three elements seemed to have less of an effect than applying individual components.

So even if you could equate cyber rule-breaking with dishonesty, there are no simple answers; this is a complex picture. The one thing that we can be relatively sure of is that letting people know that their actions are visible to others tends to reduce levels of dishonesty. Herath and Rao also reported changes in behaviour when people thought they might be called out for their actions. Burnett [63, p233] provides further evidence, in that just the anticipation of guilt may be sufficient to change behaviours. The corollary being that when we're *not* being watched, we must have some way of dealing with those guilty feelings.

Neutralisations

In the 1950s, Sykes and Matza [64] were looking into how people could knowingly break society's rules but, at the same time, acknowledge that the rules were important, and that they personally believed in the value of those rules.

Sykes and Matza proposed the idea of a neutralisation – an excuse we make for ourselves when we're knowingly non-compliant with a rule that we believe in. Their original paper identified five scenarios:

- Denial of injury ("no-one was hurt").
- Denial of responsibility ("it wasn't my choice").
- Denial of the victim ("they deserved it").
- Condemnation of the condemners ("you're picking on me").
- Appeal to higher loyalties ("there was a bigger issue at stake").

Since then, the number of proposed neutralisations has been extended, and further research has been carried out into the underlying theory [65–72]. Siponen and Vance in particular [73] looked into the application of neutralisations in the context of information security and found that by hinting at a specific neutralisation (e.g. defence of necessity – "maybe you had to break the security rules to get the job done?"), people were more than happy to take that as an excuse for their behaviour. Offering the neutralisation provided a way out, and as a consequence people were more likely to be non-compliant. Barlow and Warkentin [74] tried the reverse – they used messages designed to suppress the use of neutralisations and found their messaging resulted in increased levels of compliance.

Suppressing the use of neutralisations is at the heart of the cyber community's approach. If the cyber team can prevent users from making excuses for their non-compliance, then, by definition, those users will be more compliant. That's what awareness courses are aimed at – "you were told". No excuses. The use of "fear appeals" has been reviewed as a means of getting users to toe the line [75], but in truth, it's much more about applying guilt.

SECURITY DECISION-MAKING

COMING TO TERMS WITH OUR DECISIONS

When we're asked to make an actual decision, why does the outcome differ from the answer we give when we're asked to imagine ourselves in the same situation? Some of that is due to "social desirability bias" – we tend to give answers that we think the questioner wants to hear [76]. But a lot of it may be to do with the decision-making process itself.

There's a commonly used model of consumer decision-making [77] that divides the process into five sequential stages:

1. **Need recognition.** When I go out in the rain, my feet get wet. Clearly, what I need right now is a new pair of shoes.
2. **Search.** What shoes are available? Seems like my choice is limited to either open-toed sandals or hiking boots.
3. **Comparison.** Using some criteria or other (aesthetics, price, the weather forecast), I compare the options.
4. I make my **decision**.
5. **Rationalisation.** I explain the decision to myself, so that I feel it was the right choice. I hate feeling that I've made a bad decision.

As we progress through the stages, the degree of irrationality is imagined to rise, until it reaches a peak in the decision itself, so that by default we make the decision mostly on "gut feel". The fifth and final stage allows us to take a result driven primarily by instinct and explain it to ourselves, so that we feel as though we'd been thinking rationally all along.

For example, the need for a new pair of shoes is likely to be based on logic – your feet get wet when it's raining. The search for alternatives is also likely to be carried out rationally – you look in a shoe shop. But when we start to compare options, it all gets a bit shaky. Suppose the two options are hiking boots and open-toed sandals. As you approach the decision itself, the lure of open-toed sandals, worn with dark woollen socks and knee-length shorts, starts to make its presence felt. That's a good look. Very few people could carry that look, but I could... and before you know it, you've left the hiking boots on the shelf, and you're headed home with a pair of sandals.

But then you get home. And you realise your feet are still going to get wet. But actually that's ok – it's nearly Summer, and the sandals will be so much more comfortable than those big boots. Also, they were cheaper. Good call.

That uncomfortable feeling you experienced when you got home and opened the box is generally referred to as cognitive dissonance, and luckily for us, we're very good at handling it. And we need to be. Because as summarised by Feddersen [78], "*no rationalisation, no decision*".

THE ROLE OF EMOTION

It might seem odd to state that decision-making seems to be quite so capricious. However, the reality is that while emotion may not dominate, it does seem to occupy a necessary role.

Mandel and Vartanian [79] found that the strategy adopted for decision-making was dependent on the way in which the question had been framed. Crucially, they also offered evidence that the integration of emotional cues was a key component of the decision-making process, possibly through the attachment of an emotional weighting to each option. Ip [80, p158] and Gupta [81] cite a number of results suggesting that when the emotional centres of the brain are damaged, people find it difficult to make appropriate decisions. Bechara [82] summarises the evidence, saying that "... *decision making is a process critically dependent on neural systems important for the processing of emotions*".

SECURITY DECISIONS

It should come as no surprise that similar issues were found in an experiment on email classification tasks. In terms of sequencing, the first stage of need recognition doesn't really apply, but to quote Janis and Mann [83], "*we are reluctant decision-makers*". So the first stage can be replaced by something like "ownership" in which we think about the problem and then accept that we have to make the decision. Other than that, the process seemed to proceeds as per the case of consumer decision-making (see Figure 3.1).

The nudges applied in the experiment were intended to reduce error rates in security decisions e.g. "is this an appropriate sensitivity marking for the email, given the content?" and "what sensitivity marking should this email have on it?". The aim of the intervention being to prompt more rational consideration of the problem.

Instead, the nudge seemed to reduce the overall time needed to make a choice, although the decisions themselves were to all intents and purposes the same as those

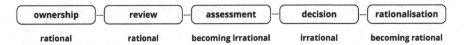

FIGURE 3.1   Decision-Making model. (Leapfrog Creative Ltd, reproduced with permission.)

made by the individuals in the "no-nudge" group. That is, the nudge reduced processing times, but it had no effect on error rate. A feasible explanation being that the post-decision rationalisation phase was being shortened – the nudge seemed to be making it easier for people to "forgive" themselves for their gut feel decision. But since that took place after the decision, it didn't affect their choice.

Interestingly however, the error rates for emails that needed to be downgraded (i.e. the sensitivity marking was too high) were three times the corresponding rates for emails that should have had their marking increased. The significance of that is that on occasion, we look ahead to predict whether or not we might feel uncomfortable having taken our preferred option [84, 85]. In consumer decision-making, that's referred to as "anticipatory regret". In this case, it would map to something like "if I reduce the sensitivity marking on this email, I might regret it, but if I leave it alone it's not my fault if it's wrong".

To be clear, this was one experiment conducted at one point in time, involving one group of people. It constitutes potential evidence, it's not a fact. Nonetheless it does point to the idea that we want to feel comfortable about our security decisions, and it suggests that the process of excusing our behaviour can be made easier. By implication, it can therefore also be made harder.

NAMING AND SHAMING

BACKGROUND

There's evidence both for and against [67], but neutralisations seem to be applied after the decision has been made. On that basis, suppression probably works by interfering with the process of post-decision rationalisation, perhaps by attaching a negative emotional label to one or more options, so that if we look ahead, we associate a guilty feeling with those options, and therefore rate them less favourably.

In other areas, this effect has been achieved through posters with images of staring eyes, with some form of admonition underneath. The idea being to convince the viewer that someone is watching their behaviour (and being very disappointed with it), in the expectation that feelings of guilt will reduce the likelihood of the individual engaging in the unwanted action [86]. An example from an intervention designed to deter bicycle theft is reproduced below (see Figure 3.2).

This technique has been used in other areas of crime reduction, such as deterring pet owners from leaving dog poo in alleyways [87], to reduce levels of bicycle theft as noted above [88, 89], to reduce the incidence of littering [90], and to discourage drink-driving [91]. Readers may also recall the use of the same technique to encourage compliant behaviour during the pandemic [92].

FIGURE 3.2   Cycle Theft poster. (Nettle et al. [89]. Reproduced under the Creative Commons Attribution License.)

It's also been used in cases of suspected rather than actual crime. Most supermarkets now have forward-facing cameras and screens on their self-checkout (SCO) terminals. You can see you're being monitored as you're scanning the things you want to buy. In effect, you're presented with a message saying "we have eyes on you – we know you're a thief – we just haven't caught you stealing anything yet". Looking at the problem in isolation, that makes sense. The business needs to reduce theft, and if increasing discomfort amongst potential shoplifters does that, then where's the problem? Well, the problem is that the measure is indiscriminate. Honest shoppers are presented with the same message. The reaction from (presumably honest) customers has been predictable – I'm making profits for you, I'm doing the work of your staff for nothing, and at the precise point of my doing so, you're calling my honesty into doubt [93, 94].

The same technique has been applied in cases where they may have been no actual crime at all. There's a well-known intention/behaviour gap when it comes to buying Free Trade products, for example, in which stated beliefs don't always get translated into actual sales [95, 96]. Working on the principle of anticipated guilt [97], Lindenmeier et al. [98] nonetheless successfully increased sales of those products, by using guilt-inducing nudges, which suggested to consumers that they would feel bad as they walked out of the shop carrying the cheaper, non-Free Trade option.

And inevitably, it has been used in security. As far back as 2009, Boss et al. [99] suggested that users could be made more compliant with security guidance if they could be convinced that the issued guidance was mandatory, and that therefore close monitoring of their behaviour was a legitimate action. To quote from the abstract: "... *if individuals believe that management watches, they will comply*".

So yes, it's possible to exploit feelings of guilt, in order to improve levels of compliance [100]. But on the examples quoted, that doesn't come for free.

The replication experiment conducted by Schild et al. [62] on the REVISE model operationalised the "visibility" construct by creating a situation in which participants might reasonably assume that the experimenter had access to the same information as them and would therefore be able to detect acts of dishonesty. In an office environment, those circumstances would translate into an atmosphere in which everybody believed that their every action was open to being monitored, i.e. everyone in the office has a set of eyes on them, all the time. It's perhaps worth noting that Posey et al. [101] found that levels of monitoring perceived to be excessive created a feeling of social injustice, which in turn led to higher levels of unwanted behaviour. Essentially, if I feel that my integrity is being unfairly called into doubt, then I'm going to be less inclined to follow the security guidance [102]. I might even be inclined to break it [103]. In this respect, cyber isn't a "special case". Ravid et al. [104] looked into the effectiveness of code monitoring of employee performance using Electronic Performance Management (EPM), concluding that:

[r]esults provide no evidence that EPM improves worker performance. Moreover, findings indicate that the presence of EPM increases worker stress and strain, regardless of the characteristics of monitoring. Findings also demonstrate that organizations that monitor more transparently and less invasively can expect more positive attitudes from workers.

More recently, Siponen et al. [105] took counter-neutralisations as the basis for an intervention to improve password creation and management. Their experiment deliberately invoked cognitive dissonance amongst users, by challenging their use of neutralisations in direct, face-to-face meetings. Compared with a group that did not go through this treatment, those that did expressed a lower level of intention to contravene password guidance, both immediately after the session, and also three weeks later. On the face of it, that seems like a good result. However, setting aside the fact that as with many papers on neutralisations, the experiment drew on self-reported intentions rather than actual behaviour, and admittedly on a purely personal note, I think there are some wider issues that need to be thought through. While it's not universal, the introductory text for most reports on neutralisations tends to frame them as excuses for law-breaking. The paper under discussion, for example, cites evidence of neutralisations being applied to deer poaching, hate crimes, rule-breaking in military environments, drug use, corporate crime, and workplace theft, and then extends the list to cyberloafing (i.e. wasting company time online). The implication seems to be that non-compliance with security rules is on a par with criminal activity, and that consequently, any means of reducing non-compliance is justifiable. And further, that any organisational costs arising from reducing non-compliance simply have to be accepted.

Neocleous [106, p124 et seq.] uses the growth of McCarthyism to illustrate shifts in attitudes over time: from the possibility of large numbers of US citizens being communists, to the possibility that just one dissident could bring down the entire nation; from the idea of individuals asserting loyalty, to the requirement for them to refute disloyalty; from the idea of "reasonable grounds" to the concept of "reasonable doubt". That is, a shift from searching for evidence of positive behaviours to considering simply the possibility of misbehaviour. All of which was conducted in the name of improving security through driving increased levels of compliance.

Demonstrable compliance with security guidance it seems, is a goal that has to be achieved at any price. Consequently, it's perfectly reasonable to treat users as criminals who just haven't been caught yet. Drawing a parallel between security non-compliance and law-breaking has allowed cyber practitioners to legitimise the exercise of control, and at the same time, to excuse any subsequent costs to the organisation.

Security activities, and awareness training in particular, are conducted within a wider business environment, and within a wider social environment. They are not conducted in isolation. Cyber practitioners generally pay lip service to the idea that security should align with business interests, but when it comes down to it, it's not the security team that sees the downsides. My local supermarket chain, for example, spends millions on PR each year, trying to get across the idea that they're compassionate retailers, in the hope of engendering goodwill across their client base. A default assumption of criminality, publicised through the use of technology, is clearly at odds with that message. But on the other hand, the security team doesn't do PR. That's not our job. Someone else does that.

I-FRAMES VS S-FRAMES

BACKGROUND

Chater and Lowenstein [107] suggest that societal problems can be framed in one of two ways: as a matter relating to individual behaviour (the "i-frame"), or as a problem relating to wider systemic issues (the "s-frame"). As described in their paper, the opioid abuse problem in the United States, for example, can be seen either as a matter of individual behaviour (people recklessly abusing prescription painkillers) or as a systemic problem (the over-prescribing of very strong painkillers, thereby leading to addiction). Chater and Lowenstein argue that in many instances, what has been presented as an i-frame problem, to be solved through the application of behavioural science, might perhaps be more effectively addressed through an s-frame solution. They point out, for example, that other nations such as Germany did not go along with pharmaceutical industry pressure to adopt drugs such as OxyContin on a wide basis and hence managed to avoid the addiction problem, at least on the same scale as in the United States, largely because in Europe the "rules of the game" are different – there is less financial incentive for practitioners to issue prescriptions [108]. A central point in the paper is that where there is a strong commercial vested interest, i-framing is often used by industries as a tactic to avoid changing their economic model. In the case of opioids, one solution would have been to reduce the scale on which painkillers were being prescribed. That, however, would have affected the pharmaceutical industry's profits (sales of OxyContin in 2000 stood at about US$1Bn [109]). Consequently, the industry reframed the problem as an issue of personal responsibility. The paper quotes the head of the pharmaceutical company at the centre of the debate [107, p25] seeking to portray addiction victims as weak-willed: *"[w]e have to hammer on the abusers in every way possible. They are the culprits and the problem. They are reckless criminals"*. Other studies (funded by the pharmaceutical industry) claimed that in fact only 1% of patients became addicted, and suggested that patients suffering from withdrawal symptoms were actually being under-prescribed [107, p25], i.e. they were suffering these symptoms because they were not being given *enough* opioids.

Chater and Lowenstein cite President Obama's comments [107, p22] on the difficulty of systemic reform in the face of extensive industry lobbying:

> *Unlike the insurance companies or Big Pharma, whose shareholders expected them to be on guard against any change that might cost them a dime, most of the potential beneficiaries of reform – the waitress, the family farmer, the independent contractor, the cancer survivor – didn't have gaggles of well-paid and experienced lobbyists roaming the halls of Congress.*

Their paper argues that although well-intentioned, the use of behavioural science has implicitly supported the use of i-framing by industries intent on maintaining profits. The authors suggest that [107, p5] *"corporations consistently cast societal problems as issues of individual weakness and responsibility, the solutions to which involve 'fixing' individual behavior"*. In doing so, those industries deflect attention away from the idea that their own actions might be in need of reform. The paper suggests a number of examples: the opioid problem as discussed above; the debate on climate change, reframed away from institutional reform of the petroleum giants, and focused instead on personal behaviour; smoking and the tobacco lobby; obesity and the sugar industry; pension savings; healthcare; and plastic bag recycling. On plastic bag recycling, specifically, the authors point out that the movement was *started* by the packaging industry in order to establish it as an i-frame issue, and that one effect of charging for single-use bags has been to drive up the overall use of plastic, as consumers buy more bin bags to meet a role that the single-use bag used to fill [107, p19].

Building on previous work [110], the authors propose that behavioural science, rather than being used as a means of solving i-framed questions, should instead be used as a means of informing s-framed solutions. That is, a knowledge of human behaviour should be used to find ways in which the wider, underlying issues might be addressed.

In line with previous reviews, the paper quotes studies such as Della Vigna and Linos [111], who found that while laboratory results show relatively large effect sizes for nudging (around 9%), practical applications tend to show much smaller effects (around 1.4%). The primary reason for the discrepancy, as noted by e.g. Mertens et al. [112] and also by Ritchie [113] being "publication bias" – the tendency for journals to only publish attention-grabbing results. That doesn't mean that the nudge isn't worth applying, just that it shouldn't be seen as "the answer", and that it should perhaps be combined with other, system-level measures [107, p10]. The use of economic disincentives, combined with behavioural pressure for example, is quoted as having been highly successful in the case of anti-smoking campaigns [107, p26].

The paper also makes a strong point that [107, p32]:

Designing policy around the consumer can frequently make the difference between success and failure, and policy design should be guided primarily by behavioral insights. Policy, like any complex good or service, is best designed by multidisciplinary teams, with subject experts, designers, user-experience specialists, ethnographers, anthropologists, and psychologists, alongside behavioral insights specialists.

In the words of the paper, perhaps it's time to rethink some policy assumptions [107, p9]. This might sound odd, but here goes. Rather than concentrating on the individual, a more enlightened approach to security behaviour change might be to look at the problem in the round, taking into account the context for cyber.

That is, to view security behaviours as a systems issue, rather an issue of control.

APPLICATION

Practitioners like to claim that security and usability are compatible. What they really mean is that the technology is going in, whether the users like it or not. That kind of thinking is more about redefining usability, rather than achieving any kind of balance. Instead, when deciding on the implementation of a particular security technology, it might be worth asking: "in reality, is this technology likely to drive users to engage in workarounds?". In which case, in a practical sense, is it actually going to improve the situation?

Similarly, it might be worth asking whether the technology is going to shield the user to such a degree that they will assume that the system "has their back". That is, whether or not the interaction of technology and behaviour will again worsen the situation. Instead of micromanagement, it might be an idea to allow users to make some security decisions themselves. In the safety field, Dekker [114, p121] calls this "freedom in a frame". Within the framework of a limited number of red lines, users are free to work in whatever way they find best.

Rather than implementing some kind of technical panopticon [115] to be used as the basis for issuing punishments, it might be an idea to provide feedback to users on the outcomes of their decisions, but only when those decisions look to be outside the stated boundaries. That isn't simply a matter of courtesy – there's empirical evidence that doing so is more effective than outright refusal, and also more effective than refusal combined with threats of punishment [116, 117]. That is, to use technology to shape behaviours, rather than constrain them. An example might be the use of a DNS firewall to check for attempted accesses to a domain less than 30 days old. Instead of triggering a punishment, a more effective approach might be to suggest to the user "that's probably not what you wanted to do, but if it is, let us know, and we may be able to make an exception".

Instead of gathering huge amounts of logging data and then sifting through for evidence of misbehaviour, possibly it might be more efficient to start from what behaviours you would prefer not to see, to determine what events in the logs would be created under those circumstances, and then to alert on those events. It makes much more sense to use technology and behavioural science in an interleaved way rather than as two separate strands, and it's much more efficient to do the sense-making up front rather than after the event.

It's been shown by Isler et al. [118] that a brief session on noticing and correcting cognitive biases, in combination with asking people to justify their decision, leads to more reflective decision-making. There's also generally agreed evidence that offering people a way of coping with cyber threats is more productive than simply offering them a scary view of the problem [31, 75, 119–122]. The practice of security is conducted in a business and social environment, and it doesn't make any sense to simply ignore that context. As an example, consider the use of a process known as a "pre-mortem", where users are encouraged to imagine that their decision has gone wrong, and they have been asked to explain their security choice to a third party. If they can come up with a rationale that seems acceptable, chances are that it was probably a good decision. If not, then maybe a second opinion might be a good idea.

Finally, as set out by Michael Brunton-Spall et al. [123], link security functionality to use cases. Because if security isn't supporting a use case, then what is it achieving?

There's nothing in this book that suggests that we should never ever buy any security tech again. What's strongly suggested, however, is that we need to view the application of technology within a wider context. The "problem" of user behaviour can be seen in one of two ways: as a failing on the part of the individual, that requires control and correction; or as a wider systems issue. Addressing it as an i-frame problem doesn't seem to have worked. It might be time to look at the alternative.

AWARENESS TRAINING: CONCLUSIONS

THE CURRENT SITUATION

There's evidence that we make decisions on the basis of gut feel and rationalise the choice afterwards. If that's true, then there may be a route to adjusting security decisions, by working on the potential for guilty feelings arising from decisions that aren't in accordance with security guidelines. The suppression of those feelings is referred to as "neutralisation", and there may be scope for interfering with the neutralisation process, as a way of driving up levels of compliance.

These methods may well work. However, they're based on the idea that non-compliance can be equated to law-breaking. The underlying logic being that any actions by the security team can therefore be justified, irrespective of any impact on the organisation, if they're aimed at enforcing compliance.

A DIFFERENT APPROACH

An examination of i-frames and s-frames indicates that the psychology of the situation could and should be considered in parallel with wider, system-level issues such as the technical environment, and the business context. That is, by taking a systems view. Doing so would embed security training and/or behaviour change within a more appropriate and possibly more productive setting.

REFERENCES

1. Herley, C., So long, and no thanks for the externalities: the rational rejection of security advice by users. In Proceedings of the 2009 *Workshop* on *New Security Par*adigms. 2009. ACM.

2. Kruger, H.A. and W.D. Kearney, Measuring information security awareness: A West Africa gold mining environment case study. 2005. Proceedings of the 2005 ISSA Conference. Johannesburg , p. 1–10.

3. Stewart, G. and D. Lacey, Death by a thousand facts: Criticising the technocratic approach to information security awareness. *Information Management & Computer Security*, 2012. 20(1): p. 29–38.

4. Reeves, A., D. Calic, and P. Delfabbro, "Get a red-hot poker and open up my eyes, it's so boring" 1: Employee perceptions of cybersecurity training. *Computers & Security*, 2021. 106: p. 102281.

5. Stanton, B., et al., Security fatigue. *It Professional*, 2016. 18(5): p. 26–32.

6. D'Arcy, J., T. Herath, and M.K. Shoss, Understanding employee responses to stressful information security requirements: A coping perspective. *Journal of Management Information Systems*, 2014. 31(2): p. 285–318.

7. Renaud, K., et al., Exploring cybersecurity-related emotions and finding that they are challenging to measure. *Humanities and Social Sciences Communications*, 2021. 8(1): p. 1–17.

8. Reeves, A., P. Delfabbro, and D. Calic, Encouraging employee engagement with cybersecurity: How to tackle cyber fatigue. *SAGE Open*, 2021. 11(1): p. 21582440211000049.

9. Scott, J. and J. Ophoff, Investigating the knowledge-behaviour gap in mitigating personal information compromise. In HAISA. 2018.

10. Parsons, K., et al., Phishing for the truth: A scenario-based experiment of users' behavioural response to emails. In IFIP *I*nternational *I*nformation Security Conference. 2013. Springer.

11. Ackoff, R.L. and J.R. Emshoff, Advertising research at Anheuser-Busch, *I*nc. (1963–68). In *Marketing classics*, B.M. Enis and K.R. Cox, Editors. 1988: Allyn and Bacon, p. 495–506.

12. Barry, P., *The advertising concept book: Think now, design later (third)*. 2016: Thames & Hudson.

13. Weldon, M.S. and H.L. Roediger, Altering retrieval demands reverses the picture superiority effect. *Memory & Cognition*, 1987. 15(4): p. 269–280.

14. Hinojosa, J.A., et al., Common basal extrastriate areas for the semantic processing of words and pictures. *Clinical Neurophysiology*, 2000. 111(3): p. 552–560.

15. Paivio, A., *Imagery and verbal processes*. 2013: Psychology Press.

16. Glaser, W.R. and M.O. Glaser, Context effects in stroop-like word and picture processing. *Journal of Experimental Psychology: General*, 1989. 118(1): p. 13.

17. Houwer, J.D. and D. Hermans, Differences in the affective processing of words and pictures. *Cognition & Emotion*, 1994. 8(1): p. 1–20.

18. Bullée, J.-W., et al., Telephone-based social engineering attacks: An experiment testing the success and time decay of an intervention. in SG-CRC. 2016. Proceedings of the Singapore Cyber-Security Conference (SG-CRC) 2016, p. 107–114. IOS Press.

19. Junger, M., L. Montoya, and F.-J. Overink, Priming and warnings are not effective to prevent social engineering attacks. *Computers in Human Behavior*, 2017. 66: p. 75–87.

20. Sawaya, Y., et al., Self-confidence Trumps knowledge: A cross-cultural study of security behavior. In Proceedings of the 2017 CHI Conference on *H*uman *F*actors in Computing *S*ystems. 2017. ACM.

21. D'arcy, J. and T. Herath, A review and analysis of deterrence theory in the IS security literature: Making sense of the disparate findings. *European Journal of Information Systems*, 2011. 20(6): p. 643–658.

22. Herath, T. and H.R. Rao, Encouraging information security behaviors in organizations: Role of penalties, pressures and perceived effectiveness. *Decision Support Systems*, 2009. 47(2): p. 154–165.

23. Bada, M. and A. Sasse, *Cyber security awareness campaigns: Why do they fail to change behaviour?* 2015. International Conference on Cyber Security for Sustainable Society, Global Cyber Security Capacity Centre, p. 1–11.

24. ISF, From promoting awareness to embedding behaviours. 2014 [Accessed 14 January 2023]; Available from: www.prlog.org/12319007-information-security-forum-embedding-positive-information-security-behaviors-in-employees-is-key.html

25. Odebade, A.T. and E. Benkhelifa, Evaluating the impact of government *cyber secu*rity initiatives in the UK. arXiv preprint arXiv:2303.13943, 2023.

26. Gordon, S., Privacy: A study of attitudes and behaviors in US, UK and EU information security professionals. In *Symantec White Paper*, 2004.

27. Barth, S., M.D. de Jong, and M. Junger, Lost in privacy? Online privacy from a cybersecurity expert perspective. *Telematics and Informatics*, 2022. 68: p. 101782.

28. Barth, S., et al., Putting the privacy paradox to the test: Online privacy and security behaviors among users with technical knowledge, privacy awareness, and financial resources. *Telematics and Informatics*, 2019. 41: p. 55–69.

29. Tischer, M., et al., Users really do plug in USB drives they find. In 2016 IEEE Symposium on Security and Privacy (SP). 2016. IEEE.

30. Langner, R., Stuxnet: Dissecting a cyberwarfare weapon. *IEEE Security & Privacy*, 2011. 9(3): p. 49–51.

31. Van Steen, T., et al., What (if any) behaviour change techniques do government-led cybersecurity awareness campaigns use? *Journal of Cybersecurity*, 2020. 6(1): p. tyaa019.

32. Nijland, S.H., *Nudge me correctly: Social proof and reciprocity nudges and the online privacy protection behavior of Generation X and Generation Y.* 2020: University of Twente.

33. Das, S., et al., Increasing security sensitivity with social proof: A large-scale experimental confirmation. In Proceedings of the 2014 ACM SIGSAC *Conference* on *Computer* and *Communications Security*. 2014.

34. Cialdini, R., *Influence: The psychology of persuasion.* 2007: Collins.

35. Cialdini, R., *Pre-suasion: A revolutionary way to influence and persuade.* 2016: Simon and Schuster.

36. Burger, J.M., Replicating Milgram: Would people still obey today? *American Psychologist*, 2009. 64(1): p. 1.

37. Miller, A.G., Reflections on "Replicating Milgram" (Burger, 2009). *American Psychologist*, 2009. 64: 20–27.

38. Doliński, D., et al., Would you deliver an electric shock in 2015? Obedience in the experimental paradigm developed by Stanley Milgram in the 50 years following the original studies. *Social Psychological and Personality Science*, 2017. 8(8): p. 927–933.

39. Cialdini, R., Principles of *persuasion*. 2016 [Accessed 10 April 2021]; Available from: www.influenceatwork.com/principles-of-persuasion

40. Parsons, K., et al., Predicting susceptibility to social influence in phishing emails. *International Journal of Human-Computer Studies*, 2019. 128: p. 17–26.

41. Akbar, N., *Analysing persuasion principles in phishing emails.* 2014: University of Twente.

42. Ferreira, A. and S. Teles, Persuasion: How phishing emails can influence users and bypass security measures. *International Journal of Human-Computer Studies*, 2019. 125: p. 19–31.

43. DCMS, Cyber security breaches survey 2017. 2017 [Accessed 9 April 2021]; Available from: https://assets.publishing.service.gov.uk/government/uploads/system/uploads/attachment_data/file/609186/Cyber_Security_Breaches_Survey_2017_main_report_PUBLIC.pdf

44. Leukfeldt, R. and J. Jansen, Financial cybercrimes and situational crime prevention. In *The human factor of cybercrime*, R. Leukfeldt and T.J. Holt, Editors. 2019, Routledge. p. 216–239.

45. Krombholz, K., et al., Advanced social engineering attacks. *Journal of Information Security and Applications*, 2015. 22: p. 113–122.

46. Quiel, S., *Social engineering in the context of Cialdini's psychology of persuasion and personality traits.* 2013: Technische Universität Hamburg.

47. Bullée, J.W.H., et al., On the anatomy of social engineering attacks – A literature-based dissection of successful attacks. *Journal of Investigative Psychology and Offender Profiling*, 2018. 15(1): p. 20–45.

48. Steinmetz, K., R. Goe, and A. Pimentel, On social engineering. In *The human factor of cybercrime*, R. Leukfeldt and T.J. Holt, Editors. 2019: Routledge. p. 173–193.

49. Nabb, J., Can information about the behaviour of colleagues make laggards onboard cybersecurity training? 2022. Masters thesis, Hanken School of Economics.

50. Ariely, D. and S. Jones, *The (honest) truth about dishonesty: How we lie to everyone, especially ourselves.* Vol. 336. 2012: HarperCollins.

51. Mazar, N., O. Amir, and D. Ariely, The dishonesty of honest people: A theory of self-concept maintenance. *Journal of Marketing Research*, 2008. 45(6): p. 633–644.

52. Verschuere, B., et al., Registered replication report on Mazar, Amir, and Ariely (2008). *Advances in Methods and Practices in Psychological Science*, 2018. 1(3): p. 299–317.

53. Kristal, A., et al., When we're wrong, it's our responsibility as scientists to say so. 2020 [Accessed 10 April 2021]; Available from: https://blogs.scientificamerican.com/observations/when-were-wrong-its-our-responsibility-as-scientists-to-say-so

54. Hagger, M.S., et al., A multilab preregistered replication of the ego-depletion effect. *Perspectives on Psychological Science*, 2016. 11(4): p. 546–573.

55. Kristal, A.S., et al., Signing at the beginning versus at the end does not decrease dishonesty. *Proceedings of the National Academy of Sciences*, 2020. 117(13): p. 7103–7107.

56. Prochazka, J., Y. Fedoseeva, and P. Houdek, A field experiment on dishonesty: A registered replication of Azar et al. (2013). *Journal of Behavioral and Experimental Economics*, 2021. 90: p. 101617.

57. Engelmann, J.B. and E. Fehr, The slippery slope of dishonesty. *Nature Neuroscience*, 2016. 19(12): p. 1543–1544.

58. Garrett, N., et al., The brain adapts to dishonesty. *Nature Neuroscience*, 2016. 19(12): p. 1727.

59. Gneezy, U., A. Kajackaite, and J. Sobel, Lying aversion and the size of the lie. *American Economic Review*, 2018. 108(2): p. 419–453.

60. Pascual-Ezama, D., et al., Cheaters, liars, or both? A new classification of dishonesty profiles. *Psychological Science*, 2020. 31(9): p. 1097–1106.

61. Ayal, S., et al., Three principles to REVISE people's unethical behavior. *Perspectives on Psychological Science*, 2015. 10(6): p. 738–741.

62. Schild, C., et al., Revisiting REVISE:(Re) Testing unique and combined effects of REminding, VIsibility, and SElf-engagement manipulations on cheating behavior. *Journal of Economic Psychology*, 2019. 75: p. 102161.

63. Burnett, D., *Happy brain: Where happiness comes from, and why*. 2018: WW Norton & Company.
64. Sykes, G.M. and D. Matza, Techniques of neutralization: A theory of delinquency. *American Sociological Review*, 1957. 22(6): p. 664–670.
65. Collins, M.D., *Neutralization theory: An empirical application and assessment*. 1994, Oklahoma State University Stillwater.
66. Cromwell, P. and Q. Thurman, The devil made me do it: Use of neutralizations by shoplifters. *Deviant Behavior*, 2003. 24(6): p. 535–550.
67. Harris, L.C. and A. Dumas, Online consumer misbehaviour: An application of neutralization theory. *Marketing Theory*, 2009. 9(4): p. 379–402.
68. Hinduja, S., Neutralization theory and online software piracy: An empirical analysis. *Ethics and Information Technology*, 2007. 9(3): p. 187–204.
69. Maruna, S. and H. Copes, What have we learned from five decades of neutralization research? *Crime and Justice*, 2005. 32: p. 221–320.
70. Minor, W.W., Techniques of neutralization: A reconceptualization and empirical examination. *Journal of Research in Crime and Delinquency*, 1981. 18(2): p. 295–318.
71. Thurman, Q.C., Deviance and the neutralization of moral commitment: An empirical analysis. *Deviant Behavior*, 1984. 5(1–4): p. 291–304.
72. Webber, C. and M. Yip, Humanising the cybercriminal: Markets, forums and the carding subculture, In *The Human Factor of Cybercrime*, R. Leukfeldt and T.J. Holt, Editors. 2019: Routledge. p. 258–285.
73. Siponen, M. and A. Vance, Neutralization: New insights into the problem of employee information systems security policy violations. *MIS Quarterly*, 2010: p. 487–502.
74. Barlow, J.B., et al., Don't make excuses! Discouraging neutralization to reduce IT policy violation. *Computers & Security*, 2013. 30(1): p. e1–5.
75. Renaud, K. and M. Dupuis, Cyber security fear appeals: Unexpectedly complicated, In *Proceedings of the New Security Paradigms Workshop*. 2019.
76. Shotton, R., *The choice factory: 25 behavioural biases that influence what we buy*. 2018: Harriman House Limited.
77. Keller, K.L. and P. Kotler, *Marketing management*. 2016: Pearson.
78. Feddersen, T. Rationalization in decision making. 2009 [Accessed 10 April 2021]; Available from: https://insight.kellogg.northwestern.edu/article/rationalization_in_decision_making
79. Mandel, D.R. and O. Vartanian, Frames, brains, and content domains: Neural and behavioral effects of descriptive context on preferential choice. *Neuroscience of Decision Making*, O. Vartanian and D. R. Mandel, Editors, 2011: Routledge, p. 45–70.
80. Ip, G., *Foolproof: Why safety can be dangerous and how danger makes us safe*. 2015: Hachette UK.
81. Gupta, R., et al., The amygdala and decision-making. *Neuropsychologia*, 2011. 49(4): p. 760–766.
82. Bechara, A., Human emotions in decision making: Are they useful or disruptive. *Neuroscience of Decision Making*, O. Vartanian and D. R. Mandel, Editors, 2011: Routledge, p. 73–95.
83. Janis, I.L. and L. Mann, *Decision making: A psychological analysis of conflict, choice, and commitment*. 1977: Free Press.
84. Zeelenberg, M., Anticipated regret, expected feedback and behavioral decision making. *Journal of Behavioral Decision Making*, 1999. 12(2): p. 93–106.
85. Wolfson, S. and P. Briggs, Locked into gambling: Anticipatory regret as a motivator for playing the National Lottery. *Journal of Gambling Studies*, 2002. 18(1): p. 1–17.

86. Dear, K., K. Dutton, and E. Fox, Do "watching eyes" influence antisocial behavior? A systematic review & meta-analysis. *Evolution and Human Behavior*, 2019. 40(3): p. 269–280.

87. Keep_Britain_Tidy, Keeping an eye on it. 2014. Available from: www.keepbritaintidy.org/sites/default/files/resource/Keeping%20an%20eye%20on%20it_Final%20report.pdf

88. Savage, D., "Watching eyes" poster reduces bicycle thefts. 2013 [Accessed 10 April 2021]; Available from: www.bbc.co.uk/news/av/uk-22275952

89. Nettle, D., K. Nott, and M. Bateson, "Cycle thieves, we are watching you": Impact of a simple signage intervention against bicycle theft. *PLoS One*, 2012. 7(12): p. e51738.

90. Ernest-Jones, M., D. Nettle, and M. Bateson, Effects of eye images on everyday cooperative behavior: A field experiment. *Evolution and Human Behavior*, 2011. 32(3): p. 172–178.

91. Think, 50 years of drink drive campaigns. 2017 [Accessed 10 April 2021]; Available from: www.think.gov.uk/campaign/50-years-of-drink-drive-campaigns

92. Magee, K., Will the government's new emotive Covid ad make people obey the rules? 2021 [Accessed 10 April 2021]; Available from: www.campaignlive.co.uk/article/will-governments-new-emotive-covid-ad-people-obey-rules/1705634

93. Khaliq, Z., Sainsbury's shoppers furious after being made to scan receipts to leave stores. 2022 [Accessed 3 January 2023]; Available from: www.mirror.co.uk/money/sainsburys-making-shoppers-scan-receipts-28746658

94. Nazir, S., Sainsbury's faces backlash as it makes shoppers scan receipts before exiting store. 2022 [Accessed 3 January 2023]; Available from: www.retailgazette.co.uk/blog/2022/12/sainsburys-scan-receipts-exit

95. Carrington, M.J., B.A. Neville, and G.J. Whitwell, Why ethical consumers don't walk their talk: Towards a framework for understanding the gap between the ethical purchase intentions and actual buying behaviour of ethically minded consumers. *Journal of Business Ethics*, 2010. 97(1): p. 139–158.

96. Chatzidakis, A., S. Hibbert, and A.P. Smith, Why people don't take their concerns about fair trade to the supermarket: The role of neutralisation. *Journal of Business Ethics*, 2007. 74(1): p. 89–100.

97. Steenhaut, S. and P. Van Kenhove, The mediating role of anticipated guilt in consumers' ethical decision-making. *Journal of Business Ethics*, 2006. 69(3): p. 269–288.

98. Lindenmeier, J., et al., Anticipated consumer guilt: an investigation into its antecedents and consequences for fair-trade consumption. *Journal of Macromarketing*, 2017. 37(4): p. 444–459.

99. Boss, S.R., et al., If someone is watching, I'll do what I'm asked: Mandatoriness, control, and information security. *European Journal of Information Systems*, 2009. 18(2): p. 151–164.

100. Holmes, D., Staring eyes are anxiety-provoking. 2013 [Accessed 10 April 2021]; Available from: www.bbc.co.uk/news/av/uk-22275956

101. Posey, C., et al., When computer monitoring backfires: Invasion of privacy and organizational injustice as precursors to computer abuse. *Journal of Information System Security*, 2011. 7(1): 24–47.

102. Jiang, H., et al., Examining the side effects of organizational Internet monitoring on employees. *Internet Research*, 2020. 30(6), p. 1613–1630.

103. Thiel, C., et al., Monitoring employees makes them more likely to break rules. 2022 [Accessed 29 September 2022]; Available from: https://hbr.org/2022/06/monitoring-employees-makes-them-more-likely-to-break-rules

104. Ravid, D. M., Tomczak, D. L., White, J. C., and Behrend, T. S., EPM 20/20: A review, framework, and research agenda for electronic performance monitoring. *Journal of Management*, 2020. 46(1): p. 100–126.

105. Siponen, M., P. Puhakainen, and A. Vance, Can individuals' neutralization techniques be overcome? A field experiment on password policy. *Computers & Security*, 2020. 88: p. 101617.

106. Neocleous, M., *Critique of security*. 2008: Edinburgh University Press.

107. Chater, N. and G. Loewenstein, The i-frame and the s-frame: How focusing on the individual-level solutions has led behavioral public policy astray. Available at SSRN 4046264, 2022.

108. DeWeerdt, S., Tracing the US opioid crisis to its roots. *Nature*, 2019. 573(7773): p. S10–S10.

109. Van Zee, A., The promotion and marketing of oxycontin: commercial triumph, public health tragedy. *American Journal of Public Health*, 2009. 99(2): p. 221–227.

110. Loewenstein, G. and N. Chater, Putting nudges in perspective. *Behavioural Public Policy*, 2017. 1(1): p. 26–53.

111. DellaVigna, S. and E. Linos, RCTs to scale: Comprehensive evidence from two nudge units. *Econometrica*, 2022. 90(1): p. 81–116.

112. Mertens, S., et al., The effectiveness of nudging: A meta-analysis of choice architecture interventions across behavioral domains. *Proceedings of the National Academy of Sciences*, 2022. 119(1): p. e2107346118.

113. Ritchie, S., *Science fictions: Exposing fraud, bias, negligence and hype in science*. 2020: Random House.

114. Dekker, S. and T. Conklin, *Do safety differently*. 2022: Pre-Accident Investigation Media.

115. Galič, M., T. Timan, and B.-J. Koops, Bentham, Deleuze and beyond: An overview of surveillance theories from the panopticon to participation. *Philosophy & Technology*, 2017. 30(1): p. 9–37.

116. Nudge, Making security work for modern work. 2022 [Accessed 11 January 2023]; Available from: www.nudgesecurity.com

117. Nudge, Debunking the "stupid user" myth in security. 2022 [Accessed 11 January 2023]; Available from: www.nudgesecurity.com/debunking-the-stupid-user-myth-in-security

118. Isler, O., O. Yilmaz, and B. Dogruyol, Activating reflective thinking with decision justification and debiasing training. *Judgment & Decision Making*, 2020. 15(6): p. 926–938.

119. van Bavel, R., et al., Using protection motivation theory in the design of nudges to improve online security behavior. *International Journal of Human-Computer Studies*, 2019. 123: p. 29–39.

120. Braakman, R., *The effect of cybersecurity messages and personality on cybersecurity behavior*. 2021: University of Twente.

121. ENISA, Cybersecurity culture guidelines: Behavioural aspects of cybersecurity. 2019 [Accessed 10 April 2021]; Available from: www.enisa.europa.eu/publications/cybersecurity-culture-guidelines-behavioural-aspects-of-cybersecurity

122. Dupuis, M. and K. Renaud, Scoping the ethical principles of cybersecurity fear appeals. *Ethics and Information Technology*, 2020. 23(3): p. 265–284.

123. Bell, L., Brunton-Spall, M., Smith, R., and Bird, J., *Agile application security: enabling security in a continuous delivery pipeline*. 2017: O'Reilly Media, Inc.

4 Security = Confidentiality + Integrity + Availability

THE GENERAL IDEA

BACKGROUND

The so-called triad of Confidentiality, Integrity, and Availability (CIA, conveniently) is a staple of security folklore. Pretty much any security practitioner you encounter will bring this out at some point, although there's no precisely worded explanation of the thinking behind it.

The general principle is that security is about preventing people who shouldn't see specific bits of information from seeing them (confidentiality), preventing information from being changed when we didn't want it to be changed (integrity), and making sure that information and services are accessible when they're needed (availability). The implication being that the triad is a complete set, i.e. there's nothing else, and also that these three aspects are orthogonal – they're different from each other. It follows that any security problem ought therefore to fall into one of those three pots, and only one. However, such a clear division doesn't seem to work out in practice.

Suppose I'm running an IT department with a converged communications strategy, and I've provided mobile phones to employees so that they can pick up emails when they're on the road, and so that they can be contacted Monday to Friday, from 09:00 to 17:00, when their colleagues need to speak to them. Now suppose one enterprising employee sets up their own premium rate phone number that pays them commission based on connection time. Every Friday at five minutes past five, they call that number from their work phone. They leave it connected all weekend, hanging up at five to nine on the following Monday morning, having earned some revenue at the company's expense. That seems to be something that security ought to be concerned about, but it's hard to see why. Confidentiality hasn't been affected – no data has been leaked. Integrity hasn't been affected – nothing's been corrupted. Availability hasn't been affected, because even if someone needed to contact that employee, the caller could leave a voicemail and expect a call back. After all, it's the weekend. But still, something has happened that we wouldn't want to happen. This type of fraud doesn't seem to be captured by the model.

Arguably, there are also security concerns that don't fit into just one pot. Malicious software ("malware" – viruses, Trojans, etc.) can have a range of potential outcomes.

DOI: 10.1201/9781003380962-4

It's possible that files could be deleted or encrypted (affecting availability), but it's also possible that information could be corrupted (affecting integrity) or leaked out (breaching confidentiality). In fact, a malware infection could affect just one, any two, or all three of the triad of attributes. Malware breaks the assumption that security problems relate to one and only one category.

There must be something missing from the model, if there are security concerns that won't fit into any of the three buckets. And when we have impacts that won't fit into just one of the buckets, that in turn implies the absence of one or more additional categories.

THE PARKERIAN HEXAD

Donn B. Parker wrote a piece some years ago, called "*Our excessively simplistic information security model and how to fix it*" [1, 2]. His proposal is now referred to as the Parkerian Hexad [3], because it expanded the original triad to a total of six components, adding authenticity ("Has this information come from a reliable source?"), possession ("I want to maintain control over my data"), and utility ("I have my data, but is it useable?"). You can see that the concept of utility captures the outcome of, say, ransomware encrypting my files, but in a much more subtle way than saying it's an availability problem. I may still have the files, but they're of no use to me. The Parkerian Hexad adds three more characteristics to the basic model and, in doing so, produces a richer picture.

MISSING COMPONENTS

As part of an assignment for a UK Government Department, I was involved in developing a similar model, to support a more agile approach to risk analysis. After some thinking, we added the concepts of "ownership" and "purpose" to the standard CIA model. Attacks on ownership include malware and the use of unauthorised software generally. If I own the system, then I get to decide what software runs on it. Someone trying to introduce software that I haven't sanctioned isn't an attack on C, I or A – it's an attack on ownership. Fraud, generally speaking, is an attack on purpose. The purpose of a converged communications system is to ensure that people can be contacted when necessary, not to enable employees to make pocket money over the weekend. Any attempt to do that is an attack on the purpose of the system.

We also implemented two fundamental shifts in viewpoint. Rather than taking CIA plus those two new characteristics as attributes of a secure system, we used them as search terms when looking for attack scenarios. That is, we used them not as a definition of security (that seemed an optimistic thing to do) but as categories of attacks that we might want to consider.

The second shift involved a recognizing that any model with a finite number of categories was unlikely to stay that way for long. The more we thought about attack types, the more categories we came up with. In the final analysis, we went with ownership and purpose, but placed them within a wider category of "other" (making it the CIAO model). The category of "other" accommodated the idea that there could be further types of attack, but without requiring us to spell them out.

Overall, the method seemed to be well received, and certainly, adding that open branch to the CIA model helped enormously when we were asking people to be creative in thinking up attack scenarios. However, we achieved those benefits by turning a closed model into an open one, with an implicit acknowledgement that no matter how many categories we added, it would never be complete. Samonas and Coss [4] provide a summary of other, previous attempts to put back something that seemed to be absent from the basic triad. Their review identified eight additional dimensions [4, Table 3], although two of the parameters proposed by Donn Parker are missing from that list, so adding in those brings the count up to ten. Adding in the two that we suggested makes a round dozen. All of which indicates that perhaps we should be thinking about a continuum rather than a finite set of characteristics.

Approaches such as the standard CIA model, ones that split problems down into a finite number of sub-problems, are usually referred to as reductionist. A reductionist approach implicitly assumes that any problem can be broken down into smaller/simpler problems. That's perfectly fine for, e.g., space stations, car engines, and even laptops, because you can capture the relationships between the constituent parts. You know the required relationship between the piston, the piston rings, and the cylinder. That allows you to analyse and construct the constituent parts in isolation, with a reasonable expectation that when they're put together, the physical relationships between them will be as designed. But in almost all cases that stops being true when you have a human as one of the components, and it almost never seems to be true when there's more than one human involved. Not the least important reason being that it's difficult and maybe impossible to predict the ways in which the human components will interact with each other, let alone how they will interact with the technology. That sort of situation simply isn't amenable to a nice clean breakdown.

Reductionism assumes that the decomposition can be carried out *without losing any information*. In fact, what's lost when you break down security into C, I and A is the original context for the problem. An implicit assumption in a reductionist, engineering view is that context is irrelevant, that you can analyse security without any consideration of its setting. In practice, in situations involving human beings and decision-making, the setting of the security event is central. Samonas and Coss noted that the majority of the items seemingly missing from the model came from a socio-technical view of security – a view that says security is made up of people and technology interacting, not just technology. The implication being that whatever is missing from the CIA model, it has something to do with people.

THE IMPORTANCE OF CONTEXT

SECURITY AND MORALITY

Siponen [5] relates the story of a Finnish dive school operator in Indonesia following the Boxing Day tsunami. Frustrated at not being able to help the families of both victims and survivors, the operator put up the names of those who had been seen and were known to be alive and well on the dive school website. However, publishing the names of those individuals without their explicit consent was illegal under Finnish data protection legislation. The Finnish government investigated, but concluded that under the circumstances, what had been done was for the best, and therefore took no action.

Whether or not you think publishing the names was a good security decision depends on your point of view. Most practitioners I guess would take the view that the rules had been broken, and that's that. For me, security controls are there to maintain the value of information until it comes to be used for a legitimate purpose. If the controls continue to prevent access beyond that point, then they're not to do with security anymore. So I think the decision to publish was not only a good decision morally but also a good decision in a security sense. That information was never going to be more valuable than it was at that point, and it was time to cash it in. The issue of morality in relation to security decision-making has been noted by a number of others, e.g. Myyry et al. [6]. In the same vein, Alter [7] demonstrates that there can be beneficial outcomes from non-compliance with corporate policies, and also that there can be detrimental outcomes from unthinking compliance, i.e. having users demonstrate complete compliance with the rules isn't always the best option for the organisation. It depends on the context for their actions.

A DIFFERENT VIEWPOINT

Taking all this into consideration, maybe what's needed is for users to have the ability to interpret security rules within the prevailing context [8], rather than just following them. Perhaps the necessary skill might be an ability to interpret security policy – to be able to understand when a security policy makes sense and when it doesn't [9, 10].

That leads to a strong argument for a greater level of participatory design in security policy development – an argument that users and managers should be involved in deciding what "good security" looks like. Rostami [11] found very few examples of users being engaged as part of the process of developing information security policies; however, Olivos [12] cites the importance of the "IKEA effect" – that when people are actively engaged in the development or construction of something, then they feel a greater sense of ownership and buy-in. Renaud and Flowerday [13, p80] make a similar point:

> Back in 1999 Adams and Sasse [14] shone the light on the divide between information security professionals and end users. Almost two decades have passed and that divide has not yet been bridged. Those who secure systems still fail to understand why users behave the way they do. This category of disruption asks us to start listening to our end users, and to stop telling them what to do without considering their perspectives.

All of which leads us towards the idea of social construction as an alternative to the use of reductionism.

SECURITY AS A SOCIAL CONSTRUCT

CREDIT CARD FRAUD

In 2018, the cost of credit and debit card fraud in the UK amounted to £671M, at least according to UK Finance, who claim to be *"...the collective voice for the banking and finance industry... [r]epresenting more than 250 firms across the industry"* [15], which as far as I can see makes them a reasonably authoritative source.

In the same period, an additional £1.12Bn in attempted credit card fraud was prevented, against total spending of about £800Bn.

Now imagine that you make a little over two short hops in the car every day – say out to the railway station and back to get to work each weekday, and out to the shops and back and maybe one or two other equal-length trips over the weekend. That comes to about 800 trips in a year. If the same statistics apply, one interpretation is that in a typical year, you could expect two of those trips to result in an accident. Don't worry about the grinding sound, that's just the teeth of my statistics tutor. I should perhaps have used numbers of transactions rather than transaction values, but road accident rates are expressed in terms of accidents per passenger mile, which maps more comfortably to transaction value. Sorry, Dr. S.

Interpreting the fact that (again, by value) about one third of attempted fraud is successful, that means that there's a reasonable chance that in one of those two yearly accidents, your seat belt won't work, and your airbags will fail to deploy.

On the face of it, that doesn't seem to be an acceptable situation. How can an industry losing around three quarters of a billion pounds annually be seen as secure?

Klein and Kleinman [16] summarise some key ideas in the social construction of technology – the idea that the accepted meaning of a technology is defined through the interpretation put on it by relevant sections of society, after they've engaged in a negotiation. The sections are referred to as social groups – parties who at least within their group, share a common view of a particular technology. A similar term, "worldview", is used by Checkland [17, p192].

Because each social group may have different views, they go through a process of negotiation, to arrive at an agreed position [18]. Negotiation on a technological issue ceases, i.e. closure comes about, through various mechanisms. Redefinition is one, when it's declared that the remaining issues aren't relevant (*"it's not a bug, it's a feature"* [16, p30]). Rhetorical closure is another, when it's agreed by all relevant parties that there are no remaining problems to be concerned about.

In the case of credit and debit card frauds, the relevant social groups might be users, banks/issuers, and regulatory bodies. Card holders are ok with the situation. They want to keep spending [19], and apart from Authorised Push Payments, fraudulent card transactions are repaid 98% of the time [15, p12] (see also [20] and [21, p8]). In effect, the banks absolutely guarantee that if your airbags fail to deploy, they will provide you with free healthcare and a new car (in fact, the situation certainly ought to be acceptable to the general public, since about 15% of them admit to engaging in some type of consumer fraud themselves [22]). The banks are ok with the situation, since the marginal cost of reducing fraud is higher than the cost of just living with it [23]. Regulators are ok, as long as the banks are seen to be doing something about the problem, such as enforcing the use of one-time SMS passwords [24], even though it's well known that almost everyone has their phone set to display text messages when the device is locked.

Essentially, the social groups involved have all declared that there's no problem here, and that the situation is secure. We've all agreed that by and large, it's safe to use credit and debit cards. Although mostly because we want to keep using them, and also because the banks want us to keep using them (see Figure 4.1).

Security, in this sense, is very much what the relevant social groups see it as. It isn't a thing, there's no definition of it – it's a social construct. It's something we decide is there on the basis of our individual viewpoints. If the prevailing circumstances meet the views of security as held by each of the relevant parties, then we have security.

In truth, the idea of security as a social construct is hardly rocket science. Arguments that the parallel concepts of risk and safety are social constructs have been around for some time [25, 26]. A 2018 ENISA report concluded that a number of the studies they examined "… *show that security is ultimately a social construct and as such needs to be negotiated between the different stakeholders in the ecosystem*". Das et al. [27] also suggest that "… *security behaviors – as any human behavior – should*

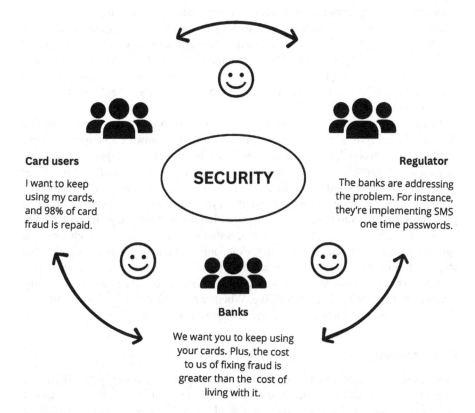

FIGURE 4.1 Security as a social construct. (Leapfrog Creative Ltd, reproduced with permission.)

be viewed within the context of a social system". Nevertheless, despite the fact that the social construction argument has been around for some time and despite the fact that it's still being promoted, the cybersecurity industry, for whatever reason, hasn't taken it on board.

CYBER INSURANCE

The discussion regarding cyber insurance (ongoing, at the time of writing) provides another example. There's an argument that as an increasing number of companies carry insurance, more and more lovable little scamps will engage in writing ransomware [28]. Since the default position of insurance companies is to pay out, there's no incentive for victims to resist, and indeed potentially no incentive to protect. Consequently (the argument goes), writers of ransomware are encouraged to try their hand, because there's a reasonable chance of being paid.

The social groups involved in this case can be seen as writers, victims, and insurance companies. The victims, assuming they have insurance, are ok with the situation, because the costs of cleaning up and recovering their data are likely to be much higher than the costs of simply paying the ransom, which will be covered by the insurance company anyway. The insurance companies are ok with it, because they're riding the growth curve. At this stage, as long as they have happy customers, then they're capturing more and more of an expanding market. Once they've established a customer base, they can start hiking premiums, as per the standard model. The ransomware writers are perfectly fine with it. As long as their demands are lower than the costs of a clean-up, then they're highly likely to get paid. So we have a stable situation.

But here comes a new social group – cybersecurity practitioners, protesting that their job is being made harder by rising levels of ransomware. So now we have another party involved, and because a new viewpoint has been expressed, we need to go through another round of negotiation as part of the process of "securing" (as suggested by Burdon and Coles-Kemp [29]). You can see that reflected in the reports put out by the insurance industry, saying that cyber insurance is helping the situation [30, 31], vs blogs from cyber people arguing that it's making things worse [32, 33]. The most likely resolution, it seems to me, is that we'll see closure through a general agreement that it's the customer's fault. Companies need to get their act together and stop their employees from clicking on dodgy links in emails. The insurance companies might therefore mandate some form of standard security awareness training, specifically training relating to phishing. Whether or not that will have any effect is a different question, but it looks as though it might, which is the point.

OTHER EXAMPLES

You can see similar themes in a study by Dupont into the ecology of cybercrime [34]. Dupont expands the concept of a stakeholder to include malicious actors, such as cybercriminals, and suggests that we should "... *think in an integrated way about how diametrically opposed groups (banking institutions, Internet fraudsters, and the police, for example) are intertwined and inexorably connected through the shifting, yet balanced, relationships that make up a single process ...*". Drawing on the concept of "figuration" as described by Elias [35], Dupont suggests that [34, p389]:

> *Cybersecurity is understood as the product of constant interactions between three interdependent communities: an industrial community, which is the source of a major technological revolution launched some 20 years ago that has also spawned major digital risks; a criminal community, which was able to capitalize on this revolution to take advantage of criminal opportunities on an unprecedented scale; and, a security community, which has struggled to effectively manage cybercrime.*

Zimmermann and Renaud take a similar view, suggesting that the parties involved in the negotiation of security consist of government(s), hackers, and the cyber industry [36].

This kind of thinking views security as an ongoing, complex process rather than a static position, and contrasts somewhat with the view taken by cyber practitioners, who typically summarise the security landscape through a one-off linear risk analysis. Possibly the most important difference however, is that seeing security as a social construct allows us to view it through the eyes of other stakeholders, rather than simply breaking it down into a limited set of characteristics that are of interest only to the security community.

APPLYING THE MODEL

SECURITY AS A NEGOTIATION

Using the idea of social construction, we can see how the situation on card fraud might evolve. At the time of writing, although consumers and banks seem to be content, the UK Government isn't, at least not when there are votes to be gained. It's an outrage apparently, that banks and card issuers haven't done more to prevent the related problem of Authorised Push Payment fraud [15, p7]. Clearly, additional pressure [37] and possibly legislation will be required to make banks step up and address the problem [38, 39].

What's happened is that another relevant social group (politicians) has entered the picture, and they aren't happy, even though everyone else is. So before we get back to a stable situation where everyone agrees that we're secure, we have to go through another cycle of negotiation. That's why, when you bank online, you may be asked to tick a little box when you move money (even between your accounts with the same bank), acknowledging that you guarantee that you aren't being scammed, i.e. if it turns out that in fact you are being scammed, then it's your fault and not the fault of the bank. Let's see how that pans out. What appears to have been the first test case has gone in favour of the consumer and not the bank [40], although it's fair to say that the negotiation between the banks and the regulators (and the public) has only just [got] started [41–49].

In this case, nothing fundamental has changed, it's just that another social group has become relevant. I guess the corollary is that if you want to change the way security is seen and managed, then you have to introduce a new social group – or have a set of stakeholders that aren't content that the current conditions map to their interpretation of security. You might see echoes of that in the earlier argument regarding the bargaining power of customers wanting something different from cyber.

This theme of social negotiation also chimes with a number of other points made earlier. The summary of social constructionism by Humphreys, for example [50], notes that "*[t]hrough advertising, marketers can convey that a technology will solve a problem and thus convince users that the technology is closed*". To expand on that – where the meaning of a technology is socially constructed, there is ample room for hype.

It may also be relevant to note that trying to impose a common view of security across a number of social groups (i.e. trying to lay down a security culture) isn't likely to be successful, precisely because each group has a different understanding of what security looks like.

The commonality of approaches embodied in national cyber strategies was noted earlier [e.g. 51]. As discussed by Burgers [52], that leads to a sub-optimal situation – a cyber arms race – because, as with the "prisoner's dilemma", although it might make more sense for the collection of nations to de-escalate, the safest option for individual countries is to "arm up". That's a situation that comes up again and again in the context of game theory [53]. Viewing security as a negotiated set of circumstances, however, suggests a different route, as proposed by Dunn Cavelty: "*[t]hus, the type of cyber-power that the European Union needs is expressed through finding common ground between the different stakeholders involved and by building collective strength with and among these stakeholders*" [54]. van de Meer [55] makes a similar point: "*[i]n the long term, cooperation between states to establish confidence and commonly accepted norms of behaviour in cyber space are the most promising ways available to achieve enduring cyber security and stability*".

The social construction of security offers not just a means of explaining real-world effects that we see in relation to cyber, but also a means of predicting them and managing them. And it's a more business-oriented approach – rather than one detached group of people within an organisation deciding what security is and what it isn't, leading to unexpected side-effects, it's more productive to see the process of "securing" as a negotiation between stakeholders.

COMPLEXITY AND EMERGENCE

Academics but also some practitioners have suggested that cybersecurity is a "wicked problem" that can't be solved in the same sense that an engineering problem can be solved [56–58]. Clemente [59] provides a summary, and both Gilmore [60] and Doernberg [61] set out the characteristics that make problems "wicked", e.g. there are no right or wrong solutions, only good or bad outcomes.

This fits intuitively with the view of cyber as a problem that isn't open to reductionism, but for me it tends to sideline the issues of context and environment. More significantly, it just doesn't help. It doesn't seem enough to say that it's hard. Ideally, we would like some way of understanding it.

Others have said that by analogy with the problem of safety, security is a property of what's referred to as a "complex adaptive system". A number of sources [e.g. 62] set out the key characteristics of complex systems, such as unpredictability – *"[p]ushing on a complex system 'here' often has effects 'over there' because the parts are interdependent"* [62, para 1.3]. Check. See the examples on share price. Complex systems also exhibit non-linearity (tipping points), where a relatively small change in the input can lead to disproportional changes in output. Check. See the earlier example regarding the Wannacry virus.

Holland [63] notes that *"all [Complex Adaptive Systems] that have been examined closely exhibit trends towards increasing numbers of specialists"*. Co-evolution between agents, such as the constant interaction between a predator and its prey, leads to increasingly specialised niches. Also, check. Both of those (increasing degrees of specialisation and constant interaction with an attacker) seem to be elements of cyber.

I should be honest and point out that what's being said here isn't exactly groundbreaking. The idea that safety is a property of a complex system, and the consequent need to employ systems thinking in the safety field, as pointed out by Dekker [64], has been around for at least a decade [65, 66].

Emergence is perhaps the key property of complex systems. It's not stretching a point to say that unless there is emergence, then you're probably not looking at a complex system. An emergent property being one that exists solely because of the interaction of the components of the system [67]. A standout security example is shown in the work of Yurcik et al. [68] on the security of clusters – what happens when you link together a number of large computers.

Yurcik et al. found the security environment for the cluster to be greater than the sum of the environments for its parts. For one thing, the act of clustering seemed to bring about different behaviours. Quoting a related paper [69], the authors note that *"...even minimal overhead from the use of encrypted communications is often considered unacceptable"*, i.e. we've built this thing for speed, so it's perfectly ok to take off any security features that slow it down.

To quote the abstract from the paper:

While an individual commodity machine may have prescribed best practices for security, a cluster of commodity machines has emergent security properties that are unique from the sum of its parts.

The paper goes on to describe six ways in which cluster security is different from traditional enterprise-level security, all of which come into being because the machines have been clustered. Or to put it another way, if you un-clustered them and analysed each security environment in turn, you wouldn't get the same picture.

Emergence itself seems to be a less than straightforward concept, and a wider study has arisen looking into its underlying philosophy [70, 71]. Humphreys [72] provides a concise explanation of the different types of emergence, and also the arguments for and against. NCSC's very useful blog post on the subject ("Of Mice and Cyber" [73]) also provides an explanation of the difference between systems that are complicated (e.g. machinery) and those that are complex (mixtures of humans and technology, but also mice).

All of this has led people to say that safety (and by analogy, security) is an emergent property of a complex system. But again, that runs up against the problem of relevance. If security is something that just pops out of the ether because of the interaction of the components in a system made up of people plus technology, then that gets us nowhere if we want to predict the outcome. There's also a degree of confusion (I think so anyway), as to whether it's security that's the emergent property, or threats/hazards, i.e. a lack of security. For me the argument on safety as an emergent property is ended by the statement from Eric Hollnagel [74], who says that safety isn't a property – it's a state, or a set of states that meet a given set of criteria on acceptability. That, as far as I can see, says that while we should acknowledge that security exists within a complex and unpredictable environment, it's not so much a property, more an agreement on whether or not the current situation is acceptable.

As such, the state of security can be understood, but it isn't amenable to being broken down into components, at least not in a sensible way. Essentially, there is no such thing as "provable" security. You can argue that all parties are content and maybe even show that they are. But the state of "security" is (a) transient and (b) dependent on the views of the interested parties. As such it probably isn't really a state. It's more of a temporary pause in the discussion.

PRACTICAL ISSUES

AVAILABLE TOOLS

If we ditched the CIA model and the associated basis of reductionism, what could we use instead? If security is indeed socially constructed, what models could we use to engage it?

Dalpiaz et al. developed a socio-technical security modelling language (STS-ml) and associated analysis tool [75-–77]. Others have also developed similar approaches, e.g. Mujinga et al. [78] and Li et al. [79]. This is a possible way forward, but for me, there seems something inconsistent about using a reductionist approach to modelling socio-technical security requirements, especially when the approach is itself based on an adaptation of the CIA model [76, p14].

Reynolds and Holwell [17] identified five "systems thinking" methodologies, one of which was soft systems methodology (SSM). SSM recognises that for very complex ("wicked") problems, there may be no perfect solution, and that in many cases, the best that can be hoped for is an improvement rather than a resolution. SSM has been used for security systems design [80], security requirements gathering [81, 82], and incident investigation [83], amongst other security-based applications.

By using a combination of workshops and scenario thinking, van Deursen and colleagues [84] assembled a list of risk circumstances based on likely behaviours, e.g. losing files, sending emails to the wrong recipient, etc. Their key finding was that by using groups and workshops to generate ideas, the picture that emerged was much closer to real life than would have been the case with an approach based on risk "calculations". By acknowledging security as a product of social circumstances, and by adopting a soft systems approach, the team produced a much more realistic representation of the organisation's security requirements. That is, while this might all look like theory, there are practical benefits.

SSM suggests a number of analytical tools, a central one being the "rich picture" – a diagram showing stakeholders, their requirements, and the key problem areas. I have had personal experience of applying rich pictures in security settings, and they really help (a generic example is shown below in Figure 4.2). Rather than trying to document a set of technical boundaries, it's useful to be able to set down in a diagram the expectations of the security stakeholders, mostly because it provides context.

THE CHANCES OF SUCCESS

Armstrong et al. [85] make a strong case that reductionism has reached its limits. Others have said that we should treat cyber as a social construct [86–88], on the basis that it's likely to give us a more useful set of tools [89–91].

But to revisit a theme from an earlier chapter – is change likely? Samonas and Coss [4], in their 2014 review of the development of the CIA model, point out that security practitioners have shown a remarkable degree of resistance in the face of a strong argument for change:

> *This paper has reviewed the conception and use of the CIA triad from two, seemingly fragmented, approaches to information security. Firstly, we looked at the way in which practitioners have been consistently portraying the triad as a unique point of reference in information security. Secondly, we examined how academic research in information systems security has suggested several socio-technical extensions to the original CIA triad, in order to address the limited scope of technical controls. Our goal was to provide a plausible explanation as to why security practitioners have largely ignored these extensions and continue to place great importance in the key components of the CIA triad itself.*

It would be optimistic to suggest that the security industry is going to drop the CIA model overnight, or indeed at all. Bergstrom and West [92] cite Brandolini's Law – that to refute BS, you need to expend an order of magnitude more effort than the amount of effort that went into creating it. Nonetheless, although there's only a very small chance of a change in thinking, the adoption of components such as SSM, and rich pictures in particular, is recommended here as a real-world, practical addition to security risk analysis, because (a) it provides a social context for security and (b) it can only add to the debate, and not detract from it [93, 94].

SOCIAL CONSTRUCTION: CONCLUSIONS

SYSTEMS THINKING

The argument presented here is that security is socially constructed. It comes about through negotiation. As a result, it's not appropriate to apply reductionism. Instead, if we want to understand security, then we need to take a more rounded view, using systems thinking.

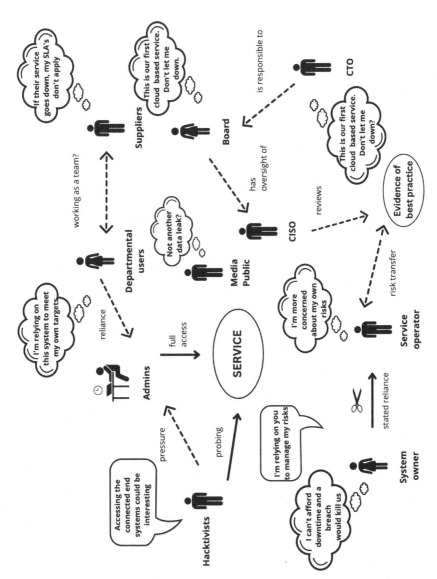

FIGURE 4.2 Example rich picture. (Leapfrog Creative Ltd, reproduced with permission.)

Acknowledging security as a social construct allows us to take a more useful view of security management. It provides a means of placing behaviour change programs within a wider context, and it explains why we see benefits from adopting more socially oriented approaches.

At a personal level, to be honest, if the security industry had owned up and said "here we are, this is the CIA model and it's a bit of a guess, but let's take it as that" then fair enough [95]. But the engineering approach adopted across much of the industry means that it's accepted as gospel, without any kind of critique. That sort of behaviour seems to be endemic throughout the industry – see [96–99] for an engaging demonstration.

LIKELY DEVELOPMENTS

It's unlikely that the necessary shift in thinking will take place any time soon. There's ample evidence that for all its faults, the CIA model is irretrievably embedded in the thinking of security practitioners.

Hielscher et al. [100] suggest that "taking out the trash" is an important part of security awareness and training – that old, possibly obsolete ideas need to be explicitly removed from the curriculum, because if they aren't taken out, they'll get in the way of any updated messages. I think that's a laudable aim, and very probably a good idea. However, as currently presented, it's aimed at employees and users, whereas it ought to be aimed at practitioners. The discussion on organisational issues in IT security, for example, has been running (to my personal knowledge) for well over 20 years [101], and yet the practice of security still hasn't taken on even the most basic of business concerns [102].

REFERENCES

1. Parker, D.B., Toward a new framework for information security? *Computer Security Handbook*, S. Bosworth, M. E. Kabay, E. Whyne, Editors. 2012: Wiley, p. 3.1–3.23.
2. Parker, D., Our excessively simplistic information security model and how to fix it. *ISSA Journal*, 2010. 8(7): p. 12–21.
3. Pender-Bey, G., *The Parkerian Hexad: The CIA Triad Model expanded*. MSc dissertation from Lewis University, 2103, p 1–31.
4. Samonas, S. and D. Coss, The CIA strikes back: Redefining confidentiality, integrity and availability in security. *Journal of Information System Security*, 2014. 10(3): p. 21–45.
5. Siponen, M., Six design theories for IS security policies and guidelines. *Journal of the Association for Information systems*, 2006. 7(1): p. 19.
6. Myyry, L., et al., What levels of moral reasoning and values explain adherence to information security rules? An empirical study. *European Journal of Information Systems*, 2009. 18(2): p. 126–139.
7. Alter, S., *Beneficial noncompliance and detrimental compliance: Expected paths to unintended consequences*. 2015. Proceedings of the 21st Americas Conference on Information Systems.
8. Kirlappos, I., A. Beautement, and M.A. Sasse., "Comply or Die" is dead: Long live security-aware principal agents. In *International Conference on Financial Cryptography and Data Security*. 2013. Springer.

9. Yevseyeva, I., et al., Addressing consumerisation of IT risks with nudging. *International Journal of Information Systems and Project Management.*, 2015. 2(1): p. 5–22.

10. Kolkowska, E., F. Karlsson, and K. Hedström, Towards analysing the rationale of information security non-compliance: Devising a value-based compliance analysis method. *The Journal of Strategic Information Systems*, 2017. 26(1): p. 39–57.

11. Rostami, E., Tailoring policies and involving users in constructing security policies: A mapping study. In HAISA 2019, Nicosia, Cyprus, 15–17 July, 2019. 2019.

12. Olivos, O., Using the IKEA Effect to improve information security policy compliance. In HAISA. 2019.

13. Renaud, K. and S. Flowerday, Contemplating human-centred security & privacy research: Suggesting future directions. *Journal of Information Security and Applications*, 2017. 34: p. 76–81.

14. Adams, A. and M.A. Sasse, Users are not the enemy. *Communications of the ACM*, 1999. 42(12): p. 41–46.

15. UKFinance, Fraud the facts 2019: The definitive overview of payment industry fraud. 2019 [Accessed 9 April 2021]; Available from: www.ukfinance.org.uk/system/files/Fraud%20The%20Facts%202019%20-%20FINAL%20ONLINE.pdf

16. Klein, H.K. and D.L. Kleinman, The social construction of technology: Structural considerations. *Science, Technology, & Human Values*, 2002. 27(1): p. 28–52.

17. Reynolds, M. and S. Holwell, *Systems approaches to managing change: A practical guide*. 2010: Springer.

18. Pinch, T., The social construction of technology: A review. *Technological Change: Methods and Themes in the History of Technology*, 1996. 35: p. 17–35.

19. UKFinance, *Card spending*. 2021 [Accessed 10 April 2021]; Available from: www.ukfinance.org.uk/data-and-research/data/cards/card-spending

20. Sims, B., UK Finance calls for urgent action on fraud prevention. 2022 [Accessed 24 October 2022]; Available from: https://securitymattersmagazine.com/uk-finance-calls-for-urgent-action-on-fraud-prevention

21. UKFinance, *2022* Half year fraud update. 2022 [Accessed 24 October 2022]; Available from: www.ukfinance.org.uk/system/files/2022-10/Half%20year%20fraud%20update%202022.pdf

22. CIFAS, One in seven (14% of) British adults has committed a type of consumer fraud, new report shows. 2019 [Accessed 10 April 2021]; Available from: www.cifas.org.uk/newsroom/wpi-report

23. Zywicki, T., The economics of credit card security. 2014 [Accessed 10 April 2021]; Available from: www.washingtonpost.com/news/volokh-conspiracy/wp/2014/01/21/the-economics-of-credit-card-security

24. FCA, FCA agrees plan for a phased implementation of *strong customer authen*tication. 2019 [Accessed 10 April 2021]; Available from: www.fca.org.uk/news/press-releases/fca-agrees-plan-phased-implementation-strong-customer-authentication

25. Simpson, R., Neither clear nor present: The social construction of safety and danger. In *Sociological Forum*. 1996. Springer.

26. Bradbury, J.A., The policy implications of differing concepts of risk. *Science, Technology, & Human Values*, 1989. 14(4): p. 380–399.

27. Das, S., et al., The effect of social influence on security sensitivity. In 10th Symposium on Usable Privacy and Security ({SOUPS} 2014). 2014.

28. Wright, R., Cyberinsurance is on the rise – And so is ransomware. 2019 [Accessed 2 March 2022]; Available from: www.techtarget.com/searchsecurity/news/252475732/Cyberinsurance-is-on-the-rise-and-so-is-ransomware

29. Burdon, M. and L. Coles-Kemp, The significance of securing as a critical component of information security: An Australian narrative. *Computers & Security*, 2019. 87: p. 101601.

30. McCabe, M., Cyber insurance is supporting the fight against ransomware. 2019 [Accessed 10 April 2021]; Available from: www.brinknews.com/cyber-insurance-is-supporting-the-fight-against-ransomware

31. Kleinman, Z., Insurers defend covering ransomware payments. 2021 [Accessed 10 April 2021]; Available from: www.bbc.co.uk/news/technology-55811165

32. Boyd, C., Cyber insurance: Here to stay, whether we like it or not. 2019 [Accessed 10 April 2021]; Available from: https://blog.malwarebytes.com/ransomware/2019/10/cyber-insurance-here-to-stay-whether-we-like-it-or-not

33. Sabbagh, D., Insurers "funding organised crime" by paying ransomware claims. 2021 [Accessed 10 April 2021]; Available from: www.theguardian.com/technology/2021/jan/24/insurers-funding-organised-by-paying-ransomware-claims

34. Dupont, B., The ecology of cybercrime. In *The human factor of cybercrime*, R. Leukfeldt and T.J. Holt, Editors. 2019: Routledge. p. 389–407.

35. Elias, N., *What is sociology?* 1978: Columbia University Press.

36. Zimmermann, V. and K. Renaud, Moving from a "human-as-problem" to a "human-as-solution" cybersecurity mindset. *International Journal of Human-Computer Studies*, 2019. 131: p. 169–187.

37. FCA. Which? Authorised push payments super-complaint: our response. 2016 [Accessed 10 April 2021]; Available from: www.psr.org.uk/publications/news/which-authorised-push-payment-super-complaint-our-response

38. Jones, R. MPs urge compulsory refunds for victims of bank transfer fraud. 2019 [Accessed 10 April 2021]; Available from: www.theguardian.com/business/2019/nov/01/mps-urge-compulsory-refunds-for-victims-of-bank-transfer

39. Parliament. Banks must do more for consumers exposed to economic crime. 2019 [Accessed 10 April 2021]; Available from: https://committees.parliament.uk/committee/158/treasury-committee/news/98709/banks-must-do-more-for-consumers-exposed-to-economic-crime

40. Byers, D., We lost £25k savings to bank payment scam. 2020 [Accessed 10 April 2021]; Available from: www.thetimes.co.uk/article/we-lost-25k-savings-to-bank-payment-scam-5k6gkrq90

41. Bryan, K., Banks plan to kill off fraud refunds. 2020 [Accessed 10 April 2021]; Available from: www.thetimes.co.uk/article/banks-plan-to-kill-off-fraud-refunds-s9x2st76q

42. Byers, D., Banks failing to protect people from scams, say regulators. 2020 [Accessed 10 April 2021]; Available from: www.thetimes.co.uk/article/banks-failing-to-protect-people-from-scams-say-regulators-bqjcwszp6

43. Whitworth, D., Banks "too often blaming customers" for fraud. 2020 [Accessed 10 April 2021]; Available from: www.bbc.co.uk/news/business-55286037

44. Taylor, J.L. and T. Galica, A new code to protect victims in the UK from authorised push payments fraud. *Banking & Finance Law Review*, 2020. 35(2): p. 327–332.

45. Parris, M., No one seems to care about phone hoaxers. 2021 [Accessed 10 April 2021]; Available from: www.thetimes.co.uk/article/no-one-seems-to-care-about-phone-hoaxers-st9vd790p

46. Brennan, H., Banks forced to refund fraud victims. 2021 [Accessed 2 March 2022]; Available from: www.telegraph.co.uk/personal-banking/current-accounts/banks-forced-refund-fraud-victims

47. BBC, Romance fraud: "I wish I hadn't given £300k to a man I met online". 2021 [Accessed 7 March 2022]; Available from:www.bbc.co.uk/news/newsbeat-59135689

48. Byers, D., Facebook and Instagram blamed for surge in scams. 2022 [Accessed 14 January 2023]; Available from: www.thetimes.co.uk/article/facebook-and-instagram-blamed-for-surge-in-scams-jqtn9sdsm

49. Whitworth, D., Fraud victim gets surprise £153,000 refund despite rules. 2023 [Accessed 25 March 2023]; Available from: www.bbc.co.uk/news/business-64981507

50. Humphreys, L., Reframing social groups, closure, and stabilization in the social construction of technology. *Social Epistemology*, 2005. 19(2–3): p. 231–253.

51. Luiijf, E., K. Besseling, and P. De Graaf, Nineteen national cyber security strategies. *International Journal of Critical Infrastructures* 6, 2013. 9(1–2): p. 3–31.

52. Burgers, T. and D.R.S. Robinson, Keep dreaming: Cyber arms control is not a viable policy option. *S&F Sicherheit und Frieden,* 2018. 36(3): p. 140–145.

53. Tadelis, S., *Game theory: An introduction.* 2013: Princeton University Press.

54. Dunn Cavelty, M., A resilient Europe for an open, safe and secure cyberspace. *UI Occasional Papers*, 2013. 23.

55. van der Meer, S., Enhancing international cyber security: A key role for diplomacy. *Security and Human Rights*, 2015. 26(2–4): p. 193–205.

56. Carr, M. and F. Lesniewska, Internet of Things, cybersecurity and governing wicked problems: Learning from climate change governance. *International Relations*, 2020. 34(3): p. 391–412.

57. Lowenstein, D. and R. Na, Cyber security: Wicked problems, messes and metaphors. 2011 [Accessed 25 November 2022]; Available from: www.zdnet.com/article/cyber-security-wicked-problems-messes-and-metaphors

58. Conti, G., Why haven't we "solved" cybersecurity? 2020 [Accessed 25 November 2022]; Available from: https://federalnewsnetwork.com/commentary/2020/08/why-havent-we-solved-cybersecurity

59. Clemente, D., Cybersecurity as a wicked problem. 2017 [Accessed 25 November 2022]; Available from: www.ihavenet.com/Technology-Cyber-Security-as-a-Wicked-Problem-The-World-Today.html

60. Gilmore, K., Cyber security: A wicked problem. 2016 [Accessed 25 November 2022]; Available from: www.dafitc.com/cyber-security-a-wicked-problem

61. Doernberg, J., The wicked problem of cybersecurity. 2017 [Accessed 25 November 2022]; Available from: www.linkedin.com/pulse/wicked-problem-cybersecurity-john-doernberg

62. Bar-Yam, Y., *General features of complex systems.* 2002: Encyclopedia of Life Support Systems (EOLSS), UNESCO, EOLSS Publishers, p. 1.

63. Holland, J.H., *Complexity: A very short introduction.* 2014: OUP Oxford.

64. Dekker, S., *Safety differently.* 2014: CRC Press London.

65. Leveson, N.G., *Engineering a safer world: Systems thinking applied to safety.* 2016: The MIT Press.

66. Leveson, N.G., *System safety engineering: Back to the future.* 2002: Massachusetts Institute of Technology.

67. Husted, N. and S. Myers., Emergent properties & security: The complexity of security as a science. In Proceedings of the 2014 New Security Paradigms Workshop. 2014. ACM.

68. Yurcik, W., et al., Cluster security as a unique problem with emergent properties: Issues and techniques. In 5th LCI International Conference on Linux Clusters. 2004.

69. Connelly, K. and A.A. Chien., Breaking the barriers: High performance security for high performance computing. In Proceedings of the 2002 *Workshop* on New *Security Paradigms*. 2002. ACM.

70. Clayton, P. and P. Davies, *The re-emergence of emergence: The emergentist hypothesis from science to religion.* 2011: Oxford University Press.

71. Kaas, M., Emergence: A philosophical account. *Dialogue: Canadian Philosophical Review/Revue canadienne de philosophie*, 2018. 57(3): p. 645–646.

72. Humphreys, P., Out of nowhere. 2018 [Accessed 10 April 2021]; Available from: https://aeon.co/essays/atomism-is-basic-emergence-explains-complexity-in-the-universe

73. GeoffE. Of *m*ice and *c*yber. 2018 [Accessed 10 April 2021]; Available from: www.ncsc.gov.uk/blog-post/mice-and-cyber

74. Hollnagel, E. Is safety an emergent phenomenon? 2015 [Accessed 12 July 2023]; Available from: https://safetysynthesis.com/safetysynthesis-facets/safety-i-and-safety-ii/is%20safety%20emergent

75. Dalpiaz, F., E. Paja, and P. Giorgini, *Security requirements engineering: Designing secure socio-technical systems.* 2016: MIT Press.

76. Paja, E., F. Dalpiaz, and P. Giorgini, Modelling and reasoning about security requirements in socio-technical systems. *Data & Knowledge Engineering*, 2015. 98: p. 123–143.

77. Salnitri, M., et al., STS-tool 3.0: Maintaining security in socio-technical systems. In CAiSE Forum. 2015.

78. Mujinga, M., M.M. Eloff, and J.H.H. Kroeze., A socio-technical approach to information security. 2017 [Accessed 10 April 2021]; Available from: www.researchgate.net/publication/320288245_A_socio-technical_approach_to_information_security

79. Li, T., J. Horkoff, and J. Mylopoulos, Holistic security requirements analysis for socio-technical systems. *Software and Systems Modeling*, 2018. 17(4): p. 1253–1285.

80. Tawileh, A., J. Hilton, and S. McIntosh, Managing information security in small and medium sized enterprises: A holistic approach. In *ISSE/SECURE 2007 Securing Electronic Business Processes*. 2007: Springer, p. 331–339.

81. Damenu, T.K. and C. Beaumont, Analysing information security in a bank using soft systems methodology. *Information & Computer Security*, 2017. 25(3): p. 240–258.

82. Craig, R., et al., Soft systems methodology in net-centric cyber defence system development. In *2014 IEEE International Conference on Systems, Man, and Cybernetics (SMC)*. 2014: IEEE.

83. AlSabbagh, B. and S. Kowalski, Security from a systems thinking perspective-applying soft systems methodology to the analysis of an information security incident. In Proceedings of the 58th *Annual Meeting* of the ISSS-2014 United States. 2015.

84. van Deursen, N., W.J. Buchanan, and A. Duff, Monitoring information security risks within health care. *Computers & Security*, 2013. 37: p. 31–45.

85. Armstrong, R., J. Mayo, and F. Siebenlist, *Complexity science challenges in cybersecurity.* 2009: Sandia National Laboratories SAND Report.

86. Pieters, W., The (social) construction of information security. *The Information Society*, 2011. 27(5): p. 326–335.

87. Wall, D.S., The devil drives a Lada: The social construction of hackers as cybercriminals. In *Constructing Crime*. 2012: Springer, p. 4–18.

88. Johnson, N., *Simply complexity: A clear guide to complexity theory.* 2009: Oneworld Publications.

89. Forrest, S., S. Hofmeyr, and B. Edwards, The complex science of cyber defense. 2013 [Accessed 10 April 2021]; Available from: https://hbr.org/2013/06/embrace-the-complexity-of-cybe

90. Gandhi, G., Complexity theory in cyber security. 2014 [Accessed 10 April 2021]; Available from: www.researchgate.net/publication/263652176_Complexity_theory_in_Cyber_Security

91. O'Connor, C. and J.O. Weatherall, How misinformation spreads – And why we trust it. 2019 [Accessed 10 April 2021]; Available from: www.scientificamerican.com/article/how-misinformation-spreads-and-why-we-trust-it

92. Bergstrom, C.T. and J.D. West, *Calling bullshit: The art of Skepticism in a data-driven world.* 2020: Random House.

93. Conklin, W.A. and G. Dietrich, Systems theory model for information security. In Proceedings of the 41st Annual Hawaii International Conference on System Sciences (HICSS 2008). 2008: IEEE.

94. Kupfersberger, V., et al., Applying soft systems methodology to complex problem situations in critical infrastructures: The CS-AWARE case study. *International Journal on Advances in Security,* 2018. 11(3 & 4), 2018.

95. Fruhlinger, J., The CIA triad: Definition, components and examples. 2020 [Accessed 5 March 2022]; Available from: www.csoonline.com/article/3519908/the-cia-triad-definition-components-and-examples.html

96. Martin-Vegue, T., The mad men of cyber security advertising. 2018 [Accessed 5 June 2021]; Available from: https://medium.com/@tdmv/the-mad-men-of-cyber-security-advertising-e383ad82f79c

97. Martin-Vegue, T., The birth of a ransomware urban myth. 2017 [Accessed 4 June 2021]; Available from: https://hackernoon.com/the-birth-of-a-ransomware-urban-myth-cf9950addb80

98. Martin-Vegue, T., Selection bias and information security surveys. 2017 [Accessed 5 June 2021]; Available from: https://hackernoon.com/selection-bias-and-information-security-surveys-c991b79aab17

99. Martin-Vegue, T., How to lie with statistics, information security edition. 2018 [Accessed 5 June 2021]; Available from: https://medium.com/@tdmv/how-to-lie-with-statistics-information-security-edition-b0f373bdf5f

100. Hielscher, J., et al., "Taking out the Trash": Why security behavior change requires intentional forgetting. In New Security Paradigms Workshop. 2021.

101. Fagan, P., Organizational issues in IT security. *Computers & Security*, 1993. 12(8): p. 710–715.

102. Reinfelder, L., R. Landwirth, and Z. Benenson, Security managers are not the enemy either. In Proceedings of the 2019 CHI Conference on Human Factors in Computing Systems. 2019.

5 Security Is Best Done with Numbers

MARKETING CONTEXT

SECURITY AND MARKETING

In 1960, Theodore Levitt wrote a piece for the Harvard Business Review [1]. The title was "Marketing Myopia", and the article became something of a marketing classic [2], partly because it challenged the business orthodoxy of the time, but also because of the appeal of two very clear messages.

The first was to do with marketing. Levitt said that when you're selling something, you can either say "this is what we're selling, buy it", or you can ask potential customers "what would you like to buy – perhaps we can build that for you". The first type of marketing is called a product-based approach, and you don't see a lot of it these days. For good reason, as it turns out. The second method is called a market-based (or customer-oriented) approach. Levitt is supposed to have summarised this second approach by saying: "*[w]hen people buy a quarter inch drill, they don't want a quarter inch drill – what they want is a quarter inch hole*". The point is that unless you consider what the customer wants as an end benefit, then you aren't going to meet their needs.

The second message was almost the reverse of the first. Levitt said that industries that don't take the time to ask themselves "why do people buy our product?" tend to find quite unexpectedly that people aren't buying their product anymore. This is the myopia angle – unless you look beyond the product, you won't see ways in which the market might be evolving around you. Levitt took as an example the US railroad industry, which stuck firmly to the idea that they were in the business of building and operating railroads. Consequently, when other forms of transport emerged, rather than riding the curve, they ignored it. Flying machines you say? A passing fad. Automobiles? A ludicrous idea, such a thing will never catch on. In fact, aeroplanes could have been used as a basis for charging premium delivery rates, and trucks could have done the "last mile" from the railhead to the homestead. Instead, the railroad industry hit the buffers, so to speak, at a time of unprecedented demand for transportation.

Levitt's point was that if the industry had seen themselves in the wider transportation business rather than occupying a narrow technological niche, then they might have fared a bit better. This sort of argument is often described as "Brunswikian",

DOI: 10.1201/9781003380962-5

after Egon Brunswik [3], who proposed that an organism and its environment interact and affect each other. Levitt said that a focus on the product rather than on the customer was unlikely to work in the longer term. Intuitively, any organism that ignores its environment can't expect to survive.

MARKET DEVELOPMENTS

Philip Kotler's book on marketing principles [4] makes the point that companies occasionally carry out a process he terms "reverse integration". If you're a business and you have someone supplying to you, but you're not satisfied with the product or service, then you have a couple of options. You can develop the same capability in-house, or you can acquire that company and fix the problems. Either way, you incorporate the role of that service provider into your own business.

It seems to me that the same process is happening in the security industry. Changes that have been emerging over the past few years bear all the hallmarks of a customer who's lost patience with a supplier that isn't listening to their needs, and has decided to do the job themselves.

According to ISACA, their CRISC security risk management qualification [5] is particularly popular among C-suite executives – about 10% of the total membership of 24,000 is made up of CIOs, CFOs, etc., indicating that those individuals now see cyber security as part of their role, rather than the job of a technical specialist.

At the time of writing, there are at least five combined business/cyber courses available from UK universities. These are either Master of Business Administration (MBA) degrees with cyber as a specialisation, or MSc degrees in cyber security that have had a chunk of business and psychology added in [6–10].

Service Operational Controls (SOC) standards [11] are increasingly being used as a means of achieving security assurance. The chief benefit of a SOC assessment is that it provides a formal attestation of how well the organisation is doing in terms of meeting its declared security targets. It's not a report on password lengths or firewall settings. It's a statement of whether or not the board is successfully managing cyber risks. It uses the same basic process as is followed in audits for commercial risk, contractual risk, financial risk, etc., so it's a process familiar to managers, and it provides information in a form that can be assimilated by shareholders and collaborating companies.

Depending on who you ask, the global cyber insurance market is predicted to be worth about US$20Bn by 2025 [12]. Impressive, since insuring against the impact of cyber security incidents wasn't a thing until a few years ago. In 2017 the US market grew by about 30% [13] (or 37%, again depending on who you ask [14]). In 2018/2019, the US market only managed a disappointing 10% year-on-year growth [14], but on the plus side, in the past five years the value of the market seems to have doubled [15]. All of which is interesting, because insurance is a business solution to a business problem. Companies have insurance to cover a wide range of risks, including loss of key personnel and public liability. So if the rise of cyber insurance follows the same logic, it means that cyber risks are now being seen as something that should have at least in part a business solution, and not a completely technical one.

A SUGGESTION

What seems to be happening is that the practice of information security is increasingly being regarded as a management discipline, rather than a technical specialisation. The cyber industry is being overtaken by market changes, as might have been predicted by Levitt, and perhaps also reflecting what we saw when we were looking for external drivers of change in the industry.

If Levitt's argument holds, then the reason underlying the shift is likely to be an excessive focus on products that the industry wants to sell, rather than looking at what the customer might want to receive. The argument presented in the rest of this section is that the cyber industry's very narrow interpretation of risk is at the heart of this conflict.

RISK AS A NUMBER

CALCULATING RISK

Security risk analysis usually embodies some kind of "risk equation", e.g.:

Risk = Threat x Vulnerability x Impact

The implicit assumption being that risk is a quantity – that it can be represented using a number. If that were true of course, then there would be a standard way of calculating it. However, that doesn't seem to be the case. A now unsupported UK Government approach, for example, combined just threat and impact, whereas the popular OCTAVE approach seems to add threat and impact together, rather than multiplying them [16, p53].

A cursory examination of any "risk equation" also throws up a couple of questions:

- If risk can be calculated, then it ought to have a scale.
- How do you measure threat and vulnerability, and what scales do they use?
- How do we assign an impact to an event before that event has taken place?

And to take the work of Frank Knight (a 1920's economist) – are we concerned with risk, or is it uncertainty [17]? They're not the same.

At best, security risk equations take two or more concepts plus a guess, and combine them in an arbitrary way to arrive at a misleading number, an approach that has been summarised as "pseudo-quantitative". Bergstrom and West, in their book "Calling Bullshit" [18] propose the very useful idea of "mathiness" – something that seems as though it has mathematical authority, when in fact it doesn't.

THE CASE AGAINST NUMBERS

The risk equation is sometimes presented in the form of a matrix, with "threat level" along one axis and "impact" along the other. That too has been assessed and discarded. Louis Cox [19] used formal logic to draw up rules that a risk matrix should adhere to and showed that in practice there were a number of intractable problems, not the least of which was the generation of misleading outcomes. Thomas et al. [20] go further and point out "... *the gross inconsistencies and arbitrariness embedded in [risk matrices]*" and conclude that "*[g]iven these problems, it seems clear to us that [risk matrices] should not be used for decisions of any consequence*" [20, p63]. Verendel [21] argues that the idea of quantified security itself constitutes "*a weak hypothesis*", largely because of the absence of any supporting evidence. Others, e.g. Pfleeger [22], have commented on the difficulty of "measuring" security.

John Adams [23] sums up the problem that arises when you focus on risk as a quantity:

> *The Kelvinist, rocket-science approach to virtual risks, with its emphasis on the quantitatively soluble, threatens to divert attention from larger, more complicated, more urgent problems with which we ought to be grappling.*

The trouble is, risk as a number is an established viewpoint, at least within the practitioner community. Perceived wisdom has it, for example, that risk appetite is some form of upper limit on the acceptability of residual risk (the security risk that's left over once you've implemented all the relevant countermeasures, presumably found as the difference between quantified risk and quantified security). Aven's work on the concept of risk appetite [24] notes that, as with the "equations" used to calculate risk, there's no commonly accepted interpretation, and consequently, no meaning can be attached to the term. Dunn Cavelty [25] goes further and argues that linear risk analysis can't be applied to real-world situations, because the socio-technical environment for security is too complex. Others have suggested the same [26].

But if the theoretical foundations are so shaky, why does the industry persist in seeing risk as a quantity? Hard to say, probably inertia, possibly because the roots of the industry are linked to reductionism and an engineering-type approach. For me the main issue is not so much the use of numbers, it's the implicit assumption that because it's a number, it must be reliable.

AN ALTERNATIVE VIEW

Risk and Reward

If you were to take a purely rational standpoint, then risk and reward would be positively linked – if there's a high level of risk then it seems reasonable to expect a high level of potential benefit. The investigation conducted by Finucane and colleagues, however, took as its basis previous findings that the two seemed to have an inverse relationship in people's minds [27]. That is, if something's very risky, then it can't possibly be beneficial. Similarly, if something's seen as enormously beneficial, then it can't be that risky.

Finucane et al. found that by presenting people with a positive message on a particular issue, judgements of the balance of associated risks and benefits could be altered. Further, they found that the inverse relationship between risk and reward was strengthened when people were put under time pressure – when they were encouraged to make a quick decision. That aligns with the findings of Meyerson et al. [28] and those of Kirlappos and Sasse [29], who found that consumers employed confirmation bias when they really (really) wanted to use a web site, even though it had been flagged up to them as being potentially dangerous.

If we can see a reward in sight, and particularly one that's emotionally important, then we tend to discount the associated risk. That is, what we perceive as risk depends on the prevailing circumstances.

RISK AS A PERCEPTION

John Adams [30] argues that at least for individuals, risk is best viewed as a perception [31] rather than as a calculation. As an illustration, there's a roundabout near my house that has peak time traffic signals on it. When the traffic lights are active, you sit and wait until you have a green light. When they aren't active, you look to the right as you approach (I live in the United Kingdom), and if the road is clear, you proceed onto the roundabout. Occasionally there's a sign saying "caution – traffic lights out of order". So I do as I'm told – I take extra care. But why? If the lights are out of action, that's no worse than having them switched off. And yet people do take more care, because the sign declaring a failure of the lights implies a higher degree of risk.

Adams provides a number of examples in the same vein. When a dangerous curve in the road is straightened out, average speeds tend to increase. Adams' explanation is that because the perceived level of risk has gone down, drivers go faster in order to compensate, so that they feel as though they are facing the same (presumably acceptable) overall level of risk. The use of seat belts, Adams argues, hasn't led to fewer deaths on the road. If you're in an accident then you're more likely to survive, but because people feel safer when they're buckled up, they tend to take more risks, leading to more accidents.

Conversely, there are towns in the United Kingdom and elsewhere that have taken away the "street furniture" – street signs, road markings, etc. (e.g. [32]). That brings about a drop in accident rates, because drivers take more care without all those reassuring signs making their decisions for them. The removal of white lines down the middle of the road, in particular, has been found to significantly reduce average speeds [33], because although the circumstances haven't changed that much, your perception of them has.

Although it may be convenient for cyber practitioners to represent risk as a number, that doesn't align with the way that we, as humans, treat risk in practice.

COMMUNICATING RISK

A survey conducted in collaboration with Nasdaq [34] indicated that amongst companies deemed to be "highly vulnerable" to cyber-attack, 91% of non-executive directors said that they couldn't interpret a cybersecurity report. Perhaps a more representative figure quoted in the report was that "*43% of all respondents can't interpret a cybersecurity report at the same level as a financial report*".

The 91% and 43% figures, or at least the reporting of them, suggest two possible situations. The first is that C-suite executives really aren't that bright (I guess that's why they're running major corporations) and that, consequently, they require education, as

shown in comments such as "*[t]he first step in maturing an organization's management of cyber risks is educating the executive team*" [35].

The second possibility is that it might have to do with poor communication by
security practitioners. Lallie et al. [36] looked at two ways of communicating the
nature of a cyber-attack, using either adapted attack graphs or fault trees. Some of
the people taking part in the study were computer science graduates, some weren't.
Amongst the computer science graduates, adapted attack graphs were found to be
more effective, as reflected in higher mean assessment scores when their comprehension of attack descriptions was tested. However, the non-computer science people
performed rather worse than the computer science group overall.

So if you want to describe cyber risks to a group of computer science graduates,
then you should probably use representations that they're familiar with, e.g. symbols
from a technical diagram. But why would you want to? What's the point of cyber
practitioners talking about risk in a way that can only be understood by other cyber
people?

Baskerville [37] makes an absolutely critical point here – that the purpose of a
risk analysis is to communicate risk, not just to document it. Lui et al. go further,
suggesting that practitioners and non-practitioners have different mental models of
cyber risks, and that this difference could "*... lead to ineffective and poor risk communication*". Therefore they suggest that "*... risk communication methods should
be designed based on the non-expert's mental models ...* " [38]. That is, the process
of risk analysis should focus on the intended audience – managers, rather than other
cyber practitioners. The same suggestion has been made by the UK National Cyber
Security Centre (NCSC) [39]:

> *Risk Management often requires a relationship between people who analyse
> risks and people who make decisions based on that analysis. Communication
> between these two groups must be clear, understandable and useful. If the
> people who make decisions can't interpret the analysis they're presented with,
> then there is little point in doing risk analysis at all.*

The obvious message being that there's no point in carrying out a risk analysis if
you can't communicate the results. Blastland and Speigelhalter, in their book on risk
perception [40], go further and suggest that we tend to make risk decisions through a
"*visceral, emotional response*" [41], within a framework of social norms [42, 43]. If
that's true, then it's going to be better to use narratives rather than numbers as a basis
for risk communication [44]. Or, as we saw with Fuzzy Trace Theory, to communicate the context for the risk, rather than using numerical, verbatim representations.
Because either way, when risk is represented as a number in a spreadsheet, people
find it difficult to gain an intuitive feel for it [45]. Quoting the findings of Kunreuther
et al., Greg Ip [46, p204] sums this up: "*... people can better evaluate risk when they
have a strong narrative context*".

To return to Levitt's argument, when practitioners concentrate on the product
(as in "there, I produced a risk analysis") rather than on what the customer wants
(an understanding of the risks they're running), then the customer's requirements
won't be met. It's that simple. Using risk "calculations" might be convenient for

practitioners, but it does nothing to help managers make decisions. It fails to effectively communicate the risks, which drives people to think that maybe they could do a better job themselves.

AVOIDING CALCULATIONS

ALTERNATIVE APPROACHES

There's plenty of advice available if you're looking for an approach to risk analysis that doesn't involve numbers.

The ISO/IEC 31000 series of standards relate to risk analysis and risk management. In particular, three central documents provide guidance to organisations and individuals on the management of risk, and in a general sense, not just relating to cyber. ISO/IEC 31010 is one of those standards – it contains a list of current risk analysis and management techniques (about 30 of them, in the most recent version [47]). After discarding those based on a numerical representation of risk and/or a risk matrix and/or a risk equation, three broad categories remain:

- Structured and semi-structured thinking. The Delphi technique is an example, in which subject matter experts are asked their opinion on how the security of a system might be compromised.
- State transition methods, such as Markov diagrams, where the conditions necessary to trigger a system to shift from a secure state to an insecure state can be identified.
- Tree breakdowns. Starting with an attacker's objective, identify the conditions and associated sub-conditions necessary to achieve that objective, as the branches on a tree. McQueen [48–50] suggests that this approach can be applied repeatedly to refine security plans, through the idea of an "iterative weakest link" [51].

The "Bow Tie" method [52] is probably the most well-known state transition method. It recognises that a change in status can be brought about by a range of possible events, and that a change in state can have a range of possible outcomes. It's an attack-based approach, which makes it particularly useful. On the downside, the experience of practitioners is that it can involve a large amount of paperwork, and that consequently it can be difficult to maintain the associated documentation.

Schneier attack trees [53] are probably the most useful of the tree breakdown structures. Similar approaches have been applied successfully to identify product security requirements, together with a set of assumptions regarding the operating environment. This approach is also amenable to the use of support tools such as concept mapping.

Of the structured and semi-structured approaches, the Structured What-If Technique (SWIFT, [54]) is probably the most relevant. To quote the standard:

[SWIFT] is a systematic, team-based study, utilizing a set of "prompt" words or phrases that is used by the facilitator within a workshop to stimulate

participants to identify risks. The facilitator and team use standard "what-if" type phrases in combination with the prompts to investigate how a system, plant item, organization or procedure will be affected by deviations from normal operations and behaviour.

As part of the process of developing a new risk analysis approach for a UK Government Department, we adopted much of the thinking behind SWIFT. The process needed to fit into an agile development environment, and crucially, in the words of one of the collaborators, needed to produce a report *"... that a senior manager could pick up, read through, and understand the risks they're running"*.

A DIFFERENT MODEL

The approach we took was based on two information-gathering workshops.

The first is a user stories session, in which business stakeholders are asked for their positively worded requirements for security in the delivered system. An example might be "As a system administrator, I want a reliable audit trail of user actions, so that I can be sure I'm meeting my regulatory obligations". Another might be "As a system owner, I want to have assurance in the delivered service so that I can be confident of the extent of my liability". This first workshop has no security people in it at all – it involves system administrators, system owners, and representatives of user communities. The aim is to gather and collate user expectations on security without the influence of security practitioners.

The second workshop gathers information on likely attack types. This session requires security people, people with knowledge of what data is held on the system (and why and to whom it might be valuable), and system architects (because they know where the weak spots might be). This session asks the group "if you personally were having a pop at the system, what would you do?". By looking at practical attack routes, the workshop avoids disaster scenarios and worst-case hypothetical situations. The information gathered from this workshop provides an indication of who would attack the system, why they would do it, and to one degree or another, how they would do it. But there's no use of pseudo-quantitative guesses at probability. An overview of the process is given in Figure 5.1.

The notes from the two workshops are combined into a single report of about a dozen pages, using diagrams, bullet point lists, and narrative. That's achieved in a third, usually smaller workshop, which combines the expressions of requirements from the first two sessions to derive a set of countermeasures, split into three economic categories (free, paid for, and can't be done).

In terms of the preceding argument on social construction, the first two workshops independently gather views on what security looks like according to the key stakeholders (i.e. the two main "social groups"), and the third workshop carries out the negotiation for them, to arrive at a situation that both should be happy with. In principle, if there's a specific third or fourth community, there's no reason why the number of workshops couldn't be expanded to accommodate their views, also. In fact, in principle, there's no reason why the process couldn't be preceded by an analysis identifying the relevant social groups.

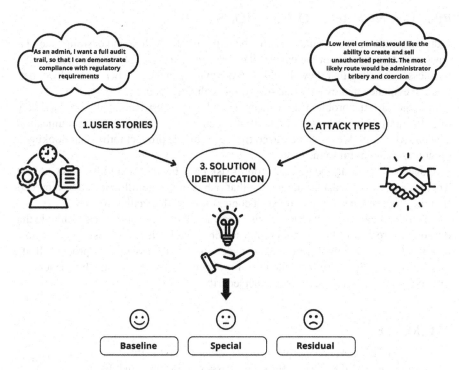

As an admin, I want a full audit trail, so that I can demonstrate compliance with regulatory requirements

Low level criminals would like the ability to create and sell unauthorised permits. The most likely route would be administrator bribery and coercion

1.USER STORIES

2. ATTACK TYPES

3. SOLUTION IDENTIFICATION

Baseline   Special   Residual

FIGURE 5.1   Risk assessment. (Leapfrog Creative Ltd, reproduced with permission.)

I have used this technique on a number of projects under a range of circumstances. The key benefits are that:

- Risk is communicated, not just documented.
- Security approval authorities get their day back. There are no thousand-page security reports to wade through.
- System owners and users get involved in the design of the system (an application of "participatory design" [55–57]).
- Security stops being a job carried out in isolation by a security "expert".

The process isn't presented here as a cure-all solution. One of the principles underpinning the method was that "there is no one true way" in risk analysis, as emphasised by NCSC [58]: *"[t]he short answer is that there is no single method for doing risk management for cyber security which can be applied universally, to good effect"*. Nonetheless, this approach was found to be a significant improvement over techniques based on exhaustive systematic searches and pseudo-calculations. To take a lead from Adams, and to slightly misinterpret the quote from Laplace regarding probabilities, the use of that type of search has come to represent *"common sense reduced to calculus"*.

RISK AS A NUMBER: CONCLUSIONS

Industries with no understanding of the benefits sought by their end customers tend to have uncertain futures. In the case of the cyber industry, the future may be driven by businesses deciding that they should own the management of cyber, and indeed there is some evidence that exactly that transition is already taking place.

In large part, the problem stems from the industry's very technically oriented view of risk, combined with a lack of attention to achieving effective risk communication. The underlying problem can be traced to a focus on the product rather than looking at outcomes meaningful to the customer.

Concepts regarding the quantisation of risk have been shown to be shaky at best. There is a body of evidence suggesting that risk is more usefully viewed as a perception, i.e., that risk has more to do with context than with calculations.

In terms of carrying out practical risk analyses, there are approaches available that do not require risk to be a number, and which provide clear business benefits, such as a greater level of involvement of managers in the risk assessment process. In the main, those benefits arise from the use of processes drawing on a much broader pool of expertise than simply technical cybersecurity.

REFERENCES

1. Levitt, T., Marketing myopia. *Harvard Business Review*, 1960. 38(4): p. 24–47.
2. Enis, B.M. and K.K. Cox, *Marketing classics*. 1988: Allyn and Bacon.
3. Brunswik, E., Organismic achievement and environmental probability. *Psychological Review*, 1943. 50(3): p. 255.
4. Keller, K.L. and P. Kotler, *Marketing management*. 2016: Pearson.
5. ISACA, *Certified in risk and information systems control (CRISC)*. 2021 [Accessed 10 April 2021]; Available from: www.isaca.org/credentialing/crisc
6. Warwick, *MSc cyber security and management (CSM)*. 2023 [Accessed 10 April 2021]; Available from: https://warwick.ac.uk/fac/sci/wmg/education/wmgmasters/courses/cyber_security/cyber_security_management
7. Coventry, *MBA (for the cyber security management sector)*. 2023 [Accessed 14 January 2023]; Available from: www.prospects.ac.uk/universities/coventry-university-3715/faculty-of-business-and-law-3716/courses/mba-cyber-security-management-110089
8. Bournemouth, *MSc cyber security & human factors*. 2021 [Accessed 10 April 2021]; Available from: www.bournemouth.ac.uk/study/courses/msc-cyber-security-human-factors
9. Sunderland, *Cybersecurity MBA*. 2023 [Accessed 25 March 2023]; Available from: https://london.sunderland.ac.uk/study/master-business-administration/mba-cybersecurity
10. Lancaster, *Cyber security executive MBA*. 2023 [Accessed 25 March 2023]; Available from: www.lancaster.ac.uk/study/postgraduate/postgraduate-courses/cyber-security-executive-mba-mba
11. AICPA, *SOC for service organizations*. 2021 [Accessed 10 April 2021]; Available from: www.aicpa.org/interestareas/frc/assuranceadvisoryservices/socforserviceorganizations.html

12. Alllianz, *A guide to cyber risk.* 2015 [Accessed 10 April 2021]; Available from: www. agcs.allianz.com/content/dam/onemarketing/agcs/agcs/reports/AGCS-Cyberrisk-rep ort.pdf

13. Amaral, R. *Here's what's happening with the U.S. cyber market.* 2019 [Accessed 10 April 2021]; Available from: https://riskandinsurance.com/u-s-cyber-insurance-mar ket-updates

14. Aon, *US cyber market update.* 2019 [Accessed 10 April 2021]; Available from: www. namic.org/pdf/resourceCenters/rerc/2019/201906-us-cyber-market-update.pdf

15. insurancejournal.com, *State of the cyber insurance market.* 2019 [Accessed 10 April 2021]; Available from: www.insurancejournal.com/news/national/2019/06/18/ 529747.htm

16. Caralli, R., et al., *Introducing octave allegro: Improving the information security risk assessment process.* 2007 [Accessed 10 April 2021]; Available from: https://resources. sei.cmu.edu/library/asset-view.cfm?assetid=8419

17. Knight, F.H., *Risk, uncertainty and profit.* New York: Hart, Schaffner and Marx, 1921.

18. Bergstrom, C.T. and J.D. West, *Calling bullshit: The art of skepticism in a data-driven world.* 2020: Random House.

19. Louis Anthony Cox Jr, What's wrong with risk matrices? *Risk Analysis: An International Journal*, 2008. 28(2): p. 497–512.

20. Thomas, P., R.B. Bratvold, and E. Bickel, The risk of using risk matrices. *SPE Economics & Management*, 2014. 6(02): p. 56–66.

21. Verendel, V., Quantified security is a weak hypothesis: A critical survey of results and assumptions. In *Proceedings of the 2009 Workshop on New Security Paradigms.* 2009. ACM.

22. Pfleeger, S. and R. Cunningham, Why measuring security is hard. *IEEE Security & Privacy*, 2010. 8(4): p. 46–54.

23. Adams, J., Risk management: It's not rocket science...... It's much more complicated. *Risk Management*, 2007. 54(5): p. 36.

24. Aven, T., On the meaning and use of the risk appetite concept. *Risk Analysis*, 2013. 33(3): p. 462–468.

25. Dunn Cavelty, M., A resilient Europe for an open, safe and secure cyberspace. *UI Occasional Papers*, 2013. 23 .

26. Björnsdóttir, S.H., et al., The importance of risk management: What is missing in ISO standards? *Risk Analysis*, 2022. 42(4): p. 659–691.

27. Finucane, M.L., et al., The affect heuristic in judgments of risks and benefits. *Journal of Behavioral Decision Making*, 2000. 13(1): p. 1–17.

28. Meyerson, D., K.E. Weick, and R.M. Kramer, Swift trust and temporary groups. In *Trust in organizations: Frontiers of theory and research*, R. Kramer and T. Tyler. 1996: SAGE, p. 166–195.

29. Kirlappos, I. and M.A. Sasse, Security education against phishing: A modest proposal for a major rethink. *IEEE Security & Privacy*, 2011. 10(2): p. 24–32.

30. Adams, J., *Risk.* 1995, Routledge.

31. Slovic, P., et al., Risk as analysis and risk as feelings: Some thoughts about affect, reason, risk, and rationality. *Risk Analysis*, 2004. 24(2): p. 311–322.

32. Kennedy, J., et al., *"Psychological" traffic calming.* 2005 [Accessed 10 April 2021]; Available from: https://pure.strath.ac.uk/ws/portalfiles/portal/120689049/Kennedy_ etal_TRL_641_2005_Psychological_traffic_calming.pdf

33. Harrison, J., *Are roads safer with no central white lines?* 2016 [Accessed 10 April 2021]; Available from: www.bbc.co.uk/news/uk-35480736

34. Nasdaq, *Bridging the accountability gap: Why we need to adopt a culture of responsibility.* 2016 [Accessed 2 March 2022]; Available from: www.nasdaq.com/articles/bridging-accountability-gap-why-we-need-adopt-culture-responsibility-2016-04-01

35. Dennis, P., Helping the C-suite assess cyberrisk. *Risk Management,* 2015. 62(8): p. 28–30.

36. Lallie, H.S., K. Debattista, and J. Bal, An empirical evaluation of the effectiveness of attack graphs and fault trees in cyber-attack perception. *IEEE Transactions on Information Forensics and Security,* 2017. 13(5): p. 1110–1122.

37. Baskerville, R., Risk analysis: An interpretive feasibility tool in justifying information systems security. *European Journal of Information Systems,* 1991. 1(2): p. 121–130.

38. Liu, D., F. Asgharpour, and L.J. Camp, Risk communication in security using mental models. *Usable Security,* 2008. 7: p. 1–12.

39. NCSC, *Risk management guidance.* 2021 [Accessed 10 April 2021]; Available from: www.ncsc.gov.uk/collection/risk-management-collection/essential-topics/fundamentals

40. Spiegelhalter, D. and M. Blastland, *The Norm chronicles: Stories and numbers about danger.* 2013: Profile Books.

41. Kahan, D.M., et al., *Affect, values, and nanotechnology risk perceptions: An experimental investigation* GWU Legal Studies Research Paper, no. 261. 2007.

42. Douglas, M. and A. Wildavsky, *Risk and culture: An essay on the selection of technological and environmental dangers.* 1983: University of California Press.

43. Kahan, D.M., H. Jenkins-Smith, and D. Braman, Cultural cognition of scientific consensus. *Journal of Risk Research,* 2011. 14(2): p. 147–174.

44. Brown, V.J., *Risk perception: It's personal.* 2014, NLM-Export.

45. Leman-Langlois, S., Privacy as currency: Crime, information and control in cyberspace. Technocrime: Technology, Crime and Social Control. 2008: Willan, p. 112–138.

46. Ip, G., *Foolproof: Why safety can be dangerous and how danger makes us safe.* 2015: Hachette UK.

47. ISO, *ISO 31010.* 2019 [Accessed 21 February 2023]; Available from: www.iso.org/standard/72140.html

48. McQueen, M., et al., *Quantitative risk reduction estimation tool for control systems, suggested approach and research needs.* 2006, Idaho National Laboratory (INL).

49. McQueen, M.A., et al., Quantitative cyber risk reduction estimation methodology for a small SCADA control system. In *Proceedings of the 39th Annual Hawaii International Conference on System Sciences (HICSS'06).* 2006. IEEE.

50. McQueen, M.A., et al., Time-to-compromise model for cyber risk reduction estimation. In *Quality of Protection,* D. Gollmann, F. Massacci, and A. Yautsiukhin, Editors. 2006, Springer. p. 49–64.

51. Bohme, R. and T. Moore, The iterated weakest link. *IEEE Security & Privacy,* 2010. 8(1): p. 53–55.

52. Cockshott, J., Probability bow-ties: A transparent risk management tool. *Process Safety and Environmental Protection,* 2005. 83(4): p. 307–316.

53. Schneier, B., Attack trees. *Dr. Dobb's Journal,* 1999. 24(12): p. 21–29.

54. Card, A.J., J.R. Ward, and P.J. Clarkson, Beyond FMEA: The structured what-if technique (SWIFT). *Journal of Healthcare Risk Management,* 2012. 31(4): p. 23–29.

55. Albrechtsen, E., A qualitative study of users' view on information security. *Computers & Security,* 2007. 26(4): p. 276–289.

56. Albrechtsen, E. and J. Hovden, Improving information security awareness and behaviour through dialogue, participation and collective reflection. An intervention study. *Computers & Security*, 2010. 29(4): p. 432–445.

57. Beckers, K. and S. Pape, A serious game for eliciting social engineering security requirements. In *2016 IEEE 24th International Requirements Engineering Conference (RE)*. 2016. IEEE.

58. NCSC, *Coming soon: *new* guidance on risk management for cyber security*. 2021 [Accessed 10 April 2021]; Available from: www.ncsc.gov.uk/blog-post/coming-soon-new-guidance-risk-management-cyber-security

6 Security Is Treated as a Business Issue

AVAILABLE BUSINESS MODELS

INTRODUCTION

In his critique of security, Mark Neocleous [1] suggests that practitioners see security as being a good thing under all circumstances, and that they hold a corresponding belief that security must always be "maximised". That is, there is no such thing as an optimal level of security. You can always have more. In my experience, that's a fair summary of the thinking across much of the industry. It reflects the idea that security exists outside the business environment.

And yet, if I had a penny for every time I've been told by security practitioners that security is a business issue, well... I'd probably have about £3.50. What does it mean, anyway – "security is a business issue"? Whenever I hear it, it seems like the person saying it wants you to believe that they understand business. They get it. Personally, I can't see any evidence that the industry as a whole has taken on any common business models.

GROWTH

Greiner [2] put forward the idea that companies grow by passing through a number of recognisable stages, and that the transition between stages is marked by some form of crisis. The stages and their crises were identified as:

1. Growth through creativity. This is the archetypal start-up, with a bright idea, attracting investment because it opens up a new market, or because it reduces costs in an existing market, or because it's disruptive and it's going to change the way the market operates. Usually a company starts out as a small number of people working together with a common cause, but eventually reality sets in, and you have to have someone making the tough decisions. That's why the transition between this stage and the next is marked by a crisis of leadership. It's only by passing through that crisis that companies can move into the next phase.

DOI: 10.1201/9781003380962-6

2. Growth through direction. Having established some form of command and control, the company benefits from managing individual parts of the enterprise. Stability is achieved, but at a price – having segmented the organisation, those segments start to differentiate. This is kind of like the growth of an animal from an embryo – at this stage you start to see cell differentiation. The individual components need room to manoeuvre, and they can't do that unless the founders give them some autonomy. It's the crisis of autonomy that marks the transition to the next stage.

3. Growth through delegation. During this stage the founders need to "let go" a bit more and allow the managers that they have brought in, to manage. Richard Branson [3] identified a willingness to delegate responsibility to the right people as one of the factors leading to his success. However, delegation of responsibility doesn't mean there's no need for control. The crisis separating this phase from the next relates to the need to either re-establish or just maintain overall control.

4. Growth through coordination. In this phase, the company grows because of successful coordination between its individual parts. But coordination requires processes and rules, and when they become so strict that the company starts to suffer, there's a "crisis of red tape".

5. By relaxing the extent of the red tape, the individual components of the organisation can work together more effectively, and the company grows through collaboration. The structure of the organisation starts to become less rigid. However, even that can only get the company so far, and sooner or later, if the enterprise gets to this stage, the only available route for growth is through alliances with external agencies. The crisis marking the transition to the next phase is termed the "growth crisis".

6. In the final stage, growth takes place through alliances and mergers, although there is an attendant risk that the company loses its way and is itself taken over.

As an example, in the first phase of growth, there are any number of reasons why a company could fail in the weeks or months ahead, the usual problem being cash flow. But maybe the founders might fall out, or a single contract that was supporting the company might finish unexpectedly. A security failure is just one of those possible reasons. So although it shouldn't be ignored, cyber needs to take its place in the queue.

As the organisation matures, security controls will be amongst the formalised processes and red tape that constrict growth. That needs to be addressed in just the same way as any of the other constraints. And when the company starts to grow through mergers and acquisitions, the reliability of the cyber measures taken by the acquired companies starts to become important. So maybe the cyber processes within the organisation need to become a little more outward-looking.

In other words, the approach to cyber ought to evolve as the company matures, and at any point in the growth pattern, the approach to cyber ought to match the company's stage of development. Possibly I haven't been asking the right people, but nothing like this seems to have been incorporated into any security model that

I've ever seen. The original paper by Greiner was written in 1997, and it's still being referenced. It's not unreasonable to expect the cyber industry to understand that companies have different priorities as they evolve.

Environment

Emery and Trist [4] suggested that the business environment for an organisation could be categorised using a two-by-two matrix, leading to four generic types of environment. The two axes were to do with the distribution of opportunities in the environment, and the pace of change in the environment. The subsequent four types of environment were identified as:

- **Placid randomised.** This sort of environment changes very slowly if at all, and the opportunities are randomly distributed. This is kind of a "vanilla" environment.
- **Placid clustered.** The rate of change in the environment is slow, but the environment is segmented. The security market itself [5] might be an example. An organisation wanting to take advantage of this type of environment would need to offer different products to each segment.
- **Disturbed reactive environments**, in which change is a constant, and the components of the environment interact with one another in a complex way.
- **Turbulent environments** are basically chaotic, and there seems to be no pattern. Organisations living with this kind of environment need to be very sensitive to change, and need to have the ability to react quickly.

The key point being that the strategy adopted by an organisation, even if it isn't uniquely driven by the business environment, should at least take notice of it. The original paper was produced about 50 years ago, but it's still being cited (e.g. [6]). Over that time the model has also been extended to include a fifth type of environment ("vortical" [7]).

The Emery and Trist model raises the possibility that the security environment might vary, just as the business environment does – that there might be different types of cybersecurity environment, e.g. some fast-changing, some not. The implicit assumption within the industry, however, is that the business environment for an organisation isn't relevant to the consideration of its position on cyber. It's only the cyber environment, expressed as a static threat picture, that matters.

Culture

Charles Handy [8] (and again, about 20 years ago) identified four broad types of organisational culture. This isn't the same use of "culture" as you might see in relation to "security culture". Handy used it as a kind of shorthand for a combination of structure and internal communication – the way companies organise themselves. The four generic types he identified were based on structure and operation:

- **Task-based organisations.** This is typified by the use of teams that are created from all corners of the business to solve a problem or to work on a project that needs a specific set of skills. Once the task is complete, the team disbands and the team members go off to work on other projects.

- **Organisations based around the individual.** A typical person-based organisation would be a university, where the individual has a great deal of autonomy based on their level of experience, and decisions generally need to be made by consensus rather than being imposed by management.
- **Power-based organisations.** These usually have a single person at the centre of the organisation, which might be viewed as a web-like structure, with power radiating out from that individual. Typically the management style in these organisations is autocratic – "my way or the highway".
- **Role-based organisations.** The UK Civil Service is often viewed as a role-based organisation, although these days that might be a little inaccurate. The power that an individual has in the organisation has nothing to do with them personally, nor with their skills. It's vested in the role that they presently occupy.

Again, I can't see this reflected in any model of cybersecurity. Surely in order to implement cyber effectively, there should be some consideration of the way in which an organisation is structured, or the way in which internal communication is achieved, or the way in which power is exercised?

CONCLUSION

On this basis, I can't see any evidence that business models are reflected in the traditional approach to cyber. Consequently, I don't see any grounds for claiming that the cyber industry treats security as a business issue.

ALTERNATIVE APPROACHES

WHAT SECURITY AS A BUSINESS ISSUE MIGHT LOOK LIKE

In the long term, it's not so far-fetched to imagine that something like the Emery and Trist model could be applied to the threat environment for an organisation, characterising it by e.g. the diversity of threats and the rates of change. Similarly, it's not hard to envisage a risk assessment process that takes into account the developmental stage of a company and/or its internal structures, when deciding on the necessary security measures. However, achieving that will involve integrating a number of basic and well-established business models into the practice of cybersecurity, and that could take some time.

I should point out that this is emphatically not a proposal for a "Cyber Security Maturity Model". Using e.g. the Greiner model or organisational growth would be kind of the reverse of a Cyber Security Maturity Model – rather than looking at cyber maturity as a standalone issue, it would fit cyber into the prevailing circumstances for the organisation. NCSC in fact, suggests the possibility of doing just that [9]:

> *If your organisation has recently moved office, this could significantly change its cyber security maturity. Equally, in a year of high staff turnover, a workforce's*

approach to security will change. If you're using a maturity assessment to track your organisation's improvement you might capture these changes, and then be able to link them to these contextual changes in your organisation.

But as noted above, applying Greiner and/or Emery and Trist, at least on any kind of scale, is likely to involve significant effort, and would require a substantial change in thinking. In the meantime, are there any measures that could be taken to link a cyber approach to the specific circumstances of an organisation or project? Possibly.

NEAR TERM SOLUTIONS

Typically a project or an organisation will set up a security forum, or some form of "Security Working Group" (SWG). It's usually a collection of security people who talk about security without any reference to any other aspect of the business, and who deal with issues such as maintaining and updating their own documentation. It's often not a very helpful arrangement, partly because it reinforces the idea that security should be handled as a separate stream.

I have in the past used a more business-focussed approach, closer to the idea of a security steering committee. The meetings are attended by representatives from:

- service delivery;
- technical architecture;
- user experience/user requirements;
- project planning;
- security.

The point of the committee is to ensure that any proposed security mechanism fits within the context of the other areas represented at the meeting, such as ensuring that the project is content (or not) with delays caused by the introduction of specific security measures, that the user experience has been considered, and that any proposed change has been accepted in terms of its impact on the technical architecture and impact to overall service delivery.

On previous occasions the remit of the group has been summarised in a small number of key principles, such as:

- We will prioritise the user experience, because unusable security features simply prompt workarounds – people are paid to achieve, not to do security.
- We will ensure that all proposed security measures are underpinned by a clear, acceptable justification.
- Security decisions will be based on evidence rather than opinion.
- We prefer to encourage positive behaviours rather than apply blanket technical constraints.
- We will not implement extensive technical controls to address requirements that could be met instead through simple hygiene.
- We will ensure that assurance activities such as penetration testing are tailored to objectives and not carried out by default.

I should be honest and say that these are all based on openly available NCSC guidance, e.g. [10], and in truth, the operation of the group is probably no different than the process you might see in e.g. a Change Approval Board or similar. But experience shows that it leads to a better level of integration between the security function and other parts of the organisation, partly because it encourages the adoption of shared, core principles, but also because it triggers discussion.

REASONS FOR INVESTING

These are measures that could improve the fit between the business and the security function, although to be honest, this may be just fiddling around the edges. They aren't going to bridge the gap.

And yet, despite a lack of integration, people do find it meaningful to invest. The standard explanation offered by the cyber industry is that cyber investments will ward off huge, inevitable losses occasioned by security breaches. It's a reasonable marketing stance, but does it stack up?

THE CASE FOR INVESTMENT: AVOIDING LOSSES

STANDARD ARGUMENT (1): THE IMPACT ON SHARE PRICE

It's been suggested that announcing a security breach has a long term, negative effect on a company's share price. To take a random example, CGI commissioned a report[1] which claimed that a company's share price dropped by an average of 1.8% after the announcement of a breach [11], and which also suggested that the drop was "*permanent*" [11, pp6, 8, 16, 23]. The implication being that it's worth investing in cyber in order to avoid that. Obviously, nobody wants an unrecoverable impact on their share price.

Digging into those figures, the analysis seems to be based on the share price on the Friday after the announcement [11, p8]. If that's the case, then it raises two concerns. The first is that academic studies indicate that timing is critical. You really need to tie the change in share price to the day of the announcement, rather than measure it at some point during the week. The second is the use of the word "permanent". In most academic studies (e.g. [12]), the effect on share price is not statistically different from zero by about the 20-day mark. The stock price recovers. But obviously, you won't see that if you only look at it for a week [13].

I should point out that there is no one correct way to conduct these sorts of analyses. Most academic studies employ event study methodology [14] and measure Cumulative Average Abnormal Return (CAAR). Based on how the stock has been doing up to the point of the breach, you compare its path after the breach with the predicted trajectory and bring statistics to bear to detect significant differences. That works for short periods around the breach [15], although different methods are needed when you look at longer timescales, e.g. comparing the company's performance against a group of peer businesses. There's also more than one way to assess statistical significance in these studies [16].

But whatever the approach, you have to take care to filter out confounding events – events that might have affected the share price anyway. An example might be the reference in the report to a 2014 breach affecting a major UK supermarket, whose share price fell by just over 12% in the same week, the implication being that the breach led to the drop [11, p9]. Assuming that to be a reference to the 2014 Morrisons incident, then as pointed out by many reports at the time (e.g. [17]), in that week the supermarket "... *posted the worst performance in the FTSE 100 as a second profit warning in three months triggered a 12% slump*". Contemporary statements from Morrisons also hint at their readiness to engage in a price war with other UK supermarkets [18], possibly in order to soften the impact on their share price compared to the sector as a whole. Under these circumstances you either have to remove that event from the sample, on the basis that the drop was more likely to have been occasioned by the profit warnings or, instead, justify why it should be included. But it's dangerous to bypass those checks and quote the case as a front-line example.

Whichever method of analysis is used, it should involve in a significance test – a figure that goes alongside each conclusion, indicating how reliable we think that conclusion is. The usual measure of validity is the "p statistic". If that's less than 0.05, then one (perhaps slightly loose) interpretation is that there is less than a 5% probability that the reported finding came about purely by chance. What *is* that grinding sound? There are other measures that should be taken into account, such as the ability to detect an effect at all. However, for better or worse, the p value is the most reported statistic. Most studies will put forward their findings as reliable when the p statistic is less than 5% ($p < 0.05$), although $p < 0.01$ is preferred. At higher values (e.g. $p < 0.10$) the finding is at best, at least in academic papers, reported as only "marginally significant". As stated openly in the report, some of their results were not statistically significant "... *at the usual statistical confidence levels*" [11, p7]. I might be misreading the text, but I can only find one figure with a significance level attached to it, and that's 10% (i.e. $p < 0.10$).

The report also had "... *a focus on 65 'severe' and 'catastrophic' breaches occurring since 2013*" [11, p23], i.e. the authors seem to have selected which events they took into the analysis and consequently they may have (unintentionally) chosen cases that were more likely to show an effect. This is usually referred to as sampling bias.

Further, as stated in the report: "*[a] share price impact was also observed in companies suffering from low grade breaches but the results were less statistically significant and therefore excluded from the main results*" [11, p24]. One possible reading of that statement is that some of the findings were removed from the analysis, in order to get a result that was closer to significance [19]. This process of setting aside "non-findings" tends to distort the overall result, usually leading to the conclusion that there was an effect when perhaps there wasn't one – this is known as publication bias, or the "file drawer effect".

The report concludes that the average drop in share price (1.8%), when applied to the average market capitalisation of an FTSE 100 company, equates to a £120M loss in company value [11, p8], and that when the same percentage drop in share price is applied to the total market capitalisation of the companies in the sample, the loss in value comes to £42Bn.

Acquisti et al. [20] and Cavusoglu et al. [21] both reported that the distribution of observed drops in share price seemed to have a relatively low median compared to the mean (i.e. the "mid-range" point was quite low compared to the overall average), indicating that the mean was being inflated by a small number of relatively severe outliers. It was also noted that larger companies tended to exhibit smaller percentage drops. Nevertheless, in most studies examining the effect of a breach, these patterns are set aside, and the figure for the average drop in share price is multiplied by the average market capitalisation of the sampled companies, in order to arrive at an "average" loss of market value.

By taking the time to multiply individual share price drops by each company's market capitalisation, and *then* calculating the average, Acquisti et al. concluded that their original estimate of the average drop in value (US$140M) should in fact have been closer to US$10M. That's about 93% less than the headline figure that would have been seen in a report using the more simplistic (and erroneous) calculation. Most statisticians will be happy to confirm that except under unusual circumstances, the product of the averages is not the same as the average of the products.

The suggestion of permanence also bears examination. Richardson et al. [22] examined 95 breach reports over the years 2005–2017 and, based on each company's relative performance in the period preceding the breach, looked for abnormal share price changes in the immediate aftermath of the breach announcement. They also looked at overall performance after one, three, and six months.

In the short term (looking at a four-day period around the day of the announcement) the abnormal returns averaged out at about -0.3%. Others have found greater levels of impact, e.g. Goel and Shawky [23], who reported a 1% drop, although with lower levels of statistical significance. The study by Richardson et al. found that after 21 days there were no statistically significant differences between expected and actual share prices, i.e. not only was the dip quite small, but it was also quite short-lived. The authors found no statistically significant differences in returns between breached firms and similar firms at the one-, three-, and six-month points. They also found no evidence that accounting measures of company performance were affected in the longer term, i.e. breached firms didn't seem to differ from their peers in terms of subsequent performance.

As the authors noted, with a few exceptions the impact "...*disappears within days*" [22, p227] and that "*[m]ost of the difference between companies disclosing breaches and matched companies is driven by the rare catastrophic incidents*" [22, p229]. They conclude that their findings indicated "*[o]verall, no material economic impacts for a company after a data breach*" [22, p229]. These results are echoed in a number of other studies (e.g. [24–34]), which found either short-term impacts, limited impacts (sometimes only within specific industries, or in relation to specific attacks), or no statistically significant evidence of any impact.

In the spirit of fairness, the report under discussion isn't a lone example. Ford et al [33] looked at the impact of GDPR fine announcements on share price, specifically in the European market, and concluded that the announcement of a fine dropped the company's share price by about 1% in the three days after the event. The report quotes an average drop in market capitalisation of €1.2Bn but goes on to note that the average may have been skewed by one event (the Alphabet fine). In fact, if you remove that entry from the calculations, then the average change in market capitalisation falls to about one quarter of the quoted figure. That's how much impact one outlier can have on the calculations. It's also worth noting that taking an absolute value of the change in market capitalisation may not be the most meaningful way to present the results. The report states, for example, that BNP Paribas saw a drop of about €1Bn in their market capitalisation as the result of a GDPR fine. The fine, by the way, was for not responding to a data deletion request within the permitted timeframe [35], and the fine imposed was €2k. That is, the report concludes that a €2k fine for a minor misdemeanour led to a €1Bn drop in company value. Does that seem likely? As far as I can tell, the share price rose the day before by about 1.8% and fell on the day of the announcement by about 1.1% – those seem like normal day-to-day shifts. But when your market capitalisation runs to about €70Bn, small shifts come to represent a large amount of money in absolute terms. And it's the headlines that count.

Ali et al. [36] conducted a comprehensive literature search on the topic and concluded that [36, p28]:

> *Most event windows extending beyond two days of an event are insignificant... we thus infer that [Information Security] events affect a company's performance briefly, which signals the presence of strong and semistrong forms of the [Efficient Market Hypothesis] for [Information Security] event announcements.*

When you're presented with scary numbers on impacted share prices, it's worth looking past the headline figures and taking the time to examine the approach to calculating those numbers.

A 2015 Harvard Business Review (HBR) report [37] asked *why* security breaches didn't seem to affect stock prices. A factor hinted at in the report was that investors might lack the skills to be able to interpret the meaning of a security breach, and it's the failure of investors to understand the significance of the incident that leads to the very minor impact on share price. However, studies looking at the results of malware outbreaks [28] and Denial of Service (DOS) attacks [26] indicate that the markets treat these incidents differently, which seems to show that investors do appreciate the differences between attack types. IT-intensive companies for example tended to see a bigger impact from DOS attacks than did other companies. Aytes et al. [38] found that for non-confidentiality-related breaches, there was no significant effect, whereas companies suffering a breach of confidentiality saw a drop of about 1.85% over a six-day period. Campbell et al. [25] found a similar picture. There's also general evidence supporting the idea that markets neither overreact nor underreact to the announcement of a security breach [27].

On the available evidence, the market reaction seems valid; investors do have the capacity to understand both the impact and the nature of a breach. The logical conclusion is that there's no long-term impact on share price because, in the general case, investors don't see any long-term impact on profitability.

There do appear to be some medium-term issues. Cardenas [29] found that measures of share price volatility ("beta") increased after a breach announcement and also found an effect on volume (the number of shares traded). However, as with share price, the effect may be transient – Lange and Burger [12] found that by the 90-day mark, there was no significant effect on beta when compared to the values for matched companies. Against that you have to take into account the findings of Malliouris and Simpson [39], who took a larger sample size and found that announcing a security breach, especially in a falling market, affected the cost of capital for the breached company and hence could lead to reduced opportunities for future investment. The converse may also be true. Havakhor et al. [40] found that announcing an investment in cyber could lead to a reduction in the cost of capital, thereby potentially making it easier for the company to invest in future growth.

As we'll see in more detail later, sometimes there are externalities – effects on other parties – following a breach announcement. For example, Chen et al. [41] examined the impact on the share price of the firm that built the IT system operated by the breached company. They found that the supplier's share price went up in the two-day period after the announcement, possibly reflecting a view that the breached firm would need to procure additional services from the supplier in order to remedy the problem. However, as the number of breached records increased, that turned into a negative return for the supplier, which was found to be greater for breaches involving technology-intensive firms. Other studies have noted that the nature of the breach seems to decide the impact on the firm's competitors (either contagion, in which the competitors' share prices fall, or competition, in which competitor companies see gains). Essentially, the impact on related companies isn't straightforward, and it seems to reflect a shift between competition and contagion. But it's not always negative.

It's hard to align these nuanced changes with the simplistic, catastrophic predictions of the cybersecurity industry, where the claimed drop in share price is multiplied by an average market value, to arrive at a figure for overall loss. That's typically touted to be in the hundreds of millions of dollars, which conveniently sets a benchmark for how much companies should be spending on security. But when the figures are examined in detail, there don't seem to be widespread catastrophic impacts on share price. Cyber incidents aren't unique in this respect – you can see similar patterns following announcements of environmental accidents [42] and product recalls [43].

The conclusion is that it doesn't make sense to invest in cyber purely to avoid large and permanent drops in share price, because in the general case, those drops are (a) much smaller than advertised and (b) not permanent.

Standard Argument (2): Unplanned Internal Costs

The claimed loss in market capitalisation is commonly cited as being much higher than the internal costs arising from a breach, so it makes a more eye-catching headline. But if the share price recovers (and maybe even gets a bounce), then that headline figure doesn't stand. Let's fall back then, to an examination of the costs of repairing the damage arising from a breach, starting with the views of the companies themselves.

Sherman [44] provides a quote from the chairman and founder of the Ponemon Institute regarding cyber breaches: "*In some cases the feedback from CEOs and board members was it's interesting, but it's not a sleepless night*".

Campbell [25] quotes a response from eBay's CEO following their hack:

When asked about the economic impact of this attack on eBay, the firm's CEO, Meg Whitman, responded:

"Minimal. If people weren't able to list items during the time that our site was unavailable, they probably listed them soon afterward. Even if you make extreme assumptions that none of those deferred listings ever got made, the maximum we could be talking about is $ 50 000 of lost revenue to eBay".

When asked about the impact on eBay's reputation Whitman stated: "Probably neutral. Most of our users were very supportive of us, and very angry at whoever did this".

Romanosky [45] undertook a painstaking investigation into the financial impact accruing to companies following different types of breach. The report is full of detail and rightly includes a number of caveats. However, the work drew upon a reliable commercial database of breach reports, and took care to look for confounding factors. Key findings were that "... *most cyber events cost firms less than 0.4% of their revenue*" [45, p132], that "... *they cost most firms less than $200k, only a fraction of the millions of dollars commonly cited*" [45, p133], and that this was "... *far less than other losses due to fraud, theft, corruption, or bad debt*" [45, p133]. That is, in the general case, there are existing unwanted financial drains on companies which are (a) more severe and (b) ongoing, rather than episodic.

A 2016 survey conducted on behalf of the Banca d'Italia [46] noted that:

More than 90 per cent of firms report having sustained a direct cost below €10,000; only about one per cent reported damages in excess of €50,000, with 0.1 per cent above €200,000.[2]

Again in 2016, Edwards et al. [47] reported that:

Neither size nor frequency of data breaches has increased over the past decade. We find that the increases that have attracted attention can be explained by the heavy-tailed statistical distributions underlying the dataset.

Richardson et al. [22] cite an analysis by Dean [48]:

- In the case of the Target breach, the company estimated its internal costs to be around US$250M. An insurance payout of US$90M and tax relief on the extra expenditure brought that down to US$105M, a figure representing about 0.1% of Target's revenue in the year of the breach.
- For the Home Depot breach, net expenses came to US$28M after insurance payouts, representing about 0.01% of revenue.
- Media estimates of the cost of the Sony Pictures hack ranged from US$100M to US$300M. Dean's article points to the costs declared in the company's subsequent financial reports (US$15M, growing to US$35M if IT improvements were included). That represents around 1–2% of revenue in the year, and as pointed out in the article, the film at the centre of the hack (*"The Interview"*) gained significant, widespread (and free) publicity.

It's been suggested that companies lack the ability to accurately assess the impact of a breach, and that consequently, their reported figures are unreliable. A recent study conducted on behalf of the UK Government looked into just that – whether or not breach costs as estimated by affected companies were accurate [49, 50]. The researchers developed an approach which systematically examined all potential areas in which there might have been a financial impact. Some 15 case studies were then used to compare the cost estimate produced by the tool with the original estimate produced by the company [51]. Setting aside a small number of cases where the estimated costs were either zero or a nominal £1 (i.e. "non-breaches"), and taking the midpoint where a range was provided rather than a single figure, then by my calculation, the detailed examination tended to produce estimates that were on average just under 20% higher than the original estimates provided by the breached company. That is, in the general case, even if you look really hard, you might find about another 20% to add to the figures reported by the companies themselves.

However, when it comes to cyber, folklore seems to override facts. At a 2015 hearing of the US House of Representatives Committee on Small Businesses, the chief operating officer of the National Cybersecurity Institute at Excelsior College quoted a statistic that you can still see widely on the web – that the financial impact of a security incident is so great, 60% of small enterprises suffering a breach go out of business within six months of the event [52]. Setting aside the fact that large numbers of start-ups tend to go broke anyway, it's worth looking at the provenance of that statistic. The alleged source (the National Cyber Security Alliance) has a statement on their web site saying: "please don't keep quoting this figure and attributing it to us, we had it on an infographic in 2011 but couldn't verify it, so we took it down" [53, 54]. But still it persists [55, 56], even on Government web sites [57]. As recently as October 2022, the BBC ran a story [58] relating to the impact of cyber-attacks on small businesses, repeating the 60% statistic and even going so far as attributing it to the National Cyber Security Alliance.

STANDARD ARGUMENT (3): REPUTATIONAL DAMAGE

So if the impact of a breach isn't related to massive drops in share price, and if there's no cash bonfire, what other impact can we take as the basis for a business case to support investment in cyber? A number of industry pundits offer up the idea of reputational damage. It's worth looking at that.

Breitinger and Bonardi [59] examined the concept of reputational damage, arguing that it's socially constructed:

Reputation loss should thus be viewed as a socially constructed phenomenon in which the framing of the issue and the person/entity who frames it matter much more than the severity of the issue or how often a firm is criticized.

Their argument is that in order for there to be any reputational damage, there must be "norm guards" – social groups that raise a flag when they see corporate actions that may have negative consequences for society in general. Their paper points to the existence of environmental groups in the case of polluting companies, and e.g. Transparency International [60] in the case of corporate corruption.

Are there norm guards for cyber security? If you treat privacy as a special case of information security, then the answer is that there are quite a few actually, e.g. Privacy International [61], Big Brother Watch [62], the Electronic Privacy Information Centre [63], the Open Rights Group [64], Privacy Rights Clearinghouse [65]. It seems there are lots of organisations who are ready to identify companies that misuse or lose personal data and to state very publicly that such behaviour is not acceptable.

So perhaps we do have the necessary ingredient for reputational damage. Let's take a look at how that works out for companies that breach privacy and are called out for it.

At this point you may be thinking "wait a minute – there was that company – Cambridge something". Ah yes. Cambridge Analytica (CA). For anyone that's been in isolation since 2018, CA was a company that allegedly employed big data techniques to profile voters, and used social media to send out highly targeted messages, thereby affecting the outcomes of some important elections and other types of poll [66]. They were closely linked to a number of unexpected election winners and (again, allegedly) accessed data from Facebook in ways that were not quite proper [67]. The affair was widely reported as a huge breach of data privacy [e.g. 68, 69, 70]. Within a short time, CA had closed down, Facebook had seen a 24% collapse in their share price (amounting to about US$130Bn), and a "delete FB" hashtag was trending on Twitter. So – reputational damage at its most obvious. Case closed.

Well, maybe. Facebook's share price, having dropped 24% in March 2018, was back up on track by May 2018, having recovered all of its losses [71], and having done so within a timeline pretty much in keeping with the research findings [20]. After appealing against the initial ruling, and hence delaying the process until things had calmed down [72], the company came to an agreement with the UK Information Commissioner's Office (ICO). The ICO imposed a fine of £500,000 (described by the UK Shadow Culture Secretary as "a drop in the ocean" [73] – or should that be "OCEAN"?) but Facebook got to retain ICO documents and did not admit liability.

In the United States, the Federal Trade Commission (FTC) imposed a US$5Bn fine and mandated a lengthy program of changes [74]. That financial penalty was the largest ever handed out for a privacy breach. But as noted at the time in a CBS News report [71], Facebook's quarterly results showed that operating income had grown by 64% over the preceding 12 months. Profits in the year stood at about US$22Bn. Other reports [75, 76] pointed out the immediate *increase* in Facebook's share price following the announcement. Conveniently, that rise in market capitalisation just about equalled the cost of the fine (which amounted to about a month's worth of revenue). As one source put it, the major impact of the ruling seemed to be that it had increased the personal wealth of Mark Zuckerberg.

Ah, but – CA went under, and that shows the power of reputational damage. Well, yes and no. But mostly "no".

Part of the problem for CA may have been that 50 or so key customers pulled out more or less immediately, leaving the staff with no fee-earning work [77]. That, I would suggest, might have been because they didn't want their own dealings to be drawn into the sunlight (known to be the best antiseptic). Part of it may also have been due to Facebook suspending CA from accessing their network [78, 79]. That may have had an impact on revenue, given that CA were a social media marketing company. Part of it may also have been due to a'sting conducted on one of its executives, which resulted in said executive being filmed apparently boasting about bribing politicians, and discussing other ways in which the company had wielded influence, such as engaging the services of Ukrainian sex workers [68]. Up until that point it seems that there had been some hope of saving the company through rebranding. But when the sting was publicised, it was obvious that the company had nowhere to go. So was it reputational damage from the privacy issues that caused CA to go under? I'd say it may have been related to reputation, but it was to do with issues far larger than privacy.

But surely all those users deserting Facebook caused damage? A mid-2018 survey by Pew [80] claimed that 26% of US Facebook users responding to their survey had deleted the app from their phones during the year (although that percentage ignored those who did not answer, and those who answered "other"). That has to be set against a reported trend away from Facebook and towards, e.g. Instagram [81], and it also has to be viewed in light of a study reported by the *same* survey company the next year [82], stating that *"[a]round seven-in-ten U.S. adults (69%) use Facebook, according to a survey conducted in early 2019. That's unchanged since April 2016, but up from 54% of adults in August 2012"*. No, me neither. According to Facebook's reported figures, *"monthly active users had risen 8% in the second quarter"* [83]. Academic studies conducted at the time (see below) indicated that most users continued to use the service. One suggestion is that users stayed because they felt that it *"wouldn't happen to them"* [84]. However, that may not be the whole story.

The "privacy paradox" [85–88] remains a somewhat contentious idea (Kokolakis [89] and Barth et al. [90] provide reviews, and Solove [91] provides a critique), but the essence of it is that people are temporarily outraged when e.g. their personal information is traded by social media firms, but when questioned, they seem quite willing to sell their browsing history for as little as €7 [92], indicating that privacy is all very well in principle, but I'll live without it if I get something in return. The idea of missing out on e.g. impromptu events organised via social media seems to be unthinkable – or at least sufficiently unthinkable to even consider deleting your account [93]. Another study [94], confirming that Facebook accounts were not deleted *en masse*, provides a telling quote: *"[f]or the majority of active users, Facebook is used in spite of the privacy challenges because it provides useful resources"* [94, p6]. There's evidence that since 2013, some users have become more alert to potential institutional misuse of their data [95], but as that paper points out, attitudes aren't always followed through into behaviour. Again, the message seems to be that people will sacrifice their privacy, providing they get something meaningful in return. But if that's true, why all the fuss about CA?

Gordon [96] provides an absorbing analysis of the social aspects of the CA/FB affair, noting that Barack Obama's 2012 campaign used very similar techniques to access Facebook data and to profile voters, although without provoking anywhere near the same reaction. To quote the paper: *"Cambridge Analytica did not significantly deviate from standard voter surveillance practices in the US, but it did draw attention to those practices*" [96, p51]. Turns out that broadly, the UK Information Commissioner's Office thought the same [97, 98]. Gordon's work also points to the (extant, at the time of writing) i360 voter database with (allegedly) 1,800 data points on each of 290 million individuals, calling it "*...an alarming invasion of privacy, [which] remains unchallenged by the public*" [96, p37]. It also references Facebook's own clandestine experiment in 2013, aimed at manipulating the emotional state of its users [96, p64].

The paper makes a critical point on privacy [96, p(iii)]:

> *A network of actors seized the momentum of this conflict to drive the message that voter surveillance is a threat to democratic elections. These actors humanized the CA conflict and created a catalyst for a large scale public outrage to these previously ignored structures. Their focus on democratic threat also allowed this conflict to transcend the typical contours of a privacy conflict and demonstrate that the consequences of CA are societal, rather than personal.*

That is, the norm groups who mobilised so much public reaction, in contrast to the lack of reaction to previous, similar events, framed the problem as having more to do with the erosion of democracy than with data privacy *per se*.

The key point for me is that it's hard to link meaningful reputational damage to a privacy breach, when people are willing to trade privacy for utility [99].

A 2016 study by the Rand Corporation [100] reported that only 11% of the people they surveyed stopped dealing with a company after a notified breach relating to their personal data. Lee et al. [101] noted that about the same proportion of customers (17%) closed their accounts with a major online retailer following a breach, at least in the short term, although the majority took no action. Any action that was taken was dependent on two factors: the perceived (rather than actual) damage and the existence of competitors to the breached company that the customer could switch to and still shop online. That is, *if there were alternatives*, then people were more likely to leave. Janakiraman et al. [102] looked at the customer response to a similar large-scale breach affecting a multichannel retailer (i.e. a retailer that in effect, provided their own alternatives). The study concluded that the amount of money spent with the retailer decreased, although the effect dissipated over time. However, the primary finding was that regular customers stayed with the retailer and simply switched to a different channel.

In their study, Acquisti et al. [20] noted that "*...there is little field evidence that the professed retaliation against offending companies has actually taken place*". That is, contrary to reports, there doesn't seem to be a general public backlash following privacy breaches. A Home Office report on cybercrime [103] concluded that both people and businesses found it difficult to understand the meaning of reputation, much less the reputational impact of a breach.

It also seems that the way in which the breach announcement is handled can make a significant adjustment to public reaction [104]. And as we'll see later, even with airline crashes and chemical spills [42], companies have to make a large number of mistakes before people start viewing them differently.

If you need any further evidence, you might look at the lack of reaction to privacy stories ongoing at the time of writing, regarding the surveillance conducted by local councils in the United Kingdom [105], the formal registration of protest by Privacy International over e.g. contact tracing apps and non-consensual temperature scanning at airports [106–108], and the voter profiling currently (still) going on in the UK [109].

WRAPPING THINGS UP: ESTIMATING LOSSES

As noted by Hovav and D'Arcy [28] in their review of the results of virus attacks, media reports of the level of impact following a breach may have been inflated. Their parallel review into the effect of DOS attacks [26] concluded that:

> *Large companies who are not "Internet-specific" might be overreacting to the media hype and may be investing resources to prevent a problem that has marginal impact on their shareholder value.*

Gordon and Loeb [110] summarised their findings by saying that:

> *Information security vendors and consultants will naturally focus on huge potential losses from security breaches in order to sell their products and services. Astute information security managers no doubt are aware that expected losses are typically an order of magnitude smaller than such potential losses.*

A 2011 report by the security services supplier Detica achieved some kind of passing fame when it claimed that cybercrime was costing the UK economy £27Bn, each and every year. You can see Professor Ross Anderson's reaction in the minutes of the Home Affairs Select Committee [111]: "*... it is truly disturbing that the Cabinet Office was willing to co-brand the Detica brochure*" [111, p126]. The problem is, eye-catching headline figures tend to be used to create, well... eye-catching headlines. Consequently the Detica figure was widely reported and widely referenced at the time, in some cases with further, implicit Government endorsement [112, 113].

The more recent and more grounded Home Office document notes the difficulty of estimating the cost of cybercrime and provides some very useful guidance on how you might go about avoiding basic traps such as methodological errors [103, p12].

CONCLUSIONS

Announcing a breach doesn't seem to significantly affect market capitalisation, with the exception of a small number of outlying cases. Academic studies indicate that internal costs, at least for the breaches examined here, don't seem to be large, at least not in comparison to company turnover. Reputational damage is hard to quantify and, in the case of cyber, may not have the necessary societal mechanisms to make it a front-line issue.

None of these issues seem to constitute a compelling case for investing in cyber, if you simply want to avoid the risk of experiencing them (on the assumption that the cyber industry can help you do that).

To be clear, I'm not saying that breaches have no impact. I'm sure the (ex) owners of Code Spaces and HBGary Federal would attest to that. And while less serious impacts might not be catastrophic, they're not non-zero either. But the industry does itself no favours when it puts out alarming headline figures, because (a) that takes attention away from the facts of the situation and (b) it draws attention to the methods used to generate those figures in the first place. If cybersecurity practitioners want to be seen as professionals, then some of this doom-mongering based on a loose interpretation of statistics will need to be cleaned up.

CASE STUDY: TRAVELEX

INTRODUCTION

I have had it suggested to me that the reported non-impacts on share price (a) do not apply in the case of more recent events and (b) are discredited by well-known examples such as the case of Travelex. That's a reasonable question. It's fair to challenge what's being said here. Let's see what happened.

BACKGROUND

The 2020 ransomware attack on the foreign exchange company Travelex is commonly cited as the reason for their subsequent collapse into administration. The case has become something of a negative poster child for the cybersecurity industry, supposedly demonstrating the catastrophic impact that a lack of cyber preparedness can have on the value and viability of a business. Yet this popular narrative is not only overly simplistic – it's also wrong.

In fact, any decline and fall into administration owes more to the market's adverse reaction to the business affairs of a major shareholder than it does to a cyber-attack. To understand what really happened, this case study explores the evidence and time-line of events to illustrate how unhelpful cyber myths like this get created – and why cybersecurity can only truly be understood by considering the context in which it operates.

HISTORY

In January 2015, a majority stake in Travelex was acquired by businessman Dr BR Shetty, who at the time also owned a UAE-based money transfer business, UAE Exchange. At the time, Dr Shetty's rise to billionaire status was widely viewed as the archetypal rags-to-riches story, starting from his birth into relatively humble circumstances.

In May 2019, a holding company incorporating both Travelex and UAE Exchange was floated on the London Stock Exchange, under the name Finablr. Dr Shetty retained a controlling stake in the holding company. At the time he also owned a controlling share in a healthcare company which he had founded (NMC Health), also based in the United Arab Emirates. This much you can find from Wikipedia. Almost all of the rest of this account can be obtained from publicly available share price data, company statements, and press releases. It's particularly worth reading the Muddy Waters article regarding NMC Health [114].

THE BREACH

On or around New Year's Eve 2019, Travelex suffered a cyber-attack that led to a number of their systems being taken offline. Following the announcement of the event (on 2 January 2020), Finablr's share price fell by about 1.4% in early trading – exactly in the middle of the bracket seen by researchers looking at the impact of security breach announcements.

From this point onwards, the narrative from the cyber security industry is that Travelex was hacked, and that as a direct result, the company ceased to exist. Simple.

SHARE PRICE DETAILS

Between 6 and 8 January 2020, Finablr's share price did indeed fall sharply, by about 20%. Now, if it was the breach at Travelex that caused the drop, then it must have been due to some strange delayed-action effect. The only relevant press release issued by the company over the period stated that they expected the breach to have no material impact on their 2019 figures and no material impact on trading in 2020. So what caused the fall in share price?

Perhaps coincidentally, on or about 6 January, it was announced that two business associates of Dr Shetty had offloaded about US$0.5Bn worth of shares in NMC Health and Finablr, reportedly to meet personal debts. The shares were sold at a steep discount (up to 19.7%), a figure which almost exactly matches the observed drop in Finablr's share price. One interpretation is that given an indication of what a couple of major investors thought the share price should be (i.e. 20% less than the closing price on the previous day), the markets took note and responded accordingly.

It's also interesting to look at why those shares might have been sold. On or around 18 December 2019 (i.e. two weeks before the hack took place), there was a similar fall in Finablr's share price. That aligns perfectly with the publication of an article on the Muddy Waters analyst web site, alleging that NMC Health (the sister company to Finablr) had sought to arrange US$200M of loans that were "off balance sheet", i.e. that the owners had allegedly tried to bolster the financial position of the company by taking on debt, but without revealing that debt to the markets.

There were also some quite serious allegations of misrepresentation, as you can see in the Muddy Waters article, which concludes:

> We are unsure how deep the rot at NMC goes, but we do not believe that its insiders or financials can be trusted.

That is, we don't trust the people running the business, and we don't trust their financial reporting.

Given that Finablr was also being managed by Dr Shetty, it's reasonable to assume that the impact on Finablr's share price was a spillover from the allegations relating to NMC Health. And in case it needs restating, this event took place a full two weeks before the breach.

So one explanation would be that the markets were simply reacting to the perceived business dealings of key individuals and reflecting those sentiments in the company's share price. That, however, doesn't fit the narrative. So, let's ignore the drop that took place before the hack, let's ignore the shorting of NMC Health, let's attribute the second drop to some hitherto unknown delayed-action effect arising from the attack, and let's ignore the fact that on the day there was only a minimal effect. What happened next?

Subsequent Events

In the weeks after the breach, Finablr's share price steadily recovered. The rise continued up until about 23 January 2020, when there was another precipitous fall. Another delayed-action effect? Possibly. Or it could have been driven by the announcement that Dr Shetty had apparently pledged over 50% of the shares in Finablr as security to re-finance the debts taken on when buying his stake in Travelex. The deal included a clause relating to the transfer of ownership in the event of default on repayments, thereby raising questions over the future ownership of the company. Finablr subsequently (and publicly) called on Dr Shetty to clarify his holdings in the company and, specifically, to clarify the role of another company part-owned by Dr Shetty, which was used to route the transactions in Finablr's shares.

Towards the end of February 2020 (around the 21st), Dr Shetty is reported as calling in advisers to review "strategic options" in relation to his level of debt. At this point it begins to become publicly acknowledged that the fate of NMC Health and the fate of Finablr are closely linked.

On March 2, 2020, Finablr issue a profit warning, saying that the combined effects of the breach and something to do with an infection originating in Asia were going to hit their bottom line by about US$25M. They note, however, that they expect the impact of the breach to be materially covered by their cyber insurance. Finablr's share price falls 2% on the day and then recovers.

On March 4th, Standard and Poor hint at concerns arising from circumstances "… that might be interpreted as weak corporate governance" and revise the company's credit rating. They revise it quite substantially downwards, citing a level of debt described as "unsustainable". Finablr subsequently (on March 12th) announce that they are carrying out an urgent cashflow review – basically, they acknowledge that without the ability to borrow money, they will be unable to meet the obligations arising from just keeping the company going. Luckily there was just enough time between those two statements for NMC Health to announce (on March 9) that their debt, previously reported as US$2.1Bn, was in fact closer to US$5Bn. Later that same month, Finablr reveal previously undisclosed debt amounting to ca. US$100M and suggest that COVID travel restrictions are going to materially impact the business on an ongoing basis.

In late March, trading in Finablr shares is suspended.

Epilogue

The chart below (Figure 6.1) summarises the sequence of events. The solid line indicates share price, and the vertical bars indicate trading volume.

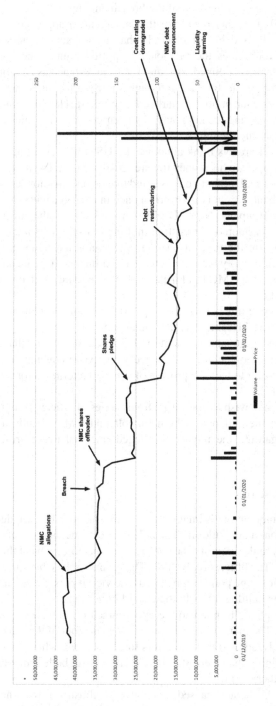

FIGURE 6.1 Finablr share price. (Leapfrog Creative Ltd, reproduced with permission. Data Source: Yahoo Finance.)

You can see a peak in volume as people bail out following the liquidity warning (c.f. the lack of any spike at the time of the breach announcement).

Since March 2020, further details of the management approach at Finablr have come to light. Finablr's debt, for example, has been found to be something like US$1.3Bn, about four times the previously reported figure. The board has been replaced, administrators appointed, etc., and EY have resigned as auditors to the company. Travelex were put up for sale, although shortly afterwards their credit rating was cut, and they were taken off the market. Happily, Travelex have since been taken over by their creditors, and the company has been given a cash injection which has enabled them to continue trading.

In January 2021, Barclays Bank announced a US$130M claim against Dr Shetty in respect of a loan made to his money transfer business UAE Exchange (another part of Finablr). In response, Dr Shetty has asserted that he had no knowledge of what was going on, and that bank accounts etc. were opened in his name without his agreement.

Finablr's sister company NMC Health (the subject of the allegations in the December article) has entered administration. Finablr itself looks like it will be taken over. The company (at the time of writing, under new management) has initiated a formal investigation into what they believe to be historical financial wrongdoing. A similar investigation at NMC Health claimed to have found evidence of "significant financial irregularities".

It's worth looking at this Forbes article [115] for a summary, including an allegation that shares in NMC Health were also pledged to cover debts.

You might also want to take a look at the FT article suggesting that another of Dr Shetty's companies (Neopharma) was allegedly involved in raising false orders to go to NMC Health in order to feed the process of reverse factoring, a form of off-balance sheet financing [116].

As a coda, you may wish to leaf through this series of articles from Reuters [117–122], summarising the collapse of both Finablr and NMC Health, and especially the statements regarding the impact of alleged financial irregularities and undisclosed debt.

TRAVELEX: CONCLUSION

Parking this for a moment, let's imagine that sadly someone has decided to end their life by jumping from a tall building. The police investigate, and the officers involved are called to testify at the inquest. The coroner asks the officers what they believe was the cause of death. The officers reply "flu". The coroner asks why, since that seems to be an odd conclusion. The police reply that as the victim passed the 14th floor, one of the witnesses in the building thought they heard him sneeze.

It is at best simplistic to point to the cyber-attack on Travelex as the reason for Finablr's collapse. The market's perception of the behaviour of the principals for both Finablr and NMC Health led their investors to desert them, while the markets themselves, after examining the levels of debt associated with both companies, restricted their access to further credit.

Claiming that the breach caused this outcome illustrates the linear, simplistic approach to cause and effect which is so prevalent in the cyber industry. The phenomenon of "superstitious learning" would seem to apply here – a situation in which the mere coincidence of a breach and a poor outcome is enough to establish an argument that one inevitably led to the other [123].

It also says that you can only understand cybersecurity by considering the business context in which it operates. It cannot be viewed as a standalone issue. At least, not sensibly.

THE CASE FOR INVESTMENT: GAINING BENEFITS

INTRODUCTION

It's difficult to find evidence of direct organisational benefits arising from investments in cybersecurity. I don't mean that people have looked and failed to find any. It's more that to date, nobody seems to have spent much time looking. It was noted earlier that the industry tends to see risk as a topic that can be viewed in the absence of any link to rewards. That seems to be highlighted quite clearly in the paucity of evidence identifying positive outcomes from cyber investments. The one piece of work you might come across is the study by Doherty and Fulford [124], who looked for a link between the existence of an Information Security Policy and corporate benefits such as reduced numbers of incidents and/or reduced severity of incidents. The paper examined a number of related hypotheses, such as the idea that you might expect to see greater reductions the longer a policy had been in place, ditto for more broadly-based policies, and also for those based on best practice and for those that were more frequently updated. It won't come as any surprise to hear that there was no statistically significant correlation in any of the cases they examined. The authors summarise the results as "... *somewhat surprising, as they show no statistically significant relationships between the adoption of information security policies and the incidence or severity of security breaches*".

An unfortunate result, given that at the time of writing, the industry justifies cyber investment as a way of avoiding inevitable losses and general catastrophe. But, in the interests of balance, let's ask the question – "are there any benefits that automatically accrue when companies invest in cyber?".

BENEFITS: SHARE PRICE

Szubartowicz and Schryen [125] investigated the effect of timing, specifically the relative timings of breach announcements and announcements of investment. In broad terms, their findings were that:

- Investing in cyber security (or announcing an intention to invest) with no prior breach announcement generally led to a *fall* in share price.
- If there had been a recent breach announcement in the same industry, a declaration of intent to invest led to a rise in share price for the announcing company. That is, the company didn't actually have to invest, it just had to say that it was going to. But it had to say that *after* a breach.

- Companies that announced an actual investment after news of a breach saw a bigger rise than breached companies that simply announced an intention to invest.

As summarised in that paper [125, p1]:

Overall, the lowest abnormal return can be expected when the intention to invest is announced before a fundamental information security incident and the highest return when actually investing after a fundamental information security incident in the respective industry.

Essentially, the markets were seen to punish companies investing in cyber for no good reason. Chai [126] also found that there were no statistically significant market returns for companies making security investments purely to meet best practice [126, Table 7]. The same paper noted, however, that companies did see benefits in cases where the investment had a potential for commercial exploitation through e.g. the creation of strategic partnerships. Dos Santos [127] and Bose [128] also found that IT and cyber investments could lead to market benefits, providing they were seen as innovative.

It's not a massive amount of work to figure out a decision matrix based on these results. A reasonable strategy might be to wait until a competitor has a breach, then announce the intention to invest, and then later announce the actual investment, so you get a double impact. And in case it hasn't already occurred to you – and please don't take this as an incentive to commit share fraud – why not announce a "breach" (if you get my drift), ride out the dip, and then make a couple of positive announcements regarding investments in cyber security? Works for me.

Xu et al. [129] looked at the short-term impact on share price when a company announced an investment in cyber. The summary findings [129, Table 10] indicate that positive market returns occur when the presentation of the strategy for investment is aligned with the timing. That is, markets react positively when proactive investment in advance of any breach is presented as leading to opportunities for commercial exploitation, or when reactive investment in the wake of a breach is presented as leading to improvements in security. Misalignment (e.g. reacting to a breach but presenting the investment as strategic for example) leads to a negative reaction. Companies can therefore gain a positive market reaction whether they decide to invest up front or invest after a breach, providing they can associate a commercially positive outcome with the first option.

However, taken overall, if you want your share price to go up following an investment in cyber, then you need to manage the circumstances surrounding that investment. That is, you need to recognise the business setting. The outcome is by no means automatic.

Benefits: Affecting Your Competitors

Jeong et al. [130] examined the impact of breach/investment announcements on the share prices of competitors. Their findings can be summarised as:

- In some cases, announcing a breach will bump up your competitors' share price, albeit with a slight delay.
- In some cases, announcing your own investment in cyber will drive down your competitors' share price.
- If you invest in cyber and subsequently have a breach, your competitors will see a greater benefit than they would have seen had you not made the investment.
- If you invest after a breach, your competitors don't see any benefit.

So again, there's no logic in investing upfront, at least not if your intention is to impact your competitors. The best you can hope for is that it will temporarily depress their share price. But if you go ahead and invest anyway, and then suffer a breach, your competitors could see a benefit. Whereas if you leave it until you have a breach and then invest, they don't seem to gain. The best option again seems to be to wait until you have a breach and then announce an intention to invest.

BENEFITS: GAMING THE MARKET

Impacts on share price are driven by information transfer [131], which means that you see either contagion (all the companies in the sector see a drop in share price if one has an incident) or competition (the breached company sees a drop, their competitors see a rise). That seems like a clear split between two possible outcomes. However, irritatingly the findings for cyber tend to be inconsistent – sometimes you see competition, sometimes you see contagion [127, 130, 132, 133].

This might seem morbid, but there's a much clearer picture when you look at the effect of aircraft disasters on airline share prices. Bosch [134] found that the effect on the share prices of competitors was mediated by the degree of overlap between routes. That makes sense, because if Airline B shares no routes with Airline A, then Airline B won't see any additional business when passengers stop flying the routes offered by Airline A after an accident (i.e. when passengers "switch"). In the study by Bosch, airlines that had very little overlap on routes with the affected airline saw contagion (their share price also went down), whereas those that shared a number of routes with the affected airline saw their share price go up. The key point being that contagion and competition were seen to co-exist within the same industry, which may explain why in the case of cybersecurity incidents, both effects also seem to be present. But there's no clear explanation of why there should be contagion in some cases and competition in others.

Although… it's interesting to look at what happens as the number of fatalities goes up. Ho et al. [135] found that for low numbers of fatalities (less than ten), the effect was based on competition. The airline suffering the crash saw a dip in share price and their competitors saw a small rise a matter of days afterwards. When the number of fatalities rose into the tens however, that small rise for competitors became a small drop, i.e. competition turned to contagion. It also occurred a little earlier than the date that was associated with the rise. When the number of fatalities became very large (over 100), the contagion effect was seen much more strongly, to the extent that the impact on competitors was also significantly negative, and looking at the timings presented by Ho et al., it occurred at about the same time as the impact on the airline that had suffered the accident.

If you look closely, you can see the same kind of pattern emerging in relation to cyber incidents, in the event window timings given by Yayla [31, Table 12]. It's almost as though a rational, considered (and slow) positive response is being replaced by a faster, more instinctive negative response. The report by Jeong [130] also indicates the potential for a similar pattern in cyber breaches – that competition (i.e. a rise in share price for non-breached companies in the same industry) tends to happen a couple of days after a breach, whereas contagion is almost immediate.

Taken overall, this might mean that at the minute we're seeing only low levels of the cyber equivalent of casualties, so the picture wobbles between contagion and competition, depending on some factor that isn't yet clear, such as industry type. There's some (admittedly weak) evidence that the financial sector, for example, tends to display contagion after a breach, whereas other sectors tend to display competition [e.g. 130]. There's also some evidence that the nature of the breach affects the outcome [38], in that incidents involving confidential data show a smaller rise for competitors than other types of breaches.

The one conclusion that we can be relatively sure about is that this is a complex situation – literally, as there's a strong argument that stock markets act as complex systems [136]. However, it seems that there are no automatic benefits in this area either, largely because the outcome depends so much on context.

BENEFITS: REPUTATION

There doesn't seem to be a great deal of research linking cyber investments to company reputation. That doesn't mean that there isn't any, just that I couldn't find it. There are some papers on the reputational impact of a breach, such as the paper by Makridis [137], who found that reputational damage only seemed to occur in severe, outlying cases. In the general case there was a *positive* (albeit statistically insignificant) boost to brand familiarity and brand power following a breach, although the effects overall did seem to vary according to industry type.

BENEFITS: MANAGING THE NEWS

Listed companies tend to bundle up announcements of bad news [138], whereas they tend to leak good news in advance of a formal announcement, in order to achieve some sort of double knock. Kothari et al. [139] provided empirical evidence of that and suggested that it was partly because bad news carries with it a stronger impact than good news. The practice doesn't always work out in the case of cyber however. Amir et al. [140] found that withholding news of a breach, to the extent that investors strongly suspected that there had been an incident, led to greater impacts on share price. It seemed to take some time for investors to sense that information was being withheld, but when they did, the impact on share price was much higher than in the case of simple disclosure. Gatzlaff and McCullough [141] also found that where a company refused to answer direct enquiries about a suspected breach, the eventual impact on their share price was greater than it would otherwise have been.

Bolster et al. [142] found that the news outlet used for a breach announcement also seemed to make a difference. When the news broke in one of the "big four" outlets (New York Times, Wall Street Journal, Washington Post, and Dow Jones News Retrieval Service), there were significant negative abnormal returns for the breached company. For other outlets, the abnormal returns weren't statistically significant. The study's conclusion was that the credibility of the source had an impact on the interpretation of the announcement. There's also evidence that the wording of the breach announcement affects the impact on share price [143], with those based on security and stakeholder issues leading to better outcomes than those based on business factors or technology.

In a really interesting piece of work, Wang et al. [144] linked the results of a textual analysis of security breach reports with the observed effects on share price and trading volume. Their study was based on a distinction between general investors and sophisticated investors (i.e. it adopted a complex model). They found that general investors reacted quickly to a breach report, whereas sophisticated investors such as industry analysts waited until more information became available, and that the difference was more pronounced when the original statement was short on detail. Overall, the researchers were able to "*... determine the price and volume reactions to breach announcements based on the textual contents of the news articles*". That allowed them to act as general investors, predict when there would be a dip in share price and exploit the difference between that short-term effect and the longer term analyst response. On the basis of a trial, they estimated that they could achieve a 300% return on investment (ROI) over the course of a year (presumably as long as there were enough breaches). Setting aside the possibilities for more direct funding of security research, the point here is that there are options for framing the announcement of a breach, and that some are better than others. In passing, Cohen [145], citing a number of research papers [146–149], suggests that cybercriminals and company insiders are now using advance information on security breaches to exploit the same short-term dip in share price.

CONCLUSION

The bottom line is that there may not be all that many business benefits that come for free when you invest in cyber. If you want to see any direct benefits, then you have to take into account the context for the investment, and you have to actively manage the circumstances of that investment. On that basis, whatever outcome you eventually get to probably can't be classed as "automatic". Further, if you do want to achieve benefits, then you need to view cyber as a means to an end (e.g. enabling access to new markets, or enabling strategic partnerships), and not as an end in itself.

THE CASE FOR INVESTMENT: CONSTRUCTING A BUSINESS CASE

BACKGROUND

It's proving a bit difficult to find reasons to invest. There don't seem to be any clear automatic benefits, and in the general case the financial downsides don't seem to be catastrophic.

At least some of this is implicitly acknowledged by practitioners when they seek to demonstrate the value of cyber investments. Typically, that takes place when the cyber team are asked to justify their budget. It's difficult to identify actual positive benefits, so the standard method is to work on the basis that the investment will reduce the likelihood and/or impact of security breaches, and that therefore it's worth putting up the money. The standard argument rests on two concepts: Annualised Loss Expectancy (ALE) and Return on Security Investment (ROSI).

Annualised Loss Expectancy is supposedly a measure of how much you might expect to lose through cybersecurity incidents in an average year. To get to this figure, you multiply the annual likelihood of a breach (based on a guess, usually) by the expected financial impact of the breach (again, a guess) and then you sum those products over all the breach types you think might be relevant. The number you get is usually interpreted as the amount you should spend on security per year. Assuming years tend towards an average, you'd then be spending as much as you might have expected to lose.

ALE is usually taken forward into the ROSI calculation [150] as:

$$ROSI = (\delta ALE - investment) / investment$$

where "δALE" is the reduction in Annualised Loss Expectancy brought about by the investment in security, i.e. the saving in costs arising from the security breaches that it's assumed will not occur, as a direct result of making the investment (although it's not clear to me at least, how the reduction in ALE can be assessed in an objective way).

Gordon and Loeb [151] examined the idea of ROSI and concluded that the underlying concept of ROI had been badly applied, in that accounting ROI is not the same as economic rate of return (the accrued benefits of an investment). Others [28, 38, 126] make the point that the application of ROI to cyber is dependent on accurate and reliable source data, which in most cases simply isn't available. Schneier [152] suggests that since ALE is based primarily on guesswork, it may not be wholly reliable. Others (e.g. [153]) provide a breakdown of why these methods don't (and perhaps can't) work.

And in passing, the people defining those likely losses and likely probabilities of attack are the same people trying to justify their budget. Just saying.

SOME REALITIES

So zooming out a little, and looking not for an explanation of why people invest, but instead thinking about how to create a case for investing, the industry's approach still doesn't seem to have any firm foundations. The use of ALE to justify security investments doesn't stack up, and while the logic underlying Discounted Cash Flow (DCF) calculations such as Internal Rate of Return (IRR) and Net Present Value (NPV) may be sound, there's no reliable information to feed into them.

In a move similar to the work on Prospect Theory [154], Gordon and Loeb [110] suggested that there may be non-linearities in the ways organisations manage security spending. For example, there's no point investing to prevent an incident where the cost is very significant, because it's likely to use up a disproportionate amount of the budget. And why spend money on issues that are likely to be no more than an irritation? Their study suggested that most companies should spend money on the middle ground, and empirical evidence from Tanaka et al. [155] seemed to find exactly that behaviour "in the wild". That is, people allocated spend where it would be most effective, rather than where the risk was greatest. Linear models of expenditure against risk might seem logical according to cyber people, but they don't reflect business realities [156].

Gordon and Loeb also demonstrated that because of those non-linearities, expenditure on cyber shouldn't exceed 37% of the maximum expected losses. That is, the optimal level of expenditure on cyber, even in the worst case, seems to be only around one-third of the expected financial impact of the anticipated incidents.

Value Chains

Value chains [157] have been suggested as an alternative way of identifying benefits accruing from investing in security and hence building a business case. The original concept was proposed by Michael Porter in the mid-1980s, and is usually depicted as a set of interlinked manufacturing stages, as shown in the diagram below (see Figure 6.2). Value chains identify those processes where value is created, and hence where greater value might be achieved. The analysis also flags up activities where no value is being created, hence placing a question mark over why that work is being carried out in the first place.

The idea of information as a source of competitive advantage has been put forward by Porter [158] in the context of value chains, but the analysis of cyber security as a means of gaining advantage has not been so easy [159]. Primarily that's because it's difficult to find a "home" for cyber. Most people put it in as a part of infrastructure, which perhaps hides it away a little.

In the intervening period, the model has been subject to a number of criticisms, mostly that it's linear, and that sort of "goods in, goods out" model may not be so widely applicable these days. It can also be difficult to incorporate intangible benefits such as market presence.

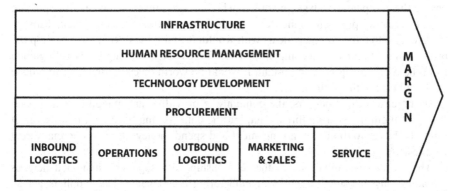

FIGURE 6.2 Porter's value chain. (Leapfrog Creative Ltd, reproduced with permission. After: Porter [157]).

Because of this, network-based approaches have been suggested as an alternative [160–162]. Possibly the most well-known is Value Network Analysis (VNA) as described by Verna Allee [163, 164]. VNA was incorporated into the IT Infrastructure Library (ITIL), at least for Version 3.

VALUE NETWORKS

Rather than looking at an organisation in isolation, VNA looks at the organisation within its environment, which could include e.g. competitors, suppliers, customers, regulatory bodies, etc. The analysis provides a way of understanding (a) the nature of the consequent relationships and (b) the expectations of each party in those relationships. There are some basic rules, e.g. each party has to contribute a benefit which is valued by at least one other party in the network. When a specific party does *not* offer a benefit that's valued by someone else, the network excludes that party and rearranges the remaining relationships. VNA also incorporates the notion of intangible benefits as well as tangible ones, and it's flexible enough to allow the analysis to be updated as circumstances change. Crucially, it examines the organisation in its environment rather than as a standalone entity. On that aspect you may see echoes of the argument made by Levitt.

Rather than choose one method over another (and/or run the risk of copyright infringement), I've drawn up a simple generic illustration in the diagram below (Figure 6.3). The key parties that the central business interacts with are shown, together with the associated exchanges of tangible and intangible benefits.

The relationship with trading partners, for example, is imagined here in the form of agencies acting as intermediaries, thereby providing channels to market. The benefits of that relationship are critical to the business, but not so much to the agencies, consequently it's not a balanced relationship. As far as the agencies are concerned, the company is just a revenue stream, and probably one that's not very important to any one individual agency, because the agencies also act as channels for other manufacturers. However, the agencies represent a significant channel for the company into their key market. Having the central company's email system hacked and used to send out phishing emails to the agencies would definitely sour the relationship, as would having the company's web site go down, which would prevent agencies from placing orders and hence put them in the front line dealing with frustrated customers. Most of the agencies that the company deals with wouldn't find it too difficult to just drop the product line and move to a competitor. Therefore, since the intangible benefit gained from the relationship is so important, it would be worth investing in cyber to reduce the likelihood of that outcome.

In the case of competitors, the company is providing an intangible benefit to a subset of them, by sharing threat data, but the data coming back isn't that useful. It might be better to ditch that arrangement and spend money on a commercial threat feed instead.

There's also an imbalance in the relationship with suppliers, imagined here as providing physical goods such as manufacturing components. The suppliers get an intangible benefit from being seen as suppliers to the company, but there's no similar

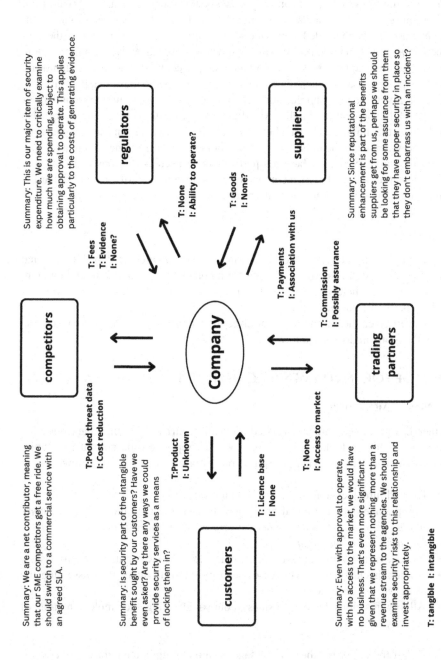

FIGURE 6.3 Business interactions. (Leapfrog Creative Ltd, reproduced with permission.)

T: tangible I: intangible

Summary: We are a net contributor, meaning that our SME competitors get a free ride. We should switch to a commercial service with an agreed SLA.

Summary: Is security part of the intangible benefit sought by our customers? Have we even asked? Are there any ways we could provide security services as a means of locking them in?

Summary: Even with approval to operate, with no access to the market, we would have no business. That's even more significant given that we represent nothing more than a revenue stream to the agencies. We should examine security risks to this relationship and invest appropriately.

Summary: This is our major item of security expenditure. We need to critically examine how much we are spending, subject to obtaining approval to operate. This applies particularly to the costs of generating evidence.

Summary: Since reputational enhancement is part of the benefits suppliers get from us, perhaps we should be looking for some assurance from them that they have proper security in place so they don't embarrass us with an incident?

competitors

regulators

suppliers

Company

customers

trading partners

T:Pooled threat data
I: Cost reduction

T: Fees
T: Evidence
I: None?

T: None
I: Ability to operate?

T: Goods
I: None?

T: Payments
I: Association with us

T: Commission
I: Possibly assurance

T:Product
I: Unknown

T: Licence base
I: None

T: None
I: Access to market

intangible benefit returned. One option for the business might be to shift to a set of suppliers with assurance in their back-end systems (e.g. Cyber Essentials), which might then enable limited access to the company's own systems so that the suppliers can check stock inventory. Moving to a new set of suppliers is likely to be a pain, and some development work would be needed to provide secure, controlled access. However, the consequent intangible benefit to the business would be to have e.g. early warning of supply shortages and reduced costs of managing their supply chain. If those are of significant benefit to the organisation, then it's worth investing in cyber to make that happen.

This is a very basic example. For one thing it doesn't look at any secondary or indirect relationships that might exist between external parties. There are also stakeholders that might be relevant but haven't been shown here, such as shareholders, service providers, and the public. However, I hope it gets across the idea that an analysis of the value exchanges between parties can be used as a means of identifying potential sources of benefit when companies invest in cybersecurity. It's not so hard to imagine that this sort of diagram could be drawn up as part of a risk analysis.

CONCLUSIONS

An article by Townsend [165], quoting a former Technical Director of the UK National Cyber Security Centre, suggests that messaging on cyber amounts to not much more than medieval witchcraft, as in "buy this magic amulet and you'll be ok", which is hardly a justifiable business case.

However, given the current levels of investment enjoyed by the cyber industry, the "amulet" argument does seem to work. Why?

THE CASE FOR INVESTMENT: COMPLIANCE

THE MANAGEMENT VIEW

Gartner has provided a business-based view of security for some years now. It's instructive to take a look at their February 2020 report on the current and future business environment for cyber [166]. I've paraphrased the key points below:

- Expenditure does not necessarily lead to protection.
- Compliance does not equal protection. In fact, to quote the report: "... *compliance forces us to spend money where we don't need it and keeps us from investing where we should*".
- The use of risk appetite assumes the existence of a measurable scale for risk.
- Audits check for the existence of security controls rather than assessing the effectiveness of those controls.
- All organisations have a business context affecting the implementation of security.

Lots of stuff there. For me the key message is summed up in the phrase: "... *compliance forces us to spend money where we don't need it and keeps us from investing where we should*" [166, p4]. It's worth looking at that in a little more detail.

EXTERNAL PRESSURES

Cavusoglu et al. [167] carried out a really interesting examination of the way in which external pressures drove organisations to invest in cyber. The structured equation modelling diagram from that paper is reproduced below (Figure 6.4).

The box labelled "ISNA" stands for Information Security Needs Analysis (i.e. the business case for investment), "ISCR" stands for Information Security Control Resources, i.e. the levels of investment made by the company in the areas of Information Security Technology (IST), qualified security personnel (QSP), and AOU (security awareness of organisational users). The numbers on each arrow represent the weightings for linkages between the factors that they're connected to, and any path with two or more asterisks on it indicates a statistically significant result. You can see for example that Mimetic Pressure (the box at the top left) has only a very low influence on the level of investment (the "0.07" on the line linking it to ISCR), and in fact we can't say with any confidence that it makes any contribution at all (there are no asterisks).

The report was based on the findings of a survey asking why companies made the effort to produce a business case for security investments, and also why they invested generally in cybersecurity. There was a particular interest in three types of pressure:

- Coercive: pressure to meet regulatory standards such as GDPR and/or the mandatory requirements of e.g. card issuers.
- Normative: pressure to follow the examples of business partners to meet best practice or to show compliance with standards such as ISO 27001.
- Mimetic: pressure to do what others are doing.

In terms of the linkages between the identified pressures and the decision to invest, the results explained about 80% of the variance in the measurements, which is relatively high. Basically, the findings seemed to provide a robust explanation.

Some of the key findings are reproduced below, with my interpretations:

> *"All coefficients on hypothesized paths except for the path coefficient from mimetic pressure to ISCR were found to significantly differ from zero"*.
> Nobody invests in cyber just because their competitors do.
> *"As expected, the results also suggest that coercive pressure influences an organization's decision to invest in ISCR. This result is consistent with the emerging view that government regulations significantly affect organizations' information security practices"*.
> Companies tend to invest in cyber as a result of external pressure to show alignment with standards.
> *"Our findings indicate that coercive and normative pressures predominate in motivating organizational investments in ISCR"*.
> Companies invest in cyber to demonstrate alignment with standards and/or meet regulatory requirements.
> *"... we assessed the indirect effects of coercive and normative pressures through ISNA on ISCR ... the indirect effect of normative pressure was significant*

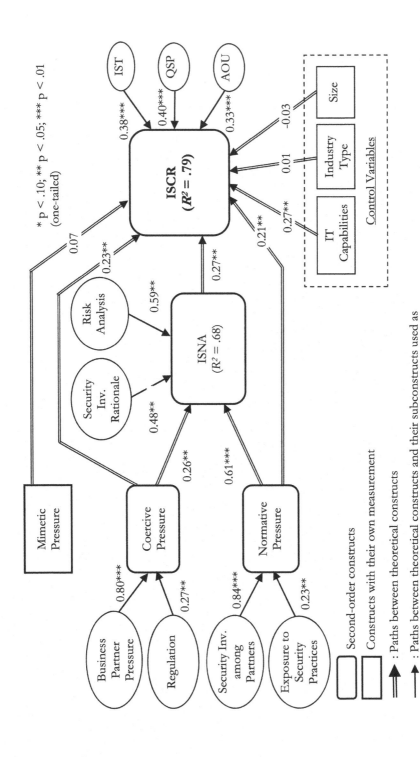

FIGURE 6.4 Structured Equation Modelling diagram. (Cavusoglu, et al. [167]. Republished under STM guidelines.)

... on the other hand, the indirect effect of coercive pressure was marginally significant".

If you suggest that the company should invest in cyber in order to meet best practice, then you have to provide a justification for spending the money. If you say you want to invest to meet regulatory pressures, then you may not need to produce a business case.

Based on their analysis of a number of security investment case studies, Weishäupl and colleagues [168] found a similar picture, concluding that (these are verbatim extracts):

- Firms' investments in information security are largely driven by external environmental and industry-related factors;
- Firms do not implement standardized decision processes;
- The security process is perceived to impact the business process in a disturbing way;
- Both the implementation of evaluation processes and the application of metrics are hardly existent;
- Learning activities mainly occur at an ad-hoc basis.

Taken together, these results and the Gartner report suggest that investment in cybersecurity is driven by external coercive pressures, and that the key benefit sought by organisations is a certificate of compliance against industry standards. Paradoxically perhaps, justifying expenditure on cyber in order to meet best practice has a harder time – businesses want to see a supporting rationale before committing any money to implement security for security's sake. Training seems to have a very low priority, primarily because it's not strongly attached to achieving compliance. And since the emphasis is on gaining a certificate, once that's been achieved, nobody feels it necessary to go back and check that the security is actually working.

To answer the earlier question on why the amulet argument works, it's because buying amulets has been made compulsory. The cyber industry not only holds control of the narrative, but also has control of the solution. And in the meantime, the security problems persist. But then, as pointed out by Mark Neocleous [1, p154], they'd have to, if the industry itself is going to persist.

OUTCOMES

It was hinted at earlier [169] that companies tend not to look too hard at whether or not their cyber defences are working. In the same vein, the Gartner report suggests that when cyber industry audit teams come in to assess security, they look at whether or not a technology is in place, rather than whether or not it's effective. Sales [170, p1559] quotes Bruce Schneier:

Firewalls are ubiquitous because auditors started demanding firewalls. This changed the cost equation for businesses. The cost of adding a firewall was expense and user annoyance, but the cost of not having a firewall was failing an audit.

Echoing the point in the Gartner report, the "Debate Security" report referenced earlier [171] notes that companies don't routinely assess the effectiveness of the technical products they buy, and indeed many don't even think to do so [171, p9]. A key driver for simply buying technology, installing it and "*crossing your fingers*" is that boards are seeking compliance as the primary outcome [171, p17]. Bruce Schneier (I think) coined the phrase "security theatre", to describe a show of security that has little to no actual effect, but looks as though it might [172]. The idea that compliance equals protection must be the biggest piece of security theatre ever promoted.

PEOPLE ISSUES

Via some additional analysis, the report from Cavusoglu et al. makes a number of specific points regarding investment in user awareness:

- "*Coercive pressure has a significant impact on information security technologies and qualified security personnel but not on security awareness of organizational users*".
  Increasing user awareness doesn't seem to be viewed as relevant to the primary business benefit of achieving compliance. As the report notes, that's probably due to an almost exclusive focus on technology within existing security standards.
- "*Mimetic pressure had a marginally significant impact on security awareness of organizational users but did not have a significant impact on information security technologies and qualified security personnel. On the other hand, normative pressure was found to have a significant impact only on security awareness of organizational users*".
  Companies invest in security awareness not because they're forced to, but because they think they're expected to.
- "*Despite the recognition that today's information security problems cannot be effectively resolved by solely focusing on technology and that the human factor must be part of the framework addressing security issues, organizations seem to remain focused mainly on technology-based solutions to address their security-related issues*".
  I'm not sure that needs any expansion. Although I can provide a standout example of the consequences, in the form of the Target hack, where a US$1.6M investment in cybersecurity technology failed because of the human context for its use [173, 174].

We've already seen that the majority of security incidents tend to arise from "people issues". And yet, at least under current circumstances, there's no incentive to invest in solving those issues. The implicit view is that any cyber problem can be fixed using technology. In his paper defending the role of the human in cybersecurity, and arguing against the cliché of a "weakest link", McMahon [175] apologises for not providing more answers, but does suggest a number of additional areas for research in the form of a list of questions. Last on the list is this: "*Fundamentally, why are we pushing such a negative vision of human capability? Who exactly are we serving with such*

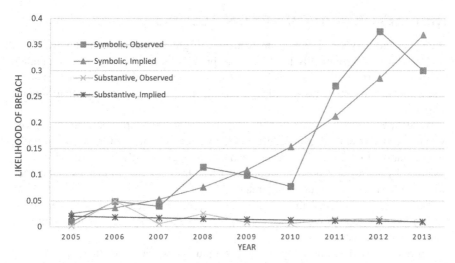

FIGURE 6.5 Outcomes of symbolic investment in cyber security. (Angst, et al. [176]. Republished with permission via Copyright Clearance Centre.)

a message?". Indeed. Who would benefit from a view that humans are a component that needs to be designed out using more technology?

The outcome of all this is shown in the work by Angst et al. [176], who looked at two groups of US hospitals. One group was classified as being "symbolic" adopters of IT security, i.e. they adopted it mostly to achieve demonstrable compliance with legislation and industry regulations. The other group were classified as "substantive" adopters, in that they took on IT security not as something separate from their main business activities, but as an integrated part. The work compared the predicted number of security breaches with the actual numbers of breaches suffered by the two groups. The key diagram from the paper [176, Figure 2] is reproduced in Figure 6.5 above.

The conclusion reached in the paper was simple. Purely symbolic adoption of IT security measures was not effective in defending the organisation against attacks.

If you want to be on the lower line, i.e. you want to achieve effective security, then you've got to move away from the idea that compliance equals protection. Second, security has to be interleaved with day-to-day operations, and you aren't going to get to that point by treating security as something separate and special. In short, you aren't going to achieve effective security by leaving it to the security team. It has to be owned by the management team.

CONCLUSIONS

Compliance against industry standards seems to be the most widely accepted argument for investment in cyber. And if instead, you want to implement security for its own sake, then you're going to have to work harder to get a budget.

On that basis, fixing the cyber behaviour problem isn't difficult. It's just not economically attractive. The cyber industry is already delivering what the customer has been conditioned to want – compliance against the industry's own standards.

THE CASE FOR INVESTMENT: CONCLUSIONS

The cyber industry's claims that investment will prevent catastrophic losses, either in the form of a permanently lowered share price or in the form of huge unplanned internal costs arising from a breach, don't seem to align with the evidence. In some cases, doubts can also be expressed regarding the methodologies employed to support those claims.

Academic studies indicate that the majority of impacts are relatively low level, with publicised average figures being driven by a small number of outliers. Similarly, the reputational damage of a breach seems to be significantly less than advertised. As noted by Acquisti, reports of a consumer backlash against companies that breach privacy rules may have been exaggerated.

There's some evidence that investment in cyber will lead to benefits, in terms of drip-feeding good news to the markets. That's interesting, but it's not enough to support a business case.

Current methods utilised by the cyber industry when estimating the value of investment, such as Annualised Loss Expectancy and ROSI, are based largely on guesswork. If you want to get a feel for the likely impact on your business, it's probably best to do that through multi-party workshops.

Methods such as VNA can be employed, if you want to look at the relevance of cyber to your relationships with trading partners, suppliers, competitors, and regulatory agencies.

The key finding from this section is that compliance seems to be the benefit sought by companies investing in cyber, although that may be because the cyber industry equates compliance with protection, and subsequently enforces compliance through their own, largely technically based standards. As we'll see in the next section, they have someone helping them to do that.

NOTES

1 This document has since been archived. The reference in the text provides a link to a summary page; if you would like to see the entire document, it's possible that the original poster may be able to provide one.
2 It's fair to point out that the authors were surprised that no larger scale impacts were found and suggested that these findings may have arisen from the choice of sampling method. However, as acknowledged in the paper, their findings broadly supported the findings of the (contemporary) UK Cyber Security Breaches Survey.

REFERENCES

1. Neocleous, M., *Critique of security*. 2008: Edinburgh University Press.
2. Greiner, L.E., *Evolution and revolution as organizations grow*. 1998: Harvard Business Review, p. 76.
3. Virgin, How to delegate. 2019 [Accessed 10 April 2021]; Available from: www.virgin.com/richard-branson/how-delegate
4. Emery, F.E. and E.L. Trist, *The causal texture of organizational environments. Human Relations*, 1965. 18(1): p. 21–32.

5. BIS, Competitive analysis of the UK cyber security sector. 2013 [Accessed 10 April 2021]; Available from: https://assets.publishing.service.gov.uk/government/uplo ads/system/uploads/attachment_data/file/259500/bis-13-1231-competitive-analysis-of-the-uk-cyber-security-sector.pdf

6. Baba, M., R. Mahmood, and A. Halipah, The moderating role of environmental turbulence on the relationship between organizational learning and firm innovativeness. *International Journal of Management Research and Reviews*, 2017. 7(2): p. 148.

7. Baburoglu, O.N., The vortical environment: The fifth in the Emery-Trist levels of organizational environments. *Human Relations*, 1988. 41(3): p. 181–210.

8. Handy, C., *Understanding organizations*. 1993: Penguin UK.

9. NCSC, Maturity models in cyber security: What's happening to the IAMM? 2018 [Accessed 10 April 2021]; Available from: www.ncsc.gov.uk/blog-post/maturity-mod els-cyber-security-whats-happening-iamm

10. Richard, C., NCSC IT: How the NCSC built its own IT system . 2017 [Accessed 10 April 2021]; Available from: www.ncsc.gov.uk/blog-post/ncsc-it-how-ncsc-built-its-own-it-system-0

11. CGI, The cyber-value connection [Accessed 14 January 2023]; Available from: www. consultancy.uk/news/13366/severe-cybersecurity-incidents-cost-shareholders-billi ons-says-cgi

12. Lange, R. and E.W. Burger, Long-term market implications of data breaches, not. *Journal of Information Privacy and Security*, 2017. 13(4): p. 186–206.

13. Choong, P., et al., Protecting the brand: Evaluating the cost of security breach from a marketer's perspective. *Journal of Marketing Development and Competitiveness*, 2017. 11(1): p. 59–68.

14. Sorescu, A., N.L. Warren, and L. Ertekin, Event study methodology in the marketing literature: An overview. *Journal of the Academy of Marketing Science*, 2017. 45(2): p. 186–207.

15. Konchitchki, Y. and D.E. O'Leary, Event study methodologies in information systems research. *International Journal of Accounting Information Systems*, 2011. 12(2): p. 99–115.

16. McWilliams, A. and D. Siegel, Event studies in management research: Theoretical and empirical issues. *Academy of Management Journal*, 1997. 40(3): p. 626–657.

17. Butler, S., Thousands of Morrisons staff personal details leaked online. 2014 [Accessed 21 April 2021]; Available from: www.theguardian.com/business/2014/mar/14/morris ons-staff-personal-details-stolen-published-online

18. Butler, S. and S. Farrell, Price war fears wipe £2bn off value of UK supermarkets. 2014 [Accessed 21 April 2021]; Available from: www.theguardian.com/business/2014/mar/ 13/morrisons-shares-profit-warning-supermarket-price-cutting

19. Aschwanden, C., We're all "P-Hacking" now. 2019 [Accessed 10 April 2021]; Available from: www.wired.com/story/were-all-p-hacking-now

20. Acquisti, A., A. Friedman, and R. Telang, Is there a cost to privacy breaches? An event study. In *ICIS 2006 Proceedings*, 2006: p. 94.

21. Cavusoglu, H., B. Mishra, and S. Raghunathan, The effect of internet security breach announcements on market value: Capital market reactions for breached firms and internet security developers. *International Journal of Electronic Commerce*, 2004. 9(1): p. 70–104.

22. Richardson, V., M.W. Watson, and R.E. Smith, Much ado about nothing: The (lack of) economic impact of data privacy breaches. *Journal of Information Systems*, 2019. 33(3): p. 227–265.

23. Goel, S. and H.A. Shawky, Estimating the market impact of security breach announcements on firm values. *Information & Management*, 2009. 46(7): p. 404–410.

24. Patel, N., *The effect of IT hack announcements on the market value of publicly traded corporations*. 2010: Duke J Econ, p. 22.

25. Campbell, K., et al., The economic cost of publicly announced information security breaches: Empirical evidence from the stock market. *Journal of Computer Security*, 2003. 11(3): p. 431–448.

26. Hovav, A. and J. D'Arcy, The impact of denial-of-service attack announcements on the market value of firms. *Risk Management and Insurance Review*, 2003. 6(2): p. 97–121.

27. Hilary, G., B. Segal, and M.H. Zhang, Cyber-risk disclosure: Who cares? *Georgetown McDonough School of Business Research Paper*, 2016 (2852519).

28. Hovav, A. and J. D'Arcy, The impact of virus attack announcements on the market value of firms. *Information Systems Security*, 2004. 13(3): p. 32–40.

29. Cardenas, J., et al., *The economic impact of security breaches on publicly traded corporations: An empirical investigation*. 2012. AMCIS 2012 Proceedings, 7: p. 1–10.

30. Ko, M.S., K.-M. Osei-Bryson, and C. Dorantes, *Investigating the impact of publicly announced information security breaches on organizational performance*. 2007: UTSA, College of Business.

31. Yayla, A.A. and Q. Hu, The impact of information security events on the stock value of firms: The effect of contingency factors. *Journal of Information Technology*, 2011. 26(1): p. 60–77.

32. Azzimonti, M. and A. Marks, *Hacking induced externalities and the apathy of stockholders*. 2016. Working Paper, Federal Reserve Bank of Richmond.

33. Ford, A., et al., The impact of data breach announcements on company value in European markets. In *WEIS 2021: The 20th Annual Workshop on the Economics of Information Security*. 2021.

34. Avery, A. and C. Ranganathan, *Financial performance impacts of information security breaches*. 2016. Work-shop on Information Security and Privacy (WISP), Dublin, Ireland, p. 1–16

35. DataGuidance, Romania: ANSPDCP fines BNP Paribas Personal Finance €2,000 for GDPR violations. 2019 [Accessed 4 August 2024]; Available from: www.dataguidance.com/news/romania-anspdcp-fines-bnp-paribas-personal-finance-2000

36. Ali, S.E.A., et al., Stock market reactions to favorable and unfavorable information security events: A systematic literature review. *Computers & Security*, 2021. 110: p. 102451.

37. Kvochko, E. and R. Pant, *Why data breaches don't hurt stock prices*. 2015: Harvard Business Review, p. 31.

38. Aytes, K., S. Byers, and M. Santhanakrishnan, The economic impact of information security breaches: Firm value and intra-industry effects. In *AMCIS 2006 Proceedings*, 2006: p. 399.

39. Malliouris, D.D. and A. Simpson, Underlying and consequential costs of cyber security breaches: Changes in systematic risk. In *Workshop on the Economics of Information Security*. 2020.

40. Havakhor, T., M.S. Rahman, and T. Zhang, *Cybersecurity investments and the cost of capital*. 2020, SSRN.

41. Chen, J.V., et al., Did IT consulting firms gain when their clients were breached? *Computers in Human Behavior*, 2012. 28(2): p. 456–464.

42. Capelle-Blancard, G. and M.-A. Laguna, How does the stock market respond to chemical disasters? *Journal of Environmental Economics and Management*, 2010. 59(2): p. 192–205.

43. Davidson, W.N. and D.L. Worrell, Research notes and communications: The effect of product recall announcements on shareholder wealth. *Strategic Management Journal*, 1992. 13(6): p. 467–473.

44. Sherman, E., The reason companies don't fix cybersecurity. 2015 [Accessed 10 April 2021]; Available from: www.cbsnews.com/news/the-reason-companies-dont-fix-cybersecurity

45. Romanosky, S., Examining the costs and causes of cyber incidents. *Journal of Cybersecurity*, 2016. 2(2): p. 121–135.

46. Biancotti, C., The price of cyber (in) security: Evidence from the Italian private sector. Bank of Italy Occasional Paper, 2017(407).

47. Edwards, B., S. Hofmeyr, and S. Forrest, Hype and heavy tails: A closer look at data breaches. *Journal of Cybersecurity*, 2016. 2(1): p. 3–14.

48. Dean, B., Why companies have little incentive to invest in cybersecurity. 2015 [Accessed 9 April 2021]; Available from: https://theconversation.com/why-compan ies-have-little-incentive-to-invest-in-cybersecurity-37570

49. Heyburn, H., et al., Analysis of the full costs of cyber security breaches: Literature Review Annex. 2020 [Accessed 30 July 2021]; Available from: https://assets.pub lishing.service.gov.uk/government/uploads/system/uploads/attachment_data/file/ 901570/Analysis_of_the_full_cost_of_cyber_security_breaches_-_literature_rev iew.pdf

50. Heyburn, H., et al., Analysis of the full costs of cyber security breaches. 2020 [Accessed 30 July 2021]; Available from: https://assets.publishing.service.gov.uk/gov ernment/uploads/system/uploads/attachment_data/file/901569/Analysis_of_the_full_ cost_of_cyber_security_breaches.pdf

51. Heyburn, H., et al., Analysis of the full costs of cyber security breaches: Case studies Annex. 2020 [Accessed 30 July 2021]; Available from: https://assets.publishing. service.gov.uk/government/uploads/system/uploads/attachment_data/file/901572/ Analysis_of_the_full_cost_of_cyber_security_breaches_-_case_studies.pdf

52. LeClair, J., Protecting small businesses from cyber attacks. 2015 [Accessed 9 April 2021]; Available from: https://docs.house.gov/meetings/SM/SM00/20150422/ 103276/HHRG-114-SM00-20150422-SD003-U4.pdf

53. NCSA, National cyber security alliance statement regarding incorrect small business statistic. 2022[Accessed 15 October 2023]; Available from: https://staysafeonline.org/ press-release/national-cyber-security-alliance-statement-regarding-incorrect-small-business-statistic

54. Chabrow, E., 60% of hacked small businesses fail. How reliable s that stat? 2017 [Accessed 21 April 2021]; Available from: www.bankinfosecurity.com/blogs/60-hac ked-small-businesses-fail-how-reliable-that-stat-p-2464

55. Johnson, R., 60 percent of small companies close within 6 months of being hacked. 2019 [Accessed 21 April 2021]; Available from: https://cybersecurityventures.com/ 60-percent-of-small-companies-close-within-6-months-of-being-hacked

56. Shepherd, M., 30 surprising small business cyber security statistics (2021). 2023 [Accessed 15 October 2021]; Available from: www.fundera.com/resources/small-business-cyber-security-statistics

57. SBIR, The impact of cybersecurity on small business. 2017 [Accessed 9 April 2021]; Available from: www.sbir.gov/sites/all/themes/sbir/dawnbreaker/img/documents/ Course10-Tutorial1.pdf

58. Jimenez, N., Cyber-attacks on small firms: The US economy's "Achilles heel"? 2022 [Accessed 10 November 2022]; Available from: www.bbc.co.uk/news/business-63260648

59. Breitinger, D. and J.-P. Bonardi, *Firms, breach of norms, and reputation damage.* *Business & Society*, 2019. 58(6): p. 1143–1176.

60. Transparency International. [Accessed 10 April 2021]; Available from: www.transpare ncy.org/en

61. Privacy International. [Accessed 10 April 2021]; Available from: https://privacyintern ational.org

62. Big Brother Watch. [Accessed 10 April 2021]; Available from: https://bigbrotherwa tch.org.uk

63. Electronic Privacy Information Centre. [Accessed 10 April 2021]; Available from: https://epic.org

64. Open Rights Group. [Accessed 10 April 2021]; Available from: www.openrightsgr oup.org

65. Privacy Rights Clearinghouse. [Accessed 10 April 2021]; Available from: https:// privacyrights.org

66. Scott, M., Cambridge Analytica did work for Brexit groups, says ex-staffer. 2019 [Accessed 10 April 2021]; Available from: www.politico.eu/article/cambridge-analyt ica-leave-eu-ukip-brexit-facebook

67. Cadwalladr, C. and E. Graham-Harrison, Revealed: 50 million Facebook profiles harvested for Cambridge Analytica in major data breach. 2018 [Accessed 10 April 2021]; Available from: www.theguardian.com/news/2018/mar/17/cambridge-analytica-facebook-influence-us-election

68. Lapowski, I., How Cambridge Analytica sparked the great privacy awakening. 2019 [Accessed 10 April 2021]; Available from: www.wired.com/story/cambridge-analyt ica-facebook-privacy-awakening

69. BBC, SNP met Cambridge Analytica before election. 2018 [Accessed 10 April 2021]; Available from: www.bbc.co.uk/news/uk-scotland-scotland-politics-43822311

70. Kleinman, Z., Cambridge Analytica: The story so far. 2018 [Accessed 10 April 2021]; Available from: www.bbc.co.uk/news/technology-43465968

71. Mirhaydari, A., Facebook stock recovers all $134B lost after Cambridge Analytica data scandal. 2018 [Accessed 10 April 2021]; Available from: www.cbsnews.com/ news/facebook-stock-price-recovers-all-134-billion-lost-in-after-cambridge-analyt ica-datascandal

72. Hamilton, I.A., Facebook shouldn't be appealing a tiny fine over Cambridge Analytica if it's really committed to privacy regulation, says data cop. 2019 [Accessed 10 April 2021]; Available from: www.businessinsider.com/ico-calls-on-facebook-to-drop-appeal-over-cambridge-analytica-fine-2019-4

73. Woodcock, A., Facebook agrees to pay £500,000 fine over Cambridge Analytica scandal. 2019 [Accessed 10 April 2021]; Available from: www.independent.co.uk/ news/uk/politics/facebook-fine-cambridge-analytica-user-personal-information-liabil ity-latest-a9177471.html

74. FTC, FTC imposes $5 billion penalty and sweeping new privacy restrictions on Facebook. 2019 [Accessed 10 April 2021]; Available from: www.ftc.gov/news-events/press-relea ses/2019/07/ftc-imposes-5-billion-penalty-sweeping-new-privacy-restrictions

75. Patel, N., Facebook's $5 billion FTC fine is an embarrassing joke. 2019 [Accessed 10 April 2021]; Available from: www.theverge.com/2019/7/12/20692524/facebook-five-billion-ftc-fine-embarrassing-joke

76. Rodriguez, S. and L. Feiner, *FTC slaps Facebook with record $5 billion fine, orders privacy oversight.* 2019 [Accessed 10 April 2021]; Available from: www.cnbc.com/ 2019/07/24/facebook-to-pay-5-billion-for-privacy-lapses-ftc-announces.html

77. Zadrozny, B. and B. Collins, Inside the final days of Cambridge Analytica: Failed rebrands, fleeing clients and Nerf basketball. 2018 [Accessed 10 April 2021]; Available from: www.nbcnews.com/business/business-news/inside-final-days-cambridge-analytica-failed-rebrands-fleeing-clients-nerf-n875321

78. Rosoff, M., Facebook suspends Cambridge Analytica for misuse of user data, which Cambridge denies. 2018 [Accessed 10 April 2021]; Available from: www.cnbc.com/2018/03/16/facebook-bans-cambridge-analytica.html

79. Grewal, P., Suspending Cambridge Analytica and SCL Group from Facebook. 2018 [Accessed 16 June 2023]; Available from: https://about.fb.com/news/2018/03/suspending-cambridge-analytica/

80. Perrin, A., Americans are changing their relationship with Facebook. 2018 [Accessed 10 April 2021]; Available from: www.pewresearch.org/fact-tank/2018/09/05/americans-are-changing-their-relationship-with-facebook

81. Martin, C., Millions of Facebook users migrating to Instagram: Report. 2019 [Accessed 10 April 2021]; Available from: www.moneycontrol.com/news/trends/millions-of-facebook-users-migrating-to-instagram-report-3623781.html.

82. Gramlich, J., 10 facts about Americans and Facebook. 2019 [Accessed 10 April 2021]; Available from: www.pewresearch.org/fact-tank/2019/05/16/facts-about-americans-and-facebook

83. BBC, Facebook to pay record $5bn to settle privacy concerns. 2019 [Accessed 10 April 2021]; Available from: www.bbc.co.uk/news/business-49099364

84. Hinds, J., E.J. Williams, and A.N. Joinson, "It wouldn't happen to me": Privacy concerns and perspectives following the Cambridge Analytica scandal. *International Journal of Human-Computer Studies*, 2020. 143: p. 102498.

85. Norberg, P.A., D.R. Horne, and D.A. Horne, The privacy paradox: Personal information disclosure intentions versus behaviors. *Journal of Consumer Affairs*, 2007. 41(1): p. 100–126.

86. Acquisti, A., L. Brandimarte, and G. Loewenstein, Privacy and human behavior in the age of information. *Science*, 2015. 347(6221): p. 509–514.

87. Acquisti, A., L.K. John, and G. Loewenstein, What is privacy worth? *The Journal of Legal Studies*, 2013. 42(2): p. 249–274.

88. Gerber, N., P. Gerber, and M. Volkamer, Explaining the privacy paradox: A systematic review of literature investigating privacy attitude and behavior. *Computers & Security*, 2018. 77: p. 226–261.

89. Kokolakis, S., Privacy attitudes and privacy behaviour: A review of current research on the privacy paradox phenomenon. *Computers & Security*, 2017. 64: p. 122–134.

90. Barth, S. and M.D. De Jong, The privacy paradox – Investigating discrepancies between expressed privacy concerns and actual online behavior – A systematic literature review. *Telematics and Informatics*, 2017. 34(7): p. 1038–1058.

91. Solove, D.J., *The myth of the privacy paradox*. Available at SSRN, 2020.

92. Carrascal, J.P., et al., Your browsing behavior for a big mac: Economics of personal information online. In Proceedings of the 22nd International Conference on World Wide Web. 2013.

93. Fiesler, C. and B. Hallinan, "We Are the Product" public reactions to online data sharing and privacy controversies in the media. In Proceedings of the 2018 CHI Conference on Human Factors in Computing Systems. 2018.

94. Brown, A.J., "Should I Stay or Should I Leave?": Exploring (Dis) continued Facebook use after the Cambridge Analytica Scandal. *Social Media+ Society*, 2020. 6(1): p. 2056305120913884.

95. Shipman, F.M. and C.C. Marshall, Ownership, privacy, and control in the wake of Cambridge Analytica: The relationship between attitudes and awareness. In Proceedings of the 2020 CHI Conference on Human Factors in Computing Systems. 2020.

96. Gordon, J., *When data crimes are real crimes: Voter surveillance and the Cambridge Analytica conflict*. 2019. Masters thesis, University of Saskatchewan.

97. ICO, ICO letter to parliament. 2020. [Accessed 10 April 2021]; Available from: https://ico.org.uk/media/action-weve-taken/2618383/20201002_ico-o-ed-l-rtl-0181_to-julian-knight-mp.pdf

98. Kaminska, I., ICO's final report into Cambridge Analytica invites regulatory questions. 2020 [Accessed 12 October 2020]; Available from: www.ft.com/content/43962679-b1f9-4818-b569-b028a58c8cd2

99. Sherman, N., TikTok users shrug at China fears: "It's hard to care". 2023 [Accessed 13 March 2023]; Available from: www.bbc.co.uk/news/business-64827885

100. Ablon, L., et al., *Consumer attitudes toward data breach notifications and loss of personal information*. 2016: Rand Corporation.

101. Lee, M. and J. Lee, The impact of information security failure on customer behaviors: A study on a large-scale hacking incident on the internet. *Information Systems Frontiers*, 2012. 14(2): p. 375–393.

102. Janakiraman, R., J.H. Lim, and R. Rishika, The effect of a data breach announcement on customer behavior: Evidence from a multichannel retailer. *Journal of Marketing*, 2018. 82(2): p. 85–105.

103. HOSAC, Understanding the costs of cyber crime. 2018 [Accessed 10 April 2021]; Available from: https://assets.publishing.service.gov.uk/government/uploads/system/uploads/attachment_data/file/674046/understanding-costs-of-cyber-crime-horr96.pdf

104. Masuch, K., et al., Do I get what I expect? An experimental investigation of different data breach recovery actions. In ECIS. 2020.

105. PI, When local authorities aren't your friends. 2020 [Accessed 10 April 2021]; Available from: https://privacyinternational.org/long-read/3586/when-local-authorities-arent-your-friends

106. PI, Fighting the global Covid-19 power-grab. 2021 [Accessed 10 April 2021]; Available from: https://privacyinternational.org/campaigns/fighting-global-covid-19-power-grab

107. bigbrotherwatch.org.uk, Big brother watch tells airports to drop thermal surveillance. 2020 [Accessed 10 April 2021]; Available from: https://bigbrotherwatch.org.uk/2020/06/big-brother-watch-tells-airports-to-drop-thermal-surveillance-2

108. openrightsgroup.org, NHSX scraps centralised model for COVID-19 app. 2020 [Accessed 10 April 2021]; Available from: www.openrightsgroup.org/campaign/protecting-digital-rights-during-covid-19

109. openrightsgroup.org, Who do they think you are? 2021 [Accessed 10 April 2021]; Available from: www.openrightsgroup.org/campaign/who-do-they-think-you-are

110. Gordon, L.A. and M.P. Loeb, The economics of information security investment. *ACM Transactions on Information and System Security (TISSEC)*, 2002. 5(4): p. 438–457.

111. Home_Affairs_Committee, E-crime fifth report of session 2013–14. 2013 [Accessed 10 April 2021]; Available from: https://publications.parliament.uk/pa/cm201314/cmselect/cmhaff/70/70.pdf

112. BBC, UK cyber crime costs £27bn a year – Government report. 2011 [Accessed 10 April 2021]; Available from: www.bbc.co.uk/news/uk-politics-12492309

113. City_of_London_Corporation, The implications of economic cybercrime for policing. 2015 [Accessed 10 April 2021]; Available from: https://orca.cf.ac.uk/88156/1/Econo mic-Cybercrime-FullReport.pdf

114. muddywatersresearch.com, MW is short NMC health plc. 2019 [Accessed 9 April 2021]; Available from: www.muddywatersresearch.com/research/nmc/mw-is-short-nmc

115. Bahree, M., Former Indian billionaire's Gulf dream turns sour. 2020 [Accessed 9 April 2021]; Available from: www.forbes.com/sites/meghabahree/2020/05/12/former-indian-billionaires-gulf-dream-turns-sour/?sh=5ea931046559

116. Kerr, S. and C. O'Murchu, False invoices at centre of new NMC probe. 2020 [Accessed 9 April 2021]; Available from: www.ft.com/content/a22b75df-f37f-4e4f-a024-3dc1c 1df82ee

117. Reuters, NMC founder says private probe shows alleged fraud at NMC, Finablr. 2020 [Accessed 4 October 2022]; Available from: www.reuters.com/article/nmc-health-shareholders-idUKL5N2CH3TU

118. Reuters, Troubled Finablr reports nearly $1 billion more debt. 2020 [Accessed 4 October 2022]; Available from: www.reuters.com/article/us-finablr-debt-idINKB N22C28N

119. Reuters, UPDATE 1-Troubled Finablr reports nearly $1 billion more in debt. 2020 [Accessed 4 October 2022]; Available from: www.reuters.com/article/finablr-debt-idUSL4N2CI4PI

120. Reuters, Finablr founder Shetty resigns, UK suspends units' registrations. 2020 [Accessed 20 June 2022]; Available from: www.reuters.com/article/us-finablr-chair man-idUKKCN25D24N

121. Reuters, UPDATE 1-Troubled payments firm Finablr gets takeover bid from Prism. 2020 [Accessed 4 October 2022]; Available from: www.reuters.com/article/finablr-ma-prism-advance-solutions-idINL4N2GX1GE

122. Reuters, Israeli-UAE consortium buys payments firm Finablr – Statement. 2020 [Accessed 4 October 2022]; Available from: www.reuters.com/article/finablr-m-a-idUSKBN28R1GX

123. Vigen, T. Spurious correlations. 2023 [Accessed 18 January 2023]; Available from: www.tylervigen.com/spurious-correlations

124. Doherty, N.F. and H. Fulford, Do information security policies reduce the incidence of security breaches: An exploratory analysis. *Information Resources Management Journal (IRMJ)*, 2005. 18(4): p. 21–39.

125. Szubartowicz, E. and G. Schryen, *Timing in Information Security: An Event Study on the Impact of Information Security Investment Announcements.* 2018.

126. Chai, S., M. Kim, and H.R. Rao, Firms' information security investment decisions: Stock market evidence of investors' behavior. *Decision Support Systems*, 2011. 50(4): p. 651–661.

127. Dos Santos, B.L., K. Peffers, and D.C. Mauer, The impact of information technology investment announcements on the market value of the firm. *Information Systems Research*, 1993. 4(1): p. 1–23.

128. Bose, I. and A.C.M. Leung, The impact of adoption of identity theft countermeasures on firm value. *Decision Support Systems*, 2013. 55(3): p. 753–763.

129. Xu, F., et al., Do strategy and timing in IT security investments matter? An empirical investigation of the alignment effect. *Information Systems Frontiers*, 2019. 21(5): p. 1069–1083.

130. Jeong, C.Y., S.-Y.T. Lee, and J.-H. Lim, Information security breaches and IT security investments: Impacts on competitors. *Information & Management*, 2019. 56(5): p. 681–695.

131. Ettredge, M.L. and V.J. Richardson, Information transfer among internet firms: The case of hacker attacks. *Journal of Information Systems*, 2003. 17(2): p. 71–82.

132. Haislip, J., et al., The economic cost of cybersecurity breaches: A broad-based analysis. In Workshop on the Economics of Information Security (WEIS). 2019: Boston, MA.

133. Zafar, H., M. Ko, and K.-M. Osei-Bryson, Financial impact of information security breaches on breached firms and their non-breached competitors. *Information Resources Management Journal (IRMJ)*, 2012. 25(1): p. 21–37.

134. Bosch, J.-C., E.W. Eckard, and V. Singal, The competitive impact of air crashes: Stock market evidence. *The Journal of Law and Economics*, 1998. 41(2): p. 503–519.

135. Ho, J.C., M. Qiu, and X. Tang, Do airlines always suffer from crashes? *Economics Letters*, 2013. 118(1): p. 113–117.

136. Foster, J., From simplistic to complex systems in economics. *Cambridge Journal of Economics*, 2005. 29(6): p. 873–892.

137. Makridis, C.A., Do data breaches damage reputation? Evidence from 45 companies between 2002 and 2018. *Journal of Cybersecurity*, 2021. 7(1): p. tyab021.

138. Segal, B. and D. Segal, Are managers strategic in reporting non-earnings news? Evidence on timing and news bundling. *Review of Accounting Studies*, 2016. 21(4): p. 1203–1244.

139. Kothari, S.P., S. Shu, and P.D. Wysocki, Do managers withhold bad news? *Journal of Accounting Research*, 2009. 47(1): p. 241–276.

140. Amir, E., S. Levi, and T. Livne, Do firms underreport information on cyber-attacks? Evidence from capital markets. *Review of Accounting Studies*, 2018. 23(3): p. 1177–1206.

141. Gatzlaff, K.M. and K.A. McCullough, The effect of data breaches on shareholder wealth. *Risk Management and Insurance Review*, 2010. 13(1): p. 61–83.

142. Bolster, P., C.H. Pantalone, and E.A. Trahan, Security breaches and firm value. *Journal of Business Valuation and Economic Loss Analysis*, 2010. 5(1).

143. Parameswaran, S., S. Venkatesan, and M. Gupta, Cloud Computing Security Announcements: Assessment of Investors' Reaction. *Journal of Information Privacy and Security*, 2013. 9(1): p. 17–46.

144. Wang, T., K. Kannan, and J. Rees, The textual contents of information security breach reports and profitable short-term investment opportunities. *Journal of Organizational Computing and Electronic Commerce*, 2013. 23(3): p. 200–223.

145. Cohen, P., Hidden profits – How criminals are using Cyber Attacks for Stock market gain. 2020 [Accessed 16 September 2021]; Available from: www.linkedin.com/pulse/hidden-profits-how-criminals-using-cyber-attacks-stock-peter-cohen

146. Piccotti, L.R. and H.E. Wang, Informed trading in options markets surrounding data breaches. Available at SSRN 3478263, 2020.

147. Wang, H.E., Q.E. Wang, and W. Wu, Short selling surrounding data breach announcements. Available at SSRN 3554487, 2020.

148. Lin, Z., et al., Insider trading ahead of cyber breach announcements. *Journal of Financial Markets*, 2020. 50: p. 100527.

149. Mitts, J. and E. Talley, Informed trading and cybersecurity breaches. *Harvard Business Law Review*, 2019. 9: p. 1.

150. ENISA, Introduction to return on security investment. 2012 [Accessed 21st January 2023]; Available from: www.enisa.europa.eu/publications/introduction-to-return-on-security-investment

151. Gordon, L.A. and M.P. Loeb, Return on information security investments: Myths vs. realities. *Strategic Finance*, 2002. 84(5): p. 26.

152. Schneier, B. Schneier on security: Security ROI. 2008 [Accessed 10 April 2021]; Available from: www.schneier.com/blog/archives/2008/09/security_roi_1.html

153. Hoo, K.J.S., *How much is enough? A risk management approach to computer security.* 2000: Stanford University Stanford.

154. Kahneman, D. and A. Tversky. Prospect theory: An analysis of decisions under risk. In *Econometrica.* 1979. Citeseer.

155. Tanaka, H., K. Matsuura, and O. Sudoh, Vulnerability and information security investment: An empirical analysis of e-local government in Japan. *Journal of Accounting and Public Policy*, 2005. 24(1): p. 37–59.

156. Gordon, L.A., M.P. Loeb, and W. Lucyshyn, Information security expenditures and real options: A wait-and-see approach. *Computer Security Journal*, 2003. 19(2).

157. Porter, M., Competitive advantage: Creating and sustaining superior performance. *Chap*, 1985. 1: p. 3–52.

158. Porter, M.E. and V.E. Millar, *How information gives you competitive advantage.* 1985: Harvard Business Review Reprint Service.

159. Linkov, I., et al., *The case for value chain resilience.* 2020: Management Research Review.

160. Christensen, C.M., *The innovator's dilemma: When new technologies cause great firms to fail.* 2013: Harvard Business Review Press.

161. Normann, R. and R. Ramirez, From value chain to value constellation: Designing interactive strategy. *Harvard Business Review*, 1993. 71(4): p. 65.

162. Stabell, C.B. and Ø.D. Fjeldstad, Configuring value for competitive advantage: On chains, shops, and networks. *Strategic Management Journal*, 1998. 19(5): p. 413–437.

163. Allee, V., Reconfiguring the value network. *Journal of Business strategy*, 2000. 21(4): p. 36–39.

164. Allee, V., *The future of knowledge: Increasing prosperity through value networks.* 2003: Routledge.

165. Bowers, K., Fighting Cyber Security FUD and hype. 2017 [Accessed 16 September 2021]; Available from: www.securityweek.com/fighting-cyber-security-fud-and-hype

166. Proctor, P. Gartner report: The urgency to treat cybersecurity as a business decision. 2020 [Accessed 9 April 2021]; Available from: www.gartner.com/en/documents/3980891/the-urgency-to-treat-cybersecurity-as-a-business-decisio

167. Cavusoglu, H., et al., Institutional pressures in security management: Direct and indirect influences on organizational investment in information security control resources. *Information & Management*, 2015. 52(4): p. 385–400.

168. Weishäupl, E., E. Yasasin, and G. Schryen, Information security investments: An exploratory multiple case study on decision-making, evaluation and learning. *Computers & Security*, 2018. 77: p. 807–823.

169. Ponemon, The Cybersecurity illusion: The emperor has no clothes. 2019 [Accessed 9 April 2021]; Available from: www.businesswire.com/news/home/20190730005215/en/Ponemon-Study-53-Percent-of-IT-Security-Leaders-Don't-Know-if-Cybersecurity-Tools-are-Working-Despite-an-Average-of-18.4-Million-Annual-Spend

170. Sales, N.A., Regulating cyber-security. *Northwestern University Law Review*, 2012. 107: p. 1503.

171. Debate, Cyber Security Technology Efficacy: Is cybersecurity the new "market for lemons"? 2020 [Accessed 16 September 2021]; Available from: www.debatesecurity.com/downloads/Cybersecurity-Technology-Efficacy-Research-Report-V1.0.pdf

172. Schneier, B., Schneier on security: Entries tagged "security theater". 2022 [Accessed 17 January 2023]; Available from: www.schneier.com/tag/security-theater

173. Plachkinova, M. and C. Maurer, Teaching case: Security breach at Target. *Journal of Information Systems Education*, 2018. 29(1): p. 11.
174. Manworren, N., J. Letwat, and O. Daily, Why you should care about the Target data breach. *Business Horizons*, 2016. 59(3): p. 257–266.
175. Mc Mahon, C., In defence of the human factor. *Frontiers in Psychology*, 2020. 11: p. 1390.
176. Angst, C.M., et al., When do IT security investments matter? Accounting for the influence of institutional factors in the context of healthcare data breaches. *MIS Quarterly*, 2017. 41(3): p. 893–916.

7 The Enforcement of Compliance

EXTERNALITIES

INTRODUCTION

If companies do invest in cyber mostly to meet compliance requirements, then logically, they'll invest just the minimum amount necessary to pass an audit. And indeed, received wisdom has it that companies do tend to under-invest in cyber, partly because in their haste to achieve certification, they discount the issue of negative externalities (e.g. [1], para 2.1).

When a breach takes place, not all of the impact will be felt by the company itself – some of it will fall to their customers, the general public, etc. The inconveniences felt by those other parties are the "externalities" [2, 3]. So because the breached company won't see all the impact, it tends to invest less, or at least less than the optimal amount that it should invest from a societal point of view [4]. There is at least one argument against this [5], but by and large, it's accepted that leaving cyber-investment to market forces will result in societal costs. Bronk, for example [6], suggests that in relation to the widely reported 2021 US pipeline attack: *"Colonial is yet another example of firms avoiding cybersecurity responsibilities and letting the costs be borne by society"*. Malliouris and Simpson [7, p25], quoting Lam [8], also suggest that *"[f]irms which can externalise breach costs to society are not incentivised to invest in attack deterrence and hence invest more in damage control than in breach avoidance"*.

Some of this could be laid at the door of the cyber industry, since there is often no consideration given to externalities when conducting a risk analysis. However, typically the party seen to be at fault is the customer.

The two best known options for reducing negative externalities are taxation and regulation [9, 10]. Either you tax companies for, e.g., the environmental damage they cause, or you impose legislation to control their behaviour.

In the case of cyber, the United States has gone with a light touch, mostly leaving industry to decide on what would be an appropriate level of protection [11, 12]. The EU, however, has opted for a greater degree of regulation, in the form of a number of Directives, some of which have now been transposed into law. Actual and impending legislation includes the General Data Protection Regulation (GDPR) [13], the EU Cybersecurity Act [14–16], emerging parallel Directives relating to the resilience of critical entities (the RCE Directive [17]) and regulations aimed at ensuring resilience in the financial sector (the Digital Operational Resilience Act – "DORA" [18–22][1]). We also have the EU Cyber Sanctions Regime [23, 24]. Perhaps the most relevant is the EU Directive intended to bring about a common standard in cyber security across critical industries, such as water, power, and transport. This is the Network and Information Security (NIS) Directive, which has been adopted into law across the EU, and also in the UK [25–30].

Papakonstantinou [31] suggests that [31, p12]:

Regulation requires consequences to be attached to infringements of obligations... if addressees are not faced with concrete consequences, they may be tempted to be lax on their implementation of the EU cybersecurity requirements, in view of the costs and effort involved.

This idea that companies need to be coerced into buying cyber irrespective of the costs, and fined for their business insouciance if they're found to be non-compliant, is a strong theme of EU policy.

THE NATURE OF ENFORCEMENT

BACKGROUND

Under the existing NIS regulations, UK Operators of Essential Services (OESs) who fail to cooperate with the National Authority can be fined up to £1M. Companies having an incident that causes (or could have caused) a reduction of service can be fined up to £3.4M. For significant interruptions, the fine can be anything up to £8.5M. Under the current UK version of the Directive, a maximum fine of £17M can be levied for a failing that "... *has caused, or could cause, an incident resulting in an immediate threat to life or significant adverse impact on the [United Kingdom] economy*" [32, 33]. Note the conditional clause.

If all this seems overly stringent, it's worth bearing in mind that just two years after its inception, the NIS Directive is being updated to "NIS2" [34–36]. Although the original Directive has been labelled a "*success in principle*" [37], it seems that variations in interpretation and implementation across member states have impaired the desired level of harmonisation [38]. Consequently, it's been argued that a more prescriptive approach is needed [39–42].

The original Directive distinguished between OESs and operators of key digital services, with the latter being subject to a slightly lighter regime. The revised Directive differentiates instead between "essential" and "important" service providers, and (a) extends the scope of the Directive to include all firms above a certain size in specific sectors, and (b) includes additional sectors, such as couriers and postal services, food production, and social networking services. To put this in perspective, one public response to the proposals noted that "*[t]he manufacturing section would bring into scope almost every manufacturing company in Europe*" [43].

The scope of incident reporting has also been extended. The draft for NIS2 requires providers of critical services to report "*any significant cyber threat that those entities identify that could have potentially resulted in a significant incident*". Failing to report an incident that didn't take place will leave the company open to a fine, by my reading.[2]

Under the revised Directive, entities will also be responsible for ensuring security in their supply chains. That is, they will be responsible for ensuring that suppliers critical to the ongoing provision of their own services are also reliable and secure. On the face of it, entities using, e.g., penetration testing and incident response services will therefore become responsible for ensuring an adequate level of security in their security services provider (para 86 in the issued document):

> *Among service providers, managed security services providers in areas such as incident response, penetration testing, security audits and consultancy play a particularly important role in assisting entities in their efforts to prevent, detect, respond to or recover from incidents. Managed security services providers have however also themselves been the targets of cyberattacks and, because of their close integration in the operations of entities pose a particular risk. Essential and important entities should therefore exercise increased diligence in selecting a managed security services provider.*

At the time of writing, there's also a proposed "name and shame" clause that allows national authorities to publicise the names of non-compliant companies [44, p5]. As a last resort, the certification of the company (i.e. its license to operate) can be suspended [41]. Presumably, electricity companies could therefore be taken off the grid in order to avoid the possibility that they might be taken offline.

THE JUSTIFICATION FOR ENFORCEMENT

The justification for introducing NIS2 is given in a companion study [39], which concludes that: "... *the market let alone would not be enough to ensure an adequate level of cybersecurity*" [39, p72]. That is, intervention is justified in this case, because industry as a whole isn't spending as much on cyber as Government would like it to do.

The figures supporting that position seem a bit confusing, at least to me.

The accompanying report says that the cost of cybercrime amounts to 8% of global GDP [39, p30], i.e. one in a dozen employed adults on the planet is working full time to meet the costs of cybercrime. The cited source of that figure however (a 2018 report from McAfee, a cybersecurity services provider [45]), reported the economic cost as *0.8%* of global GDP [45, pp4, 6, 7]).

The subsequent calculation of the expected reduction in cybercrime takes what seems to be an annualised *internal* cost *per company* (not the cost of externalities and not the cost per breach) and combines that with the predicted number of breaches per year in 2029 (*not* the number of breached companies), to reach a total of €11.3Bn in terms of potentially achievable benefits, over a ten-year timeframe [39, p121].[3] I think I have that right.

Assuming the figure of €11.3Bn over ten years is the intended figure [46, p18], it's instructive to compare it against the EU's own estimate for the annual global cost of cybercrime in 2020/21 (i.e. €5.5Tn) [47].

On these figures, the implementation of NIS2 will reduce the global impact of cybercrime by ((€11.3Bn/10)/€5.5Tn) or about 0.02% – one fiftieth of 1%. For comparison, a UK Government assessment of the costs and benefits accruing from the implementation of NIS1 [48] concluded that the net cost would be £400M (about €0.46Bn) in the UK alone, over a ten-year timeframe.

As we'll see later, the justification for cyber investments sometimes doesn't stack up when you look at the numbers in detail. For the purposes of this section, it's enough to note that probably, the legislation would have gone ahead anyway, as a matter of harmonisation. But under those circumstances, why bother to present a business case?

THE RESPONSE FROM INDUSTRY

The industry body Business Europe "*... speak[s] for all-sized enterprises in 35 European countries whose national business federations are our direct members*" [49]. Their comments on the draft for NIS2 made a number of key points:

- "*The improvement of cybersecurity resilience itself must be the primary goal, rather than the bureaucracy or administrative costs that supports it*".
- "*... the current European enforcement cybersecurity regime punishes the victims rather than the attackers*".
- "*The obligation to report potential future events ... seems unreasonable and even unmeasurable...* ".
- "*Article 6 should oblige government agencies from Member States to immediately report any information on vulnerabilities or backdoors in IT products to the respective businesses and/or ENISA. Currently it is the case that government agencies frequently hold back such knowledge which represents a significant threat to Europe's cyber-resilience*".
- "*... we believe the Art 12 cooperation group would benefit from the involvement of a wide range of industrial stakeholders ...*".

These and other comments from industry bodies [50, 51] can be summarised as "*... there is a need to produce not simply the rules, but rather the enabling environment for our industries to ensure the cybersecure future of the EU*" [44]. That is, it's not necessarily about enforcement, it's more about engagement.

The trade organisation Digital Europe [43], in particular, raised the issue of cooperation:

Vulnerability reporting works best when both sides stand to gain from the interaction and a trusted relationship can be fostered. As it currently stands, private companies often do not always stand to gain new insights from engaging with cyber authorities.

and:

Since critical infrastructure is largely owned and managed by private entities, DIGITALEUROPE recommends more structural involvement of industry in these coordination efforts, for both better alignment and as resource for industry-specific knowledge.

The strong central message seems to be that industry would prefer to be involved in a discussion, rather than simply have legislation forced upon them [52]. In terms of the model of social construction, they would like a seat at the table, since they're directly affected by the legislation. That doesn't seem unreasonable.

THE ROLE OF GOVERNMENT

In this context, Governments wear at least two hats: as the enactor of laws to protect the citizen; and as a player themselves, who sometimes also causes externalities through, e.g., failing to protect stockpiled vulnerability information [53]. That secondary role acts to distort the market in other ways. Sales, for example [54], argues that as long as some parts of Government are willing to offer indemnity, reduced transaction costs, and a greater reward, people discovering previously unreported vulnerabilities will inevitably sell them to Government agencies for offensive purposes, rather than offering them to manufacturers to remedy weaknesses in their products. The same point has been noted by others (e.g. [55], Ch11).

As summarised by Dunn Cavelty [56, p27], one part of Government wants to see perfect security in cyberspace, while another wants to see exploitable vulnerabilities:

Furthermore, the security of cyberspace and security by (or through) cyberspace are often diametrically opposed. That becomes apparent when we bring computer vulnerabilities back into the analysis: a strategically exploitable cyberspace wants to have vulnerabilities through which to achieve one's goals. A stable and secure cyberspace should have as little as possible. Without understanding the interactions between the two images, finding good solutions will remain elusive.

Under the EU proposals, all reported vulnerabilities and threats will be gathered together in a central database – not the existing, well-established CVE database [57] – this will be a new one, under EU control and holding detailed vulnerability information on all CNI companies across Europe (para 63). That central database will be used as part of a protective cyber dome [58, 59]. Systems driven by advanced Artificial Intelligence will spot attacks before they're launched and shut them down before any damage is caused [60]. Which sounds splendid.

Notwithstanding any potential for secondary uses of that information, an implicit assumption is that the central facility will itself be completely protected against zero-day attacks (i.e. attacks exploiting previously unknown vulnerabilities) such as the attack that affected the systems of the European Banking Authority (EBA), an oversight and monitoring agency for DORA [61–63]. The operators of the central facility will presumably also seek to avoid a repetition of the incident in which the vulnerability that made possible the Wannacry and NotPetya attacks [64] was stolen from a US security agency [65] (which had allegedly kept the vulnerability secret for five years, rather than disclosing it to allow companies to protect themselves [66]). And reporting of potential incidents affecting the EU's own database will presumably also be mandated, in order to avoid, e.g., situations in which the EU embassy in Moscow was allegedly hacked, but that information was not shared (by EU officials) with the president of the European Commission, nor with the president of the European Council, nor with other EU leaders [67].

LOBBYING

The role of Government doesn't, of course, exist in a vacuum. A 2021 report from a European watchdog organisation [68] noted that nearly €100M had been spent by tech companies in the preceding 12 months, lobbying members of the European Parliament. Transparency International has made similar observations [69, 70]. There have also been comments regarding "revolving doors" with the tech sector [71, 72], enabled in part by rules that have been described by some sources as "lax" [73].

In the United States, a Wall Street Journal article in 2020 [74] noted that "*[t]he collective lobbying spending of 12 large publicly traded cybersecurity firms more than tripled to $3.94 million in 2019 from $1.21 million in 2015*". The figures for years prior to 2015 are shown in a Washington Post article [75], which noted that again, "*[t]he number of companies, associations and other groups lobbying on data and cybersecurity issues has nearly tripled since 2008...*" and that "*[t]he number of lobby firms advocating on behalf of clients on data and cybersecurity issues also tripled in the same period*". That is, not only did the number of cyber companies paying for lobbying increase, but there was also an increase in the number of companies offering those services. A 2021 Washington Post article [76] acknowledged that the level of lobbying in the sector was only going to go up. The Open Secrets web site [77], which aims to "*track the flow of money in American politics*", provides a searchable database of lobbying expenditure, should you wish to follow this up. The web site ProPublica [78] provides a similar facility.

CO-PRODUCTION

Legislators often draw on expertise from industry to assist in drafting regulations, on the assumption that those experts will be impartial and objective. But because of political and social factors ("*the social embeddedness of expertise*"), the outcome can be regulatory capture, as suggested by Slayton [79]. That is, regulations can end up being steered towards achieving private sector benefits rather than protecting public interests [80]. If you're from the cyber industry, for example, and you're asked by a legislator whether there should be more or less cyber regulation forcing people to buy cybersecurity products and services, obviously that's going to be a tricky one.

Without wishing to get all Marxist about it, a critical point here is that the cyber industry claims sole ownership of "what cyber looks like", and as suggested by Carrapico [81, p251], if you have control over the pool of expertise, then you have control over the process of regulation. Quoting Jasanoff [28], Slayton also notes that although expertise may shape cyber regulations, those regulations subsequently shape the nature of the expertise, i.e. they then "co-produce" each other.

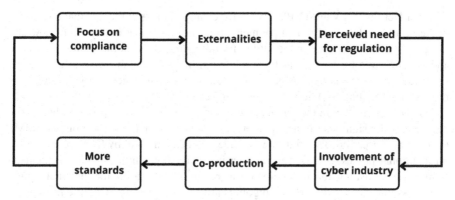

FIGURE 7.1 Outcome of co-production. (Leapfrog Creative Ltd, reproduced with permission.)

Given the increase in the severity of punishments, the increase in scope, and the increase in prescriptive detail, it's likely that as NIS1 morphs onto NIS2, we will see an increasing level of regulatory capture. The increasingly draconian legislation will then further shape the behaviour of the cyber industry. And as suggested by Cavusoglu, when companies are incentivised to achieve compliance with technically oriented standards maintained by the cybersecurity industry itself, then they're likely to ignore any other issues, including the externalities caused by their focus on compliance.

Figure 7.1 above (I think) summarises the situation.

In engineering terms, I believe this arrangement is described as "positive feedback".

Summary

The downside of regulation on this scale and with this mindset is that it sets up all the necessary conditions for a "doom loop". There's no moderating component to prevent the level of expenditure from going up and up. For example, if there were to be some evidence of a link between investment in cyber and reduced incidents and/or reduced severity of incidents, then as the number of incidents fell away, further investment might not be needed. Or perhaps if companies were encouraged to focus on externalities rather than on compliance?

DEVELOPING A BUSINESS CASE

Impact Assessments

Prior to the transposition of the NIS Directive into law, an impact assessment was carried out in the UK, looking into the likely costs of implementation, and identifying the benefits that might result [48].

For better or worse, a typical method for the production of a financial business case is to use a Discounted Cash Flow (DCF) technique, such as Internal Rate of Return

(IRR) or Net Present Value (NPV). NPV, for example, looks at the fact that payments in the future are less useful than payments right now, and that outlays right now are more of a pain than outlays in the future. By taking into account the values of outlays and benefits, and by looking at their relative timings, you can arrive at an overall net value for the investment. A negative value for NPV indicates that you're putting money in but getting back less than you're investing.

The NPV arrived at in the impact assessment, you won't be surprised to hear, was negative. Quite significantly negative in fact, the best estimate being about –£400M, over a ten-year period. That figure was made up of expenditure by CNI organisations on additional processes and security measures, and expenditure by Government in terms of establishing the necessary infrastructure. The reason for the final figure being less than zero is that while outgoings are easy to quantify, it's difficult to put a balancing monetary value on reduced externalities.

As noted in the document [48, p36], "*[i]t is not felt the negative NPV is a good reflection of the overall benefits of the regulation so it should be viewed in the context set out in this impact assessment*". That is, ignore the figures, it's the non-quantifiable benefits that matter. However, it's worth examining the quantifiable benefits for a minute.

The figures in the impact assessment were taken from the 2017 DCMS security breaches survey, which reported the average annual impact of security breaches as £1,570 per organisation, rising to £19,600 if you considered only larger firms [48, p7]. The assessment also noted that "*[t]he median cost of all breaches is zero, reflecting the fact that the majority of breaches have no actual outcome*" [48, p34]. Similar figures can be seen in the most recent (2022) survey [82], i.e. median cost zero, average cost amongst all companies reporting at least one incident £1,200 [82, Table 5.1].

For organisations within scope, the necessary additional expenditure on cyber as a result of implementing the Directive was estimated in the report to be somewhere between £100,000 and £200,000 for a large firm, and somewhere between £50,000 and £75,000 for a medium organisation. Those figures were also assumed to represent recurring annual spend [48, p25, p26]. For comparison, and going back to the most recent DCMS report, the average long-term direct cost of the most disruptive breach across those companies identifying a breach was reported as £240 [82, Table 5.3].

In passing, the Information Commissioner's Office (ICO) have a really useful feature on their web site [83] that allows you to examine and filter the outcomes of personal data breaches reported to them over the years. Unless I'm misreading the figures, you can see from their site that about 85% of the reported incidents resulted in either no further action, or only informal action. About half of the incidents (48%) affected fewer than ten individuals. About half (46%) also related to information accidentally sent to the wrong recipient, or "*other, **non cyber** incidents*" (my use of bold).

Against that background, the NIS impact assessment suggests that a 5% reduction in the number of companies suffering a breach "*… has been taken as an illustrative figure*" for quantifiable benefits [48, p4]. I can't find that calculation anywhere in the document. So in case I missed it: taking just the large companies referred to in the

2017 DCMS report, and using the average rather than the median, the annual saving in direct costs for breached companies would be $0.05 \times 19{,}600 \times 422$ (the number of large companies in scope for NIS in the UK [48, p25]), or about £413,560 per year. Over the ten years of the investment case, that amounts to savings of £4.14M, equivalent to about 1% of the projected cost of implementation.

On the face of it, this doesn't add up to a business case. Perhaps the justification for investment is more accurately reflected in a statement elsewhere in the document [48, p2]: *"[n]on-compliance with the Directive would most likely lead to infraction proceedings by the EU"*. Ah. Compliance.

The assessment moves on to consider the wider, non-quantifiable benefits [48, p3]:

The main benefits to the UK economy are improved protection of the network and information systems that underpin the UK's essential services; reducing the likelihood and impact of security incidents affecting those networks and information systems and the corresponding impact on economic prosperity. Businesses also may benefit from reduced breaches or attacks that are below the Directive thresholds. International cooperation and information sharing is also expected to improve advice and incident response for firms.

Setting aside those qualified by "may" and "expected", the chief benefit seems to be a reduction in both the likelihood and the impact of security breaches. However, as noted in the document itself [48, p35]:

Determining whether security measures implemented by businesses will lead to a reduction in the number of breaches is difficult. Little research has been conducted to quantify the link between good cyber security and the number of breaches. It faces challenges of limited data, and that not all breaches are detected, even by those with state of the art cyber security. The relationship between security measures and breaches is also not always in the direction expected.

Possibly with an eye to making the societal impacts more concrete, the document turns to a report from the Cambridge Centre for Risk Studies [84], which examined the potential impact of an attack similar to those affecting the Ukrainian power grid in 2015/2016. The Cambridge study took a number of scenarios based on different numbers of substations affected, different timeframes, etc. The figures cited in the NIS impact assessment seem to be those associated with the worst case scenario in the Cambridge report (scenario "X1"). The outcome being essentially: 13 million people affected; immediate economic impact around £85.5Bn; long-term economic damage over five years estimated at £442Bn.

The attack on the power system in Ukraine was thought to have involved just 30 substations [85, p2018], affecting an estimated 255,000 people out of a population of around 44 million [86, p119]. Whereas the Cambridge report, produced in collaboration with Lockheed Martin, a cyber security services provider, takes as a worst case 125 substations, shut down on a rolling basis over a 12-week period, affecting the City of London, all four London airports (i.e. Heathrow, Gatwick, Stansted, City), the Port of London, and the main seaports of Felixstowe and Dover. The attack takes place in the middle of winter, and attacks on substations are synchronised to cause maximum impact, based on a detailed technical knowledge of the role of each sub-station. Multiple devices are assumed to have been attached to key sites, so that the removal of one device allows the attacker to continue disrupting operations at that site. Also, at some point during the first week, an engineer is assumed to have been electrocuted, so the energy companies suspend any further manual interventions.

Based on that scenario, and taking into account the estimated costs of the Wannacry outbreak, the impact assessment concludes that "*[w]hile it has not been possible to quantify the benefits for use in the cost benefit analysis it is clear that these could be substantial where even just one significant incident is prevented*" [48, p34]. Lawson [86] quotes a phrase from Sunstein, labelling those who engage in this type of thinking as "*worst case entrepreneurs*" [86, p40]. He lists out the tactics used, such as conflation, counterfactuals, and projection, and quoting Glassner, concludes that for worst case entrepreneurs, "*scenarios substitute for facts*" [86, p42].

The summary point here is that creating an investment case for regulation founders on the difficulty of quantifying societal benefits in terms that can be compared against the level of expenditure. Consequently, the very worst case scenario is taken in order to justify the intervention on a purely intuitive basis. A couple of problems then arise. First, if you want to justify any amount of investment, all you have to do is think up a bad enough scenario. Second, if you then point to the outcome as societal benefits in the form of reduced externalities, then because those benefits can't be quantified, you don't actually have to deliver any return on investment. Not a bad position to be in, if you've been asked to help set the regulations.

But, in the real world, it's the outcome that matters. Does what seems to be a rather heavy-handed use of regulation in Europe deliver, in terms of reduced externalities?

THE OUTCOMES OF ENFORCEMENT

OUTCOMES SO FAR

In 2020, a full two years after the implementation of NIS in the UK, a Post Implementation Review (PIR) was conducted by DCMS [87]. The general conclusion (in terms of whether or not the regulations were working) was "it's too early to tell" [88]. The review noted, in fact, that the full benefits were unlikely to be seen for a number of years.

No surprises there. Greg Ip [89, p252] cites the findings of Amalberti, who looked at measures intended to reduce aviation accident rates. Assuming 20 accidents per year, if you implemented a measure intended to reduce that figure by 50%, then you'd need to leave the measure running for just over three years before you could be statistically confident that it had worked. If, however, you introduce a measure that you expect will reduce the accident rate by just 15%, then you would need to wait 32 years in order to be reasonably confident that it had worked. The original business case for the implementation of NIS not only assumed that the intervention would be effective but also assumed that benefits would be visible from Year One, with (I think) an expected reduction of 5%.

The DCMS report notes that at the time of the review, there was insufficient data available to see any trends. Nevertheless, it goes on to state that "*[w]e expect this action is leading to a reduction in the risks posed to essential services and important digital services relying on networks and information systems*" [87, p5]. In the acknowledged absence of any supporting evidence, that has to be considered as speculation.

The number of reported disruptive incidents over the period was also found to be much lower than had been anticipated in the business case. The lower bound for reported incidents was estimated in the impact assessment at 39 incidents per year, whereas the actual number of incidents had apparently been consistently below even that lower figure. The PIR concludes that reporting thresholds might need to be reduced, presumably in order to bring the actual number of reports closer to the predicted number.

The review notes that, in relation to private sector investment [87, p33]:

This set of questions has produced some useful and important data on where and how organisations are focusing their security spending, but it also makes it possible to state that a minimum of 39% of large OESs who responded to the survey spent more than the high estimated additional costs per business (£200,000). A minimum of 27% of large RDSPs who responded spent more than the high estimated additional costs per business (£50,000).

That is, actual expenditure seems to have been significantly higher than the forecasts used in the original business case. It would have been interesting for the PIR to revisit the business case, using the actual figures and timescales rather than the original estimates. However, there doesn't seem to have been room to do so. Instead, the review quotes as justification the same examples given in the impact assessment, i.e. the electricity grid attack modelling [84, 85] and the estimated impact of Wannacry on the NHS (although those figures have since been disputed [90]).

In terms of the business case for investment, the review notes that:

- *... given the nature of cyber breaches and the complex factors involved, it will not be possible to attribute incidents as having been prevented by measures taken under the Regulations.*
- *It is also not possible to quantify whether there has been a reduced impact of incidents where appropriate incident response plans have been put in place.*
- *Quantifying the benefits of avoided losses through better security and risk management approaches is an extremely difficult task ....*
- *These difficulties pose barriers to undertaking a robust cost benefit analysis ....*

So essentially, no, we can't provide evidence that the intervention is working. Nonetheless, there is apparently a clear case for continued intervention [87, p43].

The most recent PIR issued in 2022 [91] seems to carry much the same messages, i.e. no hard evidence of benefits, other than a reduction in the number of reported incidents, from 13 in 2019 to just 12 in 2020 [91, p23]. On the plus side, the report suggests that a significant positive outcome has been the creation of a security culture across the organisations affected. Against that, the financial burden on industry (the cost of compliance) seems to have been somewhere between two and four times the original estimates [91, Table 2], while the number of reported incidents seems to be about 1% of the level originally anticipated [91, Table 2].

The 2022 report again uses the Cambridge X1 scenario and the Wannacry attack as justification for ongoing spend, i.e. preventing one Wannacry attack (each year) would place the NIS implementation at or beyond the break-even point.

It seems to me that there's scope here for a standard impact quantity. Let's say a set of scales were to be attached to confidentiality, integrity, and availability impacts. Certain combinations of levels of impact in each category would add up to one incident unit. So the overall impact for an incident might involve 15 confidentiality impact units, or for a similarly serious incident, it might be made up of, e.g., 5 confidentiality impact units, plus 2 integrity units and 8 availability units. You can see plenty of scope there for practitioners to define incident types by their CIA profile. A really serious incident might see 20 C units, 15 I units, and 20 A units. Plenty of scope to justify investment on the basis of a potential 100-unit incident. And no need to link the incident scale to anything in reality. All the scales would be completely subjective.

However, we would need a name for the overall incident impact units. Something like Quantified Loss Objectives – "Quatloos". Although, thinking about it, that term may have been used before, in a similar context.

Looking Ahead

The GDPR data protection rules were implemented at the same time as NIS1 but seemed to get a lot more coverage and attention, so although the two have proceeded in parallel, it's fair to say that the implementation of GDPR may be further advanced. A review of the outcomes of GDPR might therefore provide an indication of the possible longer term benefits or otherwise of the NIS regulations.

A survey commissioned by DCMS [92] reported a number of unintended outcomes from the implementation of GDPR in the UK:

- 50% of the companies surveyed said that the legislation had led to excessive caution in handling personal data.
- 36% said that the focus on GDPR had been to the detriment of other aspects of cybersecurity.
- 78% of board members felt that the major focus in the reports they were receiving was on data rather than on security per se.
- 27% felt that the GDPR had required excessive levels of investment, significantly beyond what was felt to be necessary.

A 2022 paper by Chen [93] suggests that the implementation of GDPR also created an overall profit reduction of around 8% for affected industries. At the same time, the research found a corresponding drop of only 2% in sales, indicating that the reduction in profits was being driven by significant additional expenditure. Others (e.g. [94–97]) have reported similar downsides.

The number of incidents reported to the ICO jumped by a factor of four over the first year [98], although as noted in the parallel ICO report [99], 82% of those incidents required no action. The general conclusion being that companies were over-reporting to be on the safe side, given the threatened levels of fines for non-reporting. Anecdotally, the ICO took months to get to grips with the increased workload, and also anecdotally, other data privacy bodies across Europe were able to deal with only about 10% of the notifications they were receiving [98]. One tangible outcome of the legislation, it could be said, was that it slowed down the processing of actual incidents.

The DCMS report also states that [92, p78]:

Most interviewees reported that the GDPR was the most powerful factor influencing the changes made. The most common reason for this was that organisations wanted to be compliant with the GDPR, either because they wanted to avoid financial penalties for non-compliance or because their clients expected them to be compliant.

That is, for most organisations, it's not necessarily about achieving better security, it's about meeting expectations, an outcome fully in line with Cavusoglu's finding [100] that compliance is seen as the major benefit of investing in cyber. The DCMS report also states [92, p10] that "*[t]hough the GDPR impacted on information security in relation to data protection, there was no robust evidence of impact on other areas of cyber security to the same extent*", i.e. companies seemed to do what they needed to do to get compliant, rather than engaging in security more widely. If that's true, then the symbolic adoption of cyber, as pointed out in Angst's survey of US hospitals [101], isn't necessarily going to result in better security.

The outcome of all this can be seen in the findings of a study on risk perception [102] referenced by the DCMS report. The Marsh/Microsoft report notes that:

- Organisations believe that they can manage their cyber risk primarily through the use of technology, rather than prioritising the time, resources, and activities needed to build cyber resilience.
- Ownership of cyber security in organisations remains largely with the IT function, indicating that it's seen as a technical issue rather than as a risk management problem.
- "*There is ambivalence about the value of both government regulation and industry standards around cybersecurity. Most companies see both as having limited effectiveness, yet there is strong appetite for government leadership and support to help combat nation-state cyber threats*".

The report notes shifts in respondent attitudes between 2017 and 2019, regarding the proportion of companies having no confidence in their ability to understand and assess cyber risks (9% increasing to 18%), those with no confidence in preventing cyber threats (12% increasing to 19%), and those with no confidence in their ability to respond to, or recover from an incident (15% increasing to 22%) [102, p2].

The DCMS report makes a number of similar points, stating that [92, p21]:

While 62% of businesses invested more in cyber security in preparation for the GDPR, 49% did not believe it had made their business safer and 26% did not believe that, a year on from the GDPR deadline, their business was fully compliant.

The report notes that with hindsight, a "one size fits all" approach to security may not have been the most effective strategy. An unfortunate outcome, given that harmonisation was a key aim of the legislation [103].

The intention of this section was to examine the impact of GDPR and relate it to the possible longer term outcome of the NIS regulations. Perhaps an appropriate summary is provided by the 2019 report on risk perceptions [102]. Noting the decline in companies' confidence in their ability to meet cyber risks, the report suggests that *"[o]rganizations may be frustrated or confused when their increasing investment in cyber risk mitigation does not directly correlate to improved outcomes, as is usually the case with other areas of business investment and performance improvement"* [102, p6].

CONCLUSION

On the basis of the evidence presented, an approach based on industry-defined standards, a regime of heavy fines, and an increasing degree of regulation may well be healthy for the cyber industry, but it may not move us any closer to the stated aim of better security. Kwon and Johnson [104] examined the outcome of cyber investment in the US healthcare sector, both with and without the presence of regulation, and found that *"... proactive investments, voluntarily made, have more impact than those involuntarily made"*. Their findings indicate that organisations pressured to achieve compliance with regulations miss out on the process of learning through experience and hence see a reduced level of benefit.

As we saw elsewhere, purely symbolic adoption of security doesn't seem to lead to protection. I have seen statements to the effect that since companies voluntarily achieving compliance with e.g. Cyber Essentials tend to make fewer claims, all companies should therefore be forced to comply before being allowed to buy cyber insurance. For me, the argument runs parallel to the idea that drivers who buy their motoring insurance from Saga (a company dealing specifically for the over-50s) seem to make fewer claims. Therefore we should force all drivers to get their insurance from Saga. It just doesn't follow. A more reasonable conclusion might be that companies that have willingly chosen to engage with cyber seem to make fewer claims. Forcing companies to demonstrate compliance is likely to get you just that – compliance. What we want ideally is voluntary engagement.

COLLABORATION, NOT ENFORCEMENT

THE UK APPROACH

In 2021, the UK Financial Conduct Authority (FCA) presented proposals aimed at improving the cyber-resilience of services in the financial sector [105, 106]. If enacted, the FCA proposals will require eligible firms to identify ways in which the impact of a disruptive incident could be reduced, thereby ensuring continuity of the services provided to end customers.

On the face of it, this would appear to be similar to the route taken by EU regulators for other areas of the CNI, and especially DORA. However, there are some key differences, both in thinking and in approach.

- The FCA document stresses the primacy of services over systems [105, para 4.4].
- This approach places emphasis on the use of broader means of maintaining services through, e.g., the effective use of customer communications [105, para 7.1], and/or alternate mechanisms for service delivery [105, para 4.12], rather than simply focussing on recovering the technology [105, para 6.6].
- The process uses scenario-based assessments, rather than risk calculations. There is a specific point made in the document that this process is not about "risk appetite" [105, para 5.9].
- Rather than implementing "*security by resistance*" [107], companies are to assume that an event has taken place, and that their planning should concentrate on how they would maintain and/or restore the service to customers [105, para 6.9].
- There is an implicit assumption [105, Annex 2, para 50] that bad things happen, and that it makes no sense to rely solely on prevention. The aim is not to achieve "zero events", because that's an impossible goal.

Finally and crucially, there is the concept of "tolerances" [105, Ch5]. These are limits setting out how long a service could be down for, before causing an unacceptable level of disruption for customers. To quote the FCA proposal [105, para 5.8]:

Setting impact tolerances is intended to change the mindset of firms' boards and senior management away from traditional risk management towards accepting that disruption to business services is inevitable, and needs to be managed actively.

Under this scheme, targets are set out in terms much closer to the desired objectives. The primary objective being to keep the impact on customers within acceptable levels, rather than maintaining the percentage availability of in-house systems. As suggested by the FCA "*... firms should focus more effort and resources on achieving the continuity of their important business services in the event of severe operational disruption, and not just on recovery of the underlying systems and processes*" [105, para 4.4].

This approach also treats security as a negotiation. Eligible organisations are required to set tolerance limits, which the FCA then reviews, in order to assure themselves that the tolerances have not been set too high. That is, there is a negotiation on what security looks like. That discussion is held in advance of an incident taking place, rather than taking the form of a negotiation on what security "should have looked like" after the event. And since the negotiation takes place upfront, each party is aware of what security is defined to be in this context – basically, not exceeding the tolerance limits.

And although the document states that it's difficult to quantify benefits, the tolerance levels are in effect a quantification, or at least a representation of the benefits. For Bank "A", we will have a statement that their online service will not be out of commission for more than "x" hours even if there is a severe incident. That means that we know how much money is being put in, and we know what we're getting out of it, even if that isn't expressed in financial terms. That is more useful, I would have said, than an arrangement in which money is put in and we hope for the best.

To recap the main points: an acceptance that bad things happen; the idea that it's not about systems, it's about meeting customer needs and reducing externalities; the use of discussions rather than calculations; and the use of cross-cutting teams rather than a process managed solely by security practitioners.

Personally, I think this approach sets the benchmark for legislation intended to achieve positive outcomes. It bypasses the problems seen earlier, and it means that everyone is clear from the outset what security looks like, because it's reflected in the agreed tolerance limits. The only point I would suggest is that the negotiation could be widened to include the consumer, i.e. views could perhaps be sought from consumer groups when the tolerance limits are set. The customer is a stakeholder in the discussion and should be included alongside the regulatory body and the banks themselves. Nonetheless, for me, this is an outstanding example of what regulation might look like if it were to be more closely aligned with outcomes.

A Wider Approach

As stated in the NCSC guidance pack for NIS [26, p4]:

> In complex topic areas and rapidly changing circumstances, it may be impossible to cater for all eventualities. In such cases, which include cyber security, all attempts to devise and apply a set of prescriptive rules is almost certain to lead to unintended consequences, resources being badly misallocated, and limited benefit.

Dunn Cavelty and Suter [108] propose that the job of Government in protecting critical services should be to encourage and support appropriate business networks based on self-regulation, in order to avoid *"overly intrusive market intervention"*. Wiater [109] also suggests that establishing a formal contractual framework between Government and CNI service providers might be more effective than imposing regulation. The essence of the argument [108, p2] is that since a significant proportion of the CNI is in private hands, some form of partnership is inevitable, and the question is therefore more to do with how the partnership should be structured, rather than whether or not there should be one.

Assaf [110, Figure 1] points out that intervention isn't a simple choice from two options – it's more of a continuum. At one end, we have Government taking ownership of CNI service providers, and at the other, we have security being left to market forces. Assaf shows that there are many options between those two extremes, each with its own pros and cons. The idea of a Public Private Partnership (PPP), for example, is somewhat towards the "market forces" end of the scale and has been generally found wanting, mostly on the basis of mismatched expectations [108, 109, 111]. A "one size fits all" approach based on *"abstract, vague standards"* is singled out specifically as an approach destined to fail [109, p262].

As proposed by Wiater, a more meaningful dialogue would involve segments of the CNI being asked to offer binding standards which are then agreed with the Government, in order to bring about *"regulated self-regulation"*. You can perhaps see echoes of that in elements of the FCA approach regarding tolerance levels.

Assaf suggests a similar hybrid approach, which represents [110, p7]:

> ... *a situation where the state, through a public agency, engages in consultation, perhaps even negotiation, with regulated entities. Thus, direct regulations are tailored to individual firms or trade associations, who agree to work with the government to achieve common goals. While the state retains its discretionary power, it seeks greater acceptance (and hence compliance) from the market.*

It was suggested earlier that leaving the security of critical industries to market forces won't address the issue of externalities. However, the use of unalloyed regulation doesn't seem to be effective either. As suggested by a number of authors, e.g. Clinton [112], it might be time to try a "third way", because the use of regulation on its own is not an appropriate way to deal with complex systems. Measures need to be framed in way that looks at outcomes rather than inputs, and they should be set within a collaborative context. To quote Sales [113, p1518]: *"[r]esponsibility for defending the most sensitive systems against the most sophisticated adversaries should be shared"*. That is, the CNI sector should be actively involved rather than being seen as a problem to be controlled. This third way has been requested loudly and clearly by the CNI companies themselves, as we have seen in the responses to the public consultation on NIS2, and elsewhere [114]. Hearteningly, you can see elements of a more enlightened, more collaborative approach in the 2020 NCSC annual report [115], which sets out a number of initiatives, including the provision of tools to assist in contingency planning.

And as a closing point, if you want to see a really good example of the use of self-regulation, you could take a look at how the cyber industry governs itself [116]. If it's good enough for them...

THE ENFORCEMENT OF COMPLIANCE: SUMMARY

EXTERNALITIES

Economic theory says that when commercial organisations don't feel the full impact of a breach (i.e. when some of the impact is externalised), then their investment in security will be lower than the societally optimal amount. The primary obligation of the board is towards their shareholders. Consequently, there's no obvious reason why a company would invest to reduce potential impacts on third parties.

THE USE OF LEGISLATION

On the other hand, governments have a duty to protect their citizens. Therefore, they may step in to encourage the internalisation of those effects. In Europe, in particular, this has resulted in extensive legislation. The implicit assumption being that there exists a linear causal link between regulation and a more resilient industry, which will therefore generate fewer and/or less severe externalities. The evidence, however, points to a different possibility.

THE OUTCOMES OF LEGISLATION

Reviews of EU legislation indicate a lack of outcome (leading to the revision of the NIS Directive after only two years), and unintended side effects (as with, e.g., GDPR [96]). The erroneous assumption of cause and effect has created a situation in which CNI companies are being asked to adhere to ever more stringent technically oriented standards, thereby making them focus even less on the externalities they're generating. Much of the emphasis to date also seems to have been on harmonisation; however, as pointed out by Carrapico and Barrinha, achieving harmonisation is not the same as achieving benefits for the citizen [117, p1267].

These circumstances enable the cyber industry to promote the use of a standard model in which they own the expertise, which in turn leads to regulatory capture. Slayton et al. [79, p7] suggest that regulating complex industries isn't simply a matter of getting the right people in the room, it's also about holding them to account. With no link between regulation and benefits, that becomes impossible.

AN ALTERNATIVE VIEW

Perhaps a better way of achieving the stated aim might be to adopt a more collaborative approach, in which regulatory regimes are agreed between industry and Government, and Government's role becomes more focused on monitoring. When US President Ronald Reagan was negotiating nuclear weapon agreements with his Soviet counterpart Mikhail Gorbachev, Reagan was supposed to have borrowed a Russian phrase and used it to summarise the approach he envisaged – "*trust, but verify*". Possibly just such a third way might get us out of the problems encountered in using a simple one-track regime of enforcement.

NOTES

1   Since this book was drafted, both DORA and the RCE Directive have been formally issued.
2   Since this book was drafted, the NIS2 regulations have been formally issued. The main points set out here have survived, although non-incidents are now referred to as "near-misses", and the senior management of entities in scope have been made personally financially liable, i.e. they have been fully "responsibilised".
3   The referenced Ponemon report cites US$5.5M as the median annualised cost *per company*, drawing on a sample of breached companies. The EU report cites 450 *incidents* in 2018, the referenced source being a Eurostat report (which doesn't contain that statistic,

as far as I can see). The EU report assumes a 3% annual growth in incidents as a baseline, compared to an assumed 6% annual reduction in numbers if the legislation were to be enacted.

REFERENCES

1. Brangetto, P. and M. Aubyn, Economic aspects of national cyber security strategies. *Annex*, 2015. 1(9–16): p. 86.
2. Biancotti, C. and R. Cristadoro, *The machine stops: The price of cyber (in)security.* 2018 [Accessed 30 July 2021]; Available from: https://voxeu.org/article/price-cyber-insecurity
3. Biancotti, C., et al., *Cyber attacks: An economic policy challenge.* 2017 [Accessed 30 July 2021]; Available from: https://voxeu.org/article/cyber-attacks-economic-policy-challenge
4. Bana, S., et al., *Cybersecurity hiring in response to data breaches.* 2021 [Accessed 2 March 2022]; Available from: https://papers.ssrn.com/sol3/papers.cfm?abstract_id=3806060
5. Garg, V., *Covenants without the sword: Market incentives for cybersecurity investment.* 2021 [Accessed 2 March 2022]; Available from: https://papers.ssrn.com/sol3/papers.cfm?abstract_id=3896578
6. Bronk, C., *Don't blame the nerds: Explaining the colonial pipeline hack and what to do next.* 2021 [Accessed 26 May 2021]; Available from: www.forbes.com/sites/uhenergy/2021/05/12/dont-blame-the-nerds-explaining-the-colonial-pipeline-hack-and-what-to-do-next
7. Malliouris, D.D. and A. Simpson, The stock market impact of information security investments: The case of security standards. In *Workshop on the Economics of Information Security (WEIS)*, 2019.
8. Lam, W.M.W., Attack-prevention and damage-control investments in cybersecurity. *Information Economics and Policy*, 2016. 37: p. 42–51.
9. Rosenzweig, P., *The unpersuasiveness of the case for cybersecurity regulation – An introduction.* 2012 [Accessed 30 July 2021]; Available from: www.lawfareblog.com/unpersuasiveness-case-cybersecurity-regulation-–-introduction
10. Goldsmith, J., *Response to Paul on cyber-regulation for critical infrastructure.* 2012 [Accessed 30 July 2021]; Available from: www.lawfareblog.com/response-paul-cyber-regulation-critical-infrastructure
11. Chung, J.J., Critical infrastructure, cybersecurity, and market failure. *Oregon Law Review*, 2017. 96: p. 441.
12. NIST, *Framework for improving critical infrastructure cybersecurity.* 2018 [Accessed 30 July 2021]; Available from: https://nvlpubs.nist.gov/nistpubs/CSWP/NIST.CSWP.04162018.pdf
13. GDPR_EU, *Complete guide to GDPR compliance.* 2020 [Accessed 10 April 2021]; Available from: https://gdpr.eu
14. Saceanu, R., *The EU Cybersecurity Act enters into force – Quick facts.* 2019 [Accessed 30 July 2021]; Available from: www.smarttech247.com/news/the-eu-cybersecurity-act-enters-into-force-quick-facts
15. EU, *The EU Cybersecurity Act brings a strong agency for cybersecurity and EU-wide rules on cybersecurity certification.* 2021 [Accessed 30 July 2021]; Available from: https://digital-strategy.ec.europa.eu/en/news/eu-cybersecurity-act-brings-strong-agency-cybersecurity-and-eu-wide-rules-cybersecurity

16. Bendiek, A. and M. Schallbruch, *Europe's third way in cyberspace: What part does the new EU Cybersecurity Act play?* 2019 [Accessed 2 March 2022]; Available from: www.ssoar.info/ssoar/bitstream/handle/document/67207/ssoar-2019-bendiek_et_al-Europes_third_way_in_cyberspace.pdf?sequence=1&isAllowed=y&lnkname=ssoar-2019-bendiek_et_al-Europes_third_way_in_cyberspace.pdf

17. EU, *The Commission proposes a new directive to enhance the resilience of critical entities providing essential services in the EU.* 2020 [Accessed 30 July 2021]; Available from: https://ec.europa.eu/home-affairs/news/commission-proposes-new-directive-enhance-resilience-critical-entities-providing-essential_en

18. Armitage, V. and M. Harris, *DORA (Digital Operational Resilience Act).* 2021 [Accessed 30 July 2021]; Available from: www.grantthornton.ie/insights/factsheets/dora-digital-operational-resilience-act

19. Dentons, *DORA's debut – The EU's Digital Operational Resilience Act.* 2020 [Accessed 30 July 2021]; Available from: www.dentons.com/en/insights/articles/2020/november/12/doras-debut-the-eus-digital-operational-resilience-act

20. EU, *Digital operational resilience for the financial sector.* 2020 [Accessed 9 August 2021]; Available from: https://eur-lex.europa.eu/legal-content/EN/TXT/?uri=CELEX%3A52020PC0595

21. Mosseray, Q., et al., *The EU's Digital Operational Resilience Act for financial services.* 2021 [Accessed 30 July 2021]; Available from: www2.deloitte.com/lu/en/pages/financial-services/articles/the-eus-digital-operational-resilience-act-for-financial-services-new-rules.html

22. Scanlon, L., *The EU's Digital Operational Resilience Act for financial services.* 2022 [Accessed 4 October 2022]; Available from: www.pinsentmasons.com/out-law/analysis/dora-tech-contracting-financial-services

23. EU, *Cyber diplomacy in the European Union.* 2019 [Accessed 2 March 2022]; Available from: https://op.europa.eu/en/publication-detail/-/publication/e7194c9f-1197-11ea-8c1f-01aa75ed71a1

24. Moret, E. and P. Pawlak, *The EU Cyber Diplomacy Toolbox: Towards a cyber sanctions regime?* 2017: JSTOR.

25. ICO, *The guide to NIS: What is NIS?* 2021 [Accessed 30 July 2021]; Available from: https://ico.org.uk/for-organisations/the-guide-to-nis/what-is-nis

26. NCSC, *The guide to NIS: What is NIS?* 2018 [Accessed 30 July 2021]; Available from: www.ncsc.gov.uk/staticjson/ncsc-content/files/NIS%20Guidance%20Collection%201.0.pdf

27. KPMG, *Are you ready to comply with the UK's Network & Information Systems (NIS) regulations?* 2018 [Accessed 30 July 2021]; Available from: https://assets.kpmg/content/dam/kpmg/uk/pdf/2018/07/are-you-ready-to-comply-with-nis-regulations.pdf

28. Jasanoff, S., Beyond epistemology: Relativism and engagement in the politics of science. *Social studies of science*, 1996. 26(2): p. 393–418.

29. gov.wales, *The Network and Information Systems Regulations 2018: Guidance to the health sector in Wales.* 2021 [Accessed 30 July 2021]; Available from: https://gov.wales/network-and-information-systems-regulations-2018-guidance-health-sector-wales-html

30. EU, *Measures for a high common level of security of network and information systems across the Union.* 2016 [Accessed 9 August 2021]; Available from: https://eur-lex.europa.eu/legal-content/EN/TXT/?uri=CELEX%3A32016L1148&qid=1628527018368

31. Papakonstantinou, V., Cybersecurity as praxis and as a state: The EU law path towards acknowledgement of a new right to cybersecurity? *Computer Law & Security Review*, 2022. 44: p. 105653.

32. HMG, *The Network and Information Systems Regulations 2018.* 2018 [Accessed 9 August 2021]; Available from: www.legislation.gov.uk/uksi/2018/506/made

33. Hall, K., *UK infrastructure firms to face £17m fine if their cybersecurity sucks.* 2018 [Accessed 30 July 2021]; Available from: https://forums.theregister.com/forum/all/2018/01/29/infrastructure_firms_to_be_slapped_with_17m_fine_for_poor_cyber_security

34. Pula, V., *NIS2: Overview of the new EU cybersecurity rules proposed.* 2021 [Accessed 30 July 2021]; Available from: www.cullen-international.com/news/2021/04/NIS2--Overview-of-the-new-EU-cybersecurity-rules-proposed.html

35. EU, *Revised directive on security of network and information systems (NIS2).* 2021 [Accessed 30 July 2021]; Available from: https://digital-strategy.ec.europa.eu/en/library/revised-directive-security-network-and-information-systems-nis2

36. Buckwell, M., *EU commission proposes to update the NIS/cybersecurity directive only two years after implementation.* 2021 [Accessed 30 July 2021]; Available from: www.twobirds.com/en/news/articles/2021/global/eu-commission-proposes-to-update-the-nis-cybersecurity-directive-only-two-years-after-implementation

37. Wessing, T., *NIS 2.0 – Reform of the European network and information security directive.* 2021 [Accessed 30 July 2021]; Available from: www.lexology.com/library/detail.aspx?g=1d625709-c17d-4cfa-92a3-8e751757f0f9

38. EU, *Summary Report on the open public consultation on the directive on security of network and information systems (NIS directive).* 2021 [Accessed 30 July 2021]; Available from: https://digital-strategy.ec.europa.eu/en/summary-report-open-public-consultation-directive-security-network-and-information-systems-nis

39. EU, *Study to support the review of directive (EU) 2016/1148 concerning measures for a high common level of security of network and information systems across the Union (NIS directive), No. 2020-665 (final study report).* 2021 [Accessed 30 July 2021]; Available from: https://op.europa.eu/en/publication-detail/-/publication/3b6ad641-d23c-11eb-ac72-01aa75ed71a1

40. EU, *Hitting the refresh button on cybersecurity rules.* 2020 [Accessed 30 July 2021]; Available from: https://op.europa.eu/en/publication-detail/-/publication/2f8456d4-5c60-11eb-b487-01aa75ed71a1/language-en

41. Chee, F.Y., *Companies may face 2% fine for breaching EU cybersecurity rules.* 2020 [Accessed 30 July 2021]; Available from: www.reuters.com/article/eu-cybersecurity-idUSKBN28Q1NS

42. Schneider, F. and C. Haid, *Cybersecurity on the rise: The NIS Directive 2.0.* 2020 [Accessed 30 July 2021]; Available from: www.lexology.com/library/detail.aspx?g=b57072ee-0313-49ed-a6a1-e8e8d91e1686.

43. Felice, A.D. and M. Bell. *DIGITALEUROPE's position on the NIS 2 Directive.* 2021 [Accessed 30 July 2021]; Available from: www.digitaleurope.org/resources/digitaleuropes-position-on-the-nis-2-directive

44. Orgalim, *Position paper on the European Commission's proposal for a directive on measures for a high common level of cybersecurity across the European Union (NIS2).* 2021 [Accessed 15 August 2021]; Available from: https://orgalim.eu/sites/default/files/attachment/Position%20Paper%20on%20NIS2%20110621_0.pdf

45. McAfee, *Economic impact of cybercrime – No slowing down.* 2018 [Accessed 14 January 2023]; Available from: www.mcafee.com/enterprise/en-us/assets/reports/restricted/rp-economic-impact-cybercrime.pdf

46. EU, *Proposal for directive on measures for high common level of cybersecurity across the Union.* 2020 [Accessed 30 July 2021]; Available from: https://digital-strategy.ec.europa.eu/en/library/proposal-directive-measures-high-common-level-cybersecurity-across-union

47. EU, *Cyber Resilience Act*. 2022 [Accessed 20 January 2023]; Available from: https://digital-strategy.ec.europa.eu/en/library/cyber-resilience-act

48. HMG, *NIS regulations: Impact assessment*. 2018 [Accessed 30 July 2021]; Available from: www.gov.uk/government/publications/nis-regulations-impact-assessment

49. BusinessEurope, *Business Europe draft position paper NIS 2.0*. 2021 [Accessed 30 July 2021]; Available from: www.businesseurope.eu/sites/buseur/files/media/position_papers/internal_market/2021-05-31_pp_nis2.0.pdf

50. Felice, A.D. and M. Bell, *Critical entities: Ensuring coherence of non-cyber and cyber resilience*. 2021 [Accessed 30 July 2021]; Available from: www.digitaleurope.org/resources/critical-entities-ensuring-coherence-of-non-cyber-and-cyber-resilience

51. CECIMO, *Position paper: Directive on security of network and information systems across the EU*. 2021 [Accessed 30 July 2021]; Available from: www.cecimo.eu/publications/position-paper-directive-on-security-of-network-and-information-systems-across-the-eu

52. Gherman, C., *DIGITALEUROPE's recommendations for a more ambitious EU cyber defence policy*. 2023 [Accessed 24 June 2023]; Available from: www.digitaleurope.org/resources/digitaleuropes-recommendations-for-a-more-ambitious-eu-cyber-defence-policy/#_ftn4

53. Jardine, E., *Optimizing cyber deterrence*. 2020: Rowman and Littlefield.

54. Sales, N.A., Privatizing cybersecurity. *UCLA Law Review*, 2018. 65: p. 620.

55. Blunden, B. and V. Cheung, *Behold a pale farce: Cyberwar, threat inflation, & the malware industrial complex*. 2014: Trine Day.

56. Cavelty, M.D., Cybersecurity research meets science and technology studies. *Politics and Governance*, 2018. 6(2): p. 22–30.

57. CVE, *CVE*. 2021 [Accessed 19 August 2021]; Available from: https://cve.mitre.org

58. AP, *EU unveils revamp of cybersecurity rules days after hack*. 2020 [Accessed 30 July 2021]; Available from: https://apnews.com/article/europe-hacking-europe-coronavirus-pandemic-32c882769dc0f3c15e471657905e3713

59. EU, *EU cybersecurity: Commission proposes a Joint Cyber Unit to step up response to large-scale security incidents*. 2021 [Accessed 30 July 2021]; Available from: https://ec.europa.eu/commission/presscorner/detail/en/IP_21_3088

60. EU, *New EU cybersecurity strategy and new rules to make physical and digital critical entities more resilient*. 2020 [Accessed 30 July 2021]; Available from: https://ec.europa.eu/commission/presscorner/detail/en/IP_20_2391

61. Winder, D., *EU banking authority hacked as Microsoft exchange attacks continue*. 2021 [Accessed 30 July 2021]; Available from: www.forbes.com/sites/daveywinder/2021/03/09/eu-banking-authority-hacked-as-microsoft-exchange-attacks-continue

62. BBC, *European banking authority hit by Microsoft exchange hack*. 2021 [Accessed 30 July 2021]; Available from: www.bbc.co.uk/news/technology-56321567

63. EBA, *EBA publishes guidelines on ICT and security risk management*. 2019 [Accessed 30 July 2021]; Available from: www.eba.europa.eu/eba-publishes-guidelines-ict-and-security-risk-management

64. Brandom, R., *It's already too late for today's ransomware victims to pay up and save their computers*. 2017 [Accessed 19 August 2021]; Available from: www.theverge.com/2017/6/27/15881110/petya-notpetya-paying-ransom-email-blocked-ransomware

65. Shane, S., N. Perlroth, and D.E. Sanger, *Security breach and spilled secrets have shaken the N.S.A. to its core*. 2017 [Accessed 28 August 2021]; Available from: www.nytimes.com/2017/11/12/us/nsa-shadow-brokers.html

66. Palmer, D., *WannaCry ransomware crisis, one year on: Are we ready for the next global cyber attack?* 2018 [Accessed 30 July 2021]; Available from: www.zdnet.com/article/wannacry-ransomware-crisis-one-year-on-are-we-ready-for-the-next-global-cyber-attack

67. Nardelli, A., *The EU's Embassy in Russia was hacked but the EU kept it a secret.* 2019 [Accessed 30 July 2021]; Available from: www.buzzfeednews.com/article/albertonardelli/eu-embassy-moscow-hack-russia

68. CEO, *Report finds tech industry spends €97 million on EU lobbying.* 2021 [Accessed 20 January 2023]; Available from: www.openaccessgovernment.org/tech-industry-eu-lobbying/118747

69. TI, *Policy position on an independent EU ethics body.* 2022 [Accessed 20 January 2023]; Available from: https://transparency.eu/wp-content/uploads/2022/01/Policy-Position-Ethics-Body.pdf

70. TI, *Deep pockets, open doors: Big tech lobbying in Brussels.* 2021 [Accessed 20 January 2023]; Available from: https://transparency.eu/wp-content/uploads/2021/02/Deep_pockets_open_doors_report.pdf

71. Blenkinsop, P., *EU parliament head to set out transparency plan to respond to scandal.* 2023 [Accessed 21 January 2023]; Available from: www.reuters.com/world/europe/eu-parliament-head-set-out-transparency-plan-respond-scandal-2023-01-11

72. LobbyControl, *The revolving door – From public officials to Big Tech lobbyists.* 2022 [Accessed 21 January 2023]; Available from: https://corporateeurope.org/en/2022/09/revolving-door-public-officials-big-tech-lobbyists

73. Wheaton, S., *Watchdogs wanted an EU ethics cop. They might get a scolding.* 2022 [Accessed 5 May 2023]; Available from: www.politico.eu/article/eu-commission-ethics-watchdog-vera-jourova-backs-light-touch-ethics-cop-to-oversee-eu-institutions

74. Rundle, J. and D. Uberti, *Cybersecurity lobbying spending mounts as privacy, security laws take shape.* 2020 [Accessed 14 November 2022]; Available from: www.wsj.com/articles/cybersecurity-lobbying-spending-mounts-as-privacy-security-laws-take-shape-11588619239

75. Ho, C., *Lobbying on data, cybersecurity has tripled.* 2014 [Accessed 14 November 2022]; Available from: www.washingtonpost.com/business/capitalbusiness/lobbying-on-data-cybersecurity-has-tripled/2014/05/11/fad0fe12-d6e9-11e3-8a78-8fe50322a72c_story.html

76. Riley, T., *The cybersecurity 202: SolarWinds hack could supercharge cybersecurity lobbying spending.* 2021 [Accessed 14 November 2022]; Available from: www.washingtonpost.com/politics/2021/01/25/cybersecurity-202-solarwinds-hack-could-supercharge-cybersecurity-lobbying-spending

77. opensecrets.org, *We are OpenSecrets.* 2022 [Accessed 14 November 2022]; Available from: www.opensecrets.org

78. propublica.org, *Investigative journalism in the public interest.* 2022 [Accessed 14 November 2022]; Available from: www.propublica.org

79. Slayton, R. and A., Clark-Ginsberg, Beyond regulatory capture: Coproducing expertise for critical infrastructure protection. *Regulation & Governance*, 2018. 12(1): p. 115–130.

80. RCL, *The revolving door.* 2022 [Accessed 21 January 2023]; Available from: https://regulatorycapturelab.ca/big-tech-revolving-door

81. Carrapico, H. and B. Farrand, "Dialogue, partnership and empowerment for network and information security": The changing role of the private sector from objects of regulation to regulation shapers. *Crime, Law and Social Change*, 2017. 67(3): p. 245–263.

82. DCMS, *Cyber security breaches survey 2022*. 2022 [Accessed 19 October 2022]; Available from: www.gov.uk/government/statistics/cyber-security-breaches-survey-2022/cyber-security-breaches-survey-2022

83. ICO, *ICO security incidents dashboard*. 2022 [Accessed 19 October 2022]; Available from: https://ico.org.uk/action-weve-taken/data-security-incident-trends

84. Kelly, S., et al., *Integrated infrastructure: Cyber resiliency in society, mapping the consequences of an interconnected digital economy*. 2016 [Accessed 30 July 2021]; Available from: www.jbs.cam.ac.uk/wp-content/uploads/2020/08/crs-integrated-inf rastructure-cyber-resiliency-in-society.pdf

85. Oughton, E.J., et al., Stochastic counterfactual risk analysis for the vulnerability assessment of cyber-physical attacks on electricity distribution infrastructure networks. *Risk Analysis*, 2019. 39(9): p. 2012–2031.

86. Lawson, S.T., *Cybersecurity discourse in the United States: Cyber-doom rhetoric and beyond*. 2019: Routledge.

87. HMG, *Post-implementation review of the network and information systems regulations 2018*. 2020 [Accessed 30 July 2021]; Available from: www.gov.uk/government/publi cations/review-of-the-network-and-information-systems-regulations

88. Davey, S., *Cyber improvements driven by UK NIS regulations*. 2020 [Accessed 30 July 2021]; Available from: www.pinsentmasons.com/out-law/news/cyber-improveme nts-uk-nis-regulations

89. Ip, G., *Foolproof: Why safety can be dangerous and how danger makes us safe*. 2015: Hachette UK.

90. Jay, J,. *WannaCry attacks cost NHS trusts £5.9 million, finds new study*. 2019 [Accessed 2 March 2022]; Available from: www.teiss.co.uk/news/wannacry-attacks-cost-nhs-tru sts-59-million-finds-new-study-7453

91. DCMS, *Second post-implementation review of the network and information systems regulations 2018*. 2022 [Accessed 6 July 2023]; Available from: www.gov.uk/governm ent/publications/second-post-implementation-review-of-the-network-and-informat ion-systems-regulations-2018

92. RSM, *Impact of the GDPR on cyber security outcomes*. 2020 [Accessed 30 July 2021]; Available from: https://assets.publishing.service.gov.uk/government/uploads/system/ uploads/attachment_data/file/906691/Impact_of_GDPR_on_cyber_security_outco mes.pdf

93. Chen, C., C.B. Frey, and G. Presidente, *Privacy regulation and firm performance: Estimating the GDPR effect globally*. 2022, The Oxford Martin Working Paper Series on Technological and Economic Change.

94. Goldberg, S., G. Johnson, and S. Shriver, Regulating privacy online: The early impact of the GDPR on European web traffic & e-commerce outcomes. *Available at SSRN*, 3421731, 2019.

95. Aridor, G., Y.-K. Che, and T. Salz, *The economic consequences of data privacy regulation: Empirical evidence from GDPR*. 2020: National Bureau of Economic Research Cambridge.

96. Johnson, G., S. Shriver, and S. Goldberg, Privacy & market concentration: Intended & unintended consequences of the GDPR. Available at *SSRN* 3477686, 2022.

97. Jia, J., G.Z. Jin, and L. Wagman, The short-run effects of the general data protection regulation on technology venture investment. *Marketing Science*, 2021. 40(4): p. 661–684.

98. Davey, S., *Report flags GDPR's impact on data breach notification*. 2019 [Accessed 30 July 2021]; Available from: www.pinsentmasons.com/out-law/news/report-flags-gdprs-impact-on-data-breach-notification-

99. ICO, *GDPR: One year on.* 2019 [Accessed 30 July 2021]; Available from: https://ico.org.uk/media/about-the-ico/documents/2614992/gdpr-one-year-on-20190530.pdf

100. Cavusoglu, H., et al., Institutional pressures in security management: Direct and indirect influences on organizational investment in information security control resources. *Information & Management*, 2015. 52(4): p. 385–400.

101. Angst, C.M., et al., When do IT security investments matter? Accounting for the influence of institutional factors in the context of healthcare data breaches. *MIS Quarterly*, 2017. 41(3): p. 893–916.

102. Marsh, *Global cyber risk perception survey.* 2019 [Accessed 2 March 2022]; Available from: www.microsoft.com/security/blog/wp-content/uploads/2019/09/Marsh-Microsoft-2019-Global-Cyber-Risk-Perception-Survey.pdf

103. Bender, D., *GDPR harmonization: Reality or myth?* 2018 [Accessed 23 February 2022]; Available from: https://iapp.org/news/a/gdpr-harmonization-reality-or-myth

104. Kwon, J. and M.E. Johnson, Proactive versus reactive security investments in the healthcare sector. *MIS Quarterly*, 2014. 38(2): p. 451–572.

105. FCA, *Building operational resilience: Impact tolerances for important business services and feedback to DP18/04.* 2019 [Accessed 30 July 2021]; Available from: www.fca.org.uk/publication/consultation/cp19-32.pdf

106. FCA, *Building operational resilience: Feedback to CP19/32 and final rules.* 2021 [Accessed 30 July 2021]; Available from: www.fca.org.uk/publication/policy/ps21-3-operational-resilience.pdf

107. Zimmermann, V. and K. Renaud, Moving from a "human-as-problem" to a "human-as-solution" cybersecurity mindset. *International Journal of Human-Computer Studies*, 2019. 131: p. 169–187.

108. Dunn-Cavelty, M. and M. Suter, Public–private partnerships are no silver bullet: An expanded governance model for critical infrastructure protection. *International Journal of Critical Infrastructure Protection*, 2009. 2(4): p. 179–187.

109. Wiater, P., On the notion of "partnership" in critical infrastructure protection. *European Journal of Risk Regulation*, 2015. 6(2): p. 255–262.

110. Assaf, D., Models of critical information infrastructure protection. *International Journal of Critical Infrastructure Protection*, 2008. 1: p. 6–14.

111. Carr, M., Public–private partnerships in national cyber-security strategies. *International Affairs*, 2016. 92(1): p. 43–62.

112. Clinton, L., A relationship on the rocks: Industry-government partnership for cyber defense. *Journal of Strategic Security*, 2011. 4(2): p. 97–111.

113. Sales, N.A., Regulating cyber-security. *Northwestern University Law Review*, 2012. 107: p. 1503.

114. DigitalEurope, *DIGITALEUROPE's recommendations for a more ambitious EU cyber defence policy.* 2023 [Accessed 4 August 2023]; Available from: www.digitaleurope.org/resources/digitaleuropes-recommendations-for-a-more-ambitious-eu-cyber-defence-policy/

115. NCSC, *The NCSC annual review 2020.* 2020 [Accessed 30 July 2021]; Available from: www.ncsc.gov.uk/news/annual-review-2020

116. UK_Cyber_Security_Council, *The chartered institute for cyber security.* [Accessed 21 January 2023]; Available from: www.ukcybersecuritycouncil.org.uk/about-the-council

117. Carrapico, H. and A. Barrinha, *The EU as a coherent (cyber) security actor? Journal of Common Market Studies*, 2017. 55(6): p. 1254–1272.

8 Aggregated Case Studies

CASE STUDY: PRIVACY

BACKGROUND

Privacy can (apparently) be easily defined as the protection of personally identifiable information (PII) – that's the general idea behind EU legislation (GDPR, [1]) and in standards such as ISO 27001 [2]. Strictly speaking I can't see a formal definition of privacy in either, although it can be inferred from the definition of "privacy breach" (e.g. [3, p7]). The implication is that privacy is a pretty straightforward concept, and that it's a simple matter to enact legislation to protect it.

This apparently clear-cut view breaks down when security practitioners try to distinguish privacy from security. Privacy is supposedly something different to security, although you need to have security to have privacy. But a privacy breach might also be a security breach. So is privacy a part of security, or is it the other way around? As noted by Smith et al.: "*[t]here are ongoing debates regarding the distinction, if any, between privacy and related constructs such as security*" [4, p5].

THE CONCEPT OF PRIVACY

This might seem an obvious statement, but privacy is quite complicated. If you look at Solove's summary of the concept of privacy (70 pages) [5], the companion paper on a taxonomy of privacy (85 pages) [6] and the summary of available research from Acquisti et al. (50 pages) [7], you get the sense that this is more complex than security practitioners would have you believe.

In fact, Solove's taxonomy of privacy states openly that: "*[p]rivacy is a concept in disarray. Nobody can articulate what it means*" [6, p477]. He goes on to quote Thomson: "*[p]erhaps the most striking thing about the right to privacy is that nobody seems to have any very clear idea what it is*". Other researchers have found the same e.g. Pavlou: "*...much ambiguity and disagreement still surrounds the concept of information privacy*" [8, p977], Acquisti et al.: "*...characterizing a single unifying economic theory of privacy is hard, because privacy issues of economic relevance arise in widely diverse contexts*" [7, p442], Smith and Dinev: "*[g]eneral privacy as a*

DOI: 10.1201/9781003380962-8

philosophical, psychological, sociological, and legal concept has been researched for more than 100 years in almost all spheres of the social sciences" [4, p992].

It's fair to say that there are other, rather simpler viewpoints. What I believe is called the Chicago School of privacy says *inter alia*, that privacy is a means of deceit, and that privacy legislation is a charter to deceive through e.g. not having to reveal everything about your past when you apply for a job [9]. This is very much the view of the rational economists. It suggests that granting individuals the right to privacy impairs the efficient functioning of markets, leading to higher interest rates and reduced levels of employment. An example of this kind of thinking can be seen in a paper by Posner [10]:

> *When people today decry lack of privacy, what they want, I think, is mainly something quite different from seclusion: they want more power to conceal information about themselves that others might use to their disadvantage.*

By all means (in fact please do) download the 1981 paper by Posner and read through it. But if you do, then to be absolutely clear, I'm neither espousing nor endorsing the wider views expressed in that paper, which might be seen to be "of their time". The section on *"efficient sorting of females to males"* being an example. I'm citing it here as a reflection of the economists' view of privacy.

For me, although it's not explicitly stated, these views run close to the phrase "nothing to hide, nothing to fear". Solove [11] takes issue with that kind of thinking, pointing out that those who propose it paradoxically assume that they have an implicit right to grant or refuse their own consent. The central argument from Solove is that it's wrong to think of privacy as a single thing. Instead, it should be viewed as a family of concepts sharing common attributes, such as a resource (I value my privacy), a state (some parts of my life are private), and a process (I take steps to ensure my privacy), and further, that it's pointless to separate out those ideas, because they belong together, even if they're different in nature. In fact, Solove calls out the reductionist approach as a particularly inappropriate way to look at privacy [5, p1125], and others have done the same. So if you disagree, and you think that privacy is actually pretty straightforward, you should look away now.

CURRENCY AND CONTROL

Two themes that recur in the literature are that privacy is a form of currency, and that privacy equates to control (over your personal data, for example).

Leman-Langlois [12] says that privacy used to be based on how far the State could intrude into the lives of its citizens (as in the early definition of privacy by Warren and Brandeis [13], usually summarised as "the right to be let alone"), but privacy has since become a form of currency, in that we each have an amount of "privacy capital" that we give up in exchange for stuff. This view of privacy as a resource that we expend in order to get something in return has been suggested by others, and you'll see it referred to in the context of Social Exchange Theory [14].

Use of the term "privacy" in legislation, however, tends to be based on the 1967 definition given by Westin: *"[t]he claim of individuals, groups, or institutions to determine for themselves when, how, and to what extent information about them is communicated to others*" [15]. That is, privacy comes about through the ability to exercise control. Westin went on to identify three types of attitudes to privacy: "privacy fundamentalists", "privacy pragmatists", and the "privacy unconcerned". The general idea I believe, is that each individual fits into one (and only one) of those three categories [16].

And in a nutshell, there you have the two main views. One camp says it's a currency that enables social exchange, the other says that privacy equates to control. Not surprisingly, the security industry has gone for the simpler option – the idea that protecting people's privacy comes from giving them control over their personal data.

Westin's approach has been challenged by some [17, 18], whereas others have suggested that the model is more complex than the interpretation placed on it [19]. Either way, it forms the basis of much of the privacy legislation in the United States and elsewhere. The approach is reflected in the so-called notice and choice model [14], which is intended to put individuals in charge of the collection and use of their personal information, by presenting them with a privacy notice followed by a choice as to whether or not to proceed. The notice and choice model has now become the *de facto* mechanism for requesting consumer consent when accessing web-based services.

However, it's fair to say that this view of "privacy as control" bypasses a number of real-world complexities, at least when it comes to online behaviours. Two of those being the illusion of control, and the importance of context.

THE ILLUSION OF CONTROL

Privacy legislation may have been based originally on a model of online retailers keeping internal records of their dealings with customers. The current reality is what van de Waerdt calls Data-Driven Companies (DDCs) [20] assembling and then selling detailed profiles of individuals, by collating information on them from across a number of sources. Under those conditions, any one decision about releasing my personal data becomes irrelevant, because it's only a single component of a wider picture. Consequently, as a consumer, I don't have any real control. I'm just being given the illusion of control [21].

And in practice, the illusion of control may simply act to convince people that it's safe to disclose their personal information.

Stutzman et al. [22] were carrying out a longitudinal study of the privacy behaviours of social network users, when halfway through the study, the network operator unexpectedly changed the granularity of their users' security controls. Prior to the change, the researchers noted that:

> *Users in our dataset... became more protective of their personal information by progressively limiting data publicly shared with "strangers".*

Whereas afterwards:

> *Policy and interface changes implemented... near the end of the period... seemingly altered that outcome and countered such privacy-seeking behavior by arresting and in some cases inverting the trend.*

> *Over time, the amount and scope of personal information that... users*
> *revealed to their... "friends" (that is, to other connected profiles) actually*
> *increased. In doing so, however – and in parallel to their reducing disclosures*
> *to stranger profiles – users ended up increasing their personal disclosures to*
> *other entities on the network as well: third-party apps, (indirectly) advertisers,*
> *and [the operator] itself.*

That is, user interface changes offering a greater degree of advertised control (but offering no more actual control) led to increased levels of disclosure. Tucker, in particular, found that personalised advertising was nearly twice as effective after users had been given a greater level of granularity over their security settings [23], even though the extent of the options was unchanged. That is, increasing the *perceived* degree of control increased people's willingness to interact. Martin and Murphy [14], citing Mothersbaugh, also concluded that increased levels of control and customisation led to a greater willingness to disclose personal information, possibly because an increased perception of control seemed to reduce people's feelings of personal vulnerability [24].

Brandimarte et al. [25] concluded that: *"[o]ur results suggest that affording more control to users may not necessarily help them to better protect their privacy, but rather it may induce them to reveal more sensitive information"* [25].

Interesting point, if you're running a social network.

THE IMPORTANCE OF CONTEXT

van de Waerdt points out that companies know the full details of how personal data will be processed, whereas consumers don't [20], and that no amount of legislation will affect the consequent degree of information asymmetry [26]. By shifting responsibility onto individuals who are not in a position to make informed decisions, the model forces consumers to rely on something other than facts when making choices on consent [27]. Brandimarte, for example, suggests that when we release information online, we tend to picture it going off to some sort of benign "imagined audience" [28].

Research by John et al. [29] found that decisions to release personal information were strongly influenced by environmental cues. When presented with web sites that looked to have been less professionally produced (i.e. web sites that were "shabbier"), people tended to disclose more personal information than they did when shown the more professionally produced version. Perhaps surprisingly, the participants in the experiment also tended to be more honest in their answers when providing information to the shabbier web site.

Samat and Acquisti [30] found that when an introductory briefing talked about "prohibiting" data sharing, participants were less likely to share their information than they were when the message talked about "allowing" data sharing. The effect was found to be greater as the level of risk increased. That is, when the audience for the disclosure was seen as less benign, the framing of the privacy message had a greater impact on behaviour. Other researchers such as Nissenbaum [31] have concluded that the meaning of privacy depends crucially on circumstances. Acquisti et al. for example [32] primed individuals with a pre-amble prompting them to think about privacy and found that they tended to release fewer details. As noted in a parallel paper [33], people do seem to care about privacy, but "...*whether they appear to care a lot or a little depends critically on context*" [33, p253].

The Concerns for Information Privacy scale (CFIP) [34, 35] is based on the idea that an individual's concerns about privacy can be broken down into four orthogonal aspects: the collection of personal information; unauthorised secondary use of personal information; errors in personal information; and improper access to personal information. The idea behind CFIP has been extended to create the Internet User Information Privacy Concern scale (IUIPC, [36]), which uses different dimensions and applies when people are using the Internet. We also have the Mobile Users Information Privacy Concern scale (MUICP, [37]), which applies when people are using their cell phones.

In that context, Alashoor et al. [38] examined four widely used scales of information privacy concerns (including CFIP and IUIPC) and found that for three of them, there were statistically significant priming effects. That is, the questionnaire used to elicit people's views on privacy triggered them to think about the issue of privacy, which in turn affected their responses, leading them to inflate "... *1) intentions to refuse to provide personal information and 2) intentions to falsify their personal information...*" [38, p11]. It seemed it was not possible to ask people about privacy without affecting their view of it.

Acquisti et al. [39, 40] looked at the kinds of disclosures that prompted regret amongst Facebook users, noting that "*unintended audience seems to be a particularly salient cause of Facebook regrets but not real-world regrets*" [39, p10]. The paper suggests that if we could find a way to identify potentially inaccurate assumptions regarding the audience for a post, then nudges could be used to prompt the user to reconsider. A subsequent study did just that [41, 42]. Two nudges were trialled – one implemented a 15-second delay on posts, while the other brought up a selection of user profile pictures showing a sample of the audience that would be able to access the post, together with an estimate of the total size of the audience. Most users in the trial found the delay to be effective but irritating. However, the "actual audience" nudge was generally seen to be useful. Almuhimedi et al. [43] carried out a similar study, with a nudge showing users how many apps had shared their location, and how many times. The work seemed to be effective in prompting users to review and if necessary, change their privacy settings. In both cases it seems that the nudge worked because it reminded the user of the actual, rather than the imagined context for their disclosure. The upshot being that privacy decisions are malleable. If you can alter the circumstances, then you can change people's feelings about what privacy means.

The bottom line is that people's willingness to provide personal details is affected by the circumstances for the disclosure. Which in turn means there's a mismatch between the assumption of consistent, rational behaviour as embodied in the notice and choice model, and the way we seem to make privacy decisions in reality. That on its own, may go some way towards explaining why there have been some spectacularly bad assumptions regarding the nature of the "imagined audience" [44, 45].

Solove concludes that: "... *the value of privacy in a particular context depends upon the social importance of the practice of which it is a part*" [5, p1093]. And if that's true, then you can't apply reductionism. In fact, Solove specifically calls out theorists who "*...look for a common set of necessary and sufficient elements that single out privacy as unique from other conceptions*" [5, p1095].

Nevertheless, for better or worse, reductionist thinking and the assumption of rationality form the cornerstones of existing privacy legislation.

THE IMPACT OF LEGISLATION

In 2019, British Airways (BA) was threatened with a fine of £183M by the UK Information Commissioner's Office (ICO), for failing to protect customer information, specifically consumer credit card details [46]. That penalty, inexplicably to me, was later reduced to £20M, £4M of that reduction (out of a total reduction of £163M) being an adjustment to take into account the impact of COVID-19 [47]. By my calculation that's a fine of about £50 per person affected, representing about 0.16% of BA's global turnover in the year [48]. Similarly, the ICO fine for the Marriott breach [49] was reduced from £99M to £18M after about a year of deliberation and negotiation [50].

In 2022, a clothing company then based in China (Zoetop) had a US$1.9M fine imposed on them by the city of New York, for failures in relation to a 2018 security breach affecting Shein, one of their component businesses [51]. The court action alleged that Zoetop had covered up the breach(es), minimised the stated impact, and that in effect, the company had been "economical with the truth" with some 39 million customers, who it turns out, had seen their personal information compromised, including credit card details [52]. The company was also alleged to have hampered a subsequent investigation by an external auditor [53]. The New York Attorney General has stated openly that the company "lied" over the extent and impact of the breach [54].

In announcing the fine, the Attorney General proclaimed that "*[t]his agreement should send a clear warning to companies that they must strengthen their digital security measures and be transparent with consumers*" and that "*anything less will not be tolerated*" [55]. The cyber industry prediction was that: "*[I]f customers find out that their data was stolen and the company tried to hide the fact, then they will be much less likely to use that company in the future due to trust*" [56]. Right.

Shein had an estimated US$16Bn turnover in 2021, and an estimated turnover of US$30Bn in 2022 [57] i.e. their volume of business doubled in the year. And to set that fine in context, in 2022 the company was valued at around US$100Bn [58], up from about US$50Bn the year before [59].

In 2018, Uber reported a breach (a year after finding it), and subsequently agreed to a US$148M settlement over the incident and the associated non-reporting [60]. Annual revenue for Uber in 2018 was around US$11.3Bn [61].

In 2014, JP Morgan Chase declared a privacy breach affecting an estimated 76 million households in the United States but successfully turned down a request to offer free credit monitoring and/or identity theft protection to customers whose data had been stolen, since (they claimed) no financial or account information had been compromised [62].

In November 2022, the ICO issued a reprimand (but no fine) to the UK Department for Education (DfE), in relation to their use of the Learning Records Service (LRS) database [63]. The Department had provided access to the database to a commercial company offering age verification checks to gambling sites. As pointed out by the ICO, that was not the original reason for gathering the data, and such use therefore contravened the principles of data protection [64]. As background, the ICO noted that:

> *The LRS database has personal information of up to 28 million children and young people from the age of 14. The database records full name, data of birth, and gender, with optional fields for email address and nationality. It also records a person's learning and training achievements. The data is kept for 66 years.*

DfE allowed the access to run for about 18 months (during which time about 22,000 searches were carried out), until they were made aware of the situation, reportedly by means of an article in a Sunday newspaper. Access was then revoked, along with access that had been granted to 2,600 other organisations that presumably didn't need it either. According to the ICO report, the original company that had been granted access had never, in fact, provided any Government-funded training.

The DfE weren't issued with a fine (the ICO argument being that there's no point in one part of Government fining another), but they were given a stiff reprimand and were asked to put in place remedial measures. Interesting to compare that with the €0.4Bn fine issued to Instagram when a number of under-18's deliberately switched from personal accounts to business accounts in order to gain some extra features, accidentally making their details public in the process [65].

A 2020 Freedom of Information (FoI) request regarding the effectiveness of the ICO in enforcing fines [66, 67] indicated that over 40% of the monetary value of fines issued between 2015 and 2019 remained unpaid at the time of the request. An ICO report in 2020 [68, 69] claimed that a total of £42M had been issued in fines across 17 cases during the year, although the majority of that related to just two (2) incidents (Marriott and BA), representing a total of £40M.

And what happens if you break banking codes rather than privacy laws? Well…

- *"[t]he Financial Conduct Authority (FCA) has fined JPMorgan Chase Bank N.A. ("JPMorgan") £137,610,000 ($220 million) for serious failings related to its Chief Investment Office (CIO). JPMorgan's conduct demonstrated flaws permeating all levels of the firm: from portfolio level right up to senior management, resulting in breaches of Principles 2, 3, 5 and 11 of the FCA's Principles for Businesses – the fundamental obligations firms have under the regulatory system"* [70].
- *"JPMorgan Chase fined $920 million for market manipulation"* [71, 72].
- *"[b]anks have been fined a staggering $243 billion since the financial crisis…. [m]ost of these fines have been assessed for misleading investors about the underlying quality of the mortgages they packaged into bonds during the housing bubble. According to Keefe, Bruyette and Woods, which compiled*

the list, Bank of America leads the ignominious tally with $76 billion in fines. JPMorgan Chase has been fined nearly $44 billion, and a number of other big money-center banks have been fined over $10 billion. Thirteen banks make up 93% of the total" [73, 74].

- *"[f]our years ago, JPMorgan Chase reached a then-record settlement with the Department of Justice after, among other things, the bank received a copy of a U.S. attorney's draft complaint documenting its alleged role in underwriting fraudulent securities in the years leading up to the 2008 financial crisis. Following the bank's $13 billion financial agreement, the draft complaint was never filed. Then the bank paid another settlement to prevent a separate legal case from potentially unearthing it"* [75].
- *"JPMorgan Chase has been fined more than $2 billion for violations of the Bank Secrecy Act tied to failure to report suspicious activity related to Bernie Madoff's decades-long, multi-billion dollar Ponzi scheme"* [76].
- *"[t]he Financial Services Authority (FSA) has fined JP Morgan Securities Ltd (JPMSL) $49 million for failing to protect client money by segregating it appropriately"* [77].

On this evidence, the fines for actual privacy violations are a fraction of those imposed for breaches of financial regulations. For most companies then, the best option is to interpret the privacy requirements word for word and take the risk on the rest of it, particularly when you can subsequently engage in a negotiation with the legislators to agree on what good security should have looked like. You asked me to put in a consent form, that's what I've done. Move on.

Supporters of e.g. GDPR might reasonably point out that the legislation was intended to reduce the likelihood of a data breach, rather than to punish transgressors after the fact. That would be a fair thing to say. However, a single-minded focus on process over potential outcomes does tend to produce anomalies, as we saw earlier. At the time of writing, the ICO web site, for example, sets out the details of a number of judgements, purportedly showing that companies who do not meet the letter of the law can expect to be dealt with very firmly. One of those cases relates to webuyanycar.com (WBAC). The judgement summary [78] indicates that WBAC *"sent 191.4 million marketing emails and 3.6 million marketing SMS messages to individuals without fully satisfying the requirements of the soft opt in, resulting in 42 complaints to the Commissioner, over a period of twelve months"*. I think I read that right. Forty-two (42) complaints out of nearly 200 million emails. Most of the complainants [78, para 47] stated that *"it made me annoyed"*. And the penalty for not *"fully satisfying the requirements of the soft opt in"*? Two hundred thousand pounds, just shy of £5,000 per complainant. About 100 times the per-person fine for BA.

According to the ICO web site [79], *"[b]etween 21 December 2019 and 16 February 2020, a total of 2,565,513 direct marketing messages were received by subscribers having been sent by SportsDirect.com Retail Ltd."*. That resulted [79, para 24], in twelve (12) complaints, unless I'm misreading the summary. The fine imposed by the ICO amounted to £70,000, or about £6k per person affected. Close to 120 times the per-person fine for BA.

In 2021, the ICO issued a fine of £150,000 to Saga, on the basis that "*[d]uring the period 29 November 2018 and 2 May 2019, a confirmed total of 128,895,718 unsolicited direct marketing messages were received by subscribers, having been sent at the instigation of Saga Services Ltd.*". The messages "*contained direct marketing material for which subscribers had not provided valid consent*" [80]. The issue seems to have been not so much to do with unsolicited marketing, more that the consent process did not meet the letter of the law [80, para 72]. It's difficult to be sure because of the timeline of events, but there seems to have been a grand total of seven (7) complaints [80, para 21]. Boomers. What can you do? My rather overworked calculator says that comes to about £21,500 per complaint. Over 400 times the per-person fine for BA.

Looking further afield, a number of sources list out the biggest data protection fines issued to date [81–83]. Top of the list is Amazon, with a proposed fine of €746M (US$794M at the time of writing). Amazon has lodged an appeal, partly on the basis that the fine is disproportionate, but mostly on the fact that there was no actual breach. The technical details of the case haven't been made public, although Amazon has re-affirmed that "*there has been no data breach and no personal data has been exposed to a third party*", and that the decision "*relies on subjective and untested interpretations of privacy law*" [84].

Right below the Amazon case is WhatsApp Ireland (€225M, for "*not being transparent enough*" [81]). The case of the Austrian postal service also catches the eye (€9.5M, for not providing an email address for data protection enquiries made via their web site [81]).

Meanwhile…

Woods and colleagues [85, 86] looked into the "commodification of consent". Although consumers may well agree to share their information with the operators of a specific web site, behind the scenes, advertisers using that data may have bought into a commercial service offered by online "consent brokers", whereby one instance of consent is shared across all members of the group. Consequently, trading in consent becomes an industry in itself. Thanks to data privacy laws based on "notice and choice", consumer consent becomes a commodity that can be bought and sold. The authors conclude that "*[i]f privacy realism holds, consent coalitions should not be understood as a novel direction for privacy, but rather as an intensification of the absurdity of consent*" [85, p19].

In a 2020 study, Nouwens et al. [87] scraped the designs of the five most popular Consent Management Platforms (CMPs) across 10,000 UK-based web sites. They found widespread use of implied consent, and extensive use of dark patterns (techniques used to "direct" the consumer – an overview is given in "Deceived by Design" [88]). Only about 12% of the sites they examined were found to meet a minimum set of requirements drawn up to reflect European law. The authors also note a report from Utz et al. [89] which analysed a random sample of 1,000 CMP usages, finding that 57% of them used dark patterns to nudge users to select "privacy-unfriendly" options, and that 86% of notices provided either no choice or confirmation only.

Again in 2020, Matte, Bielova, and Santos [90] investigated the consent signal sent from the CMP to data processors. They found that 12% of the 1,426 sites they examined sent a consent signal before the user had made a choice. They also found that implicit consent was common, in that consent was variously defined as simply visiting the site (16.8%), navigating within the site (6.2%), revisiting/refreshing the page (7.6%), scrolling or clicking on the page (5.3%) and closing the pop-up or banner (1.6%). Around 10% of the sites were found to use more than one form of implied consent.

In a 2019 study, Sanchez-Rola found that post-GDPR, cookies could still identify users on over 90% of the web sites in their sample [91]. A large number of those web sites presented deceiving information, making it very difficult for users to avoid being tracked:

> *Our results show that tracking is prevalent, happens mostly without user's consent, and opt-out is difficult... [m]ost websites perform some form of tracking, and 92% of them do it before providing any notice to the user... [m]ost websites do not let visitors avoid tracking. In fact, more than 90% create tracking cookies immediately after loading the website, even before users can take any decision on tracking.*

Call me picky, but if you were to list out the categories of fines in order of magnitude, you might see (a) breaches of financial regulations, way out in front, joint first alongside technical breaches of privacy standards (but *only* if you're a Big Tech firm), followed by (b) technical breaches of privacy standards (other firms), and (c) at the bottom, actual breaches of privacy. Meanwhile, there seems to have been no improvement in online privacy.

As a result of legislation based on enforcing control, privacy has become a justification rather than an objective. Privacy legislation in the EU no longer seems to be about privacy. It's become part of a decade-long campaign against the market dominance of Big Tech [92]. The German Economy Minister and the French Finance Minister have both indicated, for example, that they would be perfectly happy to see Facebook (Meta) permanently exit the European market [93]. You can see the same thinking reflected in forthcoming EU legislation. The Digital Markets Act (DMA) for example "... *signals the EU's continued encouragement of damages claims against monopolies within the industry, widely known for their outsized impact on the economy and wider society*" [94]. The same source notes that "*[u]nder the DMA, the EU can now punish Big Tech companies that violate antitrust laws with fines of up to ten percent of the company's annual global sales*". Other, impending legislation includes the Digital Services Act [95], which will "*make tech companies more accountable for content created by users and amplified by their platforms' algorithms*" [96]. Although it seems that even when Big Tech does something about online hate, it's still at fault, for not respecting the rights of the people posting the online hate [97, 98]. All of this legislation will apparently ensure that "*...the fundamental rights of users are protected*" [95]. Of course.

PROTECTING THE RIGHTS OF THE USER

Obar [99] gave users a privacy policy of around 8,000 words that was expected to take the average adult about 30 minutes to read, together with a Terms of Service document of just over 4,000 words (i.e. about 15 minutes of reading). Both were based on actual documents but included additional clauses stating that any information gathered would be handed over to the National Security Agency (NSA) and that by agreeing to the Terms of Service, the consumer was obliged to cede ownership of their first-born child.

About three quarters of the participants chose a "quick join" option, accepting the policies without reading them. Nine out of ten people in that group said that they used quick join on a regular basis, because regardless of the policy, they just wanted to use the service. Reading times for the privacy policy varied from three seconds to 37 minutes, with a median time of just over thirteen seconds (that's for a policy of around 8,000 words – assuming single spacing and a reasonable font, about 16 pages). Some 80% of participants spent less than one minute. A specific point to note here is that the participants were communications students, studying privacy and big data. In an empirical study reported by Martin [100], it was found that even law students tended to skip through online privacy policies [101].

Vail et al. [102] found that consumers viewed textual privacy statements as more secure than other forms, yet comprehension of those policies was relatively poor. That is, standard text-based policies might look the business, but nobody understands them [103].

Martin suggests that instead, consumers see privacy notices as a *tabula rasa* i.e. they project their own expectations onto the notice, meaning that in many cases they conclude that they're being provided with a level of protection much greater than is actually the case. Others have noted [104] that the mere existence of a privacy notice can be enough to suggest to people that their data is being protected. Given the length and detail of most notices, maybe there's some kind of mental "tick-box" exercise going on, as in "I can't be bothered to read this, I'm sure it's ok". If so, then the impact of privacy legislation has only worsened the situation. Linden et al. noted that[105, p47]:

> The GDPR has been a catalyst for a major overhaul of the privacy policies inside and outside the EU … [t]his overhaul … does not necessarily come at a benefit to the users … [p]olicies have become considerably longer (a fifth longer in the Global set and a third longer in the EU set).

On the basis of this and other evidence, Obar's paper concludes that the "notice and choice" approach is "...*deeply flawed, if not an absolute failure*". Such policies "... *leave digital citizens with nothing more than an empty promise of protection, an impractical opportunity for privacy self-management, and 'too much homework'* ". Hoffman et al. [106] go further, and suggest that leaving it all up to the consumer simply creates "privacy cynicism". That's perhaps not surprising, given the findings of Kesan et al. [107], in that online statements regarding consumer privacy tended to be more detailed when describing the user's obligations to the service provider, than they were when describing the service provider's obligations to the user.

It's reasonable to ask whether privacy legislation based on "notice and choice" has achieved even its basic aim of informed consent [33, p268]. Degeling et al. [108] sum up the situation by saying that while privacy notifications may fulfil the law's requirements, they are unlikely to help Internet users make more informed decisions. Edwards and Veale also view "notice and choice" as broken, and for much the same reasons i.e. information asymmetry and illusory control [7, p442]. They conclude that *"... it is now beyond trite to talk about a 'notice and choice fallacy'"* [27]. Warner [109] amongst others, points out that the notice and choice model has been facing this sort of criticism for about the last 20 years.

Waldman [110] discusses the process of "managerialisation" in relation to privacy laws. The argument is that even where the basis for such laws may be well-meaning, they inevitably leave room for interpretation. So-called compliance professionals [110, p776] then translate privacy requirements into corporate objectives. Compliance records become *"a means of protecting the company against consumer lawsuits or government investigations"* [110, p813]. Evidence of adherence takes the place of actual protection. The paper concludes that *"[I]n a world where compliance professionals determine what the law requires and create symbolic compliance tools, the discourse of law becomes the discourse of compliance, paper trails, and checklists"* [110, p820]. In effect, the managerial question becomes *"... 'how can we prove compliance with the least disruption and risk to production?' instead of 'how can we proceed while creating fewer privacy risks for our consumers?'"* [110, p822].

So, has an approach based on extensive legislation improved the situation for users? I'd say it's not been an unqualified success. But it has opened the door for others to adopt a similar model of enforced compliance.

THE IMPACT OF PRIVACY ACTIVISTS

The €746M fine issued to Amazon (still in dispute at the time of writing) seems to have been the result of a campaign by a privacy activist group LQDN [111], acting on behalf of around 10,000 users [112], who were invited to join in with a class action against the company [113]. To set that figure in perspective, Amazon Prime, as of 2021, reportedly had around 0.2Bn active subscribers [114].

The problem raised by LQDN relates to behavioural advertising – profiling individuals on the basis of their choices, and then using that data to target them for ads [115]. Part of the argument seems to be that Amazon's services should be free to use, without having to consent to providing the company with advertising revenue. Similar reasoning was presented by another group (noyb), who won a case against Meta regarding an assumption of consent on the basis of an agreed contract [116]. According to their web site, noyb "enforces *your* right to privacy every day". The group has 4,600 supporting members, according to their web site [117].

In both cases, the authorities that chose not to pursue the cases advanced by the activists, or at least not as aggressively as the activists would have liked, are now being disparaged in terms previously reserved for the companies themselves [118]. In the case of noyb, that's the Irish Data Protection Commission (DPC), who presumably opted to exercise the principle of proportionality when setting the fine for Meta. A number of technology companies are based in the Republic of Ireland, and presumably they contribute to the economy of a nation of some 5 million people.

Perhaps as a consequence of that pressure, the European Data Protection Board (EDPB) overturned the DPC's ruling and went on to mandate fines that were about ten times greater than those originally imposed. The EDPB also ruled that the DPC should conduct a more extensive investigation into Meta's business practices. The DPC are now considering launching an action in the European court, against the

EDPB, for overreaching its remit [119, 120]. The activist group is celebrating none-theless, for having successfully dealt "... *a huge blow to Meta's profits in the EU*" [121]. I've thought about the implications of that statement, and it seems to me that there are at least three issues at the heart of the activists' position. It could be that (a) I don't want companies like Meta using my personal details to make money, or (b) I don't want my personal details to be revealed, as a matter of principle, or (c) I don't want to receive targeted advertising.

If the problem is to do with profits, then one solution might be to redistribute the revenue – to start paying people for their personal data. If it's more to do with the data itself, then anonymisation is the answer. But I'm betting the farm that a multi-billion dollar online advertising industry isn't going to commit *seppuku* by giving up on the idea of targeted advertising. The impact of privacy legislation, combined with the behaviour of activists, is likely to force the advertising industry into solutions that look, and perhaps are compliant, but which still monetise the personal information of subscribers.

LOOKING AHEAD

Nippert-Eng [122] argues that privacy is more sensibly seen as a currency rather than as a matter of control – that it should be viewed as a commodity that we swap to-and-fro, in order to build and maintain relationships.

Moon [123] examined the idea of gradual exchanges of increasingly sensitive personal information [124] in the interaction between users and desktop computers. The dialogue initiated by the computer started out with e.g. details of its internal memory, disc storage, processor speed etc. and then followed up with a question of a personal nature directed at the user. Quoting Berg and Derlega, the study expected to find that "disclosure begets disclosure" i.e. when you receive a disclosure of personal information, you feel obliged to respond in kind. Further, based on earlier work, Moon expected to find a reflection that people are attracted not only to people who disclose to them, but also to the people to whom they make their own disclosures. The study then looked at what happened when the pattern of gradual escalation was broken. White and Zahay [125], for example, found that consumers reacted negatively when they received an overly personalised advertisement that was presented without any justification. That is, when the gradual, incremental process of establishing trust seemed to have been broken.

Long story short, Moon found all these things – exchanges of personal informa-tion led to bonding. When the computer offered its own details (i.e. it encouraged reciprocity), the responses from participants included greater levels of personal information, as they did when there was a gradual escalation of the degree of intru-siveness in the questions. When some participants were subsequently asked to move to another (identical) computer in order to rate a series of products presented on the screen, those who had bonded with the original machine consistently rated the same products displayed on the second computer as less attractive. There are some differences in detail between these findings and e.g. the work by Acquisti [32], and as noted by Moon, this was one experiment at one point in time, and the participants all knew it was an experiment. However, as pointed out in Moon's paper, "*[t]he tendency to respond socially is reflexive, occurring without extensive thought or deliberation".*

You can see that in the work by Umar et al. [126] and in the work by Matthes et al. [127], who looked at the levels of self-disclosure on Twitter and Facebook respectively, during the onset of the COVID-19 pandemic and subsequent lockdowns. The occurrence of the first death in the United States, and the formal declaration of a global pandemic triggered spikes in self-disclosures on Twitter, as people sought to obtain some form of reassurance. To quote the paper: *"[a]ccordingly, we suggest that users curate their social connections and disclose intentionally to reap social benefits during difficult times"* [126, p2]. The work by Matthes et al. also showed a clear link between concerns over COVID-19 and subsequent levels of online self-disclosure, and between levels of self-disclosure and reported levels of happiness [127, Figure 2].

Privacy is something that we want to spend, not save. The value we place on privacy comes through our ability to willingly compromise it, in order to build, maintain and exploit relationships. Barocas and Levy [128], in their examination of privacy dependencies, suggest that this process is a necessary part of a functioning society. They also note that isolation (which corresponds to perfect privacy – a situation in which it's impossible to build relationships) is often imposed as a punishment.

What we guard so jealously and defend so fiercely, is not the information itself. It's the ability to release it. An article in the Times in late 2022 illustrates the point. The columnist, having discovered that they were expecting a child, immediately looked online for some specific issues relating to pregnancy. Targeted advertising then started serving adverts for baby products, based on the original search terms. The complaint from the columnist was not so much about the adverts, but the fact that others were aware of the news *"... before I'd had a chance to tell my mum"* [129]. Brandimarte et al. [25] and Acquisti [42, p72] both found the same: that the act of release is much more important to us than what happens to the information afterwards. Largely, that seems to be because we're rewarded for disclosure.

Dean Burnett, in his book "The Happy Brain" [130] notes that *"... the mechanism that guides our desire for social interaction is embedded right in the part of the brain responsible for the experience of pleasure".* Acquisti et al. [131, p744] point to the work of Tamir and Mitchell [132], who used a combination of fMRI and behavioural experimentation to examine the link between self-disclosure and the brain's reward system. It's a fascinating piece of work, and I can't do it justice here. The researchers found that the areas of the brain associated with pleasure and reward were activated when subjects were asked to perform a piece of self-reflection (to think about their "selves"), and further, that the reward was magnified when they were asked to communicate the outcome of their reflection to another individual. That is, thinking about your "self" and communicating those thoughts to others, is inherently pleasurable. The work also found that individuals were willing to forgo financial rewards to answer questions about themselves rather than other people, concluding that:

Just as monkeys are willing to forgo juice rewards to view dominant groupmates and college students are willing to give up money to view attractive members of the opposite sex, our participants were willing to forgo money to think and talk about themselves.

The authors suggest that a reward mechanism based on self-disclosure might have evolutionary benefits, through the strengthening of social bonds. Fine and Holyfield [133] looked at the roles of trust and disclosure in a community of mushroom collectors (and do please search out a copy of this paper – e.g. in Kramer [134]). Knowing the location of a spot in the woods where a specific type of mushroom can be found confers upon that individual a special kind of status. Exchanges of knowledge regarding the location and e.g. when the mushrooms will be available, act as a kind of social "glue". Sharing information and being rewarded with respect (and potentially with sensitive information about another location from another member) is what binds the group together. With due respect to mycophiles everywhere, the themes that come out in the study probably have very little to do with fungi per se. They could relate to any activity where an individual can decide (or not) to share information which is of interest to another person in their group, in order to strengthen or establish social bonds [135].

People keep sharing their private information, despite the best efforts of legislators, because that is how we form and maintain relationships [136]. We use deliberate breaches of privacy in order to establish trust [137, p510]. So when you focus on privacy as the safeguarding of personal data, you lose its most important aspect. The paper by Fine and Holyfield provides perhaps the best and most concise summary. "*An economy of secrets exists by virtue of their breach*".

All of which leads us to a further example of the cybersecurity industry being overtaken by events. "Profila" [138] is an app[1] downloaded to your mobile device, allowing you to create an avatar, which is presented to advertising companies in lieu of presenting them with your personal data directly. The advertisers don't have access to your personal details (the solution is therefore claimed to be GDPR-compliant), but through the use of intermediate, anonymising servers, they do gain access to a representation of your interests and advertising preferences [139]. The pitch to investors claims that Profila can therefore provide access into otherwise unreachable market sectors, and that they can provide much more closely targeted advertising – that they can target "*the perfect customer*" [140, p45].

Users of the app are incentivised to register their marketing choices, such as what times of year they wish to see adverts for specific products, whether or not they're interested in particular brands, what new products they may be interested in etc. They're motivated to do so largely through the same kind of psychology as we have already seen. Users of the app are offered micropayments for sharing their profile and viewing ads, using a special to purpose cryptocurrency [138]. Techniques such as gamification are also employed. Consumers are rewarded with more significant returns if they provide more detailed information. That's implemented as a "gaming levels" structure, so you feel a sense of advancement as you progress (and therefore generate a more detailed profile). The app contains quizzes and games that are used to elicit further information about your preferences. You're encouraged to identify the brands that you see are "you". Just as with the results on self-reflection (we find it pleasurable to reflect on our "selves" and even more pleasurable to share the outcome), users are encouraged to share the avatar they have created. You're also provided with quizzes on privacy, so that you feel empowered to challenge retailers for privacy misdemeanours. In fact, the business case for Profila makes a feature of the idea that the app enables consumers to engage in a relationship with advertisers. And as we saw with e.g. Moon's work, increased levels of trust and increased feelings of control tend to be associated with greater and more personal levels of disclosure.

In this context, Leman-Langlois cites Whitaker's idea of the "participatory panopticon" [141], a situation in which people willingly participate in their own surveillance, based on a re-interpretation of what it means to grant consent. There's no implied criticism of these products, nor of the companies involved, and this is purely a personal view. But for me two issues jump out.

The first is that inbuilt reward mechanisms associated with disclosure are now being exploited in much the same way as inbuilt biases and heuristics have been exploited for marketing purposes, over the past decade or so.

The second is to note that this situation has been brought about by the widespread application of legislation based on the idea of privacy as control. I'm not sure there is such a thing as secondary irony, but if there is... we now have a situation in which the cyber industry has completely bought into a view of privacy as control, whereas the agents supposedly being controlled by the associated legislation have moved on, to adopt a view of privacy as a tradeable asset.

The consensus by the way, seems to be that payments to consumers are nowhere near the market value of their data [142, 143]. Amazon for example is offering $2 per calendar month for access to personal data, which is widely seen as just a fraction of what the data is worth to advertisers [144]. I'm guessing that the key issue for most users is the feeling of being rewarded for disclosure, rather than the size of the reward.

Other forthcoming developments include the EU Payment Services Directive 2 (PSD2) [145], which among other things, will enable third-party access to your banking details, so that you can be provided with the enhanced range of services you've been longing for. One example being the offering from companies that will reward you for real-time access to your credit card transactions, so that they can provide more accurate data on advertising performance, to subscribing retailers. At least one of those companies by the way, presumably along with similar service providers, claims full compliance with GDPR, and there's absolutely no reason to doubt that claim. Although others have pointed out that it's not necessarily the technical details of the data processing that's the issue – it's the complex web of social responsibilities that comes into being when you create this sort of situation [146].

If this trend continues, then we're likely to see a situation in which there may be near-universal compliance with existing privacy legislation, but the commercial exploitation of personal preferences continues exactly as before. Existing legislation will become increasingly obsolete. Largely, that will be a result of adopting an approach based on control over data, and because that approach in and of itself has forced advertising companies to shift to a model of privacy as a tradeable currency. Consequently, it seems to me that either the industry needs to change tack and acknowledge the way in which users see privacy, or others will decide that the existing view from the industry is no longer needed.

SUMMARY

The complexity of privacy as a concept is such that this case study has provided not much more than a summary of the main areas – a skim read. But there are a number of points emerging from this quick look, mainly that reductionism doesn't form a sound basis for a consideration of the topic. When you abstract a definition of privacy as simply "control over PII" then you separate the security practitioners' view from the views of those whose privacy is under discussion. The outcome is that practitioners then start telling people what they should believe about privacy, and how they should act to protect it. It also promotes the idea that privacy is simple and it's all about economically rational behaviour, when in fact people display behaviours relating to privacy that are anything but rational.

The extensive application of privacy legislation hasn't resulted in benefits to the consumer. It has, however, resulted in a legal framework that has been redirected towards the achievement of other objectives. The subsequent, aggressive prosecution of companies for alleged technical infringements as a means of achieving economic and political outcomes calls the legislation into disrepute and diverts attention away from the aim of providing benefits to the individual. Worse, a focus on the details of process rather than practical outcomes, simply plays into the hands of "compliance professionals".

The best way I can sum up the situation is to reference a paper by Dourish and Anderson [147], which again is rich in detail and is a strongly recommended source. The authors point to evidence indicating that privacy and security both originate from social mechanisms and that as a result, reductionism cannot provide reliable models, nor can it explain observed behaviours. And because the meanings of privacy and security are socially constructed: (a) they are constantly being re-negotiated, and (b) it is not possible to take them out of context for analysis in isolation. The paper also suggests that it's not helpful to look at information – it's the flow of information that matters. The release of information is what builds up relationships. Echoing the point made by Nippert-Eng [122], the authors conclude that "*[p]rivacy is not simply a way that information is managed, but how social relationships are managed*" [147, p327].

CASE STUDY: RANSOMWARE

BACKGROUND

Ransomware is generally considered to be malicious software placed on a target system to encrypt the contents of any accessible files, so that the data contained within them is no longer available to system users. The software leaves behind contact details, together with a ransom demand, usually payable in e.g. Bitcoin, transactions in cryptocurrencies being potentially untraceable. If the victim pays up, then a second piece of software is provided that will decrypt their files.

In some cases the company may be able to restore their files from backups, and obviously that's not a great outcome from the point of view of the criminals, so they've taken to encrypting any accessible backups as well. They may also steal data before encrypting the local copies, and threaten to make the stolen files public if the ransom isn't paid [148, 149]. That might include customer details, proprietary information, sensitive financial details, etc. More recent developments include pressuring the victim through cold calling [150], and encouraging the victim's customers to contact them and tell them to pay up [151]. Basically, these people have added social components to what is perceived to be a technical issue, in order to make it more effective. Not a bad idea.

A survey carried out on behalf of Sophos in 2020 [152] reported that 94% of ransomware victims got their data back [152, p9], either by paying the ransom (26%) or by restoring from backups (56%) or presumably through some other route (the remaining 12%). A small proportion (1%) paid the ransom but did not get their data back. A parallel Coveware report [153] noted that of those that paid the ransom, 98% received working decryption software. Obviously, the business model would fall down if it got around that people who paid the ransom didn't get their data back, so it's in the interests of the extortionists to keep their promise.

One year later, the same report for 2021 stated that on average, only 65% of encrypted data was recovered, and that only 8% of victims recovered all of their data [154, p11]. I can't find any explanation of the difference between that conclusion and the findings from the previous year, but perhaps I'm missing something.

Depending on who you ask, the cost of ransomware comes to:

- US$209M every quarter in the US [155] (about US$0.8Bn per annum);
- US$7.5Bn annually in the US [156];
- US$75Bn annually just in relation to small businesses in the US [157];
- US$350M annually [158];
- US$9M annually in the US, according to an FBI report [159, p14].

The 2023 Verizon data breach report [160], quoting an FBI source [161], suggests that in 93% of reported ransomware incidents, there was no financial impact [160, p30]. As I say, the reported scale of the problem depends on who you ask, and when you ask them [162].[2]

In October 2022, what appears to be a robust study by the US Treasury, examining suspicious cryptocurrency transactions [163, 164] suggested that in the preceding 12 months, a total of US$1.2Bn had been paid by US businesses in order to meet ransomware demands. The GDP of the United States in 2021 was around US$24Tn, so to put that ransomware statistic into perspective, it's about 0.005% of the nation's GDP. Again, for context, the US Federal Trade Commission estimated the losses from insurance fraud in the same year to be about US$5.8Bn – about five times the losses associated with ransomware [165]. In the United Kingdom, a report in late 2022 [166] suggested that, setting aside accidental over-payments, benefits fraud in 2021 amounted to some £6.5Bn (US$7.5Bn at the time of writing, about six times the figure for ransomware across the whole of the United States). HMRC estimate that each year, about 5% of the tax that should be collected, isn't in fact collected. This is known as the "tax gap". Recent figures put it somewhere in the region of £42Bn (about US$51Bn). That's an annual figure [167–170]. The most recent report I can find for the US tax gap puts it at around US$496Bn i.e. about US$0.5Tn [171]. That's the gross figure, before any remedial action is undertaken. For comparison, that US Treasury estimate for ransom payments in 2021 comes to about one quarter of 1% of the annual tax gap.

To further set things in perspective, the Wannacry attack is estimated to have caused around 19,000 appointments to be cancelled [172]. In April 2023, industrial action taken by junior doctors reportedly led to the cancellation of 196,000 appointments [173]. In the first week.

ECONOMICS

Target industries vary, but during the pandemic, the education and health sectors seemed to receive an increased amount of attention from ransomware enthusiasts [174–177]. In fact, in 2021, both the Irish Health Service and the Irish Department of Health were impacted [178]. It's been suggested that a previously unknown technical vulnerability was used to deliver the software in those specific cases [179], but as pointed out elsewhere, that would be an unusual development – a more likely option would be to persuade one or more users to release their account details, or to persuade them to absent-mindedly install the encryption software. Exploiting so-called zero-day technical vulnerabilities can be expensive. It's much cheaper to make use of people's decision-making. And for attackers at least, the economic model is important.

In reacting to the incident, the Taoiseach stated that as a matter of policy, no ransom would be paid, under any circumstances [180].

When the city of Atlanta was hit by ransomware in 2018 [181],[3] the attackers demanded a ransom of around US$51,000 (it's difficult to be precise, given the volatility of the exchange rate for Bitcoin). On a point of principle, the city refused to pay, even though they were reportedly covered by a state-wide cyber insurance policy [182]. Unconfirmed reports of the clean-up costs to date suggest a figure in the region of US$17M [183]. It's not clear whether the additional expenditure was covered by the insurance policy.

When the city of Baltimore was attacked, their position was also "we don't pay ransoms". Clean-up costs to date have been unofficially reported to be in the region of US$18M, against an original ransom demand of about US$70,000 [184]. Most of those costs, it has been noted, have fallen to Baltimore residents [185] i.e. the local community has borne the majority of the externalities arising from the city's decision.

In May 2019, the city of Cartersville was reportedly hit with ransomware and an associated demand of US$2.8M [186]. The city engaged professional negotiators who managed to reduce the demand to US$380,000 (about 15% of the original figure). The decryptor key was received after 48 hours, and the city's services were back up within six days [187]. It's reported that the city's insurance provider covered the majority of the fees.

It's generally seen as logical just to pay up, since if you have an appropriate insurance policy, it will cover the cost of the ransom, and also some part of the clean-up. Recovery from scratch can be expensive, and while it's usually possible to negotiate the ransom demand down a little bit, it's much more difficult to negotiate with

IT service providers. So it makes more sense for the victim, and for the insurance company, to pay the ransom, because it's likely to be the lower of the two figures [188, p12]. All of which of course, assumes that the victim has a choice, since there is an argument from the cyber industry that paying ransoms should be made illegal [189–192].

The Chief Executive of the Irish Health Service [193] has indicated that the total costs arising from their attack could be in the region of €100M, partly due to the need to rebuild their ageing networks: *"[w]e have a really old legacy network in the HSE. It needs investment for the security and protection of data for the future, and we will have many lessons from reports that we will get through this process"*. Lacey [194, p9] suggests that in comparison to e.g. aviation safety practices *"... the security posture of many organisations is shaped by knee-jerk reactions to major incidents that occur unexpectedly after years of neglect in maintaining controls and a failure to probe below the tip of the iceberg of visible incidents"*. The Irish Health Service has been praised for taking "a strong stance" [195], although it could be argued that a stronger stance would have been to upgrade from Windows 7™ [196]. Consequently, it's debatable whether or not these costs (also reported as having been incurred by Baltimore and Atlanta) should be ascribed to ransomware, rather than being seen as an investment that should have been made anyway.

In 2021 the French arm of a major insurance company decided not to issue any new policies covering ransom payments, pending a decision on legality, at least in France [197, 198]. Predictably, the statement was met with a ransomware attack on the insurance company itself [199]. That might be viewed as a simple retaliation, although similar attacks e.g. [200] have been seen as attempts to gain detailed information on companies holding cyber policies, so that the criminals can be better informed in subsequent negotiations regarding the size of the ransom. Interesting that the criminals go to some efforts to understand the wider business context. Also interesting that the criminals target an outcome rather than just focusing on assets.

Figures from the insurance industry [201] suggest that up until about 2019, the loss ratio on cyber policies was quite healthy – around 35% (2017), 34% (2018), and 47% (2019). The figure for 2020 is expected to be 73% – that is, about three quarters of the value of premiums taken in by the insurance companies is expected to be paid out in claims. These figures are referred to as direct loss ratios and don't take into account the expenses involved in setting up the policy. One source [202] points out that if you add in that figure for the previous year, the combined loss ratio exceeds 100% i.e. in theory, the insurance industry is losing money by providing cyber cover [203]. Payouts also seem to be becoming more polarised in terms of the median value vs the mean i.e. notwithstanding the total number of claims, the outliers are becoming larger [204]. I guess as a result of increasing levels of claims, premiums rose sharply during 2020 (year on year rises were 4.4% in Q1, 6.5% in Q2, 7.7% in Q3, and 11.1% in Q4) [200]. Premiums are now expected to continue rising [205], in combination with increased constraints on cover [206].

Overall, the insurance industry has proven itself capable of adapting to change [207], so unless Governments make it illegal to pay a ransom, insurers will probably continue to cover the risk [184, p10], although premiums will rise, and limits may be imposed [208]. Consequently some organisations might become uninsurable, and smaller companies might be priced out of the market [209]. There are more detailed sources available if you would like to look into this effect [210, 211].

CONTEXT

It was argued earlier that security comes about through negotiation i.e. that security is socially constructed. The actors involved in the ransomware negotiation were identified as insurance companies, writers of ransomware, and victims. It was suggested that as long as ransom demands remained below the costs of clean-up and recovery, then the criminals would be content, because they were likely to be paid. The insurance companies would be content, providing they can subsequently adjust premiums to maintain their margin. It would probably be a simplification to say that victims were content. However, their situation is probably seen as tolerable, so long as insurers remain willing to cover the ransom, and perhaps a proportion of the clean-up costs.

It was also noted that security practitioners had entered the discussion, and that they were not happy with the situation. The practitioners' argument being that paying ransoms makes their job of protecting systems more difficult. Consequently, it was proposed that another round of negotiation would be necessary, in order to achieve closure. And indeed, recently an industry group (the Ransomware Task Force – RTF) has issued a report setting out their plan to reduce the global impact of ransomware [212].

Around 50 contributing organisations are named in the RTF report. Of those, cybersecurity companies, technology companies, cybersecurity consultancies, cybersecurity insurance companies, Government cyber agencies and other organisations related to cyber make up a total of 41. The others are e.g. police organisations with an interest in cyber, universities with an interest in cyber, etc. I may have missed them, but I couldn't find any representatives of victims. So I think it's fair to say that the document broadly reflects the position of the wider cyber industry. Plus Government.

In October 2022, the White House hosted the second conference of the Counter Ransomware Initiative (CRI) [213], at which international delegates were invited to "*address the growing threat of ransomware and other cyber crime*". The US Government also invited thirteen (mostly US) cyber organisations to attend, in order to "*represent a diverse range of size, regional reach, and focus*", although there doesn't seem to have been room to invite any victims. As noted in the pre-event briefing given by "a senior administration official" [214], the two-day conference was "closed press" (i.e. no external reporters were allowed in to see what was going on), so we have no idea what happened when representatives of the cybersecurity industry were allowed free rein over the cyber lawmakers of 37 countries.

From the Government's point of view, it makes perfect economic sense to support a growing, vibrant cyber industry. However, as noted by Mark Neocleous, the creation of such a cyber-industrial complex then leads to "...*the commodification of security, at the heart of which is a security industry working hand in glove with the state...*" [215, pp9, 153]. It probably depends on your point of view, but for me this is what happens when the objectives of Government (to have a growing and vibrant cybersecurity industry) become aligned with the objectives of the cyber industry (also, to have a growing and vibrant cybersecurity industry).

Neocleous points out that once you've established an industry selling security, the last thing you should do is actually deliver any [215, p154]. Instead, what's needed is a constant stream of insecurities to keep the industry working, because the private sector element of the arrangement is more likely to be interested in profit rather than social change. Consumption of goods then becomes the objective, rather than the provision of protection [215, p155].

Key Recommendations

The RTF report employs a recurring theme of societal impact i.e. ransomware is not just an issue affecting organisations – there are effects on society at large, and something must be done, before there are *"human casualties"* [212, p8].

By framing ransomware as a societal problem, the industry draws Government into the discussion. Of the 48 actions set out in the report, 44 are identified as tasks to be led by Government bodies or agencies. The costs of defending against ransomware therefore move away from being financial decisions for individual organisations (who may be reluctant to spend yet more money) and towards a form of societal investment, funded by Government. An implicit assumption being that the expenditure of tax dollars involves no cost to society i.e. it's not as though that money could have been spent on something else. In case it needs pointing out, this emphasis on cyber funding as a top priority for Government spending came in the middle of a global pandemic, when whole sections of national economies had been "parked".

It's difficult to pick and choose from nearly 50 recommendations, but to indicate the flavour of the report, the task force suggests [212, p52 et seq.]:

- Creating an international coalition.
- Setting up a global network of investigation hubs.
- Taking action against countries that refuse to take part.
- Making ransomware a priority for funding.

The idea seems to be that a whole new anti-ransomware industry should be set up, with its objectives reflected in national and international policies, backed up by legislation, all funded by the taxpayer.

For some time, I was confused about why the cyber industry was so vehemently anti-ransomware. I thought initially that it was simply capitalising on an opportunity for further investment. But that didn't seem quite right, given the rhetoric and the phrasing of the argument. The story is almost certainly apocryphal, but a standard if somewhat dated business story relates to the incoming CEO of Parker pens in (I think) the 1990s [216]. The CEO asked the board to identify their major competitor. Easy, that's Schaeffer pens. Nope. Well then it must be Bic, who makes disposable pens. Nope. Our major competitor is Ronson, the makers of expensive cigarette lighters. We aren't in the market for writing implements. We're in the market for expensive but very personal gifts. We aren't competing against other pen makers, we're competing for a share of the "gift" market. The Parker pens story is generally used as an example of market definition – who are your competitors, and why do people buy your products? It's entirely possible that ransomware writers aren't the enemy of the cyber industry; they're a competitor, working to obtain a share of the same budget. So why wouldn't you do whatever is necessary to make things difficult for a competitor? Up to and including making it illegal to give them any money.

THE BUSINESS CASE

Despite the emphasis on societal impacts, there are no figures that I can find in the report regarding how much the implementation of the recommended measures might cost. Nor are there any estimates (that I could find) regarding the benefits that might accrue from implementing the recommended actions, such as a likely percentage reduction in global impact.

The justification for investment seems to rely instead on figures taken from a cyber industry report [156], itself based on estimated figures for downtime and the ratio of reported vs unreported cases [217]. As has been openly stated by the source of that report [218]:

The intention of this report is not to accurately estimate the costs, which is impossible due to a dearth of data, but rather to shine a light on the massive economic impact of these incidents in the hope that doing so will help governments and law enforcement agencies formulate a proportionate response to the ransomware crisis.

This figure has no basis in reality and we have included it simply to illustrate the enormity of the costs. The actual costs are almost certainly much higher.

I can't reconcile the sense of absolute certainty on the scale of the problem with the statements regarding the unimportance of accuracy and the absence of reliable source data, but that's just a personal view. The underlying argument seems to be that Government money (i.e. taxes) should be fed into the cybersecurity industry to enable it to address ransomware on an appropriate scale, despite the industry having failed to address it effectively to date. At the same time, it's unclear what the benefits might be, and it's equally unclear what level of investment will be required. In fact, it's not even clear that those questions have been asked.

Nevertheless, the industry has pulled Government into the negotiation. So what might be the Government response? Not for me to say. But if it were, I'd probably major on two questions: how much do you want, and what are you going to do with it?

HOW MUCH SHOULD WE SPEND?

In 2019/2020 (i.e. pre-pandemic) the total commissioning budget for the NHS in the United Kingdom was £120Bn [219, p9], or about £328M per day (see also [220]). On the assumption that ransomware is such a pernicious problem that we would be willing to spend the equivalent of 1% of the NHS budget in order to completely eradicate it from the UK (assuming that were possible), then the necessary investment would be about £3.3M per day.

The average ransomware payment in about the same period according to the RTF report was US$312,493 [212, p7], or about £220,000 at the time of writing. Unless I'm misinterpreting the report, in more or less the same period (2020/2021) the UK suffered around 29 confirmed organisation ransomware attacks [212, p15]. On those figures, ransomware payments in the UK average out at (29 x £220,000/365) or about £17,500 per day. That is, the cost of simply living with ransomware comes to about 0.5% (one half of one percent) of the projected cost of dealing with it, assuming a 1% budget in comparison to the NHS.

The daily cost of servicing the UK's national debt, at the time of writing, and purely for comparison, is about £0.3Bn [221]. That's daily.

Let's say instead that we would be prepared to spend as much as we save i.e. ransomware becomes cost-neutral. Let's also assume that the reported figures are actually only one quarter of the actual case numbers, and that the additional costs of clean-up and recovery are about as much again as the direct cost of paying the ransom (these multiples, although seemingly arbitrary, are presented in a number of cyber industry reports). On that basis, we should be looking to spend about 0.04% of what we spend on the NHS. That's about £51M p.a., equivalent to a modest proportion (about 13%) of the yearly budget for the UK National Cyber Security Strategy, 2016/ 2021 [222, p4]. Whether or not you see that as a more appropriate level of spend will of course depend on your position.

WHAT SHOULD WE BE SPENDING IT ON?

The Irish Health Service Executive, courageously, in my opinion, commissioned and subsequently published an independent report into the circumstances of their ransomware attack [223]. The Stack [224] provides a useful summary (these are verbatim quotes from that article):

- The HSE did not have a Chief Information Security Officer (CISO) or a "single responsible owner for cybersecurity at either senior executive or management level to provide leadership and direction".
- It had no documented cyber incident response runbooks or IT recovery plans (apart from documented AD recovery plans) for recovering from a wide-scale ransomware event.
- Under-resourced Information Security Managers were not performing their business as usual role (including a NIST-based cybersecurity review of systems) but were working on evaluating security controls for the COVID-19 vaccination system. Antivirus software triggered numerous alerts after detecting Cobalt Strike activity but these were not escalated (The antivirus server was later encrypted in the attack).
- There was no security monitoring capability that was able to effectively detect, investigate and respond to security alerts across HSE's IT environment or the wider National Healthcare Network (NHN).

- There was a lack of effective patching (updates, bug fixes etc.) across the IT estate and reliance was placed on a single antivirus product that was not monitored or effectively maintained with updates across the estate. (The initial workstation attacked had not had antivirus signatures updated for over a year.)
- Over 30,000 machines were running Windows 7 (out of support since January 2020).
- The initial breach came after an HSE staff member interacted with a malicious Microsoft Office Excel file attached to a phishing email; numerous subsequent alerts were not effectively investigated.

It seems more sensible surely, if the overall aim is to minimise the net cost to society, to spend what might be a relatively small amount fixing the fundamental problems, before paying the cyber industry to create global coordinating bodies and a network of ransomware hubs, and allocating Government funds to sponsor corporate network rebuilds. Perhaps we might see greater societal returns if organisations were persuaded to invest in basic local protective measures, rather than have the industry aiming for the total elimination of ransomware. And perhaps it might be better to invest on the basis of identified outcomes, rather than simply providing funding as an input, and hoping that the cyber industry will deliver.

Don't misunderstand the argument – I'm not a "ransomware denier". I just don't see how we're going to address the problem through the usual processes of threat inflation and profit maximisation. Assuming that is, that the aim is to reduce the impacts felt by victims, rather than to increase the size of the cyber industry. Because to be honest about it, there's not that much profit to be had in implementing cyber hygiene.

REALITIES

Contrary to the implicit assumption in the report, it's not possible to eradicate the problem of ransomware. The ransomware industry has shown a remarkable capacity to innovate and adapt. Therefore in reality, a choice has to be made as to where the impact is best sited and best managed. There has to be a victim. To quote Sales [225] "*[t]he optimal level of cyber-intrusions is not zero, and the optimal level of cyber-security investments is not infinity*". Herley in particular [226] suggests that trying to defend against all attacks leads to "*absurdities*". If the current situation is indeed a battle against ransomware, then it might be better to develop a strategy based on the things that you can control, rather than the things that you would like to control. "Zero incidents" is neither a feasible nor a sensible target.

If the choice really is between regulation and taxation, and we genuinely want to reduce societal impacts, then it might be time to look at the alternative.

TAXATION

The situation on taxation of ransom payments, at least in the UK, seems to be cut and dried, but at the same time, doesn't seem to have been followed through. Advice from HMRC [227] is that corporate payments associated with criminal activities aren't tax-deductible. An example might be slipping a bribe to someone in order to secure a contract. At the end of the financial year, the money you put behind the third washbasin along, can't be offset against tax. Interestingly the position also covers payments to terrorists, although presumably to fall foul of the regulations, you'd need to know that the ransomware had originated from a declared terrorist organisation.

Additional advice from HMRC [228] says that blackmail payments are not tax-deductible, which would seem to cover the case of ransomware, or at least the threats to publish stolen information. However, at the time of writing, there's no definitive statement, and the wider advice seems to be that companies should treat ransomware payments as legitimate business outgoings. Which means that the company's profit figure can be reduced by the amount of the payment, meaning that the basis for calculating Corporation Tax is also brought down. In effect, for large companies in the UK, 25% of the payment is taken off their tax bill for the year. An odd situation, in that on the one hand Government seems to be offering tax breaks for people paying ransoms, and on the other, encouraging people not to pay.

Nieuwesteeg et al. [229] examined the more general situation, and concluded that a direct levy on ransom payments could be expected to increase up-front expenditure on security, while also reducing the attractiveness of paying the ransom. However, their analysis assumed rational behaviour, in that victims would always choose the lowest cost option. As noted in the paper, in reality, other factors would inevitably come into play when making the decision.

The authors examined other options, such as a combination of tax on those who pay, together with a subsidy to support those that do not. The general conclusion from the paper was that a low tax rate, combined with modest subsidies, could be an effective option, if you're looking to reduce the overall impact on society. There was also some support for a high tax/high subsidy option, although when I say "high", I mean very high – the tax bill associated with paying a ransom would be about ten times as large as the ransom itself.

In broad terms, under these schemes, the aim would be to use the tax revenues to fund the subsidies. That of course, only works up to the point where the measure proves effective in preventing companies from paying up, at which point it replaces the societal burden of criminal activities funded through ransomware payments, with the societal burden of helping people with their clean-up costs.

As noted in the paper, very few researchers have examined the taxation route, and the work is therefore useful. But for me, it does rely on an assumption an investment in cyber will reduce the risk of a successful attack. In reality, investing in cyber and hoping for the best is like jiggling the inputs to a complex machine that's not open to analysis, hoping that you'll get the output you want. It's much more sensible to concentrate on effectiveness. What's needed is protection, not expenditure.

A Suggestion

Consider the Ransomware (Payments) Act 2023. Companies in specific industries would be invited to provide the results of an independent review, demonstrating that they had taken basic steps to guard against the likelihood of infection. That would form part of their annual submission to Companies House. The areas to be covered would involve no more than basic hygiene – the list of issues in the Irish Health Service report for example. No need for a multimillion pound globally distributed intrusion detection system. No need for a 200-page internationally agreed security standard.

If you're an eligible organisation, and you pay a ransom but you haven't provided any evidence of having made the necessary preparations, then x% of the ransom payment will be added to your corporate tax bill, even if the ransom was covered by your insurance. That is, you will pay additional tax to offset the impact on society if you get hit when you didn't take steps to protect yourself. If you're a Government-funded entity in that position, then x% of your ransomware payment will be deducted from the following year's funding. Whereas current EU legislation imposes fines even if you *did* take steps to protect yourself, the Ransomware (Payments) Act imposes a social levy on just those organisations that left things to chance.

The s-frame aspect here is that we're targeting externalities, not internal company compliance. The i-frame aspect is that companies might not care too much about cyber, but they do care about tax. EBIT (Earnings Before Interest and Tax) is a significant measure of company performance, but Earnings After Tax determines the level of dividends available for shareholders. And boards have a legal obligation to manage the company for the benefit of shareholders.

Implementation

In the United Kingdom at least, this would require an amendment to the Companies Act, allowing annual returns ("confirmations") to include either a certificate from an approved reviewer, or a formal declaration of exemption. Attempts to hide ransomware payments would (I think) be covered by existing legislation requiring accurate and audited accounts, together with existing legislation on corporate taxation, at least in the private sector. Essentially, under the provisions of the Act, covering up a ransomware payment would amount to tax evasion.

The levy would be assessed and applied by HMRC as part of the corporate tax bill, rather than as a fine imposed by the Information Commissioner's Office. Consequently, any negotiation over whether or not the charge should have been applied will take place *after* the money has been paid to HMRC, and not before, as seems to be the case with the ICO. With a little bit of flexibility (e.g. companies can update their Companies House records whenever they wish, rather than waiting for their annual reminder) then perhaps we might get a secondary effect, in that companies paying a ransom may decide to "update" their records with audited evidence prior to submitting their accounts, because as found by Biancotti [230], falling victim to an attack constitutes a strong incentive to invest, and the prospect of avoiding additional tax would be an extra nudge.

If large numbers of companies are hit in any particular year, then a correspondingly large number of companies should be incentivised to fix their defences before submitting their tax return. That is, the more active the ransomware industry becomes, in theory, the more extensive the defences will become.

Over time, declarations in annual accounts would provide a picture of how effective the Act has been, and should also provide some indication of ransomware activity, which would address the current dearth of baseline numbers. In terms of Government control, the "x%" figure would provide a lever to pull if the current level of taxation isn't proving sufficiently persuasive (and in principle there's no reason why "x" as a percentage needs to stay below 100).

On the face of it, these proposals might seem harsh. But consider the imposition of a congestion charge to reduce air pollution in major cities (and in doing so, to nudge people towards using "greener" transport). Consider the fact that no one expects polluting companies to be compensated for the bottom-line impact of their (in)actions. The rationale underlying the Act is that if, as a commercial organisation, you recklessly rely on *just* insurance, and as a result you risk societal damage, then you will be expected to compensate the wider community for those outcomes. It's not so much about the use or otherwise of insurance, it's more to do with the use of insurance within an appropriate context. The Act would turn insurance into... well... insurance. It's there in the same way as motoring insurance is there in case you hit a patch of ice. Under this arrangement, it still makes sense to have cyber insurance [231]. But it doesn't make sense to *just* have cyber insurance. And as a key point, spending money on cyber security stops being something done for its own sake, and starts being something that can be presented to shareholders as a strategic decision.

THE AUDIT PROCESS

The key factor here relates to the value of the audits. As we've seen, there's very little point in developing another standard setting out a checklist of security documentation to be produced, or a list of specific technical products to be installed. That just paves the way for "compliance professionals". It would be better to have a standard that sets out how the audit process itself should work, rather than what specific security mechanisms should be implemented. That way the standard can describe objectives rather than the details of implementation.

For instance:

- Show me the processes you've got in place to reduce the risk of infection. I don't care if that's a technical solution, or regular training, or phishing your own users. But walk me through it, and show me why it's going to work.
- Show me the processes that increase management ownership of the problem. That could be sending senior management groups on team exercises, or it could be making them formally responsible. Either way, show me the argument that it will work in practice.
- Show me the processes you have in place to manage the impact on your customers. That could be alternative mechanisms keeping the service going, even if it's in a reduced state, it might be protected backups, it might be a smaller backup system that will meet just the needs of critical customer groups. Show me the argument that whatever route you've followed, it's going to work in practice.

In each case the reviewer would be responsible for signing off the effectiveness of the processes, not simply checking that there are some processes in place.

As to who conducts the review, a reasonable starting point might be to take the general industry response to the NIS2 Directive (as in "we'd like to be involved please, rather than simply being told what to do"). There are already a number of appropriate industry bodies e.g. Water UK [232], Energy UK [233], and the Nuclear Industry Association [234]. Government could engage with those bodies and negotiate an agreement on what ransomware protection "looks like" in each of those industries. Under Government oversight, the industry body would then provide certified audit services to any of their members seeking to demonstrate adherence to the standard.

Because this discussion involves only Government and trade bodies (plus maybe consumer organisations), there's no risk of regulatory capture by the cyber industry. It's also an approach which is aligned with the idea of using a "minimum critical coalition" to steer negotiations towards a more socially optimal solution [235]. And if the audit team comes from within the industry body, the expertise develops within the industry. It doesn't walk out of the door when the audit is complete. If you're from Government, and you want to know what the situation is in a specific industry, you know where that knowledge lies – go and speak to the Energy UK audit team.

This could fail at the starting gate – maybe the industry association isn't interested in taking on the responsibility, or they're quite happy to see their members pay additional and potentially unnecessary tax bills. Or it could fail in terms of implementation. But if it does, I'd suggest that there would be one of three reasons:

- The original negotiation didn't arrive at an effective set of measures. Ok, that's no problem, we'll just go round the negotiation again.
- The level of adherence isn't good enough. Ok, well from now on, what was "x%" of the ransomware fine will be "x + δx%". I'm quite old, and I've seen Governments come and go. But I've never seen one that had a problem putting up taxes.
- The tools used to achieve the results aren't working as expected. Again, I'd say that's not a disaster. It means that at least, the companies involved will be in a position to specify what it is they do in fact want from their supplier.

This provides an s-frame solution, it's based on reducing externalities as an outcome, and it's collaborative. It should minimise Government spend, and it doesn't involve the cyber industry. At least, not as decision-makers. This approach also places the management of risk where it is best handled i.e. in the hands of those with domain expertise.

The argument from Ip [236, p199] is that risk managers can be grouped into ecologists or engineers, and that "… *engineers will always be tempted to intervene, trusting in their ability to make it right; ecologists will always fear the unintended consequences of that action*". The book goes on to suggest that micro-level interventions are best left to ecologists, who see the situation in the round, whereas macro level interventions are best undertaken by engineers. In cyber terms, that would mean leaving the implementation of cyber within an organisation to those who can understand the context for its implementation, while the systemic issues would be handled by Government. As Ip notes, local "small scale disasters" are valuable learning points for organisations, whereas having Governments dive down into the detail of what each individual organisation should do in terms of cyber, prevents that from taking place.

DISCUSSION

The Ransomware (Payments) Act isn't put up here as a serious option. But it does provide a mechanism for assessing the likely stakeholder reactions. Because at a simplistic level, there are two possible routes: follow the recommendations from the cyber industry; or go with something more socially focused.

If we implement the industry view as reflected in the RTF report:

- Insurance companies will probably adapt by introducing exclusion clauses and raising premiums. The insurance industry will maintain their margins whatever happens.
- Victims probably won't change their behaviour. At present the insurance companies are covering the impact. If that becomes a mixture of Government funds and insurance payouts, that's ok. Also if you want me to fill out a checklist before I get funding or cover, that's ok too. The one change in behaviour might be that if insurance premiums go up, Government will be expected to provide up-front subsidies.
- The industry itself ought to be happy, as long as Government money keeps coming in. The implied target is the elimination of ransomware, which is practically impossible, so there will always be a problem to address [237].
- Government will be ok, since it's relatively easy to spin the expenditure as a global crusade against people that would otherwise topple "our" way of life. And of course it means a healthy cybersecurity industry.

The more interesting aspect is what happens with the ransomware writers. It's been reported that in the case of the 2021 Colonial pipeline incident, the FBI were able to recover a proportion of the ransom, either because the criminals didn't take enough care in mixing the subsequent Bitcoin transactions, or because they had the misfortune to deposit most of the funds into an account to which the FBI had gained access [238–240]. As noted in a number of reports, having been alerted, it's unlikely that the criminals will make that mistake again. Dudley and Golden [241] report other occasions when cybersecurity companies boasted openly about having found a weakness in ransomware packages (presumably in order to enhance their own reputations), meaning that the criminals were then given an opportunity to close the corresponding loopholes.

So as more and more tools are employed, one possible outcome is a technical arms race between the cyber industry and the criminals, which will require ever more funding from Government. Government will therefore buy into the argument to an ever greater extent, in a continued attempt to meet the promise of reducing ransomware to zero.

Personally, my money's on the criminals. Not because of any inherent difference in skills or ability, but on the basis that if they aren't successful, they don't get paid, which seems to be the opposite of the situation with the cyber industry.

Subject to the obvious caveat that this is a table-top exercise, the bottom line is that this negotiation leads to a relatively stable situation. Most people are happy. However, it's driven primarily by the needs of one party – the cybersecurity industry. It's also based on the view that the problem of ransomware can be completely eradicated if we put enough money into it. And crucially, the discussion doesn't involve the views of the tax-paying public.

The alternative option is to look for a better outcome for society as a whole. The Ransomware (Payments) Act is one possibility.

As with the first route, in this case the insurance companies will adapt. There's nothing about this option that would force them to move away from their current business plan.

Given that potential victims will be required to invest more as a result of Government policy, it's likely that they will want a louder and more central voice – possibly (at least in the UK) through asking for representation via a central body, or through individual trade associations. And actually, strengthening their role in the discussion might not be a bad idea. The cyber security industry will of course be unhappy, with no Government funding. Government itself is also likely to be unhappy, since the cyber industry will be negatively affected.

But again, the most interesting question is what happens with the ransomware authors. Assuming that the Act's aim of achieving more effective hygiene is successful, and assuming that the Act will apply mostly to large and/or critical companies, then the extortionists will need to adapt. The most obvious solution (to me, but then I don't write ransomware) is to attack on a coordinated front, possibly by forcing a group of larger companies to coalesce into one "super-victim", or by attacking one critical supplier to a large number of companies, forcing those larger companies to assist with meeting the ransom.

That might sound bad. But consider this – it reduces the attack surface, it concentrates the attacks into a smaller number of organisations, and it permits the application of a focused response, so that expenditure only happens when it's needed. It may still be a battle, but at least the battleground has been chosen by the defender.

BACK IN THE REAL WORLD

In practice, the Ransomware (Payments) Act obviously won't make it onto the statute books. The art of government involves politics, which is not always about making socially optimal decisions. The US Government, for example, has already adopted some of the thinking behind the RTF approach, in that their view of security seems to be more about going after the bad guys rather than protecting against them [238, 242, 243].

In the UK, it's been pointed out that the cyber industry is growing at about 7% p.a. and that at the time of writing, it's contributing £4Bn to the UK's economy, creating an increasing number of jobs, and attracting record levels of investment [244]. So to be frank, there's no incentive to mess with the model. In fact, to be perfectly logical about it, there's no economic incentive to find an answer to ransomware, because that will only lead to reduced levels of investment in the cyber industry. Shifting the emphasis away from growing the cyber industry and towards increasing the levels of protection for the end user, simply isn't economically attractive. And critically, it doesn't meet the agenda of the two loudest voices in the room, so it's not going to lead to closure.

As we saw in the earlier examples, if you want a change of direction in the negotiation, there needs to be a change in position regarding one of the participants, or alternatively, a new participant needs to enter the picture. So as things stand, unless one of the parties (e.g. Government) speaks out for the tax-paying public, or unless a new party enters the negotiation to strengthen the voice of the victims, then the views of those sectors won't be part of the discussion, and the current situation will continue. Essentially, at the moment, although there's no trace of a supporting business case, the voice of the cybersecurity industry prevails, because of the social dynamics of the situation. The good news, if there is any, is that by viewing security as a negotiation and as a social phenomenon, we can at least understand why.

NOTES

1 At the time of writing, in pre-launch.
2 I've left this reference in, although you probably won't be able to find the source document anywhere – it seems to have disappeared. It was an article asking whether or not the ransomware threat was being exaggerated.
3 This reference provides a link to Atlanta's ISO27001 precertification audit report. If you do follow the link, be aware that at the time of writing, perhaps ironically given the content, their site uses an incorrect certificate. There's an http version of the URL that does work, if you're content to use it.

REFERENCES

1. GDPR_EU, Complete guide to GDPR compliance. 2020 [Accessed 10 April 2021]; Available from: https://gdpr.eu
2. ISO, ISO/IEC 27701:2019. 2019 [Accessed 10 April 2021]; Available from: www.iso.org/standard/71670.html
3. BSI, Understanding the role of ISO/IEC 27701. 2021 [Accessed 10 April 2021]; Available from: www.bsigroup.com/globalassets/localfiles/en-gb/isoiec-27701-privacy-information-management/resources/privacy-regulation-white-paper.pdf
4. Smith, H.J., T. Dinev, and H. Xu, Information privacy research: An interdisciplinary review. *MIS Quarterly*, 2011. 35(4): p. 989–1015.
5. Solove, D.J., Conceptualizing privacy. *California Law Review*, 2002. 90: p. 1087.
6. Solove, D.J., A taxonomy of privacy. *University of Pennsylvania Law Review*, 2005. 154: p. 477.
7. Acquisti, A., C. Taylor, and L. Wagman, The economics of privacy. *Journal of Economic Literature*, 2016. 54(2): p. 442–492.
8. Pavlou, P.A., State of the information privacy literature: Where are we now and where should we go? *MIS Quarterly*, 2011. 35(4): p. 977–988.
9. Hamilton, F., Employers won't be told of minor crimes. 2020 [Accessed 10 April 2021]; Available from: www.thetimes.co.uk/article/employers-wont-be-told-of-minor-crimes-d3whm6z3s

10. Posner, R.A., The economics of privacy. *The American Economic Review*, 1981. 71(2): p. 405–409.

11. Solove, D.J., I've got nothing to hide and other misunderstandings of privacy. *San Diego Law Review*, 2007. 44: p. 745.

12. Leman-Langlois, S., Privacy as currency: Crime, information and control in cyberspace. In *Technocrime: Technology, crime and social control*, 2008: Willan, p. 112–138.

13. Warren, S.D. and L.D. Brandeis, The right to privacy. *Harvard Law Review*, 1890, 4(5): p. 172–183.

14. Martin, K.D. and P.E. Murphy, The role of data privacy in marketing. *Journal of the Academy of Marketing Science*, 2017. 45(2): p. 135–155.

15. Westin, A.F., Privacy and freedom. *Washington and Lee Law Review*, 1968. 25(1): p. 166.

16. Woodruff, A., et al., Would a privacy fundamentalist sell their DNA for $1000... if nothing bad happened as a result? The Westin categories, behavioral intentions, and consequences. In Symposium on Usable Privacy an d Security (SOUPS). 2014.

17. Kumaraguru, P. and L.F. Cranor, *Privacy indexes: A survey of Westin's studies*. 2005: Carnegie Mellon University, School of Computer Science.

18. Hoofnagle, C.J. and J.M. Urban, Alan Westin's privacy homo economicus. *Wake Forest Law Review*, 2014. 49: p. 261.

19. Austin, L.M., Re-reading Westin. *Theoretical Inquiries in Law*, 2019. 20(1): p. 53–81.

20. van de Waerdt, P.J., Information asymmetries: Recognizing the limits of the GDPR on the data-driven market. *Computer Law & Security Review*, 2020. 38: p. 105436.

21. Langer, E.J., The illusion of control. *Journal of Personality and Social Psychology*, 1975. 32(2): p. 311.

22. Stutzman, F.D., R. Gross, and A. Acquisti, Silent listeners: The evolution of privacy and disclosure on Facebook. *Journal of Privacy and Confidentiality*, 2013. 4(2): p. 2.

23. Tucker, C.E., Social networks, personalized advertising, and privacy controls. *Journal of Marketing Research*, 2014. 51(5): p. 546–562.

24. Martin, K.D., A. Borah, and R.W. Palmatier, Data privacy: Effects on customer and firm performance. *Journal of Marketing*, 2017. 81(1): p. 36–58.

25. Brandimarte, L., A. Acquisti, and G. Loewenstein, Misplaced confidences: Privacy and the control paradox. *Social Psychological and Personality Science*, 2013. 4(3): p. 340–347.

26. Acquisti, A., et al., Nudges for privacy and security: Understanding and assisting users' choices online. *ACM Computing Surveys (CSUR)*, 2017. 50(3): p. 1–41.

27. Edwards, L. and M. Veale, Slave to the algorithm: Why a right to an explanation is probably not the remedy you are looking for. *Duke Law and Technology Review*, 2017. 16: p. 18.

28. Marwick, A.E. and D. Boyd, I tweet honestly, I tweet passionately: Twitter users, context collapse, and the imagined audience. *New Media & Society*, 2011. 13(1): p. 114–133.

29. John, L.K., A. Acquisti, and G. Loewenstein, Strangers on a plane: Context-dependent willingness to divulge sensitive information. *Journal of Consumer Research*, 2011. 37(5): p. 858–873.

30. Samat, S. and A. Acquisti, Format vs. content: The impact of risk and presentation on disclosure decisions. In Thirteenth Symposium on Usable Privacy and Security (SOUPS 2017). 2017.

31. Nissenbaum, H., Privacy as contextual integrity. *Washington Law Review*, 2004. 79: p. 119.

32. Acquisti, A., L.K. John, and G. Loewenstein, The impact of relative standards on the propensity to disclose. *Journal of Marketing Research*, 2012. 49(2): p. 160–174.

33. Acquisti, A., L.K. John, and G. Loewenstein, What is privacy worth? *The Journal of Legal Studies*, 2013. 42(2): p. 249–274.
34. Smith, H.J., S.J. Milberg, and S.J. Burke, Information privacy: Measuring individuals' concerns about organizational practices. *MIS Quarterly*, 1996: p. 167–196.
35. Stewart, K.A. and A.H. Segars, An empirical examination of the concern for information privacy instrument. *Information Systems Research*, 2002. 13(1): p. 36–49.
36. Malhotra, N.K., S.S. Kim, and J. Agarwal, Internet users' information privacy concerns (IUIPC): The construct, the scale, and a causal model. *Information Systems Research*, 2004. 15(4): p. 336–355.
37. Xu, H., et al., Measuring mobile users' concerns for information privacy. 2012. 33rd International Conference on Information Systems.
38. Alashoor, T., G. Fox, and H. Jeff Smith, The priming effect of prominent is privacy concerns scales on disclosure outcomes: An empirical examination. In Pre-ICIS Workshop on Information Security and Privacy. 2017.
39. Wang, Y., et al., "I regretted the minute I pressed share" a qualitative study of regrets on Facebook. In Proceedings of the Seventh Symposium on Usable Privacy and Security. 2011.
40. Wang, Y., et al., A field trial of privacy nudges for Facebook. In Proceedings of the SIGCHI Conference on Human Factors in Computing Systems. 2014.
41. Adjerid, I., et al., Sleights of privacy: Framing, disclosures, and the limits of transparency. In Proceedings of the Ninth Symposium on Usable Privacy and Security. 2013.
42. Acquisti, A., I. Adjerid, and L. Brandimarte, *Gone in 15 seconds: The limits of privacy transparency and control. IEEE Security & Privacy*, 2013. 11(4): p. 72–74.
43. Almuhimedi, H., et al., Your location has been shared 5,398 times! A field study on mobile app privacy nudging. In Proceedings of the 33rd Annual ACM Conference on Human Factors in Computing Systems. 2015.
44. Ronson, J., How one stupid tweet blew up Justine Sacco's life. 2015 [Accessed 10 April 2021]; Available from: www.nytimes.com/2015/02/15/magazine/how-one-stupid-tweet-ruined-justine-saccos-life.html
45. Ames, J., Woman who claimed whiplash caught out climbing Sydney Harbour Bridge. 2022 [Accessed 9 November 2022]; Available from: www.thetimes.co.uk/article/woman-who-claimed-whiplash-caught-out-climbing-sydney-harbour-bridge-87xpd350t
46. Hudgins, V., What ever happened to the proposed GDPR fines against Marriott, British Airways? 2020 [Accessed 10 April 2021]; Available from: www.law.com/legaltechnews/2020/07/27/what-ever-happened-to-the-proposed-gdpr-fines-against-marriott-british-airways/?slreturn=20201101112906
47. Edwards, C., British Airways fined £20m over GDPR breach. 2020 [Accessed 10 April 2021]; Available from: www.pinsentmasons.com/out-law/news/british-airways-fined-20m-over-gdpr-breach
48. Prinsley, M.A., et al., British Airways ultimately fined £20m for personal data breach by the UK ICO under the GDPR (reduced from £183.39m). 2020 [Accessed 16 January 2023]; Available from: www.mayerbrown.com/en/perspectives-events/publications/2020/10/british-airways-ultimately-fined-20m-for-personal-data-breach-by-the-uk-ico-under-the-gdpr
49. BBC, Marriott Hotels fined £18.4m for data breach that hit millions. 2020 [Accessed 10 April 2021]; Available from: www.bbc.co.uk/news/technology-54748843
50. Baines, J., Further delay in proposed ICO GDPR fine for Marriott. 2020 [Accessed 10 April 2021]; Available from: www.mishcon.com/news/further-delay-in-proposed-ico-gdpr-fine-for-marriott

51. BBC, Shein owner Zoetop fined $1.9m over data breach response. 2022 [Accessed 19 October 2022]; Available from: www.bbc.co.uk/news/technology-63255661

52. Liao, R., Shein owner fined $1.9M for failing to notify 39M users of data breach. 2022 [Accessed 19 October 2022]; Available from: https://techcrunch.com/2022/10/13/shein-zoetop-fined-1-9m-data-breachPF

53. Schwartz, M.J., Not so fast: Retailer Shein fined $1.9M for breach cover-up. 2022 [Accessed 19 October 2022]; Available from: www.bankinfosecurity.com/so-fast-retailer-shein-fined-19m-for-breach-coverup-a-20263

54. TFL, Shein owner to pay $1.9 million to settle probe over 2018 data breach. 2022 [Accessed 19 October 2022]; Available from: www.thefashionlaw.com/shein-owner-to-pay-1-9-million-to-settle-probe-after-failing-to-remedy-data-breach

55. Clark, M., Parent company of fast-fashion brand Shein to pay New York state $1.9m for data breach. 2022 [Accessed 19 October 2022]; Available from: www.independent.co.uk/life-style/fashion/shein-fined-returns-data-breach-b2201885.html

56. Mascellino, A., Shein holding company fined $1.9m for not disclosing data breach. 2022 [Accessed 19 October 2022]; Available from: www.infosecurity-magazine.com/news/zoetop-fined-dollar19m-for-data

57. Curry, D., Shein revenue and usage statistics (2023). 2023 [Accessed 2 June 2023]; Available from: www.businessofapps.com/data/shein-statistics

58. Liao, R., *Shein said to be raising $1 billion at $100 billion valuation.* 2022 [Accessed 19 October 2022]; Available from: https://techcrunch.com/2022/04/04/shein-said-to-be-raising-1-billion-at-100-billion-valuation

59. Curry, D., Shein revenue and usage statistics (2022). 2022 [Accessed 19 October 2022]; Available from: www.businessofapps.com/data/shein-statistics

60. BBC, Uber pays $148m over data breach cover-up. 2018 [Accessed 10 April 2021]; Available from: www.bbc.co.uk/news/technology-45666280

61. CNBC, Uber's growth slowed dramatically in 2018. 2019 [Accessed 10 April 2021]; Available from: www.cnbc.com/2019/02/15/uber-2018-financial-results.html

62. Roman, J., Chase breach affects 76 million households. 2014 [Accessed 10 April 2021]; Available from: www.bankinfosecurity.com/chase-breach-affects-76-million-households-a-7395

63. Scroxton, A., Department for Education escapes £10m fine over data misuse. 2022 [Accessed 9 November 2022]; Available from: www.computerweekly.com/news/252526975/Department-for-Education-escapes-10m-fine-over-data-misuse

64. ICO, Department for Education warned after gambling companies benefit from learning records database. 2022 [Accessed 9 November 2022]; Available from: https://ico.org.uk/about-the-ico/media-centre/news-and-blogs/2022/11/department-for-education-warned-after-gambling-companies-benefit-from-learning-records-database

65. Gold, J., Instagram faces $402 million fine for alleged mishandling of children's data. 2022 [Accessed 21 January 2023]; Available from: www.csoonline.com/article/3672212/instagram-faces-402-million-fine-for-alleged-mishandling-of-childrens-data.html

66. Cazalet, H., ICO fines collection crisis – 42% of fines remain unpaid. 2020 [Accessed 21 May 2021]; Available from: https://thesmsworks.co.uk/ico-fines-collection-crisis

67. Muncaster, P., ICO still failing to collect fines from unlawful companies. 2020 [Accessed 21 May 2021]; Available from: www.infosecurity-magazine.com/news/ico-still-failing-collect-fines

68. Muncaster, P., ICO issued over £42 million in fines last year. 2020 [Accessed 21 May 2021]; Available from: www.infosecurity-magazine.com/news/ico-issued-over-42-million-in

69. Watson, P., Fines of £42 million issued to UK companies in breach of data laws. 2021 [Accessed 21 May 2021]; Available from: https://futurescot.com/fines-of-42-million-issued-to-uk-companies-in-breach-of-data-laws

70. FCA, JPMorgan Chase Bank N.A. fined £137,610,000 for serious failings relating to its Chief Investment Office's "London Whale" trades. 2013 [Accessed 10 April 2021]; Available from: www.fca.org.uk/news/press-releases/jpmorgan-chase-bank-na-fined-£137610000-serious-failings-relating-its-chief

71. Finextra, JPMorgan Chase fined $920 million for market manipulation. 2020 [Accessed 10 April 2021]; Available from: www.finextra.com/pressarticle/84292/jpmorgan-chase-fined-920-million-for-market-manipulation

72. Economist, JPMorgan Chase faces a fine of $920m for market manipulation. 2020 [Accessed 10 April 2021]; Available from: www.economist.com/finance-and-econom ics/2020/10/03/jpmorgan-chase-faces-a-fine-of-920m-for-market-manipulation

73. DSNews, How much have banks been fined since the crisis? 2018 [Accessed 10 April 2021]; Available from: https://dsnews.com/daily-dose/02-21-2018/much-banks-fined-since-crisis

74. MarketWatch, Here's the staggering amount banks have been fined since the financial crisis. 2018 [Accessed 10 April 2021]; Available from: www.marketwatch.com/story/banks-have-been-fined-a-staggering-243-billion-since-the-financial-crisis-2018-02-20

75. VanityFair, Jamie Dimon's $13 billion secret – Revealed. 2017 [Accessed 10 April 2021]; Available from: www.vanityfair.com/news/2017/09/jamie-dimon-billion-dollar-secret-jp-morgan

76. Kitten, T., JPMorgan Chase fines exceed $2 billion. 2014 [Accessed 10 April 2021]; Available from: www.bankinfosecurity.com/chase-a-6356

77. McGlasson, L., JP Morgan Securities fined $49 million. 2010 [Accessed 10 April 2021]; Available from: www.bankinfosecurity.com/jp-morgan-securities-fined-49-million-a-2599

78. ICO, We buy any car limited. 2021 [Accessed 9 November 2022]; Available from: https://ico.org.uk/action-weve-taken/enforcement/we-buy-any-car-limited

79. ICO, SportsDirect.com Retail Ltd. 2021 [Accessed 9 November 2022]; Available from: https://ico.org.uk/action-weve-taken/enforcement/sportsdirectcom-retail-ltd

80. ICO, Saga Services Limited. 2021 [Accessed 9 November 2022]; Available from: https://ico.org.uk/action-weve-taken/enforcement/saga-services-limited-mpn

81. Chazal, E.d., 20 biggest GDPR fines of 2018, 2019, 2020, 2021 & 2022. 2022 [Accessed 9 November 2022]; Available from: www.skillcast.com/blog/20-bigg est-gdpr-fines

82. Tessian, 30 biggest GDPR fines so far (2020, 2021, 2022). 2022 [Accessed 9 November 2022]; Available from: www.tessian.com/blog/biggest-gdpr-fines-2020

83. Hill, M., The 12 biggest data breach fines, penalties, and settlements so far. 2022 [Accessed 9 November 2022]; Available from: www.csoonline.com/article/3410278/the-biggest-data-breach-fines-penalties-and-settlements-so-far.html

84. Burgess, M., Why Amazon's £636m GDPR fine really matters. 2021 [Accessed 9 November 2022]; Available from: www.wired.co.uk/article/amazon-gdpr-fine

85. Woods, D.W. and R. Böhme, The commodification of consent. In 19th Workshop on the Economics of Information Security (WEIS 2020). 2020.

86. Hils, M., D.W. Woods, and R. Böhme, Measuring the emergence of consent manage-ment on the web. In Proceedings of the ACM Internet Measurement Conference. 2020.

87. Nouwens, M., et al., Dark patterns after the GDPR: Scraping consent pop-ups and demonstrating their influence. In Proceedings of the 2020 CHI Conference on Human Factors in Computing Systems. 2020.

88. Radet, F., Deceived by Design. How tech companies use dark patterns to discourage us from exercising our rights to privacy. 2018 [Accessed 10 April 2021]; Available from: https://fil.forbrukerradet.no/wp-content/uploads/2018/06/2018-06-27-deceived-by-design-final.pdf

89. Utz, C., et al. (Un) informed consent: Studying GDPR consent notices in the field. In Proceedings of the 2019 ACM SIGSAC Conference on Computer and Communications Security. 2019.

90. Matte, C., N. Bielova, and C. Santos, Do cookie banners respect my choice?: Measuring legal compliance of banners from IAB Europe's transparency and consent framework. In 2020 IEEE Symposium on Security and Privacy (SP). 2020. IEEE.

91. Sanchez-Rola, I., et al., Can I opt out yet? GDPR and the global illusion of cookie control. In Proceedings of the 2019 ACM Asia Conference on Computer and Communications Security. 2019.

92. Lynn, M., Why the EU should fear an exodus of Big Tech companies. 2022 [Accessed 21 January 2023]; Available from: https://moneyweek.com/investments/stocks-and-shares/tech-stocks/604461/why-the-eu-should-fear-an-exodus-of-big-tech

93. Horobin, W. and Z. Schneeweiss, We're fine without Facebook (FB), German and French Ministers say. 2022 [Accessed 21 January 2023]; Available from: www.bloomberg.com/news/articles/2022-02-07/we-re-fine-without-facebook-german-and-french-ministers-say

94. Rook, C., EU Digital Markets Act sets stage for future claims against Big Tech. 2022 [Accessed 21 January 2023]; Available from: www.burfordcapital.com/insights/insights-container/eu-digital-markets-act

95. EU, The Digital Services Act package. 2022 [Accessed 21 January 2023]; Available from: https://digital-strategy.ec.europa.eu/en/policies/digital-services-act-package

96. AP, Big Tech faces "Major" EU law on hate speech, disinformation. 2022 [Accessed 21 January 2023]; Available from: https://apnews.com/article/technology-business-europe-media-social-c81d310c79be1b86fbf141977b68ab1e

97. Goujard, C., German Facebook ruling boosts EU push for stricter content moderation. 2021 [Accessed 21 January 2023]; Available from: www.politico.eu/article/german-court-tells-facebook-to-reinstate-removed-posts

98. Busvine, D., Top German court strikes down Facebook rules on hate speech. 2022 [Accessed 21 January 2023]; Available from: www.reuters.com/technology/top-german-court-strikes-down-facebook-rules-hate-speech-2021-07-29

99. Obar, J.A. and A. Oeldorf-Hirsch, The biggest lie on the internet: Ignoring the privacy policies and terms of service policies of social networking services. *Information, Communication & Society*, 2020. 23(1): p. 128–147.

100. Martin, K., Privacy notices as tabula rasa: An empirical investigation into how complying with a privacy notice is related to meeting privacy expectations online. *Journal of Public Policy & Marketing*, 2015. 34(2): p. 210–227.

101. Bakos, Y., F. Marotta-Wurgler, and D.R. Trossen, Does anyone read the fine print? Consumer attention to standard-form contracts. *Journal of Legal Studies*, 2014. 43(1): p. 1–35.

102. Vail, M.W., J.B. Earp, and A.I. Antón, An empirical study of consumer perceptions and comprehension of web site privacy policies. *IEEE Transactions on Engineering Management*, 2008. 55(3): p. 442–454.

103. Reidenberg, J.R., et al., Disagreeable privacy policies: Mismatches between meaning and users' understanding. *Berkeley Technology Law Journal*, 2015. 30: p. 39.

104. Hoofnagle, C.J. and J. King, What Californians understand about privacy offline. Available at SSRN 1133075, 2008.

105. Linden, T., et al., The privacy policy landscape after the GDPR. *Proceedings on Privacy Enhancing Technologies*, 2020. 2020(1): p. 47–64.

106. Hoffmann, C.P., C. Lutz, and G. Ranzini, Privacy cynicism: A new approach to the privacy paradox. *Cyberpsychology: Journal of Psychosocial Research on Cyberspace*, 2016. 10(4): Article 7.

107. Kesan, J.P., C.M. Hayes, and M.N. Bashir, Information privacy and data control in cloud computing: Consumers, privacy preferences, and market efficiency. *Washington and Lee Law Review*, 2013. 70: p. 341.

108. Degeling, M., et al., We value your privacy... now take some cookies: Measuring the GDPR's impact on web privacy. arXiv preprint arXiv:1808.05096, 2018.

109. Warner, R., Notice and choice must go: The collective control alternative. *SMU Science & Technology Law Review*, 2020. 23: p. 173.

110. Waldman, A.E., Privacy Law's False Promise. *Washington University Law Review*, 2019. 97: p. 773.

111. LQDN, La Quadrature du Net. 2023 [Accessed 21 January 2023]; Available from: www.laquadrature.net/en

112. LQDN, Amazon fined 746 million Euros following our collective legal action. 2021 [Accessed 21 January 2023]; Available from: www.laquadrature.net/en/2021/07/30/amazon-fined-746-million-euros-following-our-collective-legal-action

113. Moody, G., The tiny nation of Luxembourg slaps Amazon with the biggest GDPR fine yet: Nearly $900 million. 2021 [Accessed 21 January 2023]; Available from:www.privateinternetaccess.com/blog/the-tiny-nation-of-luxembourg-slaps-amazon-with-the-biggest-gdpr-fine-yet-nearly-900-million

114. Curry, D., Amazon statistics (2023). 2023 [Accessed 21 January 2023]; Available from: www.businessofapps.com/data/amazon-statistics

115. noyb, noyb win: Personalized Ads on Facebook, Instagram and WhatsApp declared illegal. 2022 [Accessed 21 January 2023]; Available from: https://noyb.eu/en/noyb-win-personalized-ads-facebook-instagram-and-whatsapp-declared-illegal

116. nyob, Meta advertising ban – Decision published. 2023 [Accessed 21 January 2023]; Available from: https://noyb.eu/en/meta-advertising-ban-decision-published

117. noyb, *noyb FAQ's* [Accessed 21 January 2023]; Available from: https://noyb.eu/en/faqs

118. nyob, Irish Data Protection Authority gives € 3.97 billion present to Meta. 2023 [Accessed 21 January 2023].

119. LaCasse, A., Irish DPC fines WhatsApp 5.5M euros, fissure with EDPB continues. 2023 [Accessed 21 January 2023]; Available from: https://iapp.org/news/a/irish-dpcs-whatsapp-fine-deepens-fissure-with-edpb-over-enforcement-jurisdictions

120. Bryant, J., Irish DPC, EDPB meta decisions raise complex, fundamental questions. 2023 [Accessed 21 January 2023]; Available from: https://iapp.org/news/a/irelands-meta-decisions-raise-complex-fundamental-questions

121. noyb, BREAKING: Meta prohibited from use of personal data for advertising. 2023 [Accessed 21 January 2023]; Available from: https://noyb.eu/en/breaking-meta-prohibited-use-personal-data-advertising

122. Nippert-Eng, C.E., *Islands of privacy*. 2010: University of Chicago Press.

123. Moon, Y., Intimate exchanges: Using computers to elicit self-disclosure from consumers. *Journal of consumer research*, 2000. 26(4): p. 323–339.

124. Bibb, S. and J. Kourdi, *Trust matters: For organisational and personal success*. 2004: Springer.

125. White, T.B., et al., Getting too personal: Reactance to highly personalized email solicitations. *Marketing Letters*, 2008. 19(1): p. 39–50.

126. Umar, P., et al., Self-disclosure on Twitter during the COVID-19 pandemic: A network perspective. In Joint European Conference on Machine Learning and Knowledge Discovery in Databases. 2021. Springer.

127. Matthes, J., et al., Longitudinal relationships among fear of COVID-19, smartphone online self-disclosure, happiness, and psychological well-being: Survey study. *Journal of Medical Internet Research*, 2021. 23(9): p. e28700.

128. Barocas, S. and K. Levy, Privacy dependencies. *Washington Law Review*, 2020. 95: p. 555.

129. Freeman, L., Phone apps should come with a health warning. 2022 [Accessed 10 November 2022]; Available from: www.thetimes.co.uk/article/phone-apps-should-come-with-a-health-warning-h5bwpz87t

130. Burnett, D., *Happy brain: Where happiness comes from, and why*. 2018: WW Norton & Company.

131. Acquisti, A., L. Brandimarte, and G. Loewenstein, Secrets and likes: The drive for privacy and the difficulty of achieving it in the digital age. *Journal of Consumer Psychology*, 2020. 30(4): p. 736–758.

132. Tamir, D.I. and J.P. Mitchell, Disclosing information about the self is intrinsically rewarding. *Proceedings of the National Academy of Sciences*, 2012. 109(21): p. 8038–8043.

133. Fine, G.A. and L. Holyfield, Secrecy, trust, and dangerous leisure: Generating group cohesion in voluntary organizations. *Social Psychology Quarterly*, 1996. 59(11): p. 22–38.

134. Kramer, R.M., *Organizational trust: A reader*. 2006: Oxford University Press on Demand.

135. Calic, D., et al., Self-disclosing on Facebook can be Risky: Examining the role of trust and social capital. In HAISA. 2018.

136. Waldman, A.E., *Privacy as trust: Information privacy for an information age*. 2018: Cambridge University Press.

137. Acquisti, A., L. Brandimarte, and G. Loewenstein, Privacy and human behavior in the age of information. *Science*, 2015. 347(6221): p. 509–514.

138. Profila, Unlock your data superpower. 2023 [Accessed 6 June 2023]; Available from: https://profila.com

139. Callejo, P., et al., Zero Knowledge Advertising: A new era of privacy-preserving AdTech solutions. 2021 [Accessed 15 October 2023]; Available from: https://26847695.fs1.hubspotusercontent-eu1.net/hubfs/26847695/Web3/Profila_Zero_Knowledge_Advertising.pdf

140. Profila, Profila zero knowledge token crypto-asset whitepaper. 2022 [Accessed 6 June 2023]; Available from: https://profila.com

141. Whitaker, R., *The end of privacy: How total surveillance is becoming a reality*. 2000: New Press.

142. Hunter, T., These companies will pay you for your data. Is it a good deal? 2023 [Accessed 2 June 2023]; Available from: www.washingtonpost.com/technology/2023/02/06/consumers-paid-money-data

143. Tsukayama, H., Why getting paid for your data is a bad deal. 2020 [Accessed 2 June 2023]; Available from: www.eff.org/deeplinks/2020/10/why-getting-paid-your-data-bad-deal

144. Stern, M., Will Amazon's customers go for its pay-for-data scheme? 2022 [Accessed 2 June 2023]; Available from: https://retailwire.com/discussion/will-amazons-customers-go-for-its-pay-for-data-scheme

145. Manthorpe, R., What is *o*pen *b*anking and PSD2? WIRED explains. 2018 [Accessed 10 November 2022]; Available from: www.wired.co.uk/article/open-banking-cma-psd2-explained

146. Cavaglieri, C., Open banking: Sharing your financial data. 2022 [Accessed 10 November 2022]; Available from: www.which.co.uk/money/banking/switching-your-bank/open-banking-sharing-your-financial-data-anscq4g8p62h

147. Dourish, P. and K. Anderson, Collective information practice: Exploring privacy and security as social and cultural phenomena. *Human-Computer Interaction*, 2006. 21(3): p. 319–342.

148. Abrams, L., Conti ransomware gives HSE Ireland free *D*ecryptor, still selling data. 2021 [Accessed 1 June 2021]; Available from: www.bleepingcomputer.com/news/security/conti-ransomware-gives-hse-ireland-free-decryptor-still-selling-data

149. Dawber, A., Blackmailing hackers start to leak Washington police files. 2021 [Accessed 1 June 2021]; Available from: www.thetimes.co.uk/article/blackmailing-hackers-leak-washington-police-department-files-hq2st5pg5

150. Cimpanu, C., Ransomware gangs are now cold-calling victims if they restore from backups without paying. 2020 [Accessed 1 June 2021]; Available from: www.zdnet.com/article/ransomware-gangs-are-now-cold-calling-victims-if-they-restore-from-backups-without-paying

151. Abrams, L., Ransomware gang urges victims' customers to demand a ransom payment. 2021 [Accessed 1 June 2021]; Available from: www.bleepingcomputer.com/news/security/ransomware-gang-urges-victims-customers-to-demand-a-ransom-payment

152. Sophos, The *s*tate of Ransomware 2020. 2020 [Accessed 1 June 2021]; Available from: www.sophos.com/en-us/medialibrary/Gated-Assets/white-papers/sophos-the-state-of-ransomware-2020-wp.pdf

153. Coveware, Ransomware *c*osts *d*ouble in Q4 as Ryuk, Sodinokibi Proliferate. 2020 [Accessed 1 June 2021]; Available from: www.coveware.com/blog/2020/1/22/ransomware-costs-double-in-q4-as-ryuk-sodinokibi-proliferate

154. Sophos, The *s*tate of Ransomware 2021. 2021 [Accessed 19 June 2021]; Available from: https://news.sophos.com/en-us/2021/04/27/the-state-of-ransomware-2021

155. Fitzpatrick, D. and D. Griffin, Cyber-extortion losses skyrocket, says FBI. 2016 [Accessed 1 June 2021]; Available from: https://money.cnn.com/2016/04/15/technology/ransomware-cyber-security/index.html

156. Emsisoft, The *s*tate of Ransomware in the US: Report and *s*tatistics 2019. 2019 [Accessed 1 June 2021]; Available from: https://blog.emsisoft.com/en/34822/the-state-of-ransomware-in-the-us-report-and-statistics-2019

157. Datto, American *s*mall *b*usinesses *l*ose an *e*stimated \$75 *b*illion a *y*ear to *r*ansomware, *n*ew Datto *s*urvey *f*inds. 2016 [Accessed 1 June 2021]; Available from: www.datto.com/news/american-small-businesses-lose-an-estimated-75-billion-a-year-to-ransomware

158. McMillan, R., D. Volz, and T.D. Hobbs, Beyond *c*olonial *p*ipeline, Ransomware *c*yberattacks *a*re a *g*rowing *t*hreat. 2021 [Accessed 1 June 2021]; Available from: www.wsj.com/articles/colonial-pipeline-hack-shows-ransomware-emergence-as-industrial-scale-threat-11620749675

159. FBI, 2019 Internet Crime Report. 2019 [Accessed 1 June 2021]; Available from: www.ic3.gov/Media/PDF/AnnualReport/2019_IC3Report.pdf

160. Verizon, 2023 Data Breach Investigations Report. 2023 [Accessed 6 June 2023]; Available from: www.verizon.com/business/en-gb/resources/reports/dbir

161. FBI, Internet Crime Complaint Center (IC3) [Accessed 6 June 2023]; Available from: www.ic3.gov

162. Lemos, R., Recent ransomware attacks: Is it an epidemic or overblown? 2021 [Accessed 1 June 2021]; Available from: https://searchsecurity.techtarget.com/feature/ Recent-ransomware-attacks-Is-it-an-epidemic-or-overblown

163. Treasury, FinCEN analysis reveals ransomware reporting in BSA filings increased significantly during the second half of 2021. 2022 [Accessed 10 November 2022]; Available from: www.fincen.gov/news/news-releases/fincen-analysis-reveals-ran somware-reporting-bsa-filings-increased-significantly

164. Gillum, J., US banks reported $1 billion in 2021 ransomware payments. 2022 [Accessed 10 November 2022]; Available from: www.bloomberg.com/news/articles/ 2022-11-01/us-banks-spent-1-billion-on-ransomware-payments-in-2021-treasury-says?leadSource=uverify%20wall

165. FTC, New data shows FTC received 2.8 million fraud reports from consumers in 2021. 2022 [Accessed 21 January 2023]; Available from: www.ftc.gov/news-events/ news/press-releases/2022/02/new-data-shows-ftc-received-28-million-fraud-reports-consumers-2021-0

166. PAC, PAC: DWP excuses for "unprecedented and unacceptable" levels of benefit fraud and error don't stand up. 2022 [Accessed 10 November 2022]; Available from: https://committees.parliament.uk/committee/127/public-accounts-committee/ news/174208/pac-dwp-excuses-for-unprecedented-and-unacceptable-levels-of-bene fit-fraud-and-error-dont-stand-up

167. McDougall, M., UK tax agency failing to collect billions in revenue, MPs warn. 2023 [Accessed 11 January 2023]; Available from: www.ft.com/content/1e1f14d1-96a4-49f6-8e4a-aa55552123eb

168. Byers, D., Hunt for lockdown billions is taxing. 2021 [Accessed 11 January 2023]; Available from: www.thetimes.co.uk/article/hunt-for-lockdown-billions-is-taxing-bq9zmz6fb

169. McDougall, M., UK taxman halves target for recovering Covid schemes losses. 2022 [Accessed 11 January 2023]; Available from: www.ft.com/content/d53621a0-a133-4036-a362-51a6f8cccdc1

170. ICAEW, Estimated tax gap figure remains in line with previous year. 2023 [Accessed 19 October 2023]; Available from: www.icaew.com/insights/tax-news/2023/jun-2023/ estimated-tax-gap-figure-remains-in-line-with-previous-year

171. IRS, The Tax Gap. 2023 [Accessed 19 October 2023]; Available from: www.irs.gov/ newsroom/the-tax-gap

172. Field, M., WannaCry cyber attack cost the NHS £92m as 19,000 appointments cancelled [Accessed 10 April 2021]; Available from: www.telegraph.co.uk/technology/ 2018/10/11/wannacry-cyber-attack-cost-nhs-92m-19000-appointments-cancelled

173. Triggle, N., Junior doctor strike led to 196,000 cancellations. 2023 [Accessed 18 April 2023]; Available from: www.bbc.co.uk/news/health-65305035

174. NCSC, NCSC statement following US advisory on ransomware targeting of US health sector. 2020 [Accessed 1 June 2021]; Available from:www.ncsc.gov.uk/news/statem ent-ransomware-targeting-us-health-sector

175. NCSC, Alert: Further targeted ransomware attacks on the UK education sector by cyber criminals. 2021 [Accessed 1 June 2021]; Available from: www.ncsc.gov.uk/ news/alert-targeted-ransomware-attacks-on-uk-education-sector

176. Gatlan, S., FBI: Conti ransomware attacked 16 US healthcare, first responder orgs. 2021 [Accessed 1 June 2021]; Available from: www.bleepingcomputer.com/news/ security/fbi-conti-ransomware-attacked-16-us-healthcare-first-responder-orgs

177. NCSC, Cyber security training for school staff. 2021 [Accessed 1 June 2021]; Available from: www.ncsc.gov.uk/information/cyber-security-training-schools

178. Moloney, E., S. Molony, and A.R. Schiller, HSE set up "war room" as Department of Health subjected to separate cyber attack. 2021 [Accessed 1 June 2021]; Available from: www.independent.ie/irish-news/hse-set-up-war-room-as-department-of-health-subjected-to-separate-cyber-attack-40431351.html

179. Halpin, P. and C. Humphries, Irish health service hit by "very sophisticated" ransomware attack. 2021 [Accessed 1 June 2021]; Available from: www.reuters.com/technology/irish-health-service-hit-by-ransomware-attack-vaccine-rollout-unaffected-2021-05-14

180. Lally, C., J. Horgan-Jones, and A. Beesley, Department of Health hit by cyberattack similar to that on HSE. 2021 [Accessed 1 June 2021]; Available from: www.irishtimes.com/news/health/department-of-health-hit-by-cyberattack-similar-to-that-on-hse-1.4566541

181. Noble, A., ISO/IEC 27001 ISMS Precertification Audit – January 2018. 2019 [Accessed 14 January 2023]; Available from: www.atlaudit.org/isoiec-27001-isms-precertification-audit---january-2018.html

182. Weiss, M., City hacks – Atlanta's 2018 Cyberattack and the growing need for cyber liability insurance. 2019 [Accessed 1 June 2021]; Available from: www.fmglaw.com/FMGBlogLine/insurance/city-hacks-atlantas-2018-cyberattack-and-the-growing-need-for-cyber-liability-insurance

183. Schwartz, M.J., Atlanta's reported ransomware bill: Up to $17 million. 2018 [Accessed 1 June 2021]; Available from: www.bankinfosecurity.com/atlantas-reported-ransomware-bill-up-to-17-million-a-11281

184. Newcombe, T., Cyberinsurance evolves to meet the ransomware threat. 2019 [Accessed 1 June 2021]; Available from: www.govtech.com/security/cyberinsurance-evolves-to-meet-the-ransomware-threat.html

185. Gallagher, S., Baltimore ransomware nightmare could last weeks more, with big consequences. 2019 [Accessed 1 June 2021]; Available from: https://arstechnica.com/information-technology/2019/05/baltimore-ransomware-nightmare-could-last-weeks-more-with-big-consequences

186. Truta, F., City of Cartersville admits paying Ryuk ransomware operators $380,000. 2020 [Accessed 19 August 2021]; Available from: https://securityboulevard.com/2020/03/city-of-cartersville-admits-paying-ryuk-ransomware-operators-380000

187. Kobialka, D., Ransomware attack: Georgia city pays $380K ransom to hackers. 2020 [Accessed 19 August 2021]; Available from: www.msspalert.com/cybersecurity-breaches-and-attacks/ransomware/georgia-cartersville-city-pays-380k-ransom

188. Dudley, R., The extortion economy: How insurance companies are fueling a rise in ransomware attacks. 2019 [Accessed 27 May 2021]; Available from: www.propublica.org/article/the-extortion-economy-how-insurance-companies-are-fueling-a-rise-in-ransomware-attacks

189. Hamilton, F. and M. Bridge, Ban ransom payments to hackers, urges ex- GCHQ boss. 2021 [Accessed 1 June 2021]; Available from: www.thetimes.co.uk/article/stop-paying-hackers-ransom-demands-ex-gchq-cybersecurity-chief-warns-323fqg8zt

190. Gatlan, S., US govt warns of sanction risks for facilitating ransomware payments. 2020 [Accessed 1 June 2021]; Available from: www.bleepingcomputer.com/news/security/us-govt-warns-of-sanction-risks-for-facilitating-ransomware-payments

191. Krebs, B., Task force seeks to disrupt ransomware payments. 2021 [Accessed 1 June 2021]; Available from: https://krebsonsecurity.com/2021/04/task-force-seeks-to-disrupt-ransomware-payments

192. Tidy, J., Ransomware: Should paying hacker ransoms be illegal? 2021 [Accessed 1 June 2021]; Available from: www.bbc.co.uk/news/technology-57173096

193. O'Brien, S., Cyberattack may cost HSE hundreds of millions, predicts chief Paul Reid. 2021 [Accessed 9 July 2021]; Available from: www.thetimes.co.uk/article/cyberatt ack-may-cost-hse-hundreds-of-millions-predicts-chief-paul-reid-dkkllpn3t

194. Lacey, D., Understanding and transforming organizational security culture. *Information Management & Computer Security*, 2010. 18(1): p. 4–13.

195. NCSC, Lindy Cameron speaking to the IIEA. 2021 [Accessed 19 August 2021]; Available from: www.ncsc.gov.uk/speech/iiea-cyber-threat

196. McCormack, C., Thousands of HSE computers rely on out-of-date software. 2021 [Accessed 19 August 2021]; Available from: www.rte.ie/news/ireland/2020/1209/1183265-hse-technology/#maincontent

197. Bajak, F., Insurer AXA to stop paying for ransomware crime payments in France. 2021 [Accessed 27 May 2021]; Available from: www.insurancejournal.com/news/internatio nal/2021/05/09/613255.htm

198. Bajak, F., Insurer AXA halts ransomware crime reimbursement in France – ABC News. 2021 [Accessed 11 January 2023]; Available from: https://apnews.com/article/europe-france-technology-business-caabb132033ef2aaee9f58902f3e8fba

199. Sharma, A., Insurer AXA hit by ransomware after dropping support for ransom payments. 2021 [Accessed 27 May 2021]; Available from: www.bleepingcomputer.com/news/security/insurer-axa-hit-by-ransomware-after-dropping-support-for-ran som-payments

200. Abrams, L., CNA insurance firm hit by a cyberattack, operations impacted. 2021 [Accessed 27 May 2021]; Available from: www.bleepingcomputer.com/news/secur ity/cna-insurance-firm-hit-by-a-cyberattack-operations-impacted

201. Fitch, Sharply rising cyber insurance claims signal further risk challenges. 2021 [Accessed 1 June 2021]; Available from: www.fitchratings.com/research/insurance/sharply-rising-cyber-insurance-claims-signal-further-risk-challenges-15-04-2021

202. Kasper, D., 2020 US Cyber Loss Ratios estimated at 73%, indicating an industry-wide underwriting loss. 2021 [Accessed 1 June 2021]; Available from: www.cyber-econom ics.com/2021/04/17/2020-us-cyber-loss-ratios-estimated-at-73-indicating-an-indus try-wide-underwriting-loss

203. Howden, Cyber insurance: A hard reset. 2021 [Accessed 19 August 2021]; Available from: www.howdengroup.com/sites/g/files/mwfley566/files/inline-files/Howden%20 Cyber%20Insurance%20-%20A%20Hard%20Reset%20report_1.pdf

204. Carslaw, H., Will 2021 be the year that cyber insurance comes of age? 2020 [Accessed 1 June 2021]; Available from: www.mactavishgroup.com/coronavirus/will-2021-be-the-year-that-cyber-insurance-comes-of-age

205. Moorcraft, B., Cyber insurance market reacts to ransomware epidemic. 2021 [Accessed 1 June 2021]; Available from: www.insurancebusinessmag.com/us/news/cyber/cyber-insurance-market-reacts-to-ransomware-epidemic-252394.aspx

206. insurancejournal.com, With claims rising, cyber insurers need more than sizable rate increases: Fitch. 2021 [Accessed 1 June 2021]; Available from: www.insurancejour nal.com/news/national/2021/04/20/610631.htm

207. Hollmer, M., Insurers not quitting on cyber even as risks mount. 2021 [Accessed 1 June 2021]; Available from: www.insurancejournal.com/magazines/mag-features/2021/01/11/596795.htm

208. Mott, G., et al., Between a rock and a hard (ening) place: Cyber insurance in the ransomware era. *Computers & Security*, 2023. 128: p. 103162.

209. Hepburn, B., Why cyber is the biggest risk for 2023. 2023 [Accessed 11 January 2023]; Available from: www.strategic-risk-europe.com/home/why-cyber-is-the-biggest-risk-for-2023/1443410.article

210. IAIS, Cyber risk underwriting. 2020 [Accessed 14 January 2023]; Available from: www.iaisweb.org/uploads/2022/01/201229-Cyber-Risk-Underwriting_-Identified-Challenges-and-Supervisory-Considerations-for-Sustainable-Market-Development.pdf

211. Matthews, D., Report on the cybersecurity insurance and identity theft coverage supplement. 2020 [Accessed 1 June 2021]; Available from: https://content.naic.org/sites/default/files/inline-files/Cyber_Supplement_2019_Report_Final_1.pdf

212. RTF, Combating ransomware: A comprehensive framework for action. 2021 [Accessed 1 June 2021]; Available from: https://securityandtechnology.org/ransomwaretaskforce

213. Shalal, A., Cyber officials from 37 countries, 13 companies to meet on ransomware in Washington. 2022 [Accessed 14 November 2022]; Available from: www.reuters.com/technology/cyber-officials-37-countries-13-companies-meet-ransomware-washington-2022-10-31

214. whitehouse.gov, Background press call by a senior administration official previewing the Second International Counter Ransomware Initiative Summit. 2022 [Accessed 14 November 2022]; Available from: www.whitehouse.gov/briefing-room/speeches-remarks/2022/10/31/background-press-call-by-a-senior-administration-official-previewing-the-second-international-counter-ransomware-initiative-summit

215. Neocleous, M., *Critique of security*. 2008: Edinburgh University Press.

216. Weiss, A., A brief guide to competitive intelligence: How to gather and use information on competitors. *Business Information Review*, 2002. 19(2): p. 39–47.

217. Emsisoft, Report: The cost of ransomware in 2020. A country-by-country analysis. 2020 [Accessed 1 June 2021]; Available from: https://blog.emsisoft.com/en/35583/report-the-cost-of-ransomware-in-2020-a-country-by-country-analysis

218. Muncaster, P., Ransomware costs may have hit $170bn in 2019. 2020 [Accessed 4 October 2022]; Available from: www.infosecurity-magazine.com/news/ransomware-costs-may-have-hit-170

219. NHS, NHS England and NHS Improvement funding and resource 2019/20: supporting "The NHS Long Term Plan". 2019 [Accessed 16 June 2021]; Available from:www.england.nhs.uk/publication/funding-and-resource-2019-20

220. Harker, R., NHS funding and expenditure. 2020 [Accessed 30 July 2021]; Available from: https://commonslibrary.parliament.uk/research-briefings/sn00724

221. Duncan, H., UK national debt interest payments set to total £120.4bn this year. 2023 [Accessed 21 January 2023]; Available from: www.msn.com/en-gb/money/other/uk-national-debt-interest-payments-set-to-total-1204bn-this-year/ar-AA14f2FF

222. PAC, Cyber security in the UK [Accessed 17 June 2021]; Available from: https://publications.parliament.uk/pa/cm201719/cmselect/cmpubacc/1745/1745.pdf

223. PricewaterhouseCoopers, Conti cyber attack on the HSE: Independent post incident review. 2021 [Accessed 16 February 2022]; Available from: www.hse.ie/eng/services/publications/conti-cyber-attack-on-the-hse-full-report.pdf

224. Targett, E., PwC's HSE hack post-incident report should be a corporate textbook. 2022 [Accessed 16 February 2022]; Available from: https://thestack.technology/pwc-hse-hack-post-incident-report

225. Sales, N.A., Regulating cyber-security. *Northwestern University Law Review*, 2012. 107: p. 1503.

226. Herley, C., Security, cybercrime, and scale. *Communications of the ACM*, 2014. 57(9): p. 64–71.

227. HMRC, BIM43101 – Specific deductions: Crime (expenditure involving). 2023 [Accessed 3 July 2023]; Available from: www.gov.uk/hmrc-internal-manuals/busin ess-income-manual/bim43101

228. HMRC, BIM43160 – Specific deductions: Crime (expenditure involving): blackmail and extortion. 2023 [Accessed 4 July 2023]; Available from: www.gov.uk/hmrc-inter nal-manuals/business-income-manual/bim43160

229. Nieuwesteeg, B. and M. Faure, The uneasy case for a ransom tax. *European Journal of Risk Regulation*, 2023. 14(2): p. 382–398.

230. Biancotti, C., The price of cyber (in) security: Evidence from the Italian private sector. Bank of Italy Occasional Paper, 2017(407).

231. Skeoch, H.R., Expanding the Gordon-Loeb model to cyber-insurance. *Computers & Security*, 2022. 112: p. 102533.

232. WaterUK, Water UK [Accessed 21 January 2023]; Available from: www.water.org.uk

233. EnergyUK, Energy UK [Accessed 21 January 2023]; Available from: www.energy-uk.org.uk

234. NIAUK, Nuclear Industry Association [Accessed 21 January 2023]; Available from: www.niauk.org

235. Heal, G. and H. Kunreuther, *Interdependent security: A general model*. 2004: National Bureau of Economic Research.

236. Ip, G., *Foolproof: Why safety can be dangerous and how danger makes us safe*. 2015: Hachette UK.

237. Da Silva, J. and R.B. Jensen, "Cyber security is a dark art": The CISO as soothsayer. arXiv preprint arXiv:2202.12755, 2022.

238. Waldman, A., FBI seized Colonial Pipeline ransom using private key. 2021 [Accessed 2 March 2022]; Available from: www.techtarget.com/searchsecurity/news/252502 115/FBI-seized-Colonial-Pipeline-ransom-using-private-key

239. De, N., Federal officials recover Bitcoin Ransom from colonial pipeline attack. 2021 [Accessed 19 August 2021]; Available from: www.coindesk.com/federal-officials-reco ver-bitcoin-ransom-from-colonial-pipeline-attack

240. Ducklin, P., How could the FBI recover BTC from Colonial's ransomware payment? 2021 [Accessed 19 August 2021]; Available from: https://nakedsecurity.sophos.com/ 2021/06/09/how-could-the-fbi-recover-btc-from-colonials-ransomware-payment

241. Dudley, R. and D. Golden, The colonial pipeline ransomware hackers had a secret weapon: self-promoting cybersecurity firms. 2021 [Accessed 17 June 2021]; Available from: www.technologyreview.com/2021/05/24/1025195/colonial-pipeline-ransomw are-bitdefender

242. Scroxton, A., Government action on ransomware epidemic gathers pace. 2021 [Accessed 17 June 2021]; Available from: www.computerweekly.com/news/252501 907/Government-action-on-ransomware-epidemic-gathers-pace

243. Sigalos, M., The FBI likely exploited sloppy password storage to seize Colonial Pipeline bitcoin ransom. 2021 [Accessed 17 June 2021]; Available from:www.cnbc. com/2021/06/08/fbi-likely-exploited-sloppy-password-storage-to-seize-colonial-ran som.html

244. DCMA, Record year for UK's £8.9bn cyber security sector. 2021 [Accessed 17 June 2021]; Available from: www.gov.uk/government/news/record-year-for-uks-89bn-cyber-security-sector

9 Summary and Future Work

THEME SUMMARY

SECURITY AS A DARK ART

A number of attempts have been made to establish cybersecurity as a science, although most of them seem to have been carried out some time ago [1–5]. Cormac Herley, in particular, sought to establish a firm foundation [6–9] but concluded that [10]:

Practices on which the rest of science has reached consensus appear little used or recognized in security, and a pattern of methodological errors continues unaddressed.

Da Silva and Jensen [11] examined the idea that cybersecurity is more often seen as a "dark art" and that CISOs should therefore be seen as "soothsayers", people who use their unique and mystical gifts to interpret the auguries, to prophesy the future. The paper makes a specific point that CISOs shouldn't be compared to e.g. shamans making predictions by examining chicken entrails, but it's hard not to draw the comparison.

The key points from the work are that:

- Practitioners tend to promote cyber as something mystical – an art rather than a science [11, p6], meaning that they can act as intermediaries between "*lay people*" [11, p8] and what might be seen as The Truth, which can only be understood by "seers" (i.e. otherwise fairly ordinary individuals who are paid to act as security managers). As an example, the authors quote one interviewed CISO as saying "*[i]t is incumbent upon a CISO or any head of security in whatever guise to teach the recipient how to speak pidgin cyber or pidgin IT or something that gives them a fighting chance to understand*" [11, p6]. I had to read that statement two or three times before I believed that anyone would actually say that, but maybe that's just me. Da Silva and Jensen conclude "*[t]his suggests not just the construction of an expert identity but also one of superiority, a more knowledgeable and well-meaning parent explaining something to a less knowledgeable, naive child*" [11, p7].

DOI: 10.1201/9781003380962-9

- CISOs report feeling isolated from the business [11, pp2, 10], but at the same time, they want to identify themselves as something "special" [11, p11]. The paper suggests that as a result, those individuals are thereby placed in a position where their "unique" insights into cybersecurity perhaps create pressure to indulge in what Da Silva and Jensen describe as *"cyber sophistry"* [11, p6]. The authors point to the fact that stressing high levels of cyber-threat acts to reinforce the position of the CISO [11, pp2, 3, 11], whereas in terms of job security, it's not in the interests of the CISO for those threats to exist in reality [11, p13]. The paper notes that organisations *"... may require additional cyber-security expertise to exist at senior levels within an organisation, possibly in a non-executive capacity, in order to identify and challenge this, particularly given the inability to disprove many security-related affirmations ..."* [11, p14]. Good point.
- On the basis of the interviews with e.g. CEO's, senior managers seem to believe that CISOs *"... have a depth of knowledge and a smell and a sense for their particular area"* and that they possess *"... something beyond knowledge, an intangible, arguably mystical, 'sense' for the subject"* [11, p6]. Some of that view may be driven by CISOs laying claim to a level of understanding that transcends the abilities of normal people [11, p7]. Silva and Jensen suggest that such an attitude may be to do with job retention [11, p11], since *"... it is easier to replace a chemist than a soothsayer"* [11, p12].

Overall, CISOs themselves don't seem averse to promoting the idea that *"... 'cyber-security is a dark art... . ...most people won't understand it'"* [11, p8]. So they're happy. It makes them feel special. And managers seem to be ok with the situation, since [11, p15]:

> By relying on a soothsayer to *"read the signs"* (i.e. to provide the weather fore-cast) they may deliberately be facing away from confronting a problem more directly – or perhaps they are deliberately looking for someone to blame in the event of disaster.

Da Silva and Jensen conclude that *"[t]he association of fear with cyber security was observed throughout the data"* and that [11, p9]:

> The perception of senior leaders in particular was that a cyber security incident was something to be afraid of, summarised by the following exchange: Interviewer: *"When you hear about things like the Travelex incident, how does that tend to make you feel, how do you tend to react?"* CEO2: *"Shit!"* [laughter].

Yes. Indeed. This is what happens when you rely on soothsayers to interpret the world for you.

THE THEATRICS OF SECURITY

Contrary to the views of practitioners, cyber security is not a special case in business terms, nor is it a special case in behavioural terms. Courtesy of the argument provided by Mark Neocleous in his book "Critique of Security" [12], we can add to that the possibility that cyber security isn't even a special case in security terms. Neocleous' book isn't specifically about cyber security, it's about the concept of security in general. It opens with a wonderful quote about security people, which I can't repeat, but please do read the book (and the quote).

Neocleous cites a number of aspects that link directly to the practice of cyber:

- While security might be sold as protection, actually it's more about maintaining a desired order, through the imposition of control.
- Practitioners are wedded to idea that security always has to be maximised, and that security is always a good thing [12, pp3–4].
- The idea that people are "*objects to be administered*" [12, p4].
- The use of threat inflation, in the form of the "*theatrics of security*" [12, p137].
- The outcomes of implementing security are unpredictable [12, p1 et seq.], partly because of the absence of a universally accepted definition [12, p6].

In particular, the book notes the industry's maintenance of a state of "*permanent emergency*" [12, Ch 2 and pp65, 67, 68], which in turn requires a constant stream of disaster scenarios. And it's not just the industry that benefits. Politicians aren't above using threat inflation – as in "cyberwar is coming, and only I can save you". Sean Lawson, in his book "Cybersecurity Discourse in the United States" [13], notes that "*... cyber-doom rhetoric persists in US public policy discourse despite years of failed predictions of impending catastrophe and growing recognition that it is not reflective of the vast majority of actual threats*" [13, p65]. Reviewing a number of headline-grabbing instances [13, Ch4], Lawson shows that in most cases the consequences were significantly less severe than commonly reported, but that cyber pundits took those impacts and re-interpreted them as "just a taste of what's to come". Bruce Schneier, for example, implies that attitudes towards security will change when "*... a [cyber] disaster occurs that takes a significant number of lives*" [14, p150] and/or "*... when the Internet starts killing people*" [14, p182].

Citing Greer [15], Schneier suggests that fines for cyber indiscretions should be so severe that they drive erring companies out of business. They "*... would be taken over by Government, have all investors wiped out, and then be sold off at some later date*" [14, p125]. It's also been suggested [14, p126] that start-ups should be a focus of attention, since they're often run by people who are willing to take risks. On a purely personal note, as far as I know, small businesses account for about three-fifths of the employment and around one-half of the turnover in the UK private sector [16]. In 2022, the Office for National Statistics (ONS) [17] reported that the mortality rate for businesses in the UK was about 10.5%, against a birth rate of about 11.9%. That little sliver of difference between the birth rate and the death rate is what means we have an economy. That's the reality of it. And arguably, what creates that difference is the fact that people are willing to take risks.

The argument is extended to state that [14, p154] "*[u]nfettered innovation is only acceptable for benign technologies*". I doubt that it's taught in schools anymore, but older readers may recall the work of Edward Jenner, who noticed that people working with dairy herds (and who were therefore prone to catch cowpox) were remarkably resistant to catching smallpox. Despite opprobrium, caricature, and general disapproval, Jenner inoculated people with cowpox and found that he could reduce the incidence of smallpox, at that time a widespread and fatal disease. Smallpox has been all but eradicated from the planet, despite the fact that giving people a mild infection in order to prevent a significantly worse one was not seen at the time as a benign technology.

The proposal goes on to state that [14, p154] "... *the precautionary principle dictates that when the potential of harm is great, we should err on the side of not deploying a new technology without proof of security*". The same source [14, p136] also states that "*[w]e're butting up against some technological limits of computer science theory: our inability to declare something 'secure' in any meaningful way*". With no way of proving that a technology is secure, it seems odd (to me anyway) to suggest that products should be shown to be secure before they're used. Perhaps I'm missing the point.

To quote Lawson [13, p194]:

None of the preceding discussion should be read as suggesting that we should not take cybersecurity seriously, that we should not take measures to secure your critical infrastructures, or that we should not prepare to mitigate the effects of a cyberattack on critical infrastructure should it occur. Rather, this book should be read as suggesting that taking cybersecurity seriously requires that we re-evaluate the assumptions upon which public debate and policymaking proceed, that we can only make effective policy if we begin with a realistic assessment of current and likely future threats. To do that, we must continue to challenge and ultimately move beyond the rhetoric of cyber-doom that has persisted in the U.S. cybersecurity debate for more than two decades.

THE IMPACT OF MEDIA REPORTING

Maschmeyer et al. [18] cite evidence that the reporting of cyber-related stories is skewed towards circumstances that (a) present aspects that are unusual or unique; (b) involve a well-known victim; and (c) involve a well-known threat actor. The case of Russian spies using advanced techniques to hack into US elections, for example, satisfies all three. But as pointed out in the paper, using Government-grade technology to spy on the actions of Jamal Khashoggi, a Saudi journalist later horrifically murdered and dismembered, doesn't really tick the boxes, despite being an apparently newsworthy issue. Or at least, that was the case until a number of high-profile individuals were drawn into the story [19–21].

To be fair, Wahlberg and Sjöberg [22] argue that media representation of risk has much less of an effect than is often assumed, but others (e.g. [23]) provide evidence that "dread risks" (risks that are seen as uncontrollable, unknown, and potentially catastrophic [24]) do occupy a special place in our thinking. And the media drive home that message [13, pp51, 56] using phrases such as "*cyber Hiroshima*" and "*cyber 9/11*" [13, p114]. Lawson argues that our concerns over cybersecurity tap into a deep-seated fear regarding our dependency on technology, and that consequently, warnings from the industry threatening some form of cyber-Armageddon find an accepting and credulous audience. In the words of the paper: *"... we have a tendency to let our metaphors do the thinking for us"* [13, p135].

Kahneman and Tversky describe this as the "availability heuristic". When we have an easily accessible narrative, we tend to apply it without too much conscious thought [25].

In mid-2021, the media were much exercised by the story of a US oil pipeline company ("Colonial") which seemed to have been attacked using ransomware linked to a criminal gang based in Russia [26]. As a result, the company closed down a 5000-mile petroleum product pipeline running along the Eastern seaboard of the United States. The industrial control systems associated with the pipeline didn't seem to have been affected by the ransomware, but the pipeline was shut down as a precaution nonetheless. According to early reports, the problem arose because of a privileged remote access connection that was protected by just a password [27], a vulnerability that seems to have been exploited relatively easily.

A state of emergency was declared, so that fuel could lawfully be transported by other means [28], but local outlets nonetheless sold out of gasoline [29]. Widespread calls were made for immediate Government action [30], on the basis that ransomware clearly constitutes an existential threat to modern life.

Well, maybe. Less well-publicised is the fact that the pipeline had been shut down on a number of other occasions [31] as a result of damage, leaks, system problems, extreme weather, "integrity problems", etc. In fact, Colonial had closed down the same pipeline in August 2020 because of a massive leak. So massive that it took the company some time to discover just how massive it was, since they had no direct means of telling [32]. The company was alerted to the leak in the first place by local teenagers, who found pools of gasoline accumulating in nearby fields. The report from a Government investigation into the incident [33] sets out some interesting background:

> *Our ongoing investigation indicates that conditions may exist on the Colonial Pipeline System that pose a pipeline integrity risk to public safety, property or the environment. The conditions that led to the failure potentially exist throughout the Colonial Pipeline System. Further, Colonial's inability to effectively detect and respond to this release, as well as other past releases, has potentially exacerbated the impacts of this and numerous other failures over the operational history of Colonial's entire system. After evaluating the preliminary findings of fact described below and considering the characteristics of the Colonial Pipeline System, as well as the failure history of that system, it appears that the continued operation of the Colonial Pipeline System without corrective measures would pose a pipeline integrity risk to public safety, property, or the environment.*

Following a previous leak in 2016, actions taken by Colonial to prevent a reoccurrence led to an explosion and a fire in which one person died and a dozen others were injured. The pipeline was shut again, and various states of emergency were declared [34]. As a possibly weary local put it, even given the complications arising from the fatality, Colonial had been getting enough practice, so the pipeline shouldn't be down for too long "this time". As with the 2021 event, queues formed at gas stations, fights broke out, and eventually supplies ran out, thanks largely to panic buying, rather than due to an actual shortage [35]. Similar scenes were seen in Tennessee, and as wryly observed by the state press there, Tennessee wasn't even served by that pipeline [36]. This is what happens when people are told that there's no need to panic [37, 38].

It's highly unlikely that you will have seen any coverage of these other incidents, despite the fact that their outcomes were significantly worse than those arising from the ransomware attack. That single incident received much more exposure than the environmentally more significant, and subsequently fatal events that preceded it, because it was a cyber-related attack, with a hint that some dastardly foreign agency was behind it.

In 2000, the Maroochy Shire water treatment plant in Queensland, Australia, was hacked, leading to the release of anything up to a million litres of waste water (i.e. sewage) into local waterways and parks [39]. Not a good outcome. On the other hand, very much less than the volume of waste water released in a spill caused by unexpectedly heavy rain in the Thames Valley. In fact, about 99% less [40, 41]. But if you read any of the reports regarding the Maroochy Shire incident, there's no background provided in any of the commentaries – no context. No reporting of any non-incidents that might place the impact in perspective.

Lawson [13, p59 et seq.] cites a number of other events, including one in which a failed pump supposedly attacked by Russian hackers was in fact a simple hardware failure. The link with Russia arose because an engineer (travelling through Russia some months earlier) had logged in remotely, to access some records to go into a report [42]. When the pump subsequently burned out, the pull of "cyber-doom" was so strong that an official report into the incident (albeit subsequently disowned by the supposed authors [43]) re-interpreted the incident as "clear evidence" of an active Russian attack on US infrastructure.

The apotheosis of this is probably the 2016 Washington Post story regarding Russian cyber criminals lurking inside US critical national industries, waiting to pounce [44]. As was subsequently pointed out [45–47], the story was triggered by a utility company reporting that a single laptop infected with a common virus had been found on their premises [48, 49]. As with the burned-out pump, the facts could have been checked with a phone call. Instead, the paper went ahead with a much more interesting story.

Media reporting of shock horror headlines reinforces the industry's message of inevitable doom, because the compensating contexts, the background non-stories, simply aren't reported. The most recent records available from the US Industrial Control Systems Cyber Emergency Response Team (ICS-CERT), for example, indicate that of the 290 cyber intrusion incidents handled in 2016, 40 were to do with scans or probes, and a further 184 were deemed to have had no impact on the delivery of services [50]. Other categories were "minimal impact to non-critical services" (15), "minimal impact to ICS" (11), "unknown" (11), and "minimal impact to critical services" (10). That is, out of 290 reported cyber incidents, about 270 were non-events.

MASKING THE PROBLEM

In 2012, Saudi Aramco suffered a major cyber-attack which rendered something like 30,000 computers on their administrative networks useless, and which deleted files across the estate [51, para 2.8]. The extent of the damage was reportedly enough to justify teams being flown out to manufacturing plants to buy whole production runs of replacement hard disks [52].

In 2017, malware later named "Triton" was found in the process control network of a Saudi oil company [53, 54]. The unique aspect of the malware was that it had been designed specifically to attack the fallback safety systems on the network [55]. Pumps which had been absent-mindedly left on a "program" setting (rather than "run", presumably after a logic upgrade) had been re-programmed by the malware [56], reaching out from a compromised workstation. It's thought that the attackers had been in the system for some time [57], and also that their software had been developed specifically for the hardware configuration found in that one plant.

In 2009 malware labelled as "Night Dragon" was found to have infected a number of major gas and oil companies worldwide [51, para 2.5]. The attack used a combination of techniques to gain access to both the administrative and operational networks in order to gather data on production figures, commercial arrangements, etc. The malware also collected data of potential interest including password files and SCADA configurations [58]. Rather than causing damage there and then, the attack seemed to have been aimed at intelligence gathering for future operations.

These threats are very real, and very serious. But they aren't the whole picture. And the importance that should be attached to dealing with them is reduced when they just fade into the background noise of cyber-doom messaging. To achieve an appropriate degree of perspective, the current level of hype has got to be turned down.

In the book "Factfulness", Rosling points out that we employ an attention filter to pick out news that seems to be the most salient to us, and that media reporting is targeted at getting stories through that attention filter [59, p104]. The book concludes that:

> And yet, because of our dramatic instincts and the way the media must tap into them to grab our attention, we continue to have an overdramatic worldview. Of all our dramatic instincts, it seems to be the fear instinct that most strongly influences what information gets selected by news producers and presented to us consumers.

THE POINT

The presentation of cyber as a dark art isn't tenable. It can't continue. The problem is not so much the use of incantations and spells, more the consequence that cyber is then seen as a special case – something that can only be understood by the initiated, and that furthermore, that cyber is so special, the achievement of security overrides all other concerns. That kind of thinking creates a divide between cyber and business, and that is A Bad Thing.

FUTURE WORK

INTRODUCTION

I've used the same theme as the basis for suggestions for future work – things that could be done to reduce the gap between the folklore and the facts.

RESEARCH INTO THE APPLICATION OF DEBIASING

Someone with deep pockets could usefully fund some work into the application of debiasing to security decision-making, as demonstrated by Morewedge [60]. The current moribund and largely ineffective approach to awareness training is an area crying out to be reformed. The evidence isn't 100% compelling, but the possibility of online delivery of a method improving the quality of security decisions has got to be worth investigating.

A SABRE EQUIVALENT

Someone with an interest in the business aspects of cyber could perhaps see if there are any general principles to achieving competitive advantage through cybersecurity. Many years ago a computer system called SABRE [61] revolutionised airline booking systems and conferred a huge competitive advantage on its originator, American Airlines. Perhaps we need to find the equivalent turning point for cyber.

A WIDER LOOK AT RISK ANALYSIS

Somebody somewhere could fund research into the tags, signals, and boundaries identified by Holland [62] as mechanisms involved in the operation of complex adaptive systems. We've only just touched the surface of applying that body of knowledge to cybersecurity, and there ought to be significant benefits in applying a bit more of it.

MORE RESEARCH INTO COMPLEX SYSTEMS

It was noted earlier that because security risk analysis tends to concentrate on impacts affecting the organisation, potential externalities are overlooked. It would be interesting to extend the process of risk analysis to include a consideration of externalities, perhaps by adding e.g. customer representatives as a stakeholder.

CYBER TROLLEY PROBLEMS

I wonder if it might be useful to illustrate that not all cyber problems are soluble. Perhaps as a set of "trolley problems" [63] for cyber. The case of the dive school operator, as told by Siponen [64], could provide a useful start. Was it a good security decision to release the names of those that were known to be alive and well? As with the original trolley problem, there's probably no right answer. But asking the question would at least provoke a discussion.

PROFILING OF CYBER PRACTITIONERS

Slightly tongue in cheek perhaps, but it would be interesting to profile members of the security community, and see if there's any degree of correlation between person-ality characteristics and adherence to concepts such as the idea that risk is a number. The OCEAN (or "Big Five") model characterises personality according to the degree of Openness (the willingness to accept new ideas), Conscientiousness, Extraversion, Agreeableness (in a sense, emotional vs rational), and Neuroticism. I wouldn't want to pre-empt the results, but my guess is the traditional view might be associated with relatively low scores on Openness.

INATTENTIONAL BLINDNESS

Following on from the work by Frey [65] on cyber/manager/IT teams managing security in a fictional utility company, it might be interesting to run the same kind of experiment but with background presented to the teams beforehand, setting out e.g. the financial position of the company, its commercial history, and competitors, and see how much of that background was absorbed by each team, and the differences that it made (or not) to their decisions on security. My guess is that some form of inattentional blindness [66] is commonly exhibited by cyber practitioners, in that anything that isn't seen as directly relevant to the security issues at hand is simply ignored.

MORE SUBTLE NUDGING

Renaud and Zimmerman [67] employed what they termed a "hybrid nudge", made up of a nudge designed to exploit irrational thinking, combined with straightforward information provision, to achieve a result that was at least as good as applying a basic nudge, and occasionally better. As we saw with the findings of Isler [68] (who combined a nudge with an explanation of the nature of cognitive bias), maybe the best approach would be a combination of the two. Again, might be worth looking into.

REFRESHERS

Dekker [69, p202] expresses disappointment that having seemingly improved the situation on safety behaviours, circumstances tended to gradually migrate back to the previous state. Personal experience confirms this in the cyber context. Inevitably the situation reverts, however slowly, back to "old school" thinking. It would be interesting to see (with reference to the Anheuser-Busch story related earlier) if there might be some optimum pattern for e.g. refresher campaigns.

A WIDER PROFESSION

I don't have an answer to the general need for greater flexibility and less dogmatism throughout the industry. Even Daniel Kahneman has suggested that the dual process model developed in collaboration with Amos Tversky may not be "set in stone" [70]. However, principles such as the CIA model are put forward by the cyber industry as facts, whereas it might be better to keep a focus on evidence instead (e.g. [71–73]). Perhaps we need a new, separately managed discipline of applied research in cybersecurity.

CERTIFICATION

At present (at least in the UK), I can obtain a professional certification in penetration testing, I can obtain a professional certification in security architecture, and I can obtain a professional certification in computer forensics. But there are no professional certifications in behavioural security, business security, nor cyber policy. UK plc could help remedy this by setting up a competition in much the same way as there is for penetration testing skills [74]. The new scheme might relate to ways of gaining commercial benefit from cyber, rather than looking at technical solutions. My guess is that graduates of that scheme would be in demand to at least the same degree as those with advanced technical skills.

EXTENDING THE STANDARDS

It was noted earlier that existing cyber standards don't have a great deal of content relating to behaviours. Given the current state of the industry, if it's not part of a compliance checklist, then it's not relevant to an audit. It might be interesting to look at how behavioural issues could be linked into existing standards, in a way that wasn't just grafted on i.e. in a way that meant technology and behavioural science were working together rather than being seen as separate strands.

THANK YOU

Thank you for reading this far. I hope some of it proves useful, and if not, then I hope that it's been at least thought-provoking.

Dekker's book on safety provides a summary of the kind of change I would hope to see in the cyber field:

> *It is time for Safety Anarchists: people who trust people more than process, who rely on horizontally coordinating experiences and innovations, who push back against petty rules and coercive compliance, and who help recover the dignity and expertise of human work.*

In many ways I think the cyber industry can be seen as a victim of its own history. Security practices arose primarily from technical teams that didn't have too much involvement in business issues, such as estimating how much an initiative might cost to implement, nor were they bothered too much about what benefits might accrue.

Security was just a problem to be solved. By and large those same technicians were also treated as infallible sources of information and therefore weren't challenged. Throw in the need for hype to get the industry started, and a focus on linear development methods, and you can probably trace most of the current problems back to those starting conditions. The subsequent growth of cyber has led to venture capitalists wading in [75, p6 Exhibit 1], with a concentration on increasing company value rather than solving problems [76]. And bish-bosh, you have a situation in which the business context is ignored, albeit ironically, in order to meet the financial objectives of the industry itself.

ADDENDUM

DISCLOSURE

If you want to follow up on the key themes in this book, may I suggest "Alchemy" by Rory Sutherland [77]. It's a book on consumer behaviour. It's very engaging, and it sets out a key message – that you should look at what people actually do, and not what they tell you they're going to do.

There's another key statement in that book that also applies to this one – that at some point, some of the evidence presented here will be shown to have been wrong. There's a reason, for example, why nobody cites the tragic case of Kitty Genovese as a prime example of the "bystander effect" [78, 79], and there's a reason why nobody cites the "five monkeys and a ladder" experiment as a prime example of learned behaviour [80] (although bizarrely, you can find sources acknowledging that the experiment never took place, at least not as described, but then proceed to quote it as a "valuable lesson").

THE REPLICATION CRISIS

The background is that since about 2011, experimental psychology has been through a period of intense self-examination. A great deal of effort has been expended in attempts to replicate and hence validate the findings of key experiments in psychology. In many cases those attempts are turning out to be unsuccessful, thereby casting doubt over the original conclusions.

This is the so-called replication crisis [81–85] that has resulted in Daniel Kahneman seemingly withdrawing [86] a chapter of his well-known book, "Thinking, Fast and Slow" [87], specifically the chapter on priming, on the basis that the results published by others (and which he had originally cited) could not be repeated. On money priming[1] especially, there's evidence that if you use larger sample sizes and include previously unpublished studies (most of them unpublished because they didn't present eye-catching results), then the effect size approaches zero i.e. "money priming" ceases to be a thing [88].

Typically, the problem is viewed as three separate issues: replicability (if we re-run the experiment, do we get the same results?); reproducibility (if we re-analyse the results, do we get the same findings?); and generalisability (e.g. [89]) (can we sensibly apply the findings to a wider population?).

A central concern involves "p-hacking" (selectively interpreting your results until you get a statistically significant outcome) and/or "publication bias" – ignoring results that didn't prove what you were looking for. Most of the cases under discussion seem to reflect weak experimental procedures, such as the use of small sample sizes, and low statistical power. However, there are a couple of more egregious cases, such as that of Diederik Stapel, a Dutch psychologist [90]. It's estimated that about 30 of his peer-reviewed papers were based on fraudulent data, i.e. they presented findings from experiments that weren't actually conducted.

It's worth noting that the debate runs slightly wider than just psychology – there are similar crises reported in e.g. economics [91] and medicine [92, 93]. Stuart Ritchie [94–97] provides a balanced and comprehensive description of the replication crisis, and of the factors driving it, together with supporting detail and a sensible, structured argument. It's a great place to go if you want to look into this in more detail.

HISTORY

Much of this seems to have been triggered by a 2011 paper released by Daryl Bem [98], showing that an individual's behaviour could be affected by a nudge delivered *after* the behaviour itself. In some way, the nudge had leaked out of the future and affected the present. So far, so Rick and Morty™. But Bem provided an analysis arguing that the results were statistically valid, and his experiments drew upon a large pool of subjects, across multiple variations of the original premise [99].

A number of researchers [100] saw this as the last straw for a field that was supposed to be about understanding human behaviour. Hence the launch of a large-scale replication project looking at a number of "accepted" results [101]. The team drew up a list of studies to replicate and compared their findings with those of the original researchers.

The results made for poor reading, with a success rate of less than 40%.

Against that background, attention then turned to a paper co-authored by Amy Cuddy [102]. Dr Cuddy had gained celebrity for an experiment showing that "power posing" (e.g. standing for a couple of minutes with your legs akimbo, and holding your arms up in a victory salute) not only increased your feelings of confidence but also boosted your level of testosterone and reduced your levels of stress hormone [103]. Amy Cuddy's TED talk on power posing was and remains the second most popular talk [104].

However, all of this was based on an original study involving only about 40 people, and the project failed to (completely) replicate [105–108]. Dr Cuddy's career and reputation both took a hit, although on the plus side, the replication team got a much-needed and very public result, as reported in the New York Times article that covered the issue [109]:

> *Cuddy has emerged from this upheaval as a unique object of social psychology's new, enthusiastic spirit of self-flagellation, as if only in punishing one of its most public stars could it fully break from its past... fellow academics (or commenters on their sites) have savaged not just Cuddy's work but also her career, her income, her ambition, even her intelligence, sometimes with evident malice.*

The claimed outcome of all of this being that the field of psychology is now in "renaissance" [110]. Sunlit uplands [111]. Well, maybe.

As George Orwell said in Animal Farm [112], "whoever controls the past, controls the future". In that context, it's fair to point out that questions have been raised about the selection methods used in replication studies [113]. There's a suggestion that if you're on a replication team, you get to choose which past papers to look at, with no need to provide any specific justification. The authors picked on, however, might be a bit miffed to have been singled out. Bargh certainly was [114]. Daniel Gilbert chose instead to engage in polite discourse, the end result [115] being that the person conducting the replication admitted that they had chosen to look at Gilbert's study pretty much on the basis of personal differences between themselves and some members of the original team [116–118]. In the case of Amy Cuddy, there were one or two quite serious suggestions of misogyny [109], and what might be considered some unpleasant personal posts [119, 120]. It's hard to exclude the possibility that in some cases, the replication movement may have been used for reasons other than the stated scientific objectives.

PRE-REGISTRATION

Because of the replication crisis, some journals and funding bodies now require planned studies to undergo pre-registration. In order to have a paper considered for publication, researchers are required to lodge an upfront description of what they're planning to do, and subsequently show that they adhered to that process, exactly as described.

Strømland [121] used statistical modelling to suggest that enforcement of pre-registration would lead to a significant improvement in research credibility. Whereas Ritchie [94, p213] refers to a paper by Claesen et al. [122] (in pre-print, at the time of writing) that examined the practical effect of pre-registration, by reviewing registered and actual approaches for a number of studies. The report noted that:

In a sample of 23 papers published in Psychological Science, we found adherence and disclosure of deviations to be very low. There was no single study in which the authors adhered to the preregistration plan without any deviations. This high rate of non-adherence does not have to be problematic, however, we found that only one preregistered study disclosed all deviations. In all remaining papers, there was at least one deviation from the plan that was not fully disclosed.

The paper also notes that:

Articles with a preregistered badge should meet certain criteria as expressed in the open practice disclosure items before it can be rewarded with such a badge. Compliance with these criteria is based on self-report by the authors. Given that all of the articles in our sample have received a badge and thus have authors which have indicated compliance with the disclosure items, the low adherence is surprising. Therefore, we were interested whether the authors of these papers actually complied with the open practices disclosure items. In total, half of the sixteen included articles did not comply with all four selected disclosure items, meaning that they should not have been awarded a badge.

Goldacre [123] and Veldkamp [124], as cited by Bishop [125], reported similar outcomes in terms of the behaviour of both academic journals and researchers.

Earlier it was mentioned that after failing to replicate the original finding, Ariely had withdrawn one of his key points regarding factors driving honest behaviour. The finding being that when people were asked to sign at the top of a form before filling it out (i.e. they pledged to be honest in advance of their actions), they were indeed seen to be more honest. As Ariely has acknowledged, there's now no credible evidence to support that suggestion [126]. No comments so far on the irony of the situation, but it's early days.

REPLICATION MARKETS

In 2018, a study conducted by Camerer et al. [127] looked into the degree to which social science papers published between 2010 and 2015 in the highly regarded journals *Nature* and *Science* could be replicated. The authors went to great lengths to employ larger sample sizes than had been used in the original studies (smaller sample sizes tend to give less reliable results) and also made efforts to consult with the original researchers, in order to ensure comparability. It depends on the numbers you take from the report, but broadly speaking, only about 60-odd percent of the results could be replicated, and the effect sizes were only about 75% as large as those originally reported. Most of the differences were put down to the use of small sample sizes in the original research, although some of it may have been due to more rigorous controls around experimental procedures in the replications.

Much more interestingly, the research team ran a kind of stock market in the papers being examined. They asked an audience of social scientists to invest (or not) in "shares" in the papers that the team were examining, and looked at how the share prices developed, a low share price reflecting a belief that the replication would be unsuccessful, a high share price indicating an expectation amongst the audience that the original results would be confirmed.

You will remember that stock markets, it can be argued, are complex adaptive systems that may reflect social interpretations rather than rational judgements.

It turns out that the researchers found a strong correlation between the papers that people expected to replicate, and the actual degree of replication. That is, when people who were very similar to the researchers conducting the replications *expected* to see a confirmation of the original results, in most cases that's what the actual researchers found. Obviously this was just one study, conducted at one point in time, and it would be rash to draw conclusions. However, others have suggested that behavioural researchers might themselves be subject to the same effects that they're looking into [125, 128].

Amongst the papers that showed the highest degree of predicted replication were:

- Hauser et al. [129], a study into how psychology can be used to manage the Earth's resources for future generations.

- Janssen et al. [130], a study into the management of socio-ecological systems.
- Gneezy et al. [131], how to increase levels of donations to charities.
- Balafoutas and Sutter [132] – confirmation that positive discrimination for females promotes their position and does not affect workplace efficiency.

At the bottom of the "predicted to replicate" list were: a study co-authored by John Bargh [133], who was at that time at the centre of another replication dispute; a study [134] dealing with a topic that had already failed to replicate (the "Lady Macbeth effect" [135]); and a paper [136] which (I think, judging by the dates) had also already failed to replicate [137] and which was in the process of being publicly retracted [138]. No surprises in either list, I would say, but perhaps that's a personal view.

Following a suggestion by Hanson [139], Dreber [140] proposed the wider use of "replication stock markets" [141], on the basis that [142]:

It is great news... [i]t suggests that people more or less already know which results will replicate.

To my knowledge Bem has yet to offer any comment, although again, it's early days.

Over 2020/2021, DARPA [143] extended the idea, by creating an online replication market open to the general public, with cash rewards for successful predictions [144–146]. Participants were invited to gamble on which experiments would replicate, and which wouldn't. Effectively, members of the general public were invited to take a punt on which bit of psychology research was likely to be the most crap. Singal [147] reports on a similar exercise, asking the public to identify "silly" psychology. All in all, possibly not the best bit of messaging, given the circumstances.

The views of (professional) participants in replication markets can perhaps be seen from quotes from two related articles in The Atlantic [142, 148]:

I'm not sure I had a clear strategy... [b]eyond that, I simply used my gut instinct for whether the original finding felt plausible.
I did a sniff test of whether the results actually make sense.

Hanson [148] reviewed the outcomes of replication markets. Generally pessimistic, he believed that academics would need to be incentivised, i.e. they wouldn't take part in a market without some possibility of reward [149], and that where the publication of a paper rested on the outcome of a market "*... authors and their rivals would have incentives to trade in such markets, and others would be enticed to trade when they expect that trades by insiders, or their rivals alone, are likely to produce biased estimates*". I read that as "if you create a route to game the system, people will take it", and for what it's worth, I agree [150].

Outcomes

The replication movement has shown that it is possible for researchers to collaborate to turn a spotlight onto results that need re-examining, either because those results were in critical areas, or because they call other areas into doubt. Or, to be quite honest, because they call the practice in general into doubt.

And it's not all negative. There have been examples of successful replications, demonstrating that some key foundational findings are reliable. The movement has also increased the number of reported "null" results. The benefit of that might not seem obvious, but it's critical – it means that investigations that purportedly show a positive result can be seen in their proper context, i.e. it creates the necessary background of "non-events". And crucially, replication studies are now seen as publishable in their own right.

However, the practical application of this approach has been by no means perfect.

CONTEXT

Indications so far are that results in cognitive psychology are proving to be more robust than those in social psychology. So wherever possible, I've tried to stay in that corner, and I've tried to stick with empirical findings [151, 152]. I've also used the publicly available part of the Retraction Watch database [153] to check that for the most important papers cited here, the results have not been called into question. And I've tried not to bleat on about "heart breaking" decisions to leave authors out, on the basis that mentioning their names might affect the sales potential of the book.

I've also tried to make the content of this book robust to the debate. Where there's an ongoing argument over a result, or there are opposing views, I hope I've flagged that up in every case, so that you can come to your own conclusions. I've tried to use words like "indicates" rather than "proves". I've also tried to use examples that show a lack of findings (i.e. I've risked discounting a valid theory rather than accepting a possibly invalid one).

So please do confirm the references, and check the figures. If I've misinterpreted evidence, or I've missed some evidence entirely, or if new evidence has come to light, then call it out. The worst outcome of that would be that it kicks off a debate.

A SUGGESTION

A secondary reason for including this addendum is to suggest the establishment of some form of cybersecurity equivalent of the replication movement.

At the moment, we have claims being made on the basis of little to no evidence, and where there's no evidence at all, on occasion it's simply being made up. Where statistical methods are being used, they're often being misapplied and misrepresented. There's no baseline, and in particular, no baseline of "non-stories" to set the headline cases in their proper context. Earlier, I referenced Machiavelli, and the principle of *realpolitik* – real-world politics. I stick by that analogy. I may even have a name for what we need – *realsicherheit* – real-world security. The reality being that at some point, sooner or later, the industry has got to abandon an approach based on not much more than folklore.

As we saw with the replication movement, it's unlikely that the problems we have at the minute in cyber will be solved overnight, and there will undoubtedly be issues to resolve along the way. Nevertheless, we have that solid base of experience to build on.

NOTE

1 The idea that when you remind people of the importance of money, they seem to act more coldly towards other people.

REFERENCES

1. Kott, A., Towards fundamental science of cyber security. In *Network science and cybersecurity*, Pino, R. E., Editor. 2014: Springer, p. 1–13.

2. Schneider, F.B., *Blueprint for a science of cybersecurity*. 2012 [Accessed 10 April 2021]; Available from: www.cs.cornell.edu/fbs/publications/sos.blueprint.pdf

3. Maxion, R.A., T.A. Longstaff, and J. McHugh, Why is there no science in cyber science?: A panel discussion at NSPW 2010. In *Proceedings of the 2010 New Security Paradigms Workshop*. 2010: ACM.

4. Spring, J.M., T. Moore, and D. Pym, Practicing a science of security: A philosophy of science perspective. In *Proceedings of the 2017 New Security Paradigms Workshop*. 2017: ACM.

5. Landwehr, C.E., Cybersecurity: From engineering to science. In *Developing a blueprint for a science of cybersecurity*. 2012 [Accessed 10 April 2021]; Available from: www.landwehr.org/2012-05-cybersec-fm-engg-to.pdf

6. Florêncio, D., C. Herley, and B. Coskun, *Do strong web passwords accomplish anything? HotSec*, 2007. 7(6): p. 2–5.

7. Egelman, S., et al., Does my password go up to eleven?: The impact of password meters on password selection. In *Proceedings of the SIGCHI Conference on Human Factors in Computing Systems*. 2013: ACM.

8. Florêncio, D. and C. Herley, *Where do security policies come from?* In *Proceedings of the Sixth Symposium on Usable Privacy and Security*. 2010: ACM.

9. Herley, C., More is not the answer. *IEEE Security & Privacy*, 2013. 12(1): p. 14–19.

10. Herley, C. and P.C. van Oorschot, Sok: Science, security and the elusive goal of security as a scientific pursuit. In *Security and Privacy (SP), 2017 IEEE Symposium on*. 2017: IEEE.

11. Da Silva, J. and R.B. Jensen, *"Cyber security is a dark art": The CISO as soothsayer*. arXiv preprint arXiv:2202.12755, 2022.

12. Neocleous, M., *Critique of security*. 2008: Edinburgh University Press.

13. Lawson, S.T., *Cybersecurity discourse in the United States: Cyber-doom rhetoric and beyond*. 2019: Routledge.

14. Schneier, B., *Click here to kill everybody: Security and survival in a hyper-connected world*. 2018: WW Norton & Company.

15. Greer, J.M., *The wealth of nature: Economics as if survival mattered*. 2011: New Society Publishers.

16. FSB, *UK small business statistics*. 2023 [Accessed 19 March 2023]; Available from: www.fsb.org.uk/uk-small-business-statistics.html

17. ONS, *Business births, deaths and survival rates*. 2022 [Accessed 18 March 2023]; Available from: www.ons.gov.uk/businessindustryandtrade/changestobusiness/businessbirthsdeathsandsurvivalrates

18. Maschmeyer, L., R.J. Deibert, and J.R. Lindsay, A tale of two cybers – How threat reporting by cybersecurity firms systematically underrepresents threats to civil society. *Journal of Information Technology & Politics*, 2021. 18(1): p. 1–20.

19. Brown, D. and C. Philp, *Sheikh Mohammed hacked Baroness Shackleton's mobile phone, rules judge*. 2021 [Accessed 2 March 2022]; Available from: www.thetimes. co.uk/article/sheikh-mohammed-hacked-tory-peers-mobile-phone-rules-judge-kf3kqb5pv

20. Brown, D., *Cherie Blair is adviser to NSO, the firm behind Pegasus spyware*. 2021 [Accessed 7 October 2021]; Available from: www.thetimes.co.uk/article/cherie-blair-is-adviser-to-nso-the-firm-behind-pegasus-spyware-rjdhhvr2s

21. Times, *The times view on Sheikh Mohammed and our ties with the UAE: questionable allies*. 2021 [Accessed 2 March 2022]; Available from: www.thetimes.co.uk/article/the-times-view-on-sheikh-mohammed-and-our-ties-with-the-uae-questionable-allies-28qd338m6

22. Wahlberg, A.A. and L. Sjöberg, Risk perception and the media. *Journal of Risk Research*, 2000. 3(1): p. 31–50.

23. Jagiello, R.D. and T.T. Hills, Bad news has wings: Dread risk mediates social amplification in risk communication. *Risk Analysis*, 2018. 38(10): p. 2193–2207.

24. Slovic, P., Perception of risk. *Science*, 1987. 236(4799): p. 280–285.

25. Tversky, A. and D. Kahneman, Availability: A heuristic for judging frequency and probability. *Cognitive Psychology*, 1973. 5(2): p. 207–232.

26. Krebs, B., *Cyber incident blamed for nuclear power plant shutdown*. 2008 [Accessed 27 May 2021]; Available from: www.washingtonpost.com/wp-dyn/content/article/2008/06/05/AR2008060501958.html

27. Hoyle, B., *Colonial Pipeline hackers had to find one password*. 2021 [Accessed 9 July 2021]; Available from: www.thetimes.co.uk/article/colonial-pipeline-hackers-had-to-find-one-password-frspmspph

28. Dawber, A., *Criminal hackers blamed for closure of vital Colonial Pipeline*. 2021 [Accessed 27 May 2021]; Available from: www.thetimes.co.uk/article/criminal-hackers-blamed-for-closure-of-vital-colonial-pipeline-8vccls8xw

29. Dawber, A., *Pumps run dry after pipeline cyberattack*. 2021 [Accessed 27 May 2021]; Available from: www.thetimes.co.uk/article/pumps-run-dry-after-pipeline-cyberattack-jckz2j2mk

30. Ziady, H., *The Colonial Pipeline attackers wanted money. Should companies pay?* 2021 [Accessed 27 May 2021]; Available from: https://edition.cnn.com/2021/05/12/business/ransomware-payments-colonial-pipeline/index.html

31. Reuters, *Here are the other times when all or part of the Colonial Pipeline system was shut*. 2021 [Accessed 27 May 2021]; Available from: www.cnbc.com/2021/05/09/colonial-pipeline-cyberattack-heres-when-it-was-previously-shut-down.html

32. Edelstein, K., *Impacts of 2020 Colonial Pipeline rupture continue to grow*. 2021 [Accessed 15 July 2021]; Available from: www.fractracker.org/2021/05/august-2020-colonial-pipeline-spill-in-north-carolina

33. Boraks, D., *Feds warn colonial pipeline is at risk; company says leak is deeper than reported*. 2021 [Accessed 27 May 2021]; Available from: www.wfae.org/energy-environment/2021-04-16/feds-warn-colonial-pipeline-is-at-risk-company-says-leak-is-deeper-than-reported

34. Kumar, D.K., *Colonial may open key U.S. gasoline line by Saturday after fatal blast*. 2016 [Accessed 27 May 2021]; Available from: www.reuters.com/article/us-pipeline-blast-alabama-idUSKBN12V2FC

35. Rapier, R., *Panic buying is causing fuel shortages along the colonial pipeline route*. 2021 [Accessed 27 May 2021]; Available from: www.forbes.com/sites/rrapier/2021/05/11/panic-buying-is-causing-gas-shortages-along-the-colonial-pipeline-route/?sh=156c34726b49

36. Schmitt, B. and M. Balakit, *Worries lead to long gas lines in Nashville – Again.* 2021 [Accessed 27 May 2021]; Available from: https://eu.tennessean.com/story/money/ 2016/09/17/panic-leads-long-gas-lines-nashville-again/90575330

37. Taylor, C., *The psychology of panic buying: Why Brits are scrambling for gasoline.* 2021 [Accessed 29 November 2021]; Available from: www.cnbc.com/2021/09/29/pet rol-crisis-why-brits-are-panic-buying-gasoline.html

38. BBC, *Fuel supply: Man "pulls knife" in welling petrol station dispute.* 2021 [Accessed 10 December 2021]; Available from: www.bbc.co.uk/news/uk-england-london-58720451

39. RISI, *Maroochy shire sewage spill.* 2000 [Accessed 1 March 2022]; Available from: www.risidata.com/Database/Detail/maroochy-shire-sewage-spill

40. Shrestha, P., *Thames water fined £4m after "catastrophic" sewage spill.* 2021 [Accessed 30 July 2021]; Available from: www.energylivenews.com/2021/05/31/tha mes-water-fined-4m-after-catastrophic-sewage-spill

41. Courtney-Guy, S., *Thames water fined millions for pumping 79,000,000 litres of sewage into park.* 2021 [Accessed 28 August 2021]; Available from: https://metro. co.uk/2021/05/28/thames-water-fined-millions-for-pumping-79m-litres-of-sewage-into-park-14666084

42. Nakashima, E., *Water-pump failure in Illinois wasn't cyberattack after all.* 2011 [Accessed 19 April 2022]; Available from: www.washingtonpost.com/world/natio nal-security/water-pump-failure-in-illinois-wasnt-cyberattack-after-all/2011/11/25/ gIQACgTewN_story.html

43. Zetter, K., *Comedy of errors led to false "water-pump hack" report.* 2011 [Accessed 21 January 2023]; Available from: www.wired.com/2011/11/water-pump-hack-myst ery-solved

44. Eilperin, J. and A. Entous, Russian operation hacked a Vermont utility, showing risk to U.S. electrical grid security, officials say. 2016 [Accessed 27 May 2021]; Available from: www.washingtonpost.com/world/national-security/russian-hackers-penetra ted-us-electricity-grid-through-a-utility-in-vermont/2016/12/30/8fc90cc4-ceec-11e6-b8a2-8c2a61b0436f_story.html

45. gtm, *Fake news of Russian cyberattack on Vermont utility goes viral before truth gets its boots on.* 2017 [Accessed 27 May 2021]; Available from: www.greentechmedia. com/articles/read/Fake-News-of-Russian-Cyber-Attack-On-Vermont-Utility-Goes-Viral-Before-TrutS

46. Greenwald, G., *Russia hysteria infects WashPost again: False story about hacking U.S. electric grid.* 2017 [Accessed 27 May 2021]; Available from: https://theintercept. com/2016/12/31/russia-hysteria-infects-washpost-again-false-story-about-hacking-u-s-electric-grid

47. Leetaru, K., *How the Washington post's defense of its Russian hacking story unraveled through web archiving.* 2017 [Accessed 27 May 2021]; Available from: www.forbes. com/sites/kalevleetaru/2017/01/02/how-the-washington-posts-defense-of-its-russian-hacking-story-unraveled-through-web-archiving/?sh=455081414c9b

48. Snopes, Was *a Vermont power grid infiltrated by Russian Hackers?* 2017 [Accessed 27 May 2021]; Available from: www.snopes.com/fact-check/report-vermont-power-grid-infiltrated-by-russian-hackers

49. Walton, R., *What electric utilities can learn from the Vermont hacking scare.* 2017 [Accessed 27 May 2021]; Available from: www.utilitydive.com/news/what-electric-utilities-can-learn-from-the-vermont-hacking-scare/433426

50. NCCIC, *FY 2016 incidents by functional impact.* 2016 [Accessed 27 May 2021]; Available from: https://us-cert.cisa.gov/sites/default/files/Annual_Reports/Year_in_ Review_FY2016_IR_Pie_Chart_S508C.pdf

51. Hemsley, K.E. and E. Fisher, *History of industrial control system cyber incidents.* 2018: Idaho National Lab (INL), Idaho Falls, ID (United States).

52. Pagliery, J., *The inside story of the biggest hack in history.* 2015 [Accessed 27 May 2021]; Available from: https://money.cnn.com/2015/08/05/technology/aramco-hack/index.html

53. Slowik, J., *Evolution of ICS attacks and the prospects for future disruptive events.* 2019: Threat Intelligence Centre Dragos Inc.

54. Higgins, K., Triton/Trisis attack was more widespread than publicly known. *DarkReading.* Retrieved March, 2019. 28: p. 2019.

55. Johnson, B., et al., *Attackers deploy new ICS attack framework "TRITON" and cause operational disruption to critical infrastructure.* 2017 [Accessed 27 May 2021]; Available from: www.fireeye.com/blog/threat-research/2017/12/attackers-deploy-new-ics-attack-framework-triton.html

56. NCSC, *TRITON malware targeting safety controllers.* 2017 [Accessed 27 May 2021]; Available from: www.ncsc.gov.uk/information/triton-malware-targeting-safety-cont rollers

57. Hale, G., *S4: Warning signs before Triton attack.* 2019 [Accessed 27 May 2021]; Available from: https://isssource.com/s4-warning-signs-before-triton-attack

58. CERT, *McAfee night dragon report (update A).* 2011 [Accessed 27 May 2021]; Available from: https://us-cert.cisa.gov/ics/advisories/ICSA-11-041-01A

59. Rosling, H. *Factfulness.* 2023: Flammarion.

60. Sellier, A.-L., I. Scopelliti, and C.K. Morewedge, Debiasing training improves decision making in the field. *Psychological Science*, 2019. 30(9): p. 1371–1379.

61. Copeland, D.G. and J.L. McKenney, *Airline reservations systems: Lessons from history.* MIS Quarterly, 1988: p. 353–370.

62. Holland, J.H., *Complexity: A very short introduction.* 2014: OUP Oxford.

63. Crockett, M., *The trolley problem: Would you kill one person to save many others?* [Accessed 16 February 2022]; Available from: www.theguardian.com/science/head-quarters/2016/dec/12/the-trolley-problem-would-you-kill-one-person-to-save-many-others

64. Siponen, M., Six design theories for IS security policies and guidelines. *Journal of the Association for Information Systems*, 2006. 7(1): p. 19.

65. Frey, S., et al., The good, the bad and the ugly: A study of security decisions in a cyber-physical systems game. *IEEE Transactions on Software Engineering*, 2017. 45(5): p. 521–536.

66. Boger, T., S.B. Most, and S.L. Franconeri, Jurassic mark: Inattentional blindness for a datasaurus reveals that visualizations are explored, not seen. In *2021 IEEE Visualization Conference (VIS)*. 2021. IEEE.

67. Zimmermann, V. and K. Renaud, The nudge puzzle: Matching nudge interventions to cybersecurity decisions. *ACM Transactions on Computer-Human Interaction (TOCHI)*, 2021. 28(1): p. 1–45.

68. Isler, O., O. Yilmaz, and B. Dogruyol, Activating reflective thinking with decision justification and debiasing training. *Judgment & Decision Making*, 2020. 15(6): p. 926–938.

69. Dekker, S. and T. Conklin, *Do safety differently.* 2022: Pre-Accident Investigation Media.

70. Finlay, M., We've got thinking all wrong. In *New scientist.* 14 November 2018. p. 38–41.

71. BPS, *Foundations of sand?* 2008 [Accessed 10 April 2021]; Available from: https://thepsychologist.bps.org.uk/volume-21/edition-9/foundations-sand

72. BPS, *The line between conformity and resistance.* 2014 [Accessed 10 April 2021]; Available from: https://thepsychologist.bps.org.uk/volume-28/january-2015/line-betw een-conformity-and-resistance

73. BPS, *Why (almost) everything you know about Milgram is wrong.* 2018 [Accessed 11 January 2023]; Available from: www.bps.org.uk/psychologist/why-almost-everyth ing-you-know-about-milgram-wrong

74. CSCUK, *Cyber security challenge UK.* 2021 [Accessed 10 April 2021]; Available from: www.cybersecuritychallenge.org.uk

75. Debate., *Cyber security technology efficacy: Is cybersecurity the new "market for lemons"?* 2020 [Accessed 16 September 2021]; Available from: www.debatesecurity. com/downloads/Cybersecurity-Technology-Efficacy-Research-Report-V1.0.pdf

76. Bowers, K., *Fighting cyber security FUD and hype.* 2017 [Accessed 16 September 2021]; Available from: www.securityweek.com/fighting-cyber-security-fud-and-hype

77. Sutherland, R., *Alchemy: The surprising power of ideas that don't make sense.* 2019: WH Allen.

78. Powers, J., *"The witness" exposes the myths, misconceptions of Kitty Genovese's murder.* 2016 [Accessed 1 December 2022]; Available from: www.npr.org/2016/06/ 16/482313144/the-witness-exposes-the-myths-misconceptions-of-kitty-genoveses-murder

79. Benderly, B.L., *Psychology's tall tales.* 2012 [Accessed 1 December 2022]; Available from: www.apa.org/gradpsych/2012/09/tall-tales

80. Throwcase, *That "five monkeys experiment" never happened.* 2014 [Accessed 1 December 2022]; Available from: www.throwcase.com/2014/12/21/that-five-monk eys-and-a-banana-story-is-rubbish

81. Engber, D., *Everything is crumbling.* 2018 [Accessed 10 April 2021]; Available from: www.slate.com/articles/health_and_science/cover_story/2016/03/ego-deple tion_an_influential_theory_in_psychology_may_have_just_been_debunked.html

82. Inzlicht, M., *Reckoning with the past.* 2016 [Accessed 10 April 2021]; Available from: https://michaelinzlicht.com/getting-better/2016/2/29/reckoning-with-the-past

83. Maxwell, S.E., M.Y. Lau, and G.S. Howard, Is psychology suffering from a replication crisis? What does "failure to replicate" really mean? *American Psychologist*, 2015. 70(6): p. 487.

84. Pashler, H. and C.R. Harris, Is the replicability crisis overblown? Three arguments examined. *Perspectives on Psychological Science*, 2012. 7(6): p. 531–536.

85. Stroebe, W. and F. Strack, The alleged crisis and the illusion of exact replication. *Perspectives on Psychological Science*, 2014. 9(1): p. 59–71.

86. McCook, A., *"I placed too much faith in underpowered studies:" Nobel Prize winner admits mistakes.* 2017 [Accessed 10 April 2021]; Available from: https://retractionwa tch.com/2017/02/20/placed-much-faith-underpowered-studies-nobel-prize-winner-admits-mistakes

87. Kahneman, D., *Thinking, fast and slow.* 2011: Macmillan.

88. Rohrer, D., H. Pashler, and C.R. Harris, Do subtle reminders of money change people's political views? *Journal of Experimental Psychology: General*, 2015. 144(4): p. e73.

89. Yarkoni, T., *The generalizability crisis.* 2019 [Accessed 10 April 2021]; Available from: https://psyarxiv.com/jqw35

90. Bhattacharjee, Y., The Mind of a Con Man. [Accessed 13 October 2023]; Available from: www.nytimes.com/2013/04/28/magazine/diederik-stapels-audacious-academic-fraud.html

91. Chang, A.C. and P. Li, *Is economics research replicable? Sixty published papers from thirteen journals say "usually not"*. 2015 [Accessed 10 April 2021]; Available from: www.federalreserve.gov/econresdata/feds/2015/files/2015083pap.pdf

92. Begley, C.G. and L.M. Ellis, Raise standards for preclinical cancer research. *Nature*, 2012. 483(7391): p. 531–533.

93. Van Noorden, R., Medicine is plagued by untrustworthy clinical trials. How many studies are faked or flawed? *Nature*, 2023. 619(7970): p. 454–458.

94. Ritchie, S., *Science fictions: Exposing fraud, bias, negligence and hype in science*. 2020: Random House.

95. Ritchie, S.J., R. Wiseman, and C.C. French, Replication, replication, replication. *The Psychologist*, 2012. Available from: www.bps.org.uk/psychologist/replication-replicat ion-replication

96. Ritchie, S.J., R. Wiseman, and C.C. French, Failing the future: Three unsuccessful attempts to replicate Bem's "retroactive facilitation of recall" effect. *PLoS One*, 2012. 7(3): p. e33423.

97. Ritchie, S., *There should never be heroes in science*. 2020 [Accessed 10 April 2021]; Available from: https://unherd.com/2020/06/why-there-should-never-be-heroes-in-science

98. Bem, D.J., Feeling the future: Experimental evidence for anomalous retroactive influences on cognition and affect. *Journal of Personality and Social Psychology*, 2011. 100(3): p. 407.

99. Tressoldi, P., T. Rabeyron, and M. Duggan, *Feeling the Future: A meta-analysis of 90 experiments on the anomalous anticipation of random future events*. Daryl J. Bem Cornell University.

100. Carpenter, S., Psychology's bold initiative. *Science*, 2012. 336(6076): p. 1558–1561.

101. OSC, Psychology. Estimating the reproducibility of psychological science. *Science*, 2015. 349(6251): p. aac4716.

102. Carney, D.R., A.J. Cuddy, and A.J. Yap, Power posing: Brief nonverbal displays affect neuroendocrine levels and risk tolerance. *Psychological Science*, 2010. 21(10): p. 1363–1368.

103. Cuddy, A.J., C.A. Wilmuth, and D.R. Carney, *The benefit of power posing before a high-stakes social evaluation*. Harvard Business School Working paper series# 13-027, 2012.

104. TED, *The most popular talks of all time*. 2021 [Accessed 10 April 2021]; Available from: www.ted.com/playlists/171/the_most_popular_talks_of_all

105. Credé, M. and L.A. Phillips, Revisiting the power pose effect: How robust are the results reported by Carney, Cuddy, and Yap (2010) to data analytic decisions? *Social Psychological and Personality Science*, 2017. 8(5): p. 493–499.

106. Cuddy, A.J., S.J. Schultz, and N.E. Fosse, P-curving a more comprehensive body of research on postural feedback reveals clear evidential value for power-posing effects: Reply to Simmons and Simonsohn (2017). *Psychological Science*, 2018. 29(4): p. 656–666.

107. Crede, M., *A negative effect of a contractive pose is not evidence for the positive effect of an expansive pose: Commentary on Cuddy, Schultz, and Fosse (2018)*. 2018.

108. Ranehill, E., et al., Assessing the robustness of power posing: No effect on hormones and risk tolerance in a large sample of men and women. *Psychological Science*, 2015. 26(5): p. 653–656.

109. Dominus, S., When the revolution came for Amy Cuddy. *The New York Times*, 2017. 29.

110. Nelson, L.D., J. Simmons, and U. Simonsohn, Psychology's renaissance. *Annual Review of Psychology*, 2018. 69: p. 511–534.

111. Orwell, G., *Politics and the English language*. 1946/2021: Renard Press Limited.

112. Orwell, G., *Animal farm: A fairy story. 1945*. 1996: London: Secker and Warburg.

113. Jussim, L. Are most published social psychology findings false. *Psychology Today* 2016 [Accessed 10 April 2021]; Available from: www.psychologytoday.com/gb/blog/rabble-rouser/201602/are-most-published-social-psychology-findings-false

114. Yong, E., *A failed replication draws a scathing personal attack from a psychology professor*. 2012: Discover Magazine.

115. Morewedge, C.K., D.T. Gilbert, and T.D. Wilson, *Reply to Francis*. 2014. Available from: www2.psych.purdue.edu/~gfrancis/Publications/ConsumingExperience/MOREWEDGEREPLY.pdf

116. Galak, J. and T. Meyvis, You could have just asked: Reply to Francis (2012). *Perspectives on Psychological Science*, 2012. 7(6): p. 595–596.

117. Simonsohn, U., It does not follow: Evaluating the one-off publication bias critiques by Francis (2012a, 2012b, 2012c, 2012d, 2012e, in press). *Perspectives on Psychological Science*, 2012. 7(6): p. 597–599.

118. Simonsohn, U., It really just does not follow, comments on. *Journal of Mathematical Psychology*, 2013. 57(5): p. 174–176.

119. Gelman, A., *Statistical modeling, causal inference, and social science*. 2016 [Accessed 10 April 2021]; Available from: https://statmodeling.stat.columbia.edu

120. Letzter, R., *Scientists are furious after a famous psychologist accused her peers of "methodological terrorism"*. 2016 [Accessed 10 April 2021]; Available from: www.businessinsider.com/susan-fiske-methodological-terrorism-2016-9?r=US&IR=T

121. Strømland, E., Preregistration and reproducibility. *Journal of Economic Psychology*, 2019. 75: p. 102143.

122. Claesen, A., S.L.B.T. Gomes, and F. Tuerlinckx, *Preregistration: Comparing dream to reality*. PsyArXiv, 9 May 2019.

123. Goldacre, B., et al., COMPare: A prospective cohort study correcting and monitoring 58 misreported trials in real time. *Trials*, 2019. 20(1): p. 118.

124. Veldkamp, C.L.S., et al., Ensuring the quality and specificity of preregistrations. *PLoS Biol*, 2018. 18(12). Available from: www.cos.io/blog/improving-the-quality-and-specificity-of-preregistration

125. Bishop, D., The psychology of experimental psychologists: Overcoming cognitive constraints to improve research. 2020. The 47th Sir Frederic Bartlett Lecture. *Quarterly Journal of Experimental Psychology* 73(1): p. 1–19.

126. Kristal, A., et al., *When we're wrong, it's our responsibility as scientists to say so*. 2020 [Accessed 10 April 2021]; Available from: https://blogs.scientificamerican.com/observations/when-were-wrong-its-our-responsibility-as-scientists-to-say-so

127. Camerer, C.F., et al., Evaluating the replicability of social science experiments in nature and science between 2010 and 2015. *Nature Human Behaviour*, 2018. 2(9): p. 637–644.

128. Klein, O., et al., Low hopes, high expectations: Expectancy effects and the replicability of behavioral experiments. *Perspectives on Psychological Science*, 2012. 7(6): p. 572–584.

129. Hauser, O.P., et al., Cooperating with the future. *Nature*, 2014. 511(7508): p. 220–223.

130. Janssen, M.A., et al., Lab experiments for the study of social-ecological systems. *Science*, 2010. 328(5978): p. 613–617.

131. Gneezy, U., E.A. Keenan, and A. Gneezy, Avoiding overhead aversion in charity. *Science*, 2014. 346(6209): p. 632–635.

132. Balafoutas, L. and M. Sutter, Affirmative action policies promote women and do not harm efficiency in the laboratory. *Science*, 2012. 335(6068): p. 579–582.

133. Ackerman, J.M., C.C. Nocera, and J.A. Bargh, Incidental haptic sensations influence social judgments and decisions. *Science*, 2010. 328(5986): p. 1712–1715.

134. Lee, S.W. and N. Schwarz, Washing away postdecisional dissonance. *Science*, 2010. 328(5979): p. 709–709.

135. Earp, B.D., et al., Out, damned spot: Can the "Macbeth Effect" be replicated? *Basic and Applied Social Psychology*, 2014. 36(1): p. 91–98.

136. Gervais, W.M. and A. Norenzayan, Analytic thinking promotes religious disbelief. *Science*, 2012. 336(6080): p. 493–496.

137. Sanchez, C., et al., Direct replication of Gervais & Norenzayan (2012): No evidence that analytic thinking decreases religious belief. *PLoS One,* 2017. 12(2): p. e0172636.

138. Gervais, W.M. and A. Norenzayan, Analytic atheism revisited. *Nature Human Behaviour*, 2018. 2(9): p. 609–609.

139. Hanson, R., Could gambling save science? Encouraging an honest consensus. *Social Epistemology*, 2008. 9(1): p. 3–33.

140. Dreber, A., et al., Using prediction markets to estimate the reproducibility of scientific research. *Proceedings of the National Academy of Sciences*, 2015. 112(50): p. 15343–15347.

141. Forsell, E., et al., Predicting replication outcomes in the Many Labs 2 study. *Journal of Economic Psychology*, 2019. 75: p. 102117.

142. Yong, E., *Online bettors can sniff out weak psychology studies*. 2018 [Accessed 10 April 2021]; Available from: www.theatlantic.com/science/archive/2018/08/scientists-can-collectively-sense-which-psychology-studies-are-weak/568630

143. DARPA, *Reliable research replicates… You can bet on it*. 2021 [Accessed 10 April 2021]; Available from: www.replicationmarkets.com

144. Almenberg, J., *Prediction markets for Science*. 2016 [Accessed 10 April 2021]; Available from: www.citationfuture.com

145. Rajtmajer, S., et al., *A synthetic prediction market for estimating confidence in published work*. arXiv preprint arXiv:2201.06924, 2021.

146. Menard, A.d., *How I made $10k predicting which studies will replicate*. 2021 [Accessed 2 March 2022]; Available from: https://fantasticanachronism.com/2021/11/18/how-i-made-10k-predicting-which-papers-will-replicate

147. Singal, J., *Want to know whether a psychology study will replicate? Just ask a bunch of people*. 2019 [Accessed 14 January 2023]; Available from: https://theeconomyof meaning.com/2019/10/17/want-to-know-whether-a-psychology-study-will-replicate-just-ask-a-bunch-of-people

148. Yong, E., *Can a futures market save science?* 2015 [Accessed 10 April 2021]; Available from: www.theatlantic.com/science/archive/2015/11/gambling-on-the-reliability-on-science-literally/414834

149. Michaels, D., *The Triumph of doubt: Dark money and the science of deception*. 2020: Oxford University Press.

150. Royle, M.T. and A.T. Hall, The relationship between McClelland's theory of needs, feeling individually accountable, and informal accountability for others. *International Journal of Management and Marketing Research*, 2012. 5(1): p. 21–42.

151. Klein, R.A., et al., Investigating variation in replicability. *Social Psychology*, 2014. 45: p. 142–152.

152. Schimmack, U., *The replicability-index: Quantifying statistical research integrity.* 2014 [Accessed 10 April 2021]; Available from: https://replicationindex.com/2014/12/01/quantifying-statistical-research-integrity-r-index

153. retractionwatch.com, *Retraction watch.* 2021 [Accessed 10 April 2021]; Available from: https://retractionwatch.com

Index

Printed in the United States
by Baker & Taylor Publisher Services